ONE NATION

TELEVIS

UNDER

ONE NATION UNDER TELEVISION

the rise and decline of network TV

J. FRED MACDONALD

PANTHEON BOOKS NEW YORK

All rights reserved under International and Pan-American

Copyright Conventions. Published in the United States by Pantheon

Books, a division of Random House, Inc., New York, and simul-

taneously in Canada by Random House of Canada Limited, Toronto.

Library of Congress Cataloging-in-Publication Data

MacDonald, J. Fred.

  One nation under television: the rise and decline of network TV/

J. Fred MacDonald.

    p.   cm.

  Includes bibliographical references.

  ISBN 0-394-58018-4

  1. Television broadcasting—United States—History. I. Title.

PN1992.3.U5M24   1990

384.55'4'0973—dc20   89-42564

Book design by Archie Ferguson

Manufactured in the United States of America

F I R S T   E D I T I O N

for

LESLIE W. MacDONALD—

whose understanding and support

have been indispensable

contents

preface

This is a study of the most important social and cultural force in the United States during the past four decades. Since it emerged in the late 1940s as a nationally available medium of mass entertainment and information, commercial television has been the principal window through which Americans have viewed their world. What was new or popular or influential in American life came now through TV. The medium made nationwide events out of local happenings; and it transformed national, even international, events into neighborhood concerns. It made celebrities and toppled leaders. And as it described and interpreted the recent movements of humankind, it revealed the strengths and foibles of ourselves and others. It has shown us to be neither fully moral nor invincible: through TV we have realized our limitations.

The medium has also forever linked us to the capitalist ethic, by which it has been controlled from the outset. TV has operated as a commercial billboard, rudely invading the privacy of every American with its pitches for dog food, clothing, Buicks, fast-food chains, and even candidates for the presidency of the United States. Still, the audience has never ceased to remain fascinated with the splashy spectacle. Indeed, its commercial announcements have become enduring cultural artifacts viewed devotedly for their nostalgic and artistic qualities.

Television rapidly became the cutting edge of social, political, economic, and cultural developments in the United States. It seemed to deliver the fullness of life of which the Great Depression and World War II had robbed earlier generations. It represented a reward for years of forbearance. TV was the ultimate American medium, requiring no physical labor, offering wonderful diversion, reaffirming the reliance on technology that Americans had developed in the twentieth century, and symbolizing a victory over deprivation that cut across class lines. Truly, video in the United States was the "tube of plenty," as media historian Erik Barnouw has described it.[1]

Significantly, American television has always meant network

television, TV as delivered by CBS, NBC, and ABC, with an early assist from DuMont and a late boost from Fox. If television played a key role in the civil rights movement, the Vietnam War, or the Watergate scandal, it was because of what the networks programmed. If there has been controversy about excessive violence, the manipulation of children through materialistic messages, or sexual permissiveness on TV, it is because of what the networks have provided. The history of American video is the story of the powerful control of the medium by the major networks.

Nevertheless, the history of TV has not been static. Rising from its indebted infancy to become a major force in U.S. corporate life, commercial television has fallen upon hard times. Nowadays, ABC, CBS, and NBC are threatened, faced with dwindling viewership, massive economic problems, and formidable competition from alternative video forms. Whereas watching television once meant almost everyone tuning in to network shows, by the end of the 1980s the network share of the U.S. audience had fallen to two-thirds of the TV audience. Americans are deserting traditional television. There has even been talk of the inevitable demise of one of the three networks.

This book is a study of the American experience with television. It is at once the history of a dream come true and a dream transcended, for what had been dearly anticipated, TV as an exciting forum of diversion and edification, became a mystifying reality—but the audience is moving on. While not fully an analysis of cultural and economic collapse, it is the story of a cultural industry, the marriage of business and artistry that has permeated American civilization through the past forty years.

In his insightful screenplay *Network*, the brilliant dramatist Paddy Chayefsky once limned television as a charade believed in by too many:

Television is not the truth! Television is a goddamned amusement park, that's what television is! Television is a circus, a carnival, a travelling troupe of acrobats and storytellers, singers and dancers, jugglers, sideshow freaks, lion-tamers and football players! We are in the boredom-killing business. . . . We'll tell you Kojak always gets the killer, and nobody gets cancer in Archie Bunker's house. And no matter how much trouble the hero is in, don't worry: just look at your watch—at the end of the hour he's going to win. We'll tell you any shit you want to hear! We deal in illusion, man! None of it is true![2]

This book offers no passionate condemnation of the business or hosanna concerning its sociological contribution. Both as enterprise and social force, television has had marvelous achievements that have diverted, bemused, informed; likewise it has exerted disastrous influences that have brutalized, skewed, and otherwise misrepresented reality. This book attempts to consider both sides of the legacy. There are no calls here for the nationalization or dissolution of TV as an act of moral service; neither is there a hidden agenda intending to applaud the medium for contributions to the uplifting of humanity.

Research for this study was conducted in a number of sources. Trade journals such as *Broadcasting, Variety, Electronic Media,* and *TV Guide* were valuable for their insights into the industry. The videocassette recorder, one of the most useful tools of the media historian, was invaluable, as, too, was my personal film archive of vintage television programs.

In acknowledging individuals for their support in writing this book, it is difficult not to name everyone influential to me through seventeen years of researching and teaching the history of radio and TV in the United States. Thanks go to the people who have helped to save the filmed record of American TV—among them Rick Prelinger, J. David Goldin, Ron Simon, and Edward M. Rider, as well as Larry Urbanski, Veto Stasiunaitis, Mike Pipher, Carl Hoglund, Sam Samuelian, Randall Meade, Ray Courts, Ray Atherton, Tom Boren, Scott Zuniga, Omer Whayne, Susan Ensley, Paul Cullins, Harry Doebel, Dick Andersen, Ron Spenser, Irv Abelson, Andy Jaysnovitch, Walter von Bosau, Phil Johnson, Steve Rebro, and Jerry Nelson.

Thanks also to other friends and colleagues for their encouragement: Robert Thompson, June Sochen, Bernard Bachrach, Les Waffen, Paul Gremley, Ray B. Browne, Edward A. Robinson, Sterling "Red" Quinlan, Dwight Ellis, Wallace Sears, Eli Segal, Ann Nykanen, Darrell Hamamoto, Michael Barson, Bill Schurk, James Briggs Murray, Pat McGilligan, Ray Narducy, and Dr. Alan Blum. At the Museum of Broadcast Communications in Chicago, my gratitude goes to President Bruce DuMont, Chairman of the Board Arthur C. Nielsen, Jr., and an able staff that includes Michael Mertz, Laura Levitt, Joan Dry, Ron Falzone, Dottie Jeffries, and Tom Cieselka. Special thanks go to Tony Mechele of the British Film Institute and Alain Marchand of the Cinemathèque Française, as well as Steve Allen, Robert Blees, and Mike Wallace. And no TV historian could work effectively without some debt to the seminal contributions to the field made by Tim Brooks, Earle Marsh, and Larry James Gianakos.

Thanks, too, to my editor, Susan Rabiner, whose critical insights and suggestions/were of great importance in the preparation of this book. Finally, thanks to my wife, Leslie W. MacDonald, whose encouragement, forbearance, and support again have been invaluable. The book is dedicated to her.

THE EMERGENCE OF AMERICAN TELEVISION

THE FORMATIVE YEARS

struggle

for an

These are confusing times for network television and for an American public that has had a forty-year romance with "the tube." Through cable TV and satellite dishes, many new channels have appeared, and further advances in delivery promise even greater selection. Whereas once television was synonymous with ABC, CBS, and NBC, plus a few rerun-filled independent stations, there now are dozens of national and regional cable networks, and they are offering a broad variety of programs and formats, including first-run series and feature films. Viewers are even making their own TV shows, using portable home camcorders to turn backyard shenanigans, birthday parties, family vacations, and the like into memorable video fare.

industry

Once the stolid, overweight centerpiece of the family living room, the mighty television set has been liberated. Transistorized, miniaturized, and now pocket-sized, portable TV can be found at the beach, on the sidewalk, in the backseat, and at the office. The audience, too, has been unshackled. Thanks to prerecorded cassettes and recordings made directly off the air, viewers who used to enjoy shows as they were being televised, now watch at their own convenience. Automatic timers allow for taping at odd hours of the day and night. And the remote-control device has given even greater control to viewers, enabling them to zip from station to station, especially when the advertisements begin, or zap through those hated commercial breaks on off-the-air tapes.

But the video revolution is costing a lot of money. Americans are spending billions of dollars on recorders, camcorders, blank and prerecorded tapes, cable service, pay channels, and pay-per-view programming. Once trumpeted as "The Greatest 'Free' Show on Earth,"[1] American television in all its glory is no longer affordable to a sizable part of the citizenry. The egalitarian implications of a medium that was mass and free have been subverted by expensive monthly cable bills and costly electronic paraphernalia. As the television experience is denied increasingly to those with insufficient cash, the United States is fast becoming a nation of TV-haves and TV-have-nots.

It was so simple when once there was only a handful of stations in any market area. Local outlets were recognizable by the network reruns and low-budget commercials they ran for community merchants. Above it all towered ABC-CBS-NBC, the trinity that was national television, beguiling the populace with the miracles and mysteries of early TV.

Although network programs were formulaic, there was security in such simplicity. In this orderly past, prepossessing national concern focused on which of the three networks would outrate the others, and what new programming trends might be coming next: comedies? Westerns? detective stories? anthology dramas? The United States may have been a country of great diversity, but cultural pluralism gained little attention from national programmers. This was broadcasting mass culture, a search for the largest possible audience at any one time, an appeal to commonalities that bound together, a denial of the differences that individualized. Those with tastes not shared by enough millions had little chance of seeing their preferences on television.

Moreover, this was broadcasting with a commercial imperative. The networks that created this one nation under television were in business to make money. Programs were meant to be profitable. Those that failed to deliver high ratings and audience shares were dispatched, replaced by others that promised success where there had just been failure. It may have been the public's air waves in theory, but it was the networks' financial bottom line in practice.

By the beginning of the 1990s, however, American TV has changed. Old media empires are in disarray, while new ones are rising. Audience numbers are tumbling. And companies known for their newspapers, magazines, movies, telephones, and traveler's checks are now operating their own networks. Whereas profanity and nudity had been chronic taboos, television now communicates the entire lexicon of expletives undeleted, and bare bodies frolic and sometimes writhe in prime time. After decades of predictable sameness on national TV, there is relative diversity in the narrower focus made possible in this new video order.

In the last decade of this century of electronic marvels, television is in a state of metamorphosis, rearranging itself under the influence of cable and satellite technology and the lure of great profits. And more change is projected for the future, everything from regularized international programming to interactive TV, with its promise of two-way communication for a medium used to dishing it out to an audience used to taking it. But innovation, actual and promised, has bred industry discontent. Fiber-optic wiring installed with home telephone lines is recommended to offset the high cost of cable and to improve picture quality; but many in the broadcast and cable industries are fearful that their early investments might be rendered worthless. The Japanese and the Europeans each have developed high-definition TV with upward of 1,000 lines of resolution (the U.S. standard is 525 lines), guaranteeing crisp, perfect TV imagery; but in the name of economics and patriotism U.S. television interests demand billions of dollars from government to produce an American HDTV alternative.

The business specifics of television are similarly uncertain. While Viacom/Showtime sues its rival Time/Home Box Office for allegedly unfair business practices, Warner Communications couples with Time, Inc., but only after a nasty public challenge by a rival suitor, Paramount Communications. Whereas domestically made receivers by RCA, Zenith, Philco, Emerson, Capehart, Hoffman, Packard-Bell, Sylvania, Admiral, and other U.S. manufacturers satisfied the first television consumers, the modern audience has Japanese- and Korean-made equipment: sets, cassette recorders, and camcorders by Sony, Panasonic, Toshiba, Mitsubishi, Sharp, GoldStar, and the like. Even if such hardware bears an RCA or General Electric (GE) name, the items are manufactured in Asia, for only Zenith survives as a TV manufacturer within the United States.

This is perplexing enough, but most of the programs on American television are transmitted from studios filled with technical equipment from abroad. Meanwhile, Asians, Europeans, and Australians are buying up the most familiar institutions in American entertainment—from movie studios to record companies—many with linkages to television, while U.S. companies are busy overseas investing heavily in entertaining foreigners.

While corporations battle for the video future, their struggle is over an instrument that has influenced the American public for more than half a century. No matter how it is viewed, television has been a powerful reality in modern life. In terms of technology alone, the ability to transmit and receive pictures and sound is among the greatest human achievements of the century. But to make such an instrument universally available, to fill its multiplicity of channels twenty-four hours a day, to charge no direct cost to the consumer, and to do all this within a generation constitutes one of the outstanding developments in the history of human communication.

5

What promise television held. This was the ultimate medium, the democratic forum that would uplift and enlighten the masses. Some anticipated that it would forge a more perfect national consensus, spreading over regional, ethnic, religious, linguistic, and cultural differences, creating a common "language" rooted in shared tastes and a popular desire to understand the world. Others saw its implications more broadly, envisioning TV as a force for amalgamating the peoples of the world. In this perspective, television would link the nationalities of the planet into one audience, never disrespectful of historic differences but always stressing the characteristics that linked humankind.

But there were mitigating realities: the prejudices and greed that adversely shaped TV; the politics, both national and global, that stifled its full flowering; monopolistic network practices that placed standardization above diversity. There were other operational shortcomings, some inherent in network broadcasting, others emanating from foibles in those creating, operating, and viewing the medium.

Certainly, American television realized much that it promised. But with endemic weaknesses it has been unable to withstand the challenges of technological innovation and enhanced competition. If there is disarray in the industry, it is due to the way it has operated since its inception. If viewers are deserting "free" TV, it is because they were never fully served by broadcasting. To comprehend the forces clashing in contemporary U.S. video, it is necessary to understand the evolution of TV as it moved from a popular expectation in the 1920s to a global utility in the 1990s.

the race for television

Americans awaited television for almost thirty years. Even before radio was fully accepted as a medium of popular appeal, video was hailed as the inevitable next step in the technological triumph that was broadcasting.

During the 1920s there was frequent speculation about the emergence of "sight radio," "radio optics," "radiovisor receivers," and in a bow to the silver screen, "radio moving pictures" and "home theaters." Newspapers and magazines regularly reported on the technical progress of TV as the competition for practical video transmission focused on two technical processes: a mechanical system that employed a rotating scanning disc to transmit images; and the eventually triumphant technology, an electronic scanning system that used the principles of the cathode ray tube to produce a picture of high definition and reliability.

In the quest for viable TV, the names of the great scientists experimenting in the United States became well known. Prominent among them was Vladimir K. Zworykin, who in 1923 developed the electronic TV camera tube ("iconoscope") and six years later a nonmechanical receiver ("kinescope"). Like most important electrical experimenters, Zworykin was employed by large communications corporations, in his case Westinghouse in the early 1920s and the Radio Corporation of America (RCA) by the end of the decade.

Other inventors who applied their talents to the race to produce TV included the Swedish genius Ernst F. W. Alexanderson, who from the General Electric laboratory in Schenectady, New York, transmitted a TV image around the world in 1930; Lee de Forest, an honored pioneer of radio technology; the Puerto Rican-born U. A. Sanabria, who experimented with mechanical systems in Chicago; C. F. Jenkins of Washington, D.C., who helped perfect the TV receiver; and Allen B. DuMont, the celebrated engineer whose facility in Passaic, New Jersey, was a leader in video research and development in the 1930s and 1940s.

Of particular significance was the engineering genius Philo T. Farnsworth, whose research in the 1920s and 1930s carried him from Salt Lake City to Los Angeles, San Francisco, and Philadelphia. In 1928 he was the first inventor to present a public demonstration of all-electronic TV. However, unlike most of his formally educated rivals with their strong corporate financing, Farnsworth was relatively self-taught, and his finances came modestly from a small group of investors. Still, as Joseph H. Udelson has pointed out, Farnsworth produced components that proved crucial to the final video product. According to Udelson, "disadvantages did not prevent Farnsworth from developing the only pickup tube to present serious competition to Zworykin's iconoscope and . . . to pose a challenge to RCA. . . . If RCA was to introduce a commercially viable television system in America it could not avoid, despite all its efforts, a reckoning with Farnsworth."[2]

With such brainpower dedicated to perfecting television, Americans anticipated the educational and entertainment values the new medium soon would bring to the nation. One journalist, impressed that the inauguration of Calvin Coolidge had been heard nationally over an ad hoc network of forty radio stations, felt confident in predicting that the next inaugural ceremony would be telecast from coast to coast, perhaps even beamed to

Europe.[3] Even more exciting were the predictions of Samuel L. "Roxy" Rothafel, a noted impresario of theater and radio. In his insightful book *Broadcasting: Its New Day*, Roxy in 1925 described the breathtaking programming to be available soon:

> *The entire program that we see in a theater will come to us. . . . The ether will vibrate with the likenesses of our favorite stars, which we will receive faithfully. . . . When the [transmission] problem is finally solved the world will indeed become a very small place to live in. The living spectacle of Niagara, with its rush and roar, or the vast abyss of the Colorado Canyon can be brought to the easy-chair at home. Our baseball players, instead of performing before a group of spectators, will perform before a radio transmitter and we shall hear the whack of the bat and the call of the umpire, and see the dust raised by the sliding player's feet. Radio vision is not an idle dream.*[4]

When a research scientist declared in 1925 that all U.S. households would have TV sets by the end of the decade, there was reason to be excited.[5] It was promising, too, when David Sarnoff, the driving force energizing the Radio Corporation of America—and on his way to the presidency of RCA in 1930—predicted in 1928 that it would take about five years for TV to become "as much a part of our life" as radio.[6] It was not even discouraging when the chairman of the board of Westinghouse sought to diminish public enthusiasm by announcing in early 1930 that television would not be commercially possible for at least two years.[7]

Even the Great Depression failed to lessen enthusiasm for television. Convinced of a brilliant future for TV, *Radio Retailing* magazine in early 1932 editorialized, "Then there is the promise of television. Who knows how great will be the ultimate development of this new science—its possibilities awes [*sic*] the imagination."[8] Comedian Eddie Cantor, too, was excited in 1936 when he envisioned TV as an irresistible theater of popular diversion—a dazzling theater that would offer viewers "such entertainment as the world has never dreamed of."[9]

As early as May 1930, one optimistic consumer had queried a newspaper columnist about whether he should buy a new radio now or wait a few months to purchase a video receiver:

> *Our radio set was built in 1925. It's high time that it be replaced by a new set. . . . But now we are up in the air. We read of television images entertaining on a theater screen in Schenectady,*

8

and the prediction that thousands of playhouses will probably book television acts. Now, the question is, should we cling to the old faithful six-tube outfit, or go ahead and buy a receiver that is improved in tone more than our 1925 product? Why should we get a new set now and have a television set make it obsolete in September? [10]

Fueling public interest were those scientific breakthroughs produced periodically by leading electrical corporations such as RCA and Westinghouse. Such developments were always spectacular and, importantly, well publicized. Typically, in September 1928 the General Electric experimental station, W2XAD in Schenectady, aired the first television drama, *The Queen's Messenger*—although technological limitations necessitated a simulcast of the sound portion of the program over radio station WGY. In another GE coup, in February 1930 the image of a familiar cartoon character, Felix the Cat, was transmitted instantaneously by television over twenty thousand miles: round trip from Schenectady to Sydney, Australia, and back. Later that year a theater audience in Schenectady marveled at a live television program as it was transmitted from the GE laboratory across town.

With the imminent availability of television as entertainer and educator, public leaders foretold its future impact on varied aspects of American life. The editor of *The New Republic* expected TV to replace newspapers, as details of the daily news could be telecast to every home.[11] Police officials felt video would help in the apprehension of criminals by facilitating the exchange of information among law enforcement agencies. Some expected the medium to improve domestic politics; others felt it would enhance international relations. There were those who felt video would be a valuable tool in waging future wars, while others argued that it could render war obsolete.

Observers predicted that even business and commerce would be affected by TV. At Pennsylvania State University, the emerging medium was quickly understood in terms of the new jobs it would create; as early as 1930 that university offered home-study courses on television engineering. A scientist in Cleveland predicted that businesses soon would be able via TV to convene meetings of executives from throughout the country. This would not only save time, he suggested, but as a collateral benefit it would "make harmless the odors from foul cigars."[12] And in 1930 inventor Lee de Forest, looking fifty years into the future, foresaw a profitable relationship between video and existing technology when he predicted that for a fee long-distance telephone operators by 1980 would be able to plug TV viewers into films and plays taking place throughout the United States—all with no interruptions for commercials.[13]

Confidence in widespread, dramatic change should not have been surprising in this era of technological revolution. It must be remembered that at the beginning of the nineteenth century Napoleon had available to him essentially the same methods of communication and transportation that Julius Caesar utilized two thousand years earlier. During the first half of the nineteenth century, however, the miracle of the telegraph rendered the Pony Express obsolete, while armies came to be moved by steam-powered locomotives. And by the early twentieth century, communications were profoundly affected by the emergence of the telephone, the first flickering motion pictures, and wireless radio, while innovations in transportation included the automobile and the airplane.

For a society in which many could remember word-of-mouth and print as the primary forms of communication, this was an electrifying time in which to live. By the 1930s it was possible not only to telephone or telegraph but also to view sound motion pictures; play electronically enhanced phonograph records; and hear radio shows broadcast from network and local stations—indeed, from transmitters around the world. Also part of this age of miracles were the refrigerator, washing machine, and electric lights—all convenient, available, and affordable.

Television was only one part of a cornucopia of entertaining merchandise predicted for the American consumer. This situation was well appreciated by an official of the Stromberg-Carlson electronics company, who proclaimed in 1937 that "television is only one of seven electronic devices which someday we may have in our homes." He envisioned the home of the future as a rich audiovisual experience equipped with a "radio, phonograph, sound film projector, sound movie camera, electric organ or electric piano, wire-recording machine, and television."[14] Interestingly, of this predicted home inventory of electronic gadgets, the two that are less popular today than twenty years ago—the movie camera and projector—have been subsumed in the American home by two offshoots of television—the video camera and the videocassette recorder.

The entry into early television by the major radio networks and electrical manufacturers only intensified popular expectations. Experimental TV stations were opened by the National Broadcasting Company (W2XBS in New York City in 1928; and, in Chicago, W9XAP, purchased in 1931 from the *Chicago Daily News*); the Columbia Broadcasting System (W2XAB in New York

City in 1931); and the Don Lee Broadcasting System (W6XS and W6XAO in Los Angeles in 1931). As well as the involvement of RCA through its National Broadcasting Company, other electrical corporations operating experimental stations were General Electric (1928); Westinghouse, in East Pittsburgh (1928); Philco, in Philadelphia (1931); and the Zenith Radio Corporation, in Chicago (1938). Several leading developers of the medium—Farnsworth in Philadelphia, Jenkins in New York City, and DuMont in Passaic—also operated early stations. There also were creditable experimental stations in Kansas City (1932); Minneapolis (1934); Boston (1934); and at Purdue University in West Lafayette, Indiana (1932); the University of Iowa (1933); and Kansas State College (1932).[15]

Significantly, the scramble to develop television was not solely an American phenomenon. Interest in developing TV was manifest in the 1920s and 1930s in Poland, Sweden, France, the Soviet Union, Czechoslovakia, and the Netherlands. In many ways, moreover, scientists and engineers in Great Britain and Germany were ahead of those working in the United States.

Since the mid-1920s John Logie Baird had been a driving force in perfecting and popularizing British television. Important, too, was Electric and Musical Industries (EMI), a corporation created in 1931 through the merger of two sound recording companies, the Columbia Gramophone Company and the Gramophone Company. Since the latter was controlled by an American company, the Victor Talking Machine Company, and Victor in turn had been merged with RCA since 1929, the arrangement afforded EMI access to research conducted by RCA. And through a merger in 1934 with a Marconi company developing transmitters and aerials, EMI became the world leader in video technology. When the British Broadcasting Corporation inaugurated regularly scheduled TV in November 1936, it quickly settled upon the EMI version as the standard.

In Germany in the 1920s scientists such as Manfred von Ardenne and Denes von Mihaly labored to develop television. Through support for sound and image experimentation from the German Post Office, a TV picture had been produced as early as March 1930. The coming to power of National Socialism in January 1933 only intensified the German efforts. Although Nazi efforts were marked by rivalries among the German Post Office; the Ministry of Propaganda, headed by Dr. Paul Joseph Goebbels; and Hermann Goering's Air Ministry, in March 1935 the Germans inaugurated the first regularly scheduled television programming in the world.

Clearly, the British effort was superior. By August 1939 there were an estimated 20,000 to 25,000 sets in use in London, and the electronic scanning system adopted by the BBC offered praise-worthy picture quality. The effort in Germany—with its inferior mechanical camera system, its lack of financial backing, and its limited availability—was stunted. By 1939 video remained lim-ited to the Berlin area; there were only about 350 receivers in private hands, and most citizens came to public viewing rooms to see the propaganda films and newsreels of Nazi television.[16]

In the United States by 1939 there were twenty-two licensed experimental TV stations, but a public-opinion survey that year suggested that optimism rested not only with the experimenters and industrialists. According to a Gallup poll there was "a large potential customer audience awaiting the new television indus-try." Four million families—that is, one-eighth of all American families—considered themselves good prospects to buy a receiver sometime in the future. That figure was all the more impressive since for many years telecasting would necessarily be restricted to the densely populated areas of the country—the East, includ-ing New England; the Chicago–Detroit axis; and parts of the West Coast—where video experimentation was centered.[17]

The Gallup figures, however, were not totally positive. This remained a troubled decade. The United States was still gripped by the uncertainties of economic and social dislocation created by the Great Depression. To this was added the disquietude gener-ated by international politics as Europe and Asia were on the verge of another world war. Furthermore, video was still in its technical infancy, and there was public apprehension that a set purchased today would become obsolete tomorrow. While Amer-icans generally wanted television, only 13 percent of those polled in 1939 were interested in purchasing a receiver at that time.[18]

Consumer television equipment had been sold in New York City as early as April 1938. This included regular TV sets as well as small, less expensive attachments for converting radio receiv-ers into TV sets. By the end of the following year, however, customers had a wider choice: more than three dozen models from several manufacturers, with screens from three to twelve inches diagonally and costing $150 to $1,000.[19]

The reason for this increased availability was the decision by RCA to launch a major TV sales effort in the New York City area. RCA bought advertising space in New York newspapers to promise the public the complete video package: programs, receiv-ers, and a network.

It is now possible for the RCA to announce the extension of its plans to provide, first, a regular television program service in the

New York area; second, the offering to the public of receiving sets at moderate prices within the reach of the average family; and, third, the initial step in the construction of a television relay system as a means of interconnecting television transmitters for simultaneous service to and from other communities.[20]

The drive was started in conjunction with the opening of the World's Fair in New York City in the spring of 1939. Regularly scheduled television programming was born on April 30 when NBC cameras televised President Franklin D. Roosevelt officially opening the fair, and Sarnoff announcing "the birth in this country of a new art so important in its implications that it is bound to affect all society."[21] Until this date telecasting had been confined to a few experimental hours per week. But RCA, through its ownership of NBC, now upgraded and expanded its offerings. Although it was still noncommercial and experimental TV, station W2XBS aired live studio productions as well as films and remote transmissions from the station's mobile units.

In its first prime-time show, on May 3, 1939, NBC indicated that the future of the medium would be an admixture of live and film presentation. That premier extravaganza included a remote pickup of interviews conducted by Ed Herlihy at the fairgrounds; and from Radio City in midtown Manhattan, a ninety-minute variety show featuring music by Fred Waring and his Pennsylvanians, composer Richard Rodgers playing piano for Broadway singer Marcy Wescott, newsman Lowell Thomas with the first made-for-TV film, a newsreel called *Teletopics*, plus a juggling act, a one-act dramatic sketch, and short films that included a Walt Disney cartoon featuring Donald Duck.[22]

During its first year the NBC station—called WNBT beginning in July 1941—was on the air for an average of two hours per day, televising more than a thousand programs totaling six hundred hours. The CBS station W2XAB—called WCBW after July 1941—offered a comparable amount of airtime. Less auspicious, but telecasting regularly since the spring of 1939, was DuMont station W2XWV.

the battle of the titans

The mass marketing of domestic TV receivers in conjunction with the inauguration of regularized TV programming was a bold business gesture precipitated for the most part by RCA and its president, David Sarnoff. The move was typical of Sarnoff and his tough business technique. An impoverished Russian immigrant who in his youth had been a telegraph messenger boy and a wireless operator, he battled to leadership of U.S. telecommunications by stressing refinement of the engineering fundamentals —"the pipes," he called them—of radio and television. He blended the scientist's understanding of wireless technology with a determined, austere management style that made his employer, the Radio Corporation of America, the most formidable electronics operation in the United States. It was Sarnoff who attracted experimenters such as Zworykin to the RCA research laboratory. It was Sarnoff who made the hard deals—usually through purchase, but, in the case of vital components controlled by Philo T. Farnsworth, through licensing arrangements—that brought to RCA technical patents strategic for transmitting and receiving TV signals. It was Sarnoff, too, who still found time to serve in the armed forces, entering World War II as a colonel and ending up a brigadier general in the U.S. Army Signal Corps.

In producing American television he had rivals in Philco, Zenith, and others, but through corporate ties to NBC only Sarnoff could combine formidable technical and financial power with the programming richness necessary for national broadcasting. As his recent biographer Kenneth Bilby has described him, Sarnoff "was perhaps the last of that remarkable strain of individualistic entrepreneurs—Rockefeller, Ford, Carnegie, Frick, Harriman were among them—whose autocratic governance of industrial oligarchies bruised the precepts of free competitive enterprise but spurred the tumultuous growth of the late nineteenth and early twentieth centuries in America."[23]

For Sarnoff the launching of television in 1939 was a double-edged business enterprise intended to sell TV sets to the public and impose RCA technical standards on the industry. If RCA/NBC could develop, produce, and market receivers as well as programs, the corporation could establish itself as the technological, manufacturing, commercial, and programming giant of television. With such advantage, it could monopolize the emerging industry from the outset.

Although many in the business felt that Sarnoff was technologically premature in offering regular home TV service, if enough consumers in the New York City area bought into RCA video at this date it would be difficult for the regulatory Federal Communications Commission (FCC) to render tens of thousands of sets obsolete by revising transmission and reception standards. Then, by extending its broadcast signal through cable and electrical relays, RCA could move on to conquer other U.S. cities. In

Television, a ten-minute promotional film created in conjunction with its marketing campaign and the New York World's Fair, RCA alluringly tied its product to public anticipation of television:

> *And so a new American industry has been born. Television is taking its place as another important and vital contribution to our daily lives. It is a modern miracle, a new public service produced by combining RCA laboratory science with manufacturing skill. The research problem of yesterday is the radio marvel of today. Another milestone of progress has been passed, and science has made a reality of the age-old dream of pictures from the sky.*

But optimism at RCA proved ill-founded. During the first six months of the sales push consumers purchased fewer than five hundred units. Where company executives had envisioned the dissemination of a hundred thousand sets by Christmas 1939, total sales for all manufacturers during the first full year were about three thousand sets. One observer wrote in 1940 that "Television during the past year suffered as stormy a fate as ever beset a branch of the radio industry." In this failure RCA had spent an estimated $10 million.[24]

There were several reasons for the fiasco. Technically, with no relay facilities television transmissions could only reach the horizon. This limited reception of TV signals—transmitted by W2XBS from atop the Empire State Building and by W2XAB from the Chrysler Building—to customers residing within a radius of about fifty miles of the point of transmissions. Further, the price of receivers was high, some costing as much as a moderately priced automobile. And by the fall of 1939 economic and political uncertainties in the United States were exacerbated by the outbreak of World War II.

RCA also met technical and programming opposition from business competitors and from the FCC. Eugene McDonald, the president of Zenith, a company that felt itself long abused by RCA's monopolization of radio, deeply distrusted Sarnoff and felt that the majordomo of RCA was about to snatch the TV industry from its cradle. McDonald even purchased newspaper advertising space to publicize Zenith's claim—and to sow seeds of doubt in the public being asked to buy TV—that the move to regularly scheduled programming was "premature both for economic and technical reasons."

At Philco, President Lawrence E. Gubb was also tenacious competition for Sarnoff. In the mid-1930s, when Philco radios were the best-selling units on the market, the company sued RCA for stealing confidential information by exploiting several Philco female employees, "intoxicating them with liquors at hotels, restaurants, and nightclubs," and seeking to involve the women in "compromising situations." RCA denied the charges, and the suit was later dropped. However, it revealed the bitterness inherent in these corporate wars.[25] By 1940 Philco was engaged in open warfare against RCA television, accusing Sarnoff of business skulduggery and arguing that nothing less than the future of the video was at stake.

These were bitter rivalries that exploded beyond simple capitalistic competition. As Sarnoff's biographer Kenneth Bilby has sketched it, "To McDonald, Sarnoff was a monopolistic predator who played scheming 'Russian tricks' to enforce RCA's illegal clutch on the industry. To Sarnoff, McDonald was a bloated 'parasite' who feasted on the products of RCA research to build a huge consumer business and a personal fortune."[26] *Fortune* magazine concluded at the time that television was "a prima donna industry, as full of feuds and temperament as an opera troupe."[27]

Sarnoff's toughest and most successful rival in the programming aspect of broadcasting was William S. Paley, president of the Columbia Broadcasting System. In his memoirs, Paley graciously referred to Sarnoff as a venerable uncle; it was sentimentality missing in their actual rivalry. "The general and I had a long, continuing, avuncular relationship down through the years," recalled Paley. "From the earliest days of radio, when he was the 'grand old man' and I was 'that bright young kid,' we were friends, confidants, and fierce competitors all at the same time, and we understood each other and our relative positions."[28]

Personally, Paley was much that Sarnoff was not. Paley was American-born, handsome, gregarious, and charming. He was "Bill"; Sarnoff was "the general" or "Mr. Sarnoff." Paley also was wealthy from the beginning, the son of a millionaire Philadelphia family that owned the Congress Cigar Company, manufacturers of La Palina (a Spanish neologism based on the Paley family name) cigars. Moreover, reflecting the fact that CBS was born as a programming enterprise while NBC sprung from the technical prowess of RCA, Paley was an impresario more concerned with the show than with the equipment used to transmit and receive it.

To embark on his long and successful career as a broadcaster, Paley and his family paid $503,000 in 1928 for controlling interest in the failing United Independent Broadcasters and its fledgling radio network, the Columbia Phonograph Broadcasting Company. The following day—two days short of his twenty-seventh birthday—young Paley became president of UIB and the network, which he soon renamed the Columbia Broadcasting System. A decade later he and his family still owned about one-third of the CBS public stock, and for more than six decades he remained a decisive force in the direction of the network and American broadcasting.

By 1936 Paley had learned that one way to better NBC radio was to raid its pool of talented performers, expending large amounts of money and great personal charm to woo to CBS established crowd-pleasers such as Al Jolson, Eddie Cantor, and Major Edward Bowes. Paley also purchased NBC's prestigous *Lux Radio Theater*—with its hour-long dramatizations of great plays and movies, usually featuring the original stars, and produced by the influential film director Cecil B. DeMille—moving it from New York City to Hollywood, where it remained a popular favorite for twenty years. Such bold actions catapulted CBS to programming supremacy during the 1936–37 radio season and established a pattern Paley would repeat for CBS-TV in the late 1940s.

While Sarnoff had long disliked the advertising aspects of commercial broadcasting, Paley was a businessman who sought the most popular entertainment because it would produce the largest and most profitable audiences. As he wrote in 1940, "Advertising may not be the best method, but no one has evolved a better one, or indeed any alternative which does not entail either government control or indirect but effective government influence on what goes on the air." [29]

CBS, like Philco, Zenith, and other companies, refused to allow RCA technology, and therefore NBC programming, to define American television. These companies argued effectively that the engineering standards advocated by Sarnoff—30 frames and 441 scanning lines per second, with AM radio sound and black-and-white capability only—were inferior to their own. Philco felt the standard should be 24 frames and 605 lines, and Allen B. DuMont of DuMont Laboratories called for 15 frames and 625 lines. Others felt that FM transmission would provide improved sound and that Americans should be offered color TV. All agreed, moreover, that mass acceptance of RCA products would lock U.S. television into a position of technical mediocrity from the outset.

For its part, the FCC refused to act precipitously in setting broadcast standards for television. Instead it vacillated, serving to confuse the matter further and prompting *Variety* in mid-1940 to describe the situation as "such a muddle . . . that no predictions of coming progress may safely be ventured."[30] The commission wavered between reluctant support for the bullying enterprise of Sarnoff and RCA, the desire to keep the new industry open to competition, and the wish to protect consumers from buying TV sets that would become obsolete quickly. While NBC and CBS had been broadcasting on a regular schedule for almost a year, and RCA and others had been manufacturing and marketing home receivers, the FCC acted and then reacted.

On February 29, 1940, the commission agreed to partial commercialization that would allow stations "to make charges against program sponsors . . . but without charge for transmission." Although the decision was to become effective in six months, it still did not allow profit-making. Stations would be allowed to charge advertisers only the production costs of the show and commercials. Still, it was considered a cautious first step toward completely commercial TV.

For David Sarnoff, however, partial commercialization was greeted as an opening through which to ram the RCA juggernaut. On March 12, less than two weeks after the FCC decision, Sarnoff was ready with a full-scale assault on consumers and the industry. NBC promised an elaborate improvement in the programming already being aired on W2XBS. RCA announced a renewed sales drive spurred by reductions of set prices by 33 percent. Then, looking beyond the fifty-mile horizon, NBC announced that a series of TV relay stations would soon link New York City and Philadelphia. NBC also filed applications to operate television stations in Philadelphia; Washington, D.C.; and Chicago.

Clearly distressed over the power grab orchestrated by RCA/NBC, the FCC quickly scuttled Sarnoff's plans by announcing on March 23 that it was suspending partial commercialization: television was returning to its experimental stage for further refinement. The commission blasted RCA's aggressive tactics and reiterated its intention not to saddle the public or the industry with receivers that many felt were inferior.

Not until the following year—after the full industry, under the auspices of the newly created National Television System Committee (NTSC), agreed on improved standards of black-and-white transmission at 30 frames and 525 lines of resolution (still inferior to the 625-line standard of European television) plus improved FM radio sound—did the FCC alter its position. It accepted an NTSC recommendation to allow commercial TV to begin July 1, 1941. Significantly, the engineering standards approved on the eve of World War II have remained operative. Only the challenge of high-definition television in the last decade of the century has threatened to force a reformulation of the technical specifications of American television.

RCA had little trouble adjusting to the NTSC standards. The company even offered to adjust at no charge RCA sets purchased earlier by the public. Sarnoff also bought advertising space to proclaim that the new specifications were really the same as those at RCA. On July 1, WNBT inaugurated the first commercial TV operation in the nation.

It was a day NBC had been anticipating. Unlike the early 1920s, when there had been strenuous debate over whether radio should remain free of commercial messages or become a self-supporting electronic billboard, there was no doubt that U.S. television would eventually be advertiser-supported. In August 1939 NBC produced the first experimental commercials when announcer Red Barber, during the telecast from Ebbets Field of a baseball game between the Brooklyn Dodgers and the visiting Cincinnati Reds, delivered live pitches for Procter & Gamble soap products, Socony oil, and General Mills. For the latter, Barber even prepared a bowl of Wheaties breakfast cereal on camera, adding cream, sugar, and a banana for the edification of those watching on about five hundred TV sets in the New York area.[31] When the FCC granted telecasters the right to charge fees for commercials, again NBC was the first to act. On July 1, WNBT aired a "Bulova time check" in which the face of a Bulova watch appeared on-screen, its second hand ticking, while an off-camera announcer told viewers what time it was. Time charges to Bulova were $9.

Although the public had not rushed to buy TV sets in New York City, at least the nation remained intrigued with the medium. From the opening days of the World's Fair, the exhibits of television at the RCA, Westinghouse, and GE pavilions were so popular that police had to be hired to control the long lines of those wishing to see the new electrical marvel. TV also went on tour. During the period 1939–40 the Farnsworth Television Company traveled the country promoting the medium. In department stores in eighty-eight cities—from Frederick & Nelson in Seattle to Leavitt's in Manchester, New Hampshire—more than three million Americans saw television for the first time.[32]

Philco and RCA conducted similar tours, introducing their receivers to retailers and future customers. Typically, in Chicago RCA constructed a TV studio in Marshall Field's department store and for two weeks presented public demonstrations for as many as ten thousand daily visitors. The excitement of the event was epitomized by a local radio announcer broadcasting from the site on June 12, 1939. Greeting television "with unmitigated enthusiasm," he hailed the new technology as "the greatest achievement of the twentieth century" and claimed that TV was proof that "we're certainly living in an advanced mechanical age."

Although the FCC permitted several stations to become fully licensed commercial operations, the weight of world events thwarted further progress. Expectations within the industry were dampened when President Roosevelt in May 1941 declared an unlimited national emergency. This austerity step, plus federal actions following U.S. entry into World War II in December, effectively froze the technical development and marketing of television. Now scientific and engineering skills—as well as the vital materials needed in TV manufacturing—were placed at the disposal of a government waging war on two fronts.

television and public interest

American broadcasting was inherently contradictory. In a society espousing capitalistic free enterprise, commercial radio and television in the United States were regulated by the government. The few networks that quickly monopolized national radio operated with tacit government approval, were allowed to exploit scarce public resources for private profit. Federal actions actually shaped the monopolistic character of U.S. broadcasting.

Until World War I radio had been in the hands of the experimenters and hobbyists. The patents and related technology necessary to create a viable wireless industry were held by a number of private, often uncooperative individuals and corporations. During the Great War, however, the U.S. Navy spearheaded the rationalization of the radio business. In other countries where it was already a government monopoly, radio had proven vital to military communications. Now the U.S. Navy used wartime laws to assume complete control of existing American radio. It compensated patentholders for their losses, and actually initiated new research intended to improve the technology. This pooling of patents and processes not only modernized American radio, it also brought the nation abreast of radio developments abroad.

With the coming of peace, the Navy proposed to maintain its monopoly controls. When this plan prompted charges that the federal government was becoming the same type of autocracy as that just defeated in imperial Germany, the Navy changed course. As an alternative, it suggested that a private American company be allowed to exercise monopoly control over radio. No matter that antitrust laws would have to be relaxed to create such an arrangement, the military wanted a powerful telecommunications force, a streamlined and vertically integrated corporation that could perfect radio transmission for national defense while competing successfully with European rivals. As Secretary of the Navy Josephus Daniels explained to a congressional committee in December 1918, "It is my profound conviction, as it is the conviction of every person I have talked with in this country and abroad who has studied the question, that it [radio] must be a monopoly."[33]

The Radio Corporation of America was created in October 1919 to be the communications monopoly envisioned by the military. Private it might have been, but RCA was monitored by the government. By its rules of incorporation, all company officials had to be U.S. citizens. No more than 20 percent of RCA stock could be owned by foreign elements. The U.S. Navy even received a place on the RCA board of directors.

Formed as a subsidiary of General Electric, RCA focused initially on international radio. The fact that GE had acquired the powerful Marconi Wireless Telephone Company of America— more commonly known as American Marconi—and melded its patents and personnel into RCA gave the fledgling monopoly a powerful start. But there were other uses for radio than sending cablegrams and codified military communications. Experimenters and electrical engineers alike had dabbled with radio as a medium of entertainment and information. As early as 1910, inventor Lee de Forest had transmitted a live opera; and in 1916 he operated a primitive radio station, playing recorded music and reporting news events for the enjoyment of those few with receiving equipment.

As a young employee of American Marconi in 1916, David Sarnoff synthesized these informal developments into a business plan. He wrote to his employer proposing to wire the homes of America to receive music via radio. "I have in mind a plan of development which would make radio a 'household utility' in the same sense as the piano or phonograph," he noted in November 1916. "The idea is to bring music into the house by wireless. . . . The 'Radio Music Box' can be supplied with amplifying tubes and a loudspeaking telephone, all of which can be neatly mounted in one box."

Through the acquisition of American Marconi by GE, Sarnoff came to RCA as commercial manager. But to enter the field of domestic radiotelephony, as he had suggested years earlier, RCA needed additional technology that was already controlled by competitors. To acquire these supplementary patents, RCA in 1921 had to cede much of its common and preferred stock to other electronic giants: Westinghouse (20.6 percent), a major developer of radio patents; American Telephone and Telegraph (10.3 percent), not only "the telephone company," but also, through its long-lines system, the common carrier needed to tie local stations into a national network; and United Fruit (4.1 percent), a major radio user experienced in linking together its Central American banana empire via radio, and holder of several key patents desired by RCA.[34] General Electric (30.1 percent), however, retained the largest block of RCA stock.

With these electronic powerhouses combining their radio technologies under a single control, the new corporation became an industrial giant more impressive than the Navy had originally envisioned. RCA had prepossessing leverage that stifled competition. From the bottom up, RCA controlled radio: from the manufacture of equipment to the technology of transmission and reception. Yet few in government seemed to worry that RCA's operations flaunted the Clayton and Sherman antitrust acts and forged a massive combine that would control even broader aspects of radio telecommunications in the United States.

RCA entered the entertainment business, turning the radio receiver into a consumer device and broadcasting into a national utility. When RCA formed the National Broadcasting Company with its two networks—NBC Red in September 1926 and NBC Blue in January 1927—it brought enormous technical and financial power to programming and station ownership just as commercial radio was becoming a reality. With government blessing NBC quickly dominated the air, offering attractive shows and exploitive contractual arrangements with its affiliated radio stations. RCA would continue to have manufacturing rivals such as Philco and Zenith, and programming competition from CBS. But RCA controlled most patents, employed many of the leading researchers, and from vacuum tubes to *Amos 'n' Andy* it produced and marketed the total broadcast package.

Importantly, because television was a function of broadcasting and the natural outgrowth of radio, decisions that structured the industry in the 1920s and 1930s necessarily shaped emerging TV. Nowhere was this more obvious than in the creation of a federal regulatory agency, the Federal Radio Commission, in 1927, and its more comprehensive successor, the Federal Communications Commission, in 1934.

The FCC was another in a series of regulatory agencies created by Congress to oversee critical areas of American economic life. The first such unit, the Interstate Commerce Commission (ICC), was organized in 1887. Others in this mold included the Federal Trade Commission (FTC), the Securities and Exchange Commission (SEC), the United States Tariff Commission, and the Federal Reserve Board. These entities operated as miniature independent governments, narrowly focused and outside the direct influence of Congress, president, or court. In fact, federal commissions and boards were allotted legislative, executive, and judicial powers on matters within their jurisdictions; some referred to them, collectively, as the fourth branch of government.

The FCC was created to regulate interstate and foreign commerce in electrical communication by wire and radio. Wire communication covered writing, signs, signals, pictures, and sounds of all kinds transmitted by aid of wire, cable, or other like connection. Radiocommunication was defined by the act as transmission by radio of writing, signs, signals, pictures, and sounds of all kinds. In essence, the FCC mandate was to oversee the development of modern "telecommunications," a comprehensive term that emerged about this time to cover radio and wire electrical transmissions.[35]

Like other commissions, the FCC may have exercised legislative, executive, and judicial prerogatives when assessing license applications, but this hardly made the commission a threat to the broadcast industry. Except to revoke or refuse renewal of a broadcaster's license, the FCC could do little to ensure that station owners abided by its rules. In 1952 Congress expanded the FCC's powers by enabling it to issue "cease and desist" orders, and in 1960 the commission was allowed to impose fines ranging from $1,000 to $10,000 for violations. Still, licenses rarely were retracted or denied renewal; and use of the newer powers has been confined largely to violations of transmission technicalities.

Federal regulation of the airwaves was a new concept in the 1920s and 1930s. There was no precedent to follow in managing broadcasting as it materialized in the United States. Unlike the print medium, where someone with something to say needed only a publisher—or his or her own press if a publisher were not at hand—stations were expensive to own and operate. Further, they were scarce, since there was a finite number of frequencies on the broadcast spectrum.

FCC regulatory power raised questions dear to the heart of political left and right. To those concerned with protecting civil liberties from the infringements of the state, the commission represented potential governmental censorship, curtailment of free speech, and undermining of precious constitutional guarantees.

23

To those dedicated to laissez-faire economic practices, government regulation of business constituted a first step toward state control of capitalistic commerce and creation of a centralized, planned economy.

With such inherent limitations, the commission from the outset was torn between regulating loosely enough to allow private enterprise to flourish, but closely enough to guarantee that broadcasters respected, as the Communications Act stipulated, "the public interest, convenience, or necessity." The first half of the charge was obvious: by processing applications and licensing stations; overseeing transmitter construction; enforcing laws prohibiting profane or indecent language; and settling disputes over signal interference, static, and the like, the FCC implemented specifically defined, noncontroversial rules.

On the matter of the public interest, however, the FCC's prerogatives were ambiguous. Although it was mandated to consider if the public interest, convenience, or necessity would be served by a specific action, no clear definition of that interest, convenience, or necessity was forthcoming from Congress. While the clause was usually interpreted to mean that whatever profits the industry profits the public, its ambiguity created the potential for an aggressive FCC to demand broadcast reform—from set manufacturing to program content—in the name of the public weal.

There were factors mitigating against aggressive demands for service to the public. The seven commissioners overseeing U.S. broadcasting were political appointees of the president of the United States, designated to fill seven-year terms—or unfilled portions of those terms when an appointee prematurely left the FCC. They tended to come from radio and television and its ancillary businesses; and they usually returned to the communications industry once their terms lapsed or they retired. This made for a reluctance to regulate and a desire to please potential employers.

Furthermore, FCC commissioners were not politicians. Unlike the president and congressmen, they did not have to placate constituents, raise campaign funds, or run for reelection. Thus, whatever they might propose to do outside a narrow, self-evident area of agreement was closely watched by the White House and Congress. To be effective, the FCC needed not only an internal majority voting for action but also support in the elected government—with anticipated concordance in the federal judiciary.

According to the leading historian of the early FCC, "only for a brief period, 1941–46, did the Federal Communications Commission take its tasks seriously." In reaching this conclusion, James L. Baughman has traced the FCC from the "ill-led and badly managed" 1930s to "the whorehouse era" of the 1950s when, mired in scandal and criminality, "the Commission lost its virginity, and liked it so much it turned pro." In his reasoned assessment, however, there was little hope that the FCC would ever perform as its supporters had hoped, for it was a weak agency, crippled from the start. "Congress and the president could not abide a strong FCC, not when its wards, local and network television, could deliver more votes than the TV editor of an opinion-leading newspaper or magazine. The commission was a small, toothless dog kept on a very short leash." [36]

To another critical student of the FCC, its members have always been "reluctant regulators." [37] But a Senate committee report in 1976 was harsher. It asserted that the FCC has always been plagued by unqualified commissioners, since presidents historically have used FCC appointments as "useful runner-up awards for persons who ricochet into the appointment as a result of a strong yet unsuccessful campaign for another position; appropriate resting berths for those who have labored long and hard in the party vineyards; and a convenient dumping ground for people who have performed unsatisfactorily in other, more important government posts." [38]

Of course, there were exceptions to the party hacks or utility executives and lawyers named to the FCC with neither expertise in American telecommunications nor sensitivity to consumer interests. As appointees of President Harry S. Truman, for example, Wayne Coy and Frieda B. Hennock—the first woman to serve on the commission—challenged network preoccupation with profits by championing the woefully neglected educational potentials of radio and television.

Of the early FCC leaders, James Lawrence Fly and Paul G. Porter stand out for the activist leadership they exerted. Taking the FCC in directions that had always been possible if not probable Fly and Porter enlarged the practical boundaries of FCC jurisdiction.

The most successful of the early regulatory mavericks, Fly became chairman of the FCC in 1939 and headed the commission with a stern demeanor and a reluctance to mollycoddle industry leaders. He openly assailed the motives of Sarnoff and Paley and once compared the National Association of Broadcasters, the chief lobbying arm of station owners and network officials, to a dead mackerel: "In the night it shines and it stinks." [39]

For Fly, broadcasting was a "great public instrument" li-

25

censed "under mandate to serve the public interest." As he explained it, the relationship between public interest and licensed
broadcasters was sacred. "While the duty to operate broadly in
the public interest may lack something of definition," he wrote in
late 1940, "it is clear beyond peradventure that possession—
indeed, trusteeship—of the frequency involves more of duty than
of right." With the pluck of a New Deal trustbuster, Fly asserted
that "The right is that claimed by one person, the duty is owed to
millions. The essential function of this publicly owned facility
cannot be appraised without primary regard for the rights of the
listening public."[40]

Unlike most commissioners, Fly was uncomfortable with
broadcast monopolies. Directing the FCC toward the regulation
of the quantitative aspects of the industry, he moved vigorously
against the domination of radio by the two major networks. During
Fly's chairmanship the FCC thwarted Sarnoff's plan to saturate
the market with television receivers built to then-existing RCA
standards. Fly also ordered sweeping reforms in the coercive contractual relationships between affiliated outlets and the networks
that gave the latter the right to force its shows onto local stations,
and his commission demanded that NBC weaken its stranglehold
on broadcasting by selling one of its two radio networks.

He met formidable resistance. At CBS Paley used his political
friendships and company lawyers to resist an FCC order giving
local stations greater freedom in their contractual relationship
with the national networks; Paley lost. Sarnoff went all the way
to the U.S. Supreme Court in seeking to vacate the commission
order that NBC sell part of its operation; he also failed. As a
result, corporate ties with affiliates were made more equitable,
and in 1943 NBC Blue was sold. Within two years the divested
network became the American Broadcasting Company.

Paul A. Porter, who became FCC chairman in December
1944, was another New Dealer with experience as a lawyer and
publicist that included the Department of Agriculture, the War
Food Administration, and the Democratic National Committee.
He was once the Washington, D.C., counsel for CBS. Porter led
where no man had gone before. He took the FCC in the direction
of regulating the quality of broadcast programming, drawing inspiration from the ruling by U.S. Supreme Court justice Felix
Frankfurter in the case brought against the FCC by NBC. In the
decision upholding the forced divestiture of NBC Blue, Frankfurter wrote that the Communications Act of 1934 "does not re-
strict the Commission merely to the supervision of traffic" but
that "it puts on the Commission the burden of determining the
composition of that traffic."

Porter led the FCC to the issuance in 1946 of a landmark report, *Public Service Responsibilities of Broadcast Licensees*, the controversial "Blue Book." The report resulted from an FCC investigation headed by another New Deal commissioner, Clifford J. Durr, which found widespread abuse of the air, which included excessive commercialism and an insufficiency of public service. As its title suggests, the report emphasized the civic responsibility that must be exercised by a licensee. It named four areas in which the FCC would look for a record of responsible accomplishment when assessing license renewal applications: (1) local and network shows carried on a noncommercial basis, (2) local live programs, (3) programs featuring discussion of public issues, and (4) efforts to limit the time devoted to commercials. The commission also ordered that stations annually submit statements and other evidence of their cooperation in providing public service programming.

For regulators such as Fly and Porter, the FCC needed to do more than review license applications and assess broadcast technical standards. To them the commission was a guardian of the public trust, and as such it was to be concerned about maintaining honest competition and quality programming. But such attention could only go so far. To channel American broadcasting toward the service of the public, a public that required more than mass entertainment and escapism, the FCC needed strong chairmen and committed commissioners plus a supportive president, Congress, and court system. When any of these ingredients was deficient—and with few exceptions, such was the case since its inception—the FCC was relegated to ineffectiveness, broken on occasion by the rhetorical outburst of an idealistic member.

Even if a particular FCC session were successful, there was no guarantee that a later session would not reverse its accomplishments. For example, Chairman Porter left his position shortly after issuance of the "Blue Book," and successive sessions of the commission did not seriously apply public service criteria when evaluating license renewals. For various reasons, including decreased FCC budgets, a postwar economic boom that dampened a regulatory climate born in the Great Depression, and new personnel appointed by Harry S. Truman and then Dwight D. Eisenhower, the commission slipped back to the narrower interests that had occupied most of its first decade. Failing egregiously bad conduct, license ownership practically guaranteed license renewal.

For their part, however, American broadcasters were neither government agents serving the public good nor philanthropists willing to lose money to enlighten the masses. Although pledged to serve the local audience, the typical station owner eagerly affiliated with one or more of the national networks, filled his station for the most part with programs produced in New York or Hollywood, and then—most importantly—invited merchandisers to rent from him the public's air to advertise their products and services. The broadcaster promised the advertiser large audiences—and to get this, he relied excessively on entertainment to attract them. And the larger the audience, the more he charged the advertiser. Without a doubt such an arrangement brought wonderful diversions to the citizenry, the biggest names in show business, and all free of direct charge to the audience. No doubt, too, such programming was approved by a majority of the population. But the surrender of the U.S. radio and television to mass marketing and mass communication limited program diversity and audience experience, this in an industry severely restricted by a scarcity of stations.

There never was a great public debate about the control of broadcasting by the networks and their affiliates. The audience simply went along with the exciting fare to be heard and then seen on NBC and CBS—and to a lesser degree on the Mutual Broadcasting System and the ABC and DuMont networks. Local programming wilted before the alluring competition of big-name entertainment. When a station or network offered educational programming, it was no match for the glamour and glitz on rival network outlets. In a medium commercially dedicated to serving a national audience, the perspectives of cultural, social, political, and racial minorities seldom appeared in counterdistinction to the common fare accepted by most listeners and viewers.

Emergent television was entering an environment in which the battle between public service and mass-taste programming had been already resolved in favor of the latter. That American radio would be dominated by pop culture was determined in the struggle in 1934 surrounding passage of the new Communications Act and the failure of passage of the Wagner-Hatfield amendment to the act.

Educators saw debate over the Communications Act as an opportunity to demand a greater educational purpose for broadcasting. The proposed Wagner-Hatfield amendment, led by Senators Robert F. Wagner of New York and Henry D. Hatfield of West Virginia, would have nullified all existing radio licenses, then reassigned them, with one-quarter reserved for educational, religious, agricultural, labor, cooperative, and similar not-for-profit associations. The amendment would have permitted educational broadcasters to accept advertising to cover operating expenses. With the defeat of the Wagner-Hatfield amendment, the question of educational radio and TV was dispatched to the new FCC for further discussion.

Nothing less than the future of American broadcasting was at stake in this debate over the educational role of broadcasting. Critics were blunt in their dislike of what radio had already become. As early as 1931 *The New Republic* magazine reported on a leading broadcaster from Great Britain—where an autonomous public agency, the British Broadcasting Corporation, ran national radio without resort to advertiser revenue—who was "astonished that Americans should be willing to turn over their marvelous instrument for communication so completely to the semi-sweet uses of advertisement."[41] In 1934 theatrical impresario Eddie Dowling described commercial broadcasting as already a cultural disaster, for radio had "sold its front page, sold its editorial page, sold anything and everything without reservation to keep that rich income coming in."[42] Surveys made throughout the early 1930s suggested, as one educator summarized them, that while listeners around the world "all find something of interest in the programs" they hear, "In no country except the United States have the press, educational groups, religious groups, and consumers' organizations expressed so much or such bitter criticism of their national broadcasting systems and programs."[43]

The networks were understandably defensive in arguing against educational stations and defending their own performance in enlightening the public. William S. Paley claimed that Americans were too good for broadcasting as envisioned by educational reformers out to undermine mass culture. "We cannot hand the critical and often restive American audience some brand of bright encyclopedic facts and expect it to listen enthralled as might an astonished European peasant who had grown up without benefit of school or newspaper," he wrote in late 1934. "If in the American audience we have perhaps the highest common denominator of cultural appreciation in the world—thanks to our democratic school system—we also have perhaps the most critical audience, and one of the most independent in establishing its own standards of appreciation and judgment."[44]

The president of NBC, Merlin H. Aylesworth, defended glamorous network diversion, asking, "What kind of radio fare would you present to an audience wishing primarily to be entertained and at the same time informed and therefore enlightened?" With justifiable pride he mentioned NBC accomplishments such as news programs, the airing of lectures by distinguished academicians, and its entertaining of a nation trapped in the despair of the Great Depression. But Aylesworth may have exaggerated NBC's divine function when he claimed that radio "has given a spiritual message to millions in the dark days of economic stress, now happily passing, and a means of worship to hundreds of thousands in remote places who have no opportunity to go to the churches of their persuasion."

The NBC president also stretched his credibility when he suggested that *Amos 'n' Andy*—the serialized comedy based on minstrel-show stereotypes of African-American life—was a praiseworthy model of the educational values inherent in network entertainment. "Who would care to miss a thrilling adventure with 'Amos 'n' Andy,' " he wondered, "where life may be lived vicariously, with those great comedians of the American scene pointing out to us our human aspirations, our petty foibles, our frequent mistakes in judgment, and, as well, the live-and-let-live attitude of fairness in human relations, so characteristic of America?"[45]

This is not to say that network radio did not offer important educational shows. Beginning in the first half of the 1930s, public discussion shows such as *The University of Chicago Roundtable* and *America's Town Meeting of the Air* were broadcast without sponsors. They endured for decades as sustaining programs. A great dramatic program, *The Columbia Workshop*, was another sustaining network series, and for many years it employed talented people such as Orson Welles, Bernard Herrmann, Archibald MacLeish, and Norman Corwin to produce imaginative, intelligent radio plays designed for "the theater of the mind." CBS broadcast performances of the Minneapolis Orchestra and the Philadelphia Symphony Orchestra, but NBC went farther by organizing its own NBC Symphony, headed by Arturo Toscanini. CBS even went into American classrooms via *The American School of the Air*, an educational supplement aired throughout the Great Depression years.

Nevertheless, by the end of the 1930s American radio and television were dominated more firmly than ever by mass tastes and commercial enterprise. The celebrated critic Gilbert Seldes —who at the time was director of programs for CBS-TV—offered a realist's credo, praising television for delivering mundane entertainment in which there was satisfying art only occasionally. "We must accept the two functions as equally legitimate; and more than that," he remarked in late 1940, "we must recognize the brutal practical circumstance that the arts live by daily bread, and only occasionally bring us honeydew and the milk of Paradise."[46]

At the same time, however, David Sarnoff offered a less equivocal assessment of TV. He announced that experiments had proven that video would be effective as an advertising medium. During the first eight months of regular programming, he declared, NBC had worked closely with advertising agencies—"at no cost to the sponsors during this experimental period"—to develop shows with advertising values. This resulted in 148 programs developed in conjunction with 67 advertisers representing 16 major industries. The RCA leader was pleased to conclude that "the audience response to these experimental programs has been excellent." [47] Sarnoff then took time to congratulate those who had nurtured the medium to this point—and to predict its wondrous future:

> *Thus, the ultimate contribution of television will be its service toward unification of the life of the nation, and, at the same time, the greater development of the life of the individual. We who have labored in the creation of this promising new instrumentality are proud to have this opportunity to aid in the progress of mankind. It is our earnest hope that television will help to strengthen the United States as a nation of free people and high ideals.* [48]

2

the

World War II dramatically slowed the developmental strategies of Sarnoff and others in the video industry. With the nation waging war in the Pacific, Asia, Europe, and North Africa, the perfecting of television ceased to be a public or a private priority. Many manufacturers abandoned their regular products to **arrival** make equipment vital to the military effort. With the retooling of the electronics industry, new radios and televisions—as well as replacement parts for receivers already in use—were practically unavailable. Construction of TV stations was also halted, and many existing outlets went off the air. In fact, of the ten commercial stations still telecasting in mid-1942, only six remained on the air throughout the war—but with severely curtailed transmission hours.

By 1945 seven stations were actively programming in the United States: the network operations of NBC **of tv** (WNBT, which eventually became WNBC), CBS (WCBW, which became WCBS), and DuMont (WABD) in New York City; the General Electric outlet (WRGB) in Schenectady; the Philco station (WPTZ) in Philadelphia; the Balaban & Katz facility (WBKB) in Chicago; and the Don Lee operation in Los Angeles (W6XAO). Although these stations averaged about two hours of airtime daily, much of it was filled with test patterns.

Typical of the outlets continuing to telecast during the war was W9XBK in Chicago, owned by the Balaban & Katz theatrical corporation and affiliated with Paramount Pictures. In March 1941 this experimental station began broadcasting for two and one-half hours weekly. With American involvement in the conflict, however, it left the air to become a radio and radar training facility for U.S. Navy enlisted men. Station personnel became the teaching staff of the new school.

The Chicago outlet resumed public broadcasting in October 1942, when it was licensed commercially as WBKB. With male technicians leaving for duty in the armed forces, the station was soon staffed with an all-female crew. Still, wartime experimental

TV was minimal. In August 1944 WBKB provided only 25 hours of programming per week—and much of this time was spent with military recruitment, appeals for War Bonds and the March of Dimes, boating education, and other public service matters. During the first five years of its existence WBKB offered only 2,659 individual shows totaling little more than 700 hours.[1]

Importantly, by early 1945 the station had attracted three commercial sponsors. The electric utility Commonwealth Edison financed a weekly afternoon cooking series, a quiz show, and a household-hints program; Marshall Field's sponsored an afternoon feature highlighting its different departments by means of variety acts and dramatic and comedic skits; and Admiral Radio presented *Young Chicago*, a weekly educational show produced in cooperation with the Chicago Board of Education and featuring local high-school students.[2]

Whatever the quality of the programs, the audience for wartime TV was small. Even after the war ended, viewership remained low. As late as October 1947, there were only 7,514 television receivers operating in Chicago: 4,139 in private homes; 2,295 in bars and grills; and 1,080 in other public places. The average daily audience for video in Chicago in the fall of 1947 was estimated at less than 96,000 viewers.[3]

World War II may have blunted the development of television, but it did not stop experimentation in programming at those stations remaining on the air. In 1943 WABD revitalized television in the New York City area when it installed a new transmitter and antenna at its studios on Madison Avenue and commenced program service. By 1944 the DuMont station had attracted enough advertisers to offer the first full schedule of commercial shows. No doubt, the DuMont achievement was partly responsible for the revival of interest in production that occurred at CBS and NBC stations in the summer of 1944.

One of the most energetic efforts in the development of programs occurred at WRGB. Seeking to discover the types of shows most practical for television, the GE station staged a wide variety of experimental shows. Among the productions at WRGB in the latter half of 1943 were the following:

July 16: *Hoe-Down Night,* a musical barn dance with square dancing and instructors to teach viewers how to square dance.

July 23: *A Day at the Circus,* an actual circus with a clown, band, ringmaster, peanut vendor, and performers emanating from the Schenectady studios.

August 6: Experimental commercial shows requiring twelve

sets and sponsored by Hamilton Watch, Goodrich Tire, and Vimms. The Vimms effort included a short comedy sketch, and the Goodrich portion consisted of an in-studio demonstration of the making of synthetic rubber plus displays of the new rubber derivative latex.

August 19: An Afro-American religious revival made possible when station personnel convinced the organizers of an actual camp meeting to move their gathering inside the Schenectady studios.

August 26: An abbreviated presentation of the Tchaikovsky opera *Pique Dame* performed in Russian by a professional troupe.

September 9: In cooperation with the J. Walter Thompson advertising agency, a stark presentation on blood plasma that included an actual blood donation made by a WRGB foreman, a lecture and demonstration explaining plasma, and a dramatization of a blood transfusion on the battlefield.

September 13: First of two experimental episodes of a soap opera using a fictitious sponsor for the commercial announcements.

October 7: *Bridge on Television* offered two expert card teams and a commentator. The players used oversized cards to make their hands visible to the camera.

October 22: A production mounted by WGRB's own light opera company.

October 28: *Calling All Hunters,* produced by the Batten, Barton, Durstine & Osborn ad agency and the Remington Arms Company and using a hunting lodge set to promote the advertiser's products and to offer safety tips to sportsmen.

November 11: A complete presentation of Shakespeare's *The Taming of the Shrew.*

December 16: First of four weekly hour-long programs devoted exclusively to discovering successful ways to televise news, art, music, and commercials, respectively.

December 23: As a special Christmas offering, a full-length mounting of the opera *Hansel and Gretel.*[4]

Although the war blunted the development of TV, its lure was not diminished. In early 1942 Chairman James Lawrence Fly of the FCC demonstrated his unflagging enthusiasm when he predicted that "demobilization day will find television a fully explored but wholly unexploited field" and that "during the postwar period television will be one of the first industries arising to serve as a cushion against unemployment and depression. . . . There is no reason now apparent why we should not aim at a 50,000,000-set television industry mirroring the present 50,000,000-set standard broadcast [radio] industry."[5]

Two years later Paul G. Hoffman, president of Studebaker Automobile, was similarly enthusiastic about postwar video. He predicted that within a decade television would become a $1 billion industry employing 4.6 million people and that the $100 billion saved by Americans through the purchase of War Bonds would be a strong force in this development.[6]

TV also retained its popular attractiveness because the eventual availability of television sets and quality programming was an important factor in maintaining domestic morale during the war. One of the most familiar projections of peacetime life was that of a private home equipped with electrical devices that would be labor-saving and entertaining. Manufacturers of refrigerators, washing machines, electric ovens, electric mixers, and the like stressed in their advertising that once peace returned the average home would be filled with their electrical wares. Clothes dryers, outboard motors, and garage-door openers as well as automatic irons, vacuum cleaners, and even personal helicopters were part of a predicted cornucopia. Video was one of the most glamorous dimensions of this bountiful consumerist future.

RCA was a leading herald of postwar TV. Publicly, throughout the country in the fall of 1944 it hailed the new medium as "Television, the 'Baby' that will *start* with the step of a Giant!" RCA looked to the future, proclaiming that "America's 'Next Great Industry' awaits only the green light of Victory to open up undreamed-of horizons in Education . . . Entertainment . . . Employment." Again there was the familiar pledge, assuring future set owners they soon would "tour the world via television," that the industry would provide jobs for returning soldiers and spur economic growth, that education would be enhanced in the home and in "the little red schoolhouse," and that soon "American manufacturers will produce sets within the means of millions."[7]

It was a rosy picture of postwar TV. However, such advertising masked the intense struggle behind the scenes between contending corporate forces. On the one side was RCA, with support from other manufacturers such as Philco, General Electric, and DuMont. The principal spokesman for this alliance was RCA's chairman, David Sarnoff, who during the mid- and late-1940s became a public cheerleader for the coming of TV. He could be mercenary, as in 1945 when he predicted that video would be a $1 billion business within a decade. And he could be poetic, as in 1947 when he rhapsodized on the American future in national

TV. "The East will see the West, and the West will see the East," he mused. "Television will project pictures across the prairies, over the mountains, and into the valleys."[8] But above all, Sarnoff was determined that TV would be marketed in its present form and that RCA would continue to set the standards for American communications.

The challenge to the RCA group came from programmers such as CBS and the American Broadcasting Company. CBS, however, was primarily a broadcast network, not a great electronic research laboratory or even a manufacturer. William Paley was reluctant to enter the technological field because, as he freely admitted, he knew nothing about the inner workings of the apparatus through which radio or television programs were transmitted. CBS had dragged its feet in the development of black-and-white TV because it could not compete against RCA's prepossessing control of patents on existing technology. But through the technical and persuasive acumen of its chief researcher, Peter C. Goldmark, Paley became convinced by the late 1930s that CBS could overtake RCA technologically through the development of color television.

As early as 1941 CBS had approached the FCC—albeit unsuccessfully—to have its color transmission system accepted as the national standard. The fact that CBS color employed a mechanical rotating disk, a throwback to the early debate between mechanical and electronic mechanisms, failed to diminish CBS's determination. Although existing television was solidly committed to electronic receivers, CBS was so sure of its colorful mechanical future that WCBW began its daily black-and-white wartime telecasts with the following proviso:

> *Good evening. We hope you will enjoy our programs. The Columbia Broadcasting System, however, is not engaged in the manufacture of television sets and does not want you to consider these broadcasts as inducements to purchase television sets at this time. Because of a number of conditions which are not within our control, we cannot foresee how long this television broadcasting schedule will continue.*[9]

Most of the blows in the RCA-CBS competition were landed in arguments before the FCC. In a crucial series of hearings in 1944 and 1945, CBS urged the commission to follow a slower schedule in making television available after the war. CBS asked for further research to improve reception, and it sought authorization to open the UHF (ultrahigh frequency) transmission spectrum because it had greater channel capacity (up to seventy channels) and better picture and sound quality than the VHF (very high frequency) band approved earlier. Also, because it still saw color technology as the means supplanting RCA as the industry leader, CBS urged the FCC to wait until color was perfected: why market monochromatic receivers when color was just around the corner?

With its technical and business advantages, however, RCA pressed the commission to allow immediate exploitation of existing video technology—meaning the NTSC standards set in 1941. These hearings were so crucial for set manufacturers that ancient enmities faded: Zenith did nothing overt to assist CBS, and Philco lined up in support of RCA's "television now" position. As a Philco executive explained, "There is no good reason why the public should not enjoy our present television while . . . research is going on." [10]

Three decades later, broadcast historians Christopher H. Sterling and John M. Kittross would argue, "It would be hard to overemphasize the importance of the 1945 decisions that stemmed from these hearings. Much of their structure remains, and they are the source of many of today's problems." [11] Indeed, CBS lost on all accounts. In a series of seminal rulings, the FCC accepted the RCA position. It made little difference that commission chairman Charles Denny resigned six months later to become a vice president at NBC, fueling speculation that RCA had worked improperly behind the scenes to secure a victory. The FCC gave the go-ahead to those wishing to produce commercial television with existing black-and-white capabilities.

Although there was agreement on both sides that for adequate TV coverage the United States would require about twenty-five to fifty channels, the commission ruled that TV transmission would be limited to thirteen channels in the VHF spectrum. Moreover, because the VHF band had to be shared with existing government and nongovernment fixed and mobile services—and since channel 1 in 1947 was reserved nationally for FM radio transmission—this restrictive FCC ruling meant that no more than seven commercial stations could transmit in a single metropolitan area—and far fewer when transmission interference between stations in nearby cities further prevented use of potential outlets.

It is difficult, however, to see how the FCC could have ruled otherwise. To arrest the demand for television when the war ended would have been to thwart a public led to expect TV as soon as possible. Postponement also would have hurt manufacturers already able to produce television according to prewar standards, and eager to make consumer products now that most military contracts were canceled. Further, the United States escaped its worst economic depression only because of World War II; and now, with wartime factories closing while millions of servicemen and servicewomen returning to civilian life were looking for jobs, the possibility of national economic disaster was obvious.

The FCC decisions affected the structure of TV in the United States. To make channels so scarce effectively guaranteed that U.S. television would be broadcast TV, dominated by those few corporations able to afford stations in the largest cities, provide attractive programs, attract national advertisers, and quickly build a chain of affiliates eager to appeal to the mass audience. Small networks would face impossible odds competing against the established order. Independent stations would survive only in the largest markets where there existed sufficient advertiser support. In its rush to make video available, the FCC inhibited competition and made monopoly inevitable.

For most Americans this would mean creation of one nation under television, network television. TV would be for broad, indiscriminate tastes. As had been the case with commercial radio, less popular interests such as educational TV, minority entertainment, and even locally oriented programming would be stunted by a few networks able to assemble large numbers of viewers and deliver them regularly to advertisers. Soon commercial video would be developing shows appealing to the common denominator. As one programmer explained in 1957, TV stations in this context would seek simultaneously to satisfy "the intelligentsia, the illiterate, the idiotic, the imbecile, the young, the old, the boy, the girl, the preacher, the teacher, the urbanite, the suburbanite and the farmer, the musician, the physician, the plumber . . . the baker. . . ."[12]

postwar television

By its promulgations in 1945 the FCC effectively set U.S. commercial television in a mold that would endure until the flowering of cable TV in the 1980s. By opting for VHF stations the commission effectively destroyed UHF and its greater ability to serve a nation of diverse tastes. When the commission finally opened UHF channels in 1953, it was already too late for meaningful exploitation of the spectrum. The networks were committed by now to VHF transmission, and the networks controlled U.S. television.

In accordance with FCC regulations, each network could own as many as five VHF stations; by 1953 these owned and operated outlets were lucrative operations situated in the largest U.S. markets. For example, ABC owned stations in New York City (WABC-TV), Los Angeles (KECA-TV), Chicago (WBKB), San Francisco (KGO-TV), and Detroit (WXYZ-TV). Furthermore, by 1953 almost all stations operating in the United States were network affiliates, and these were all VHF channels.

There was little advertiser interest in UHF. Sponsors shied away from the newer channels, in part because their messages traveled greater distances on the older stations. VHF signals could spread in a radius of sixty to seventy miles from the transmitter, while UHF transmission reached no more than thirty to forty miles. Although UHF outlets came quickly to most cities in the mid-1950s, it remained almost impossible to receive their transmissions, since most TV sets—many of them manufactured by RCA—could not receive such signals. By 1960 only 7 percent of American TV sets could receive UHF. Not until 1963 did the FCC require manufacturers to add UHF channel selectors as standard equipment on new television receivers.

Left with small audiences and little capital for developing or purchasing attractive shows, most UHF operations became small operations surviving on reruns of old network series. The networks avoided UHF even as an investment. Although the FCC allowed them to own two UHF stations each, ABC never bought into UHF, and by 1960 CBS and NBC had sold their meager UHF operations.

While the effects of the VHF decision would not be felt for years, the most immediately contentious FCC decision in 1945 was its deferral of the color TV question. This allowed CBS and NBC to wage war against each other for another expensive decade. Under Chairman Denny's replacement, Wayne Coy, an official of the Washington Post Company, which owned CBS-affiliated stations, the commission in November 1950 finally established standards for color transmission. After CBS and NBC demonstrated their color capabilities, the FCC endorsed, in part because of Coy's intense lobbying of his colleagues, the CBS mechanical system.

Confident that they owned the future, CBS officials inaugurated public demonstrations of color television five times a day at the Tiffany Building in New York City. After one screening, critic Harriet Van Horne beamed, "It's beautiful beyond words.

39

It's impossible not to marvel at it. And not to feel disappointed when the show ends and the screen goes dark." [13] On June 21, 1951, CBS broadcast the first network color program. Unfortunately for CBS, however, color telecasts were incompatible with the twelve million existing black-and-white sets; those set owners saw only a blank screen during the time the network's color premiere was on the air. Moreover, only twenty-five receivers in the United States could receive mechanical color.

The CBS product may have been wonderful to the critics, but it was an anachronism from the outset. Implementing CBS color by this date would have rendered existing sets obsolete—unless owners purchased an adapter costing about $100—since they had been built to the electronic specifications of monochromatic television.

Arguing that the FCC had been hasty in choosing CBS technology, Sarnoff in 1950 had turned to the federal courts for redress. He sought to enjoin the commission and force a re-evaluation of RCA color. In the meantime, his engineers labored to upgrade the electronic color that had lost to CBS. RCA gained time by spending eight months in litigation before the U.S. Supreme Court upheld the legality of the FCC decision.

A loser in the courts, Sarnoff still refused to concede. The RCA cause was aided when manufacturers such as Zenith and Philco balked at building color sets that were incompatible with the black-and-white models they were already producing. This move compelled CBS to invest millions to acquire its own manufacturing facilities. For $17.7 million in CBS stock, the network purchased the Hytron Radio and Electronics Corporation and its subsidiary Air King, a TV set manufacturer. Paley would produce his own CBS-brand receivers.

The RCA cause was assisted, however, by world events. With the outbreak of warfare in Korea, the federal government banned commercial production of color TV because the cobalt for the CBS system was now a military priority. There was no strategic reason, however, to halt production of black-and-white sets. During the Korean War millions of new receivers with RCA specifications were reaching American consumers while CBS sat neutralized with enormous expenses mounting daily.

By the time Washington in 1952 lifted its ban on color TV production, Sarnoff and his technicians had developed electronic color that was satisfactory and compatible. Before CBS could begin mass production, Paley was ready to surrender. The network's president, Frank Stanton, told a congressional committee in March 1953 that the CBS effort in noncompatible color was "economically foolish." [14] Indeed, CBS costs were astronomical: when Paley finally sold Hytron in 1961, the network's losses on the enterprise had reached about $100 million. In December 1953 the FCC finally reversed itself. It accepted the RCA standard for electronic compatible color.

Although NBC and ABC soon introduced regularly scheduled color transmissions, CBS continued to avoid total capitulation by refusing to broadcast in color. However, in 1965, with 95 percent of the NBC schedule slated to be in color, CBS took the inevitable step, announcing that half its nighttime shows that fall would be in color. The victory of RCA in defining American television was complete. Paley was bitter about his loss, but critic Jack Gould of *The New York Times* gushed, "The hero of color TV and the indefatigable champion is Brigadier General David Sarnoff. Almost alone he has brought the medium to what it is today." [15]

Color TV was not rapidly embraced by consumers. Sets were expensive, and there was popular concern about the obsolescence of the technology. Not until 1972 would half the TV homes have color receivers. Nonetheless, because they were electronic and compatible, all color telecasts could be received in black and white on tens of millions of monochromatic sets in American homes.

Despite their intensity, the business maneuverings of U.S. communications giants did not diminish the hopes most Americans held for television. Chairman Paul A. Porter of the FCC articulated the intellectual view that saw TV as the great instrumentality for bringing together the postwar nation. Speaking a few months before the end of hostilities in the Far East in 1945, he predicted that "television's illuminating light will go far, we hope, to drive out the ghosts that haunt the dark corners of our minds—ignorance, bigotry, fear. It will be able to inform, educate, and entertain an entire nation with a magical speed and vividness. . . . It can be democracy's handmaiden by bringing the whole picture of our political, social, economic, and cultural life to the eyes as well as the ears." [16]

Although average Americans may not have conceptualized as well as Chairman Porter, they knew of television, and they, too, expected great benefits from it. A Gallup poll in late 1945 illustrated that years of publicity had been effective: while only 19 percent of the respondents had ever seen TV in operation, 85 percent knew what it was. [17] Moreover, if the public attitude was accurately reflected in the opinions sampled by *Televiser* magazine in New York City in the summer of 1945, an eager peacetime public thought in terms of popular entertainment the medium would provide. "I'd like to see all the baseball games and sports events there are," declared a messenger boy. "I would expect television to lift the cultural level of the country," contended an interior decorator. An unemployed man remarked, "It will be a rather wonderful thing. A little theater in every home. It will be a new industry."

Those polled spoke of TV as amusement, offering films, music, and Broadway plays—plus daytime programs for women and inspiring messages for children. They also mentioned video in terms of news and commentary, of special-events coverage, and of a general educational influence that would "bring the world into the home." There were a few skeptics, such as an information clerk at Grand Central Station who remarked, "I think it's one of the promises like helicopters and such. I'll think about it when I see it!" But the general tenor of the man and woman on the street was upbeat. There was exuberance in the comments of three bobby soxers who declared, "If television will bring us stuff that is solid, jive that jumps, with Frankie and Perry Como, we are all for television."

More reasoned but no less positive was the newspaperman who placed it in historical perspective. "After the war, and I think that is when television will really go ahead, people will be hungry for escapism. If television can give us real entertainment, the kind of programs everyone will enjoy, it will do its job. Television has a great opportunity to influence the life and thought of America." [18]

Such anticipation was all the more striking given the paucity of wartime programming. Yet by June 1945 the FCC had 116 applications for new licenses, 86 of the requests coming from companies that already owned radio stations. Importantly, video was about to become a geographically broader phenomenon, for these applications affected 50 cities in 27 states.

Ahead were several years in which to convert factories for mass production of video equipment, to erect transmitters, develop and implement marketing strategies, and enhance the quantity and quality of scheduled programming. Ahead, too, were national economic adjustments.

While wartime price controls had counteracted inflationary pressures, removal of such controls quickly triggered inflation. As this was occurring, moreover, millions of demobilized servicemen and servicewomen and jobless war workers glutted the domestic work force and created high levels of unemployment. Long-postponed strikes by labor unions disrupted existing production. And consumers, frustrated by years of wartime saving, austerity, and the unavailability of certain products, created a demand for products from housing to hosiery that outstripped the capabilities of U.S. industry. In this time of economic reorientation, TV came to the American people.

embracing the new medium

Television became an acceptable, attractive, and affordable national utility in 1948–49. Whereas in January 1948 there had been 18 operating stations in 12 cities, 12 months later there were 49 stations in 28 market areas. A year later that figure doubled, to 98 stations in 58 market areas. The output of receivers in 1948 exceeded 975,000 units, more than a fivefold increase over the combined production for 1946 (6,476 units) and 1947 (178,571 units). Production surged even higher in 1949, topping 1.7 million units.

Advertisers also accepted the medium. During the experimental years of World War II, television was a buyer's dream. Stations such as WABD, WRGB, and WBKB, eager to refine video commercials, actually offered airtime free; sponsors were required only to pay talent and production costs, which ranged from $100 to several thousand dollars. During 1948, however, 933 sponsors bought television time (production costs included), a rise of 515 percent over figures for the previous year.

TV sponsorship, however, was an increasingly expensive proposition. Production costs for a network offering such as *Toast of the Town* were approximately $7,000; a week of *CBS Evening News with Douglas Edwards* totaled $4,000; and the Friday night boxing match on *The Gillette Cavalcade of Sports* cost $2,500. No longer willing to give away airtime, stations and networks began charging for use of the airwaves. By mid-1949 an hour of prime time at WNBT cost $1,500; the same time on the 19 interconnected stations of the NBC network cost $7,000; and appearance on all NBC affiliates—live on the interconnected stations and via film or kinescope on those not yet connected—totaled $10,000.

Neither the networks nor the local stations were fully booked by advertisers. In March 1949, commercial programs on the network flagship stations in New York City ranged from one-quarter of available airtime at WJZ-TV to one-third at WABD and WCBS-TV (formerly WCBW) and about one-half at WNBT. At smaller local stations rates were considerably lower, but the commitment of advertisers was not overwhelming. At KFI-TV in Los Angeles, where the hourly rate was $150 and a single one-minute

43

commercial spot cost $25, only 20 percent of the airtime was sold; at KSD-TV in St. Louis, where the same hourly rate applied and the spot rate was $40, two-thirds of station airtime was sold. Local sales figures ranged from 82 percent in WTMJ-TV in Milwaukee (spot rate, $50) to 10 percent at KOB-TV in Albuquerque (spot rate, $12).[19]

But even at this early date it became clear that a trend toward national programming and advertising was diminishing local initiatives and leading clearly toward national television dominated by a few networks. From May 1948 to May 1949 the airing of network fare jumped from 21 percent to 44 percent of the current operating schedules of 38 stations. By the end of 1949 network TV was attracting half of all advertising revenues and local programmers were complaining that there was a dearth of locally available talent and imagination, that network shows were more attractive than anything they could produce, and that sponsors were expecting too much from television advertising.

Merrill Panitt, TV columnist of the *Philadelphia Inquirer* and later editor of *TV Guide,* touched on the dilemma in local TV when he wrote in mid-1949 of the greater funding available to develop network programs, and the fact that good local shows should end up on the networks. Although Panitt felt "there are good and bad shows from NBC, CBS, and ABC," he seemed less hopeful about local fare when he explained that "some Philadelphia programs smell to high heaven, others just smell, and a few are well worth watching."[20]

Whatever the internal machinations of the industry, consumers by the fall of 1949 demonstrated their acceptance of the medium: 22 percent of all families in New York City already owned a TV set, other figures were 19 percent for Philadelphia, 15.5 percent for Los Angeles, and 13.6 percent in Chicago.[21] A trade journal that year captured the excitement of the times:

Throughout the nation there is a rustle of renewed activities—rehearsal halls are being dusted and vaudeville acts are being rejuvenated. Visual entertainment in all its forms is again coming into its own. Vaudeville, operettas, and the musical revue will be brought to the masses and no longer limited to Broadway or the Rialtos of the few larger cities. . . . With the combination of motion picture film and the television camera, coupled with the television receiver in the American home, John Q. America is about to receive the greatest treasury of enlightenment and education that has ever before been given to a free man.[22]

As far as most citizens were concerned, TV meant entertainment. And the ability of the medium to entertain expanded greatly in the late 1940s as the Bell System, a subsidiary of American Telephone & Telegraph, linked the major U.S. cities through an elaborate system of cables and radio relay stations. Via a coaxial cable buried in the ground and running through subterranean conduits, the image and sound from a single TV program could be transmitted instantaneously from one distant site to another. The radio relay method transmitted sharply focused microwave signals along a chain of relay towers.

One of the significant early achievements of this technology occurred in 1949 when the Bell System completed the coaxial cable linkage between Cleveland and Pittsburgh. This was the final span required to connect existing eastern and midwestern TV linkages. Moreover, through radio relay, outlying cities such as Milwaukee and Detroit also received network productions directly. Now productions originating in New York City, Chicago, or anywhere along the cable could be seen simultaneously from Boston to St. Louis. Although the four networks—CBS, NBC, ABC, and DuMont—had to share the single cable until more lines were laid and supplementary radio relays increased transmission capabilities, the connection tied together thirty-three stations in sixteen cities.[23]

What viewers saw emerging at the time was an unprecedented blossoming of exciting diversion and information. On January 11, 1949, a special program inaugurating East-Midwest coaxial operations—hailed by *Television Forecast* magazine in Chicago as "a history-making television show," another product of "the miracle of electronics"[24]—aptly summarized the condition of the medium. It featured short speeches by Chairman Coy of the FCC and by the mayors of New York City and Chicago, followed by a short film produced for the Bell System, *Stepping Along with Television,* which entertainingly explained the operation of the cable and radio relay technology.

The highlight of the inaugural broadcast was a one-hour sampler of how the networks intended henceforth to amuse the nation. For fifteen minutes each, the four networks displayed their best: Arthur Godfrey for CBS, Ted Steele with a musical revue for DuMont, Milton Berle and Harry Richman representing NBC, and for ABC an example of a Chicago-originated mystery show, *Stand By for Crime.* The *Chicago Tribune* reported that this linkage signified that "The end of dull, sustaining filler on television screens appears to be in sight."[25]

Indeed, the end of dullness was in sight across the nation. By the end of 1950 the spread of AT&T cable and relay stations tied together viewers from Charlotte, Atlanta, Jacksonville, and Memphis, to Indianapolis, Minneapolis, Kansas City, and Omaha, all anxious to receive network TV fare originating primarily in New York City. On the West Coast the achievement was more modest, as only San Diego, Los Angeles, and San Francisco were tied together via radio relay. Conspicuously missing from the national web was a transcontinental linkage between the Midwest and the West Coast. This situation was rectified in September 1951, when a system of interconnecting radio relay sites between Omaha and San Francisco became operational.[26]

If commercial network TV had promised a variety of popular diversion, it delivered television stars such as Ed Sullivan, Milton Berle, and Jackie Gleason as early as 1948–49. Although live dramas and films had appeared on experimental television since the early 1930s,[27] by 1948 TV offered a wide schedule of dramatic programs, ranging from live network offerings such as *The Kraft Television Theater* on NBC and *Studio One* on CBS to commercial feature films shown on local TV, and filmed series and kinescoped network fare distributed nationally.

If television had promised live sports coverage, from the beginning there was diversity. In 1948–49, for example, TV covered events as varied as boxing, baseball, basketball, football, women's softball, stock car racing, track and field, speedboat racing, tennis, golf, horse racing, bowling, roller derby, and hockey. However, no sport better exploited the visual capabilities of TV than professional wrestling, which generated an enormous following in the first years of the medium.

Aired live as a local event or on film from arenas across the nation, wrestling offered movement, spectacle, combat, and frequently the captivating melodrama of moral conflict as good, "clean" wrestlers such as Antonio Rocca, an Argentine grappler who wrestled in his bare feet, were pitted against evil, "dirty" wrestlers such as Gorgeous George, a California showman who splashed himself with Chanel No. 5 perfume and gave ringsiders the hairpins used to hold his well-coiffed blond tresses.

There were wrestlers of comic-book presence with names such as Hombre Montana, Chief Don Eagle, The Swedish Angel, and Yukon Eric. There were women wrestlers, midget wrestlers, and massive sumo competitors imported from Japan. Popular political feelings were even exploited as remaining anti-Axis emotions were taunted by wrestlers such as Baron Michele Leone, Hans Schnabel, Mr. Moto, and The Great Togo, who were among the most provocative "dirty" wrestlers; and Cold War attitudes helped make Ivan Rasputin a hated competitor.

As well as adult-oriented diversion, early commercial TV offered attractive children's shows. Especially prevalent were programs featuring hand puppets and marionettes. On *Howdy Doody* (NBC) Buffalo Bob Smith, with a cast of marionettes and costumed adults, entertained an energetic audience. *Kukla, Fran, and Ollie* (NBC) mixed the puppetry of Burr Tillstrom—with his little man Kukla, the gentle-hearted dragon Oliver J. Dragon, and a supporting cast of odd characters—to interact with real-life Fran Allison. On the West Coast, *Time for Beany* (distributed nationally through KTLA, Los Angeles) was a live hand-puppet serial that employed the vocal, puppetry, and comedic skills of Bob Clampett, Stan Freberg, and Dawes Butler to relate the adventures of young Beany: the crew of the little boat *Leakin' Lena;* the black-caped villain Dishonest John forever exclaiming "Curses, foiled again!"; and a friendly sea serpent named Cecil, who for a long time was visible to no one except his pal Beany and those in the TV audience.

Ironically, many of these juvenile programs were greatly appreciated by adults. The sensitive demeanor displayed on *Kukla, Fran, and Ollie* and the sophisticated wit of *Time for Beany* transcended age. Such a program, too, was *Lucky Pup* (CBS), which featured Foodini the evil magician and Pinhead, his none-too-bright assistant. In 1949 the distinguished writer William Saroyan lauded the warmth and universality captured by these puppets of Morey and Hope Bunin. Foodini, according to Saroyan, "is the attractive fake which all authority is: confident, loud, rude, self-centered, proud and yet a delight to behold in action because his pose is so easy to see through." And as for gentle Pinhead, Saroyan found him "irresistible" because

> *he is so much like so much that is true about everybody, including children. He is dominated, he is pushed around, he is patient, he means well, but he makes one mistake after another, for which he is punished by a clunk on the head. He is slight, odd-looking, has no vanity, and yet has the dimensions of a hero. His basic remark, "Yes, Boss," is a variant on any child's feeling about his relation to the world; or anybody's at all, for that matter.*[28]

If another promise of television was informational programming, by 1948–49 there was already a wide variety of news and public-service offerings. The networks televised filmed newsreels, live evening news programs, and talk shows such as *Meet the Press* (NBC). There also was remarkable live network coverage of important events such as debates at the United Nations in Lake Success, New York, and high points in the presidential election of 1948, ranging from the Democratic and Republican national conventions held in Philadelphia, to election eve results and the inauguration of Harry S. Truman in January 1949.

Individual stations also demonstrated their ability to inform viewers of crucial local developments. A five-alarm fire raging in a Philadelphia high school was televised live on WFIL in January 1948. Several times in early 1948, WBKB in Chicago showed its skills in covering news "on the spot" by broadcasting live from the scene of major fires in the city. And many stations soon began producing their own local news shows. These usually employed a local broadcaster reading from a script while newsreel footage (often generic stock footage) was used to visualize the story.

More elaborate, however, was the well-edited local newsreel. Typical of this, in September 1948 WBAP-TV in Dallas–Fort Worth inagurated *Texas News,* a nightly newsreel that was filmed, processed, edited, written, and narrated by station personnel. The station soon began supplying NBC with footage of local stories—spring floods, a hurricane, or an airplane crash—having national interest. After a year on the air, *Texas News* was cited as "the outstanding station newsreel" in 1949 by the National Association of Radio News Directors.[29]

The importance of the news function of local stations was evidenced most dramatically at KTLA. In April 1949 that independent station in Los Angeles stayed on the air for more than twenty-seven consecutive hours while telecasting rescue operations from a field where three-year-old Kathy Fiscus had fallen into an abandoned well shaft. Before her dead body was eventually brought to the surface, a community of millions had been forged, witnessing as might the residents of a small town an event of tragic proportions. *Variety* called the performance by KTLA "the greatest broadcast for the development, progress, and advancement of television."[30]

Clearly, video had finally arrived. This was the theme of *Television Today,* a CBS sales movie issued in May 1949 to attract advertisers. The half-hour production presented a seductive definition of TV. "Television is a party in the home," declared the announcer as happy adults and children watched attentively on household receivers. TV, he continued, is "sports right in the home." It also meant "seeing the news right in the home" because "every event of major significance is now caught by television."

In *Television Today* video was hailed as the ultimate medium, combining the power of the human voice, the drama of theater, the persuasiveness of movies, and the immediacy of electronic broadcasting. As for its effect on family life, TV was praised for the intimate way in which it "involves the family at home in what is happening on the screen." More specifically for children, it was credited with creating a "whole new world . . . of wholesome, highly acceptable entertainment."

Yet for all the enthusiasm generated by its visual potentialities, the nascent medium was heavily indebted to older, sightless radio for its popularity. It was those networks responsible for the success of radio that now nurtured television through its infancy. When NBC, CBS, and ABC first staffed their video operations, they drew on executives with radio experience. Many of the production personnel from radio found themselves working in front of and behind the cameras of early TV. Television was affected, too, by the business philosophy that shaped radio for more than two decades.

For most Americans, however, the similarity between radio and video was most obvious in programming. Many successful radio shows quickly made the transition to the new medium. Situation comedies such as *The Life of Riley* and *My Friend Irma* and comedy-variety performers such as Jack Benny, Eddie Cantor, and Red Skelton entered TV early. The popular quiz shows *Break the Bank* and *Stop the Music!* crossed over to video, as did radio personalities such as Arthur Godfrey, Don McNeill, Kate Smith, and Garry Moore. *The Lone Ranger*, a radio Western popular since 1933, appeared on ABC-TV in 1949. From *The Goldbergs*, *We, the People*, and *Studio One* to *The Aldrich Family*, *Twenty Questions*, and *One Man's Family*, radio helped shape the identity of television. According to TV chroniclers Tim Brooks and Earle Marsh, 216 network programs appeared in both media. Most of these programs appeared in the late 1940s and early 1950s, and almost always they were radio series that gravitated to television.[31]

In other ways, too, TV evidenced from the beginning its indebtedness to radio. By the 1950s series such as *Dragnet, Amos 'n' Andy*, and *Gunsmoke* created TV programs by recycling scripts already used on their radio versions. Well into the decade, several soap operas—among them *The Guiding Light* and *The Brighter Day*—used the same scripts on radio and television. And programs such as *We, the People, Queen for a Day, Arthur Godfrey's Talent Scouts*, and later *The $64,000 Question* were broadcast simultaneously on both media.

Many early TV shows had the aesthetics of radio. Wordy

comedy on *The George Burns and Gracie Allen Show*, for example, tied video to the aural traditions of radio. Crime series such as *Dragnet*—which began on radio in 1949 and came to television in 1952—utilized an unseen narrator to introduce and resolve each story, while story lines were carried along by a running commentary delivered as a voice-over by Jack Webb in the role of Sergeant Joe Friday.

Through their plot structures, reliance on unseen announcers to propel the action, and prerecorded soliloquies, early television soap operas recapitulated the essence of daytime radio serials. In the years before widespread use of TelePrompTers and off-camera cue cards, TV news seated journalists behind a desk, where they read scripts—interrupted only by visual inserts of maps, still pictures, and filmed material—much as they would do in delivering a radio newscast.

If the first TV programs borrowed significantly from radio, even more striking was the migration of advertisers from audio to video. In no small way, the national acceptance of TV was assured when American corporations discovered they could profit from using TV as an advertising medium, despite the expensive rates of the newer medium. William S. Paley might remind sponsors of their primal debt to radio—noting, as he did in 1949, that "Television is accepted by advertisers and merchandisers because of its inherent effectiveness, but the acceptance was materially hastened by the long and satisfactory experiences of radio advertising"[32]—but to a great degree the success of TV was built on the grave of network radio as it then existed.

advertisers and the rush to video

In its most popular years, network radio was dominated by a handful of corporate clients who paid millions of dollars annually to deliver commercial messages on nationally transmitted shows. By the late 1940s, for example, Procter & Gamble was spending $20 million per year to advertise on a variety of daytime and evening radio shows. According to Dr. Charles A. Siepmann, in 1948 P&G "bought enough time (19,812 station-hours) on the air to fill the entire annual program schedule of more than three stations." He noted further that almost 36 percent of one network's annual ad revenues came from only six sponsors—and that of the $400 million spent in 1949 for all radio advertising, 18.5 percent was derived from only ten corporations.[33]

In opting to buy time on television, sponsors for the most part were following the suggestion of advertising agencies that seemed convinced video would soon become a major sales medium. As early as July 1948, Sylvester "Pat" Weaver, then a vice president at the Young & Rubicam agency—and soon to become vice-president for television at NBC—sounded the charge, announcing, "In my seventeen years of advertising, in all media, and with personal experience and influence in helping to forge the radio pattern in its early days, I can truthfully say that there has been nothing like television in the opportunity to convince, to demonstrate, to sell."[34] Weaver's excitement was shared by talent agent William Morris, who wrote in June 1949 that "Television has the impact of an atomic bomb. It is increasing the people's intellect in proportion to a bomb's destructive power for blowing them to pieces. And it's a foregone conclusion that national advertisers will go into TV or go out of business."[35]

The U.S. Department of Commerce confirmed such speculation, reporting its certainty in mid-1949 that TV soon would become the nation's leading sales tool. The department emphasized that the effectiveness of "television's combination of moving pictures, sound, and immediacy produces an impact that extends television as an advertising medium into the realm of personal sales solicitation. Television makes the home the location of the point-of-sales presentation and reduces follow-up personal selling to a minimum." In predicting a glowing future for TV advertising, the Department of Commerce urged agencies to prepare for the boom. Although profitability was not yet high, the report suggested that "this appears to be an opportune time for agencies to engage more strenuously in television activities, to obtain experience, and to create a reputation."[36]

While such endorsements may have been encouraging to potential advertisers, the most persuasive argument was that wherever transmitters were made operational and video was available, listeners were abandoning their radio programs in favor of TV. Television came first and most plentifully to urban centers such as Los Angeles, Chicago, New York City, Philadelphia, and Baltimore. Here by 1950 more people viewed TV than listened to the radio. Surveys indicated that once more TV stations were available, radio was finished. As CBS vice president Hubbell Robinson, Jr., had written in 1948, this was a situation analogous to Custer's Last Stand, for "Television is about to do to radio what the Sioux did to Custer. There's going to be a massacre."[37]

When Lever Brothers, General Foods, Ford, American Tobacco, Procter & Gamble, and other major sponsors began buying television time, they were escaping the massacre. By the spring of 1949, as the rush of advertisers to video moved into high gear, there were sixty-three sponsored shows on network TV, and advertisers were spending upward of $12 million annually.[38] By late 1950 *Variety* described this exodus of national sponsors from radio as "the greatest exhibition of 'mass hysteria' in show biz annals."[39] During the last six months of 1951 expenditures for TV advertising rose 195 percent above figures for the previous year; during the same time radio advertising totals dropped more than 5 percent.[40] A list of the top ten advertisers in 1951, as seen in Table 2.1, illustrates clearly that television was attracting the bankrollers principally responsible for the success of network radio.

TABLE 2.1

top ten television advertisers in 1951[41]

AMOUNT (MILLIONS)	COMPANY
$12.2	PROCTER & GAMBLE
$12.1	GENERAL FOODS
$ 7.6	R. J. REYNOLDS
$ 6.8	COLGATE-PALMOLIVE PEET
$ 6.7	FORD MOTOR
$ 6.4	AMERICAN TOBACCO
$ 5.9	LIGGETT & MYERS
$ 4.9	LEVER BROTHERS
$ 4.8	P. LORILLARD
$ 4.1	GENERAL MILLS

Video advertising burgeoned, reaching more than $336 million in 1952 (a jump of 43 percent over the previous year). Relentlessly, the television share of broadcast advertising dollars in major markets rose from 32.7 percent in 1950 to 49.3 percent the following year and to 54.2 percent in 1952. By early 1953 TV in Los Angeles was attracting as much as 63.5 percent of all broadcast advertising billings there. FCC statistics indicated, moreover, that as new stations were made operational, particularly in metropolitan areas served by only one or two outlets, television continued to attract an increasing share of advertising revenues.[42]

Such rapid and complete acceptance of video resulted in the nearly complete destruction of its "sister" medium, network radio. Whereas the top radio program had a rating of 32.2 in April 1943—and 26.3 five years later—by April 1953 the leading show had a rating of 8.5, this despite the fact that almost every person in the nation had access to radio.[43] Conversely, the leading television show during the 1952–53 season had an average rating of 67.3. By December 1955 there was not one evening program among the top ten radio shows. And although there were 46.6 million homes with radio that year, the average prime-time radio broadcast was heard in only 786,000 households.[44]

More than simply underwriting the costs of TV programs, advertisers and their agencies were fleshing out U.S. television. Unlike European nations, which developed a few noncommercial national stations that were regulated by the state and financed through taxes or licensing fees imposed on set owners, video in the United States was shaped by private businesses. In a nation that historically distrusted governmental involvement in social life, there was never a doubt of such an outcome.

But there were glaring shortcomings in a national TV system that was based on advertiser support. None was more glaring that the failure of television to become the purposefully educational medium many had anticipated. Harkening back to the debate over the Wagner-Hatfield amendment to the Communications Act of 1934, idealists who envisioned television as a vital instrument for social enlightenment found little commitment to education in commercial video. They argued, as did General Telford Taylor on ABC radio in February 1951, that to serve the diverse tastes of the pluralistic American audience there must be a system of economic support different from advertiser-based programming for part of the television spectrum.

But Professor Charles A. Siepmann on the same broadcast was convinced already that TV had become "a liability" to the public. "Basically because of its costs of operation," he saw TV developing "as almost exclusively a medium of mass entertainment, with the accent on mass. It will, in other words, compound all of radio's many felonies, eschew the long-term cultural view in the interest of quick returns on sponsors' money, measure quality by the quantity of audience response, sell cultural minorities short, and give art, intelligence, and excellence the silent treatment." Abandoning his frontal attack, Siepmann turned then to cynicism to berate the new medium:

Left to itself, commercial television is likely to turn us all into a race physically distinguished by a hyperthyroid look about the eyes, and fannies flattened by excessive hours in easy chairs. A nation of passive gapers, instead of active intelligences, credulous instead of critical, mass-minded instead of individual, more and more de-

pendent upon outside stimulus, and progressively devoid of inward resources. And we shall continue to see our children graduate prematurely to the immaturity of their elders.[45]

Opposing such learned cynicism, Pat Weaver by mid-1952 remained as hopeful and philosophically engaged as ever about the future of broadcasting. After three years at NBC, he still anticipated wondrous results from the medium—nothing less than "a new era in human history . . . a most dramatic change in the environment of our country, a change almost wholly for good, in my opinion . . . witness the problems, attend the conferences, participate in the tragedies, watch the riots, see the misery, thrill to the inspiring deeds." Weaver enthusiastically maintained the liberal perspective in which TV would educate and uplift, and in the process offset destructive narrowness and ignorance. And the future, for him, was with the children of TV, "a generation of informed youngsters whose great point of difference from us will be that they accept diversity, individuality, differences in belief, custom, language, et cetera, as wholly natural and desirable."

At the base of this social metamorphosis was network broadcasting, corporate telecommunications in the service of the common good. As Weaver explained it:

It is because having the all-family, all-home circulation through a planned radio-television schedule, we can create a new stature in our citizens. The miracles of attending every event of importance, meeting every personality of importance in your world, getting to observe members of every group, racial, national, sectional, cultural, religious; recognizing every city, every country, every river and mountain on sight; having full contact with the explanations of every mystery of physics, mechanics and the sciences; sitting at the feet of the most brilliant teachers, and being exposed to the whole range of diversity of mankind's past, present, and the aspirations for mankind's future—these and many other miracles are not assessed yet. But I believe that we vastly underestimate what will happen.[46]

It was naive to have expected video to develop other than it did. At its core, U.S. television was capitalist enterprise, intent on forming mass audiences to sell them to advertisers. Matters such as education and public interest were not of primary importance in network TV. As the distinguished journalist Edward P. Morgan aptly epitomized the performance of commercial TV after its first two decades, "Once upon a time television was supposed to operate in the public interest, but lo and behold, it has captured the public and made it a product—a packaged audience, so to speak, which it sells to advertisers."

Hosting a documentary titled "Tomorrow's Television: Get What You Want or Like What You Get" on the NET series *PBL (Public Broadcasting Laboratory)* on February 16, 1969, Morgan recognized the impact on program diversity that had resulted from the limited monopoly over American broadcasting shared by the national networks. "With rare exceptions," he remarked, "one station or one network is not really an alternative to the others because they are all engaged in similar exercises trying to corral the biggest share of viewers."

Although such criticism was well earned, it is myopic to suggest that television in the United States displeased most Americans. As with most operations in a less-than-ordered world, the performance of commercial video has ranged from wonderful and enriching to banal and even destructive. It has educated and propagandized its audiences on matters social, political, and economic; but it has gained a following whose loyalty continues to make TV popular. Daily, it has bombarded an already materialistic society with countless advertisements urging the purchase of specific products, needed or not, affordable or not; but it has been a crucial vehicle for creating popular demand within an economy greatly dependent on mass consumption for its viability.

Relative to what Americans had experienced before television, the new medium was a phenomenal development in civilized living. The United States by the early 1950s had just emerged from twenty years of social dislocation. The Great Depression had destroyed families, cut short careers, and generally set the nation on a path of austerity and want. World War II may have alleviated the economic plight, but waging a life-and-death struggle against potential totalitarian conquerors exacerbated social dread throughout the early 1940s. And the economic dislocation of the early postwar years offered little assurance that the nation had escaped its malaise.

Against this backdrop, Americans welcomed television as material proof that their time of troubles had ended. Blending the glamour of the movies with the convenience of radio, a new TV in the house signified success, both national and personal. The wartime promises had come true, one could now watch the biggest names in show business right in the front room. As compensation for years of sacrifices, Americans were being entertained with the most amazing machine produced in this most amazing century. Paying several hundred dollars for a new Admiral or Philco or other brand of receiver was an investment in family security and participation in a national cultural community.

A TV commercial for RCA-Victor television captured the satisfaction associated with set ownership. On *The RCA-Victor Show* telecast December 21, 1951, the advertisement linked the pride of possessing a receiver with sentiments of family love on Christmas Eve. While a child slept securely in bed, a young couple—amid a Christmas tree, toys, and holiday decorations—removed the large ribbon adorning their new RCA-Victor television. Here was reward for surviving decades of deprivation and conflict. With melancholy music in the background, an announcer spoke optimistically of the new medium as a source of personal gratification and as the best hope for a civilization seeking only peace and security:

Christmas Eve. Night of great expectations. Night when children dream of candy canes, and 'lectric trains—of sugar plums, toy drums, and dolls that walk and talk. This is the night when dreams come true. Children's dreams and the dreams of their parents. For on this Christmas Eve into many homes will come a whole new world of entertainment on RCA-Victor television. Super sets like this will bring our nation's finest performers into living rooms in our great cities and many of our smallest country towns. And there's more than entertainment here, for RCA-Victor television will bring to many families opportunity for greater understanding. They will watch great historical events as they take place. They will see people from all parts of this land and others stating their opinions and explaining their ways of life. And perhaps this greater understanding will bring to more and more people the spirit of peace on Earth and good will toward men.

What U.S. television did, it did well, and it pleased most viewers for many years. The case against national TV, however, is more profitably directed against what it did not do, against what was not shown. As Edward P. Morgan concluded on the NET documentary, the dissatisfying reality of commercial TV "does not mean that it should be junked or seized by the government or run by a committee of do-gooders. Heaven forbid! What is needed is more variety to nourish the increasing numbers of people who find the mass audience diet indigestible."

Television was to be a commercial medium serving a mass audience that expected neither cultural uplift nor inventiveness in its diversion. And diversion was what TV would be all about. For most people this was a medium of escape, a dalliance, a relaxing time-passer. Those seeking cultural refinement, program diversity, or educational lessons were quickly disaffected, for television had no intention of becoming a conscious instrument of social improvement.

The disparity between what people viewed, and what many felt they should have viewed, created great consternation. Commissioner Paul A. Walker of the FCC put the blame on broadcasters as well as viewers, noting in February 1952 that "to a large extent the average level of radio and television programs reflects our immature wants and interests as much as it fosters them."[47] Another commissioner, Frieda B. Hennock, was less equivocal when she attacked American educators for the state of broadcasting. "They say that the mentality and tastes of the public are at a pretty low level," she remarked in 1950.

Well, I am not altogether blaming the commercial broadcasters. I blame you educators tonight. They have to make a living. They turn to the lowest common denominator approach, because that is the intellectual level of the public mind and that is the reason for the mediocre product you get on the air. In commercial broadcasting you have to consider the profit motive. When an advertiser uses the air, he is interested in selling his product. He is interested in reaching as many persons as possible, and that is why you have mediocrity.[48]

Nevertheless, leaders of the broadcast industry—whose tastes were generally more refined than those with which they engaged the nation—justified their performance in terms of the socially important service they were providing. There was no reason for William S. Paley to have changed his mind about the salutary effect of broadcasting. Television was simply an extension of broadcast radio, which he described in 1940 as "exerting a stabilizing influence on the physical distribution of the population." By this Paley meant that the "radio and the automobile have almost eliminated involuntary isolation in the United States," and wherever one lived, "the radio will bring you a supply of news and entertainment—the same news and the same entertainment available to you if you lived in Times Square, New York."[49]

Mortimer Loewi, the director of the DuMont Television Network, thought in similarly broad social terms. He argued in 1949 that television would meet its mandatory educational role. "In the final analysis, a race raised on a diet of entertainment will shortly display many of the characteristics of a moron," he suggested. To Loewi, TV was the ultimate communications medium, "the greatest instrument for mass dissemination of information and knowledge since the days of Gutenberg" as well as "the logical, inevitable sequel to all [man's] achievements in radio and motion pictures, in printing, photography, and the fine arts." Thus Loewi could predict that American television would solve that chronic scourge of civilization, "the curse of Babel, the confusion of countless tongues." He continued:

Television will topple the walls of misunderstanding and tolerance —the Tower of Babel of our time. Television will project ideas and ideals across international boundaries and be the greatest frontier-jumper of our day. . . . This great new medium of television makes its chief appeal to the eye, which discerns truth far more quickly than the ear.[50]

In ceding the airwaves to merchandisers who used them to make a living, Americans guaranteed that the utilitarian potential of radio and television would never be fully realized. With transmission initially limited to the few channels possible on the VHF band, competition was stifled and the potential of the medium to serve many audiences was restricted. Allowing a few similarly structured networks to program for such a richly diverse nation ensured the triumph of formula over invention, simplicity over the profound. As impressive as some network fare would be— and, indeed, much network programming was enormously popular with viewers and well received by critics—national broadcasting would always be driven by the propensity to satisfy mass tastes while disappointing the legitimate expectations of audiences with narrower interests.

Given the history of U.S. broadcasting in the twentieth century and the economic and political philosophy guiding American society, this arrangement was inevitable. The eminent dramatist Norman Corwin well understood what was transpiring. Writing in 1945 about the state of network radio, his appraisal remains applicable to TV and other commercialized media in the United States. Radio "rises no higher and sinks no lower than the society which produces it," Corwin maintained. "I believe people get the kind of radio, or pictures, or theater, or press they deserve. . . . The gist of what I am saying is that the radio of this country cannot be considered [apart] from the general culture and modes of the American people." He continued, "Radio today is neither as good as the program executive will have you believe in his statement to the interviewer; nor as bad as the intellectual guest at the dinner table makes it out to be."[51]

the freeze

The acceptance of television by the public and by advertisers was all the more impressive since in mid-1950 the United States was a nation once again at war. Little more than five years after the end of World War II, American manpower and industry were geared up for armed conflict in Korea. And just as World War II had arrested video development, so the Korean War raised the possibility of a similar fate for TV in these first years of national popularity. Radio executives even expressed confidence that wartime curbs on television would give their medium a "second chance" for survival.[52]

Although the Korean conflict remained a limited war, thereby making it unnecessary for the federal government to require a retooling of the electronics industry, throughout the 1950–53 period there persisted the chance that expanded hostilities would blunt, if not fully arrest, the television boom. Yet, except for the restrictions placed on the use of cobalt in the production of color TV, Washington did not impede the fledgling industry.

Popular confidence in TV was striking, too, because a "temporary" freeze on licensing new stations severely limited the number of outlets and the availability of the medium. The hiatus was ordered by the FCC in September 1948. Expected to last six months, it was not ended until April 1952. The freeze was the result of poor planning by the FCC. The commission had anticipated neither the sudden popularity of television nor the technical problems it quickly precipitated. Although the commission had issued 108 licenses by the fall of 1948, there were hundreds more applications pending from across the nation.

The commission used the freeze years to negotiate industry agreements on such matters as frequency allocation, signal interference between cities, tropospheric interference with broadcast signals, creation of standards for color television, establishment of educational television stations, and creation of additional channels through the opening of the UHF spectrum.

In terms of video availability, the freeze affected only the issuance of new construction permits; those companies already holding licenses were allowed to build their stations and begin operations. Television continued to spread across the continent, although at a slower pace. Whereas 37 stations were telecasting in 21 market areas at the beginning of the freeze, 108 stations were telecasting by the time it was lifted. Nonetheless, in fourteen states—New Hampshire, Maine, Vermont, South Carolina, Arkansas, Mississippi, Kansas, North Dakota, South Dakota, Montana, Colorado, Wyoming, Idaho, and Nevada—no transmitters were yet authorized. Although residents in half these states could receive transmissions from adjoining states, there remained seven states in which television was not available.

Moreover, hundreds of important U.S. cities missed the first years of popular TV. Located great distances from functioning TV transmitters, communities such as Denver (330 miles), Wichita (230 miles), and Little Rock (133 miles) had no television in the freeze years. Even in states with operating stations there were important cities too far from a transmitter to receive a signal: El Paso (225 miles); Tampa-St. Petersburg (170 miles); Fresno (152 miles); Spokane (230 miles); and Portland, Oregon (142 miles).[53]

For all the inconvenience it created, the freeze blunted neither the explosive popularity of TV nor the fierce competition being waged by the networks as they maneuvered for power in the industry. Whereas less than one-half of 1 percent of the nation had TV in 1948, by the end of 1952 more than one-third of U.S. homes owned a receiver. By the latter date, too, TV advertising revenues were already 70 percent as large as those for radio. And TV set production increased sixfold between 1948 and 1952.

The freeze years also allowed the networks, specifically NBC and CBS, to extend their dominance over national video. If network success lies in the ability to deliver large audiences, the talent pool and financial strength of NBC and CBS provided leverage absent at ABC and DuMont. In many TV markets, moreover, this leverage was magnified by the fact that in TV, operations were controlled by companies already operating NBC or CBS radio affiliates. And in small markets, where a single station was affiliated with more than one network, NBC and CBS made wide use of coercive "option time" contracts, which gave them first rights to place their shows on the air ahead of ABC and DuMont programs offered at the same time. As Allen B. DuMont explained the situation, "the freeze reserved to two networks the almost exclusive right to broadcast in all but 12 of the 63 markets which had television service. It meant that the other two networks did not have . . . more than a ghost of an opportunity to get programs into the markets so necessary . . . [to] attract advertisers from whom revenues and profits must come."[54]

Proof of DuMont's lamentation was in the statistics: between 1949 and 1952 network billings for NBC and CBS rose from $9.9 million to $152.3 million, more than 84 percent of all network time sales; figures for ABC and DuMont increased from $2.4 to $28.5 million. Were it not for a windfall of $30 million acquired through its merger with United Paramount Theaters (UPT) in 1953, ABC probably would not have survived the competition. Without a similar infusion of capital, however, the DuMont network continued to atrophy until it went out of business in 1955.

Regardless of intense business struggles behind the scenes, Americans wanted television. This was evident in the rapidity with which new outlets were approved and made operational following the lifting of the freeze. Within a year 70 new stations were on the air, and the FCC approved an additional 280 broadcast licenses. By 1955 there were 422 stations in the United States, and 485 by the end of 1958. Popular acceptance of video was obvious, too, in the dissemination of receivers. The number of households with TV, which had risen steadily throughout the freeze—from 3.8 million in 1950 to 15.3 million in 1952—swelled from 26 million (55.7 percent of all U.S. households) in 1955 to 38.9 million (78.6 percent) in 1957 and to 43.9 million (85.9 percent) in 1959.[55] There existed no better indication of the video success than the profit levels of TV stations. After a few years of losses, by 1954 the average station realized profit margins of 35 and 40 percent.[56]

With all its positives and negatives, national television had arrived by the mid-1950s. Now in control of a multibillion-dollar industry, the networks would spend the rest of the decade streamlining their business. By eliminating inefficient practices, maximizing profit potential, narrowing the scope of their operations, and holding close to the ratings as a guide to program life or death, CBS, NBC, and ABC solidified their domination of American video and spent the rest of the decade making money.

When David Sarnoff guided his son Robert to the presidency of NBC in December 1955, Sarnoff the elder observed that the network now possessed "the best and most complete organization we have had since the advent of television."[57] Indeed, it was a golden time for NBC, and for all broadcasters who had survived the formative years. After absorbing massive financial losses, television began to turn a profit in 1953 and never looked back. The freeze was now history, and the rush to TV was in high gear.

At the time Sarnoff was anointing his son, there were 39.4 million sets in use in the United States; 70 percent of all U.S. homes had television; and there were 331 VHF and 106 UHF stations operative in the United States. The president of the Radio-Electronic-Television Manufacturers' Association, H. Leslie Hoffman, was ecstatic when he hailed television in 1955 as the greatest retail value of any consumer commodity—costing only three cents an hour to watch, including set depreciation and servicing.[58]

Advertisers that year spent more than $1 billion in TV, and NBC's gross billings topped $140 million. Total profits for the three networks were $68 million—a rate of return of more than 116 percent against the value of depreciated tangible property. Although ABC, CBS, and NBC owned only 25 percent of all industry assets, they earned more than 45 percent of total industry profit.[59]

The euphoria in Sarnoff's words could certainly have been shared by William S. Paley. CBS may have lost the technological competition against RCA, but in 1955 CBS made more money than NBC. Paley and his network moved to the head of the ratings race with America's favorite television programs. He later recalled the events of the year. "Being the most popular network was a nice position to be in," Paley wrote, "and though we could hardly expect to stay there undisturbed forever, we would always try." CBS's preeminence would endure for twenty-one years.[60]

Even inglorious ABC had reason to gloat. It had avoided bankruptcy and survived the final cut. With DuMont out of the picture and with new management brought to the network through its merger with UPT, it was time for the junior network to make its move for industry respect and profitability. Soon, as the most innovative operation in network TV, ABC would be taking the company, the industry, the nation—indeed, the globe —in new directions.

PART TWO

One Nation
Under Network
Television

the *1950s*

programming

for a If by the early 1950s television in the United States was already national in its physical arrangement, it also was already network in program content. Unlike broadcast radio, where the great national programmers emerged only after years of competition and invention, the TV networks were in place as soon as video became feasible and popular. By the end of 1949 a total of 92 of the 98 operating stations were network-affiliated—the holdouts were 3 stations in New York City and 3 in Los Angeles—and by 1960 more than 96 percent of the 515 operative U.S. stations were network outlets.[1]

The leader of the new industry was NBC. As well as having the technological credentials of its parent company, RCA, the network was the entertainment champion of the first half of the **nation** 1950s. This was the TV home of Milton Berle, Sid Caesar, Bob Hope, Groucho Marx, and many of those dazzling stage personalities who quickly won customers and advertisers for early television. Here, too, were attractive shows in familiar genres: *Hopalong Cassidy, Dragnet, Your Hit Parade, The Philco TV Playhouse,* and *The Gillette Cavalcade of Sports.*

At the presidency of NBC in the early 1950s was Frank White, another is the succession of capable but obscure men who had directed the network since its inception. The real power at NBC was David Sarnoff. As chairman of the board of directors at NBC, Sarnoff was the executive overseer of network policy and direction; however, as chairman of the board and former president of RCA, Sarnoff was the gray eminence who influenced network decisions and coordinated NBC operations with the rest of the electronics empire he had forged.

Ultimately, Frank White—and after 1955, Robert W. Sarnoff—worked for the general. A reporter for *Time* magazine described the man in 1953 at the height of his corporate power.

Modesty, false or otherwise, does not disguise his power and success. His chill blue eyes shine with impatient energy, his boyish, scrubbed pink face radiates cockiness. All 5 feet 5 inches of his bull-necked, bull-chested figure bristles with authority and assurance. He dresses with conservative, expensive elegance, even carries a gold frame to hold matchbooks. . . . He says there are three drives that rule most men: money, sex, and power. Nobody doubts that Sarnoff's ruling drive is power. Says a deputy, "There is no question about it, he is the god over here."[2]

The chief rivals to Sarnoff and NBC were William S. Paley and CBS. No matter that Frank Stanton had been president of the network since the early 1940s, the driving force here was Chairman of the Board Paley. Above all Paley maintained that programming was the essence of broadcasting. When he led CBS into the engineering/technical area of the business, the results could be disastrous. His abortive attempts to overtake RCA as the technological leader of television cost Columbia millions of dollars. But through its ability to entertain, to attract the right star, or to develop the popular new series, CBS quickly emerged from its junior status to become the premier network, a distinction it maintained for decades. By 1958, CBS billings of $247.8 million surpassed NBC with $215.8 million and ABC with $103 million.

No network knew better than CBS how to entertain the American people. The average audience demanded stars, and if CBS needed celebrated entertainers to meet that demand, Chairman Paley was not chary about spending money to lure the biggest. He had done it in the mid-1930s for CBS Radio, and he repeated it at the beginning of the video age. Through his legendary "raids" on NBC comedic talent in the late 1940s, Paley brought to CBS some of the most popular performers in the nation, among them Jack Benny, Edgar Bergen, Freeman Gosden and Charles Correll, George Burns and Gracie Allen, and Red Skelton.

Paley attracted these NBC stars with an inventive bookkeeping arrangement. Because personal income taxes were so high (earnings exceeding $70,000 were taxed at 77 percent), a performer found it handsomely profitable to form his own production company, with himself as its chief asset, then sell the company to CBS for millions of dollars. The star would receive a salary while making television shows for Columbia, but income from the sale of his company was treated as a capital gain, taxable at a rate of 25 percent.

Paley and CBS were not timid, either, about gambling on new

TV forms. While NBC invested in live comedy-variety shows, Paley and CBS turned to filmed situation comedies; and led by *I Love Lucy*, sitcoms eventually destroyed stage comedy. In the early 1950s the network scheduled talk-show host Arthur Godfrey on two different weekly shows, and both ended up among the top ten. Paley brought newspaper columnist Ed Sullivan to host an hour-long variety show, and the program lasted from 1948 to 1971. A big-prize quiz show in prime time, *The $64,000 Question*, precipitated an industrywide rush to quizzers. With *Gunsmoke* CBS introduced the adult Western in 1955 and launched a program trend that lasted fifteen years, and a series that served the network for twenty years.

Of the two smaller networks, ABC and DuMont, only the former had any lasting impact. The DuMont network was programmatically underdeveloped, poorly positioned in terms of its affiliates, and insufficiently supported by advertisers. With no radio network to build on, DuMont lacked the entertainers and the affiliated stations needed to compete against CBS and NBC. When DuMont did develop a talent of any consequences, such as Jackie Gleason, CBS and NBC had little trouble outbidding DuMont for his services.

ABC might have suffered a similar condition except for its merger in 1951 (approved by the FCC in 1953) with United Paramount Theaters, which brought needed capital to the struggling operation. As late as 1954 only 40 of the 354 stations operating in the United States were primarily ABC affiliates; in fact, the network had more secondary affiliations, in which an NBC or CBS outlet agreed to broadcast a small percentage of the ABC schedule. By contrast, NBC had 164 primary affiliates and CBS had 113. Moreover, in terms of network billings that year, ABC earned only 11 percent of the industry total, while NBC totaled 39 percent and CBS received 46 percent.[3]

Although it was the home of a few successful series—*Stop the Music*, beginning in 1949; *The Adventures of Ozzie and Harriet*, launched in 1952; and Danny Thomas's *Make Room for Daddy*, in 1953—Sterling "Red" Quinlan, an ABC executive in Chicago, has written of the lean early years in which bankruptcy seemed not out of the question. Another writer recalled a quip from the time suggesting that if the Korean War had been a series on ABC it would have been canceled in thirteen weeks.[4]

Significantly for ABC, the merger with UPT brought new management that would revitalize the withering network. Leonard H. Goldenson came from UPT with experience in the exhibition of feature films. As a man who headed a chain of 651 movie theaters, he proposed to treat TV as he did the theater business. If youngsters were the major consumers of theatrical films, then bring youthful shows to network TV. Soon ABC was offering *The Mickey Mouse Club, American Bandstand, Maverick,* and *Disneyland*—and emphasizing young stars such as Edd "Kookie" Byrnes, James Garner, and Ricky Nelson. Goldenson felt, too, that since TV was a visual medium, feature movies and short filmed series—especially when produced by the major Hollywood studios —would be more attractive than the public-service features and stage productions that had dominated the ABC evening lineup.

In Robert Kintner, president of ABC-TV when Goldenson became president of both ABC and its parent company, American Broadcasting-Paramount Theaters, the network had a competent and flexible broadcast executive who later headed NBC. Kintner led ABC when its evenings were filled with offerings such as *Chicago Wrestling, Politics on Trial,* and Billy Graham's devotional series *Hour of Decision.* For lack of glitzy products in 1952, ABC even offered *All-Star News,* which appeared five times per week and consumed four and one-half hours of prime time. But Kintner survived the merger, following Goldenson along the road to Hollywood glamour that would bring to ABC filmed series produced by movie giants Walt Disney, Warner Brothers, and Metro-Goldwyn-Mayer.

If Kintner was malleable, Oliver Treyz, who headed ABC-TV from 1956 to 1962, was a true believer. In his late thirties when he became president, Treyz helped to turn the runt TV network around, driving ABC from a dismal third place to ratings equality with NBC and CBS. And he did it by avoiding public service while filling prime time with a barrage of youth-oriented action series such as *77 Sunset Strip, Adventures in Paradise, The Rifleman,* and *The Untouchables,* offerings that featured violence, predictable plots, and handsome leading men. Although his decisions helped ABC toward financial respectability, his critics were less charitable, accusing Treyz of (1) dumping "four hours of garbage onto the rugs of the American people every night," (2) becoming "the Mahatma of Mediocrity," and (3) turning ABC into the "pulp fiction network."

Treyz never repented of his programming philosophy. When some suggested that TV had a nobler mission, to uplift and elucidate as well as to divert, he was frank: "Listen, when Pat Weaver was president of NBC, he was programming for people who shopped at Saks Fifth Avenue," Treyz informed an interviewer in 1972. "I was programming for the people at Sears, Roebuck. There are more of them. They have the right to attention, too."[5]

the golden age of television

In describing the place television was to occupy in the American future, Richard W. Hubbell in 1942 essentially predicted the medium that emerged within a decade. For all its insufficiencies, national television performed for most Americans as "a combination movie theater, museum, educator, news reporter, playhouse, daily picture magazine, political forum and discussion center, propaganda and counterpropaganda dispenser, art gallery, vaudeville show, opera and ballet theater, plus a few other things rolled into one." Significantly, Hubbell added, "Television is also a new branch of the business world—a new form of advertising infinitely more powerful than any other form."[6]

Whether purchased for personal enjoyment or to placate clamoring children, whether embraced to keep up with neighbors or to satisfy personal curiosities, most Americans bought receivers and did not question the medium or its impact. Yet the sudden availability of television challenged traditional social patterns. By 1949 government statistics suggested that TV was the cause of major declines in movie attendance, book purchases, admissions to professional sport events, radio listening, and attendance at the theater and the opera. Cab drivers complained that since the arrival of TV fewer people were using taxis in the evening hours. Restaurant operators and bar owners blamed the attractiveness of TV for business losses. Educators claimed that video was undermining the study habits of students.

On a personal level, too, television made its impact. In the late 1940s and early 1950s owners of television sets were visited by neighbors and relatives eager to view the new medium, often on a recurring basis. The degree to which such socializing became a national phenomenon was apparent in the humorous guidelines for "television guests at your home" read by Don McNeill on his ABC program *Don McNeill's TV Club* on May 9, 1951:

1. **seating**: The front row, floor level is for the kids. Grownups venturing there do so at their own risk. Owner is not responsible for damage done by water pistols, half nelsons, or lollypops during Westerns, wrestling, or puppet shows. The overstuffed chairs are for members of the family, guests over eighty, or anyone with the miseries. Latter must bring own bottle of Hadacol to prove it.
2. **picture quality**: Guests will not tamper with the brightness, clearness, focus, volume, or anything else. If the picture is too bright, too dark, too high, too low, too this, or too

that, remember the set is adjusted to suit our eyes. It's much cheaper to change our guests than to change our glasses.

3. refreshments: Please don't expect food or drinks to be served. We don't have a lunch counter license. We don't believe in indoor picnics. Guests bringing lunches will be expected to share same with the family. After all, TV has changed our mealtime schedule, too. And for those who need liquid refreshments, you'll find clean glasses on the kitchen sink, and the faucet on the right is the cold.

4. comparisons: We have no interest in names, makes, or locations of television sets that are supposed to have larger screens, produce clearer pictures, are easier on the eyes, or are better in any way. Of this set we simply say that (a) It's ours; (b) It's paid for; and (c) It's a Philco, and there goes your argument.

5. exits: All doors open outward and can be used at any time. In any case they should be used within fifteen minutes after the program is terminated.

6. program termination: A simple majority of the immediate family may vote when to turn off the set.

7. a final word: Good night.

The appeal of television cut across educational and economic levels. By mid-1953 a total of 43 percent of families with grammar-school educations possessed receivers; that figure was 57 percent for the high-school-educated, and 48.4 percent for the college-educated. In occupational terms, 61 percent of those in the crafts and skilled labor owned television sets; for other professions the percentages were: laborer and operator, 53.6; professional and executive, 54.9; and clerical, sales, and service, 52.4. More reflective of poor reception than rural disdain, only 20.3 percent of farm families owned sets in mid-1953.[7]

If Americans bought television sets it was primarily because they liked what they saw; and what they saw was the visual realization of familiar types of diversion, often derived from other media and hosted by or starring celebrities from the world of entertainment. Comedic performers such as Jack Benny, Bob Hope, Red Skelton, Eve Arden, and Lucille Ball came to TV from success in the theater, motion pictures, and radio. Veteran private detectives and policemen of popular culture such as Mr. and Mrs. North, Ellery Queen, and Mr. District Attorney appeared in their own series. Western champions such as Hopalong Cassidy, Gene Autry, Roy Rogers, and the Lone Ranger—from movies, radio, novels, comic books, and comic strips—found quick approval on TV. And with the emergence of network day-time programming by the early 1950s, the networks took a popular radio art form, the serialized weekday soap opera, and adapted it to audiovisual specifications.

Network TV also produced its own pop culture heroes and celebrities. There were new crime-stoppers such as private eyes Mike Barnett of *Man Against Crime* and Martin Kane of *Martin Kane, Private Eye,* as well as stalwart police officials in series such as *The Plainclothesman* and *Rocky King, Detective.* New cowboy characters appeared: Kit Carson, the Range Rider, and Wild Bill Hickok. Video even offered renewed opportunities for those—such as Sid Caesar, Imogene Coca, Jackie Gleason, and Milton Berle—who had been unspectacular in other media.

From the outset, television established a substantial range of programming. Almost four million people saw part of the 1947 World Series live on TV (more than 87 percent of these on receivers in public places), and with its live coverage of the heavyweight boxing championship bout between Joe Louis and Jersey Joe Walcott in June 1948, TV realized what its most optimistic supporters expected in sports coverage.

As a political medium, television's network coverage of elections and government happenings suggested early that the medium would be a significant addition to American politics. Early coverage of the proceedings of the U.N. General Assembly helped to popularize that international organization and reverse traditional isolationist American foreign policy. Veteran radio newsmen such as Edward R. Murrow, Robert Trout, Eric Sevareid, and H. R. Baukhage, broadcasters who had helped inform the nation through the Great Depression and World War II, now brought their prestige and authority to television reportage. And they were joined by new broadcast journalists, among them John Cameron Swayze, Pauline Frederick, Douglas Edwards, and Walter Cronkite.

In the search for popular program forms, network TV even turned to religion. Of course, there were long-running religious series on Sunday mornings, such as *Frontiers of Faith* and *The Eternal Light* on NBC and *Look Up and Live* and *Lamp unto My Feet* on CBS. But from 1951 to 1954 evangelist Billy Graham appeared on *Hour of Decision,* a quarter-hour program in ABC prime time. More memorably, Roman Catholic bishop Fulton J. Sheen was a sermonizing presence on evening TV in *Life Is Worth Living* on DuMont from 1952 to 1955, and then *Mission to the World* on ABC from 1955 to 1957. On *Crossroads,* moreover, religious drama—half-hour stories featuring renowned movie stars, sponsored by General Motors for Chevrolet automobiles, and based on actual experiences of priests, ministers, and rabbis—was an anthology series on ABC from 1955 to 1957.

Above all, this was the Golden Age of live television, marked by achievement in two distinct types of entertainment: great comedy-variety shows that brought the leading comedians before the national audience, and dramatic showcases that temporarily turned television into a training ground for a generation of gifted writers, producers, and actors.

vaudeo to sitcom

From the outset television was dominated by humor. From lavish comedy-variety revues to predictable situation comedies, Americans laughed with TV. By April 1952 one ratings service calculated that 42.7 percent of all network TV programming (24.8 percent comedy-variety, 17.9 percent situation comedy) was comedy-based.[8] Interestingly, this dichotomy between comedic types reflected the emphases of the major networks, NBC, CBS, and ABC.

At NBC, comedy-variety programs were paramount. Here the marriage of the old vaudeville format and new video requirements produced the first great form of TV comedy, the "vaudeo" style, which dominated the Golden Age of TV. Vaudeo resurrected the essentials of stage variety entertainment. Here were singers, dancers, animal acts, acrobats, jugglers, and ventriloquists. Here, too, were live music, clamorous studio audiences, and the perception at home that this was authentic theatrical performance. But above all, the effect of vaudeo was to surrender to the comedians—historically, the most popular performers of vaudeville—the fate of television.

NBC offered, and Americans embraced, vaudeo comics such as Milton Berle on *The Texaco Star Theater,* Jimmy Durante on *All-Star Revue,* and Sid Caesar and Imogene Coca on *The Admiral Broadway Revue* and later *Your Show of Shows.* The premier network employed the premier comedians of the age, among them Dean Martin and Jerry Lewis, Bud Abbott and Lou Costello, Eddie Cantor, Jerry Lester, Danny Thomas, Martha Raye, Bob Hope, and Fred Allen.

Vaudeo meant dancing, popular songs, circus-style stunts, and big-name guest stars and/or series regulars, all sandwiched between generous portions of funny skits and monologues. Fred Allen in 1950, for example, welcomed to *The Colgate Comedy Hour* talents as diverse as opera star Risë Stevens and actor Monty Woolley; Eddie Cantor made his TV debut on another installment of *The Colgate Comedy Hour* in September 1950, complemented by guests who included the Peruvian coloratura soprano Yma Sumac; and that spring Bob Hope headed a special *Star-Spangled Revue* that included Dinah Shore; Beatrice Lillie; Douglas Fairbanks, Jr.; and the Mexico City Boys' Choir. During its five seasons *Your Show of Shows* presented not only the sketches of Caesar and Coca but also a variety of weekly performers such as soprano Marguerite Piazza and baritone Robert Merrill of the New York Metropolitan Opera; popular vocalists Bill Hayes and the Billy Williams Quartet; and such dance teams as Bambi Lynn and Rod Alexander, and Nellie Fisher and Jerry Ross.

Permeating such diversion were the fundamentals of vaudeville comedy: opening monologues filled with puns, topical references, and farcical jokes; and pratfalls, pies in the face, and spirited interchanges between comedians and their studio audiences, all delivered at frantic pace with occasional muffed lines and slips of the tongue. As Milton Berle suggested, vaudeo was nothing less than a revival of the past. "Despite the really arduous task of putting on a full hour video show each week," he wrote in 1949, "it has really been a pleasure to have had a part in bringing back to the people of the United States what I consider one of the greatest forms of entertainment we've ever seen. What I'm referring to is vaudeville—the old 'two-a-day.' " Berle continued,

> *I think America has been a lot poorer since old vaudeville passed away, and it makes a lot of us troupers who made our start and were weaned in the wings on the stage of the old Palace and other theaters, feel darn good to have television—the newest of all media —be the means of bringing back one of the happiest phases of American life.*[9]

Some hosts relied on sketches with comedic figures they had developed over the years; others created new characterizations for TV. Eddie Cantor brought his likable Maxie the taxicab driver to TV. For television Sid Caesar and Imogene Coca, alone and together, developed memorable characters, including Caesar's German-accented professor who was a self-proclaimed expert on almost everything, Coca's Chaplinesque tramp who communicated his pathos through comedic song and dance, and the quarrelsome married couple Charlie and Doris Hickenlooper. Jackie

Gleason introduced many comedy types on his TV show, among them Ralph Kramden; the hedonistic playboy Reginald Van Gleason III; Loudmouth Charlie Bratton; and a touching "loser," The Timid Soul, who appeared only in pantomime skits.

Vaudeo funnymen exploited outlandish costumes, contorted facial expressions, and other visual exaggerations. There were those, too, who employed verbal running gags—from George Gobel's new phrase "So there you are" to Jimmy Durante's classic references to his neighborhood acquaintance Umbriago (a pun on the Italian word *ubriaco,* which means drunk), as well as renditions of novelty songs such as "Inka Dinka Doo" and "I'm the Guy Who Found the Lost Chord."

Of all its humorous attractions, however, NBC—and early television, for that matter—relied on the enormous drawing power of Milton Berle. Trained in vaudeville but well experienced in feature films and radio, Berle came to *The Texaco Star Theater* on June 8, 1948. At the time the show was aired on NBC's flagship station, WNBT (New York City), and its seven-station East Coast network. It was produced by the influential William Morris talent agency and was conceived as a televised vaudeville show in seven acts—"the Palace Theater of television." Berle was to be one of several hosts who would rotate weekly until a permanent headliner was selected. [10]

But Berle overwhelmed TV audiences. By September he was the sole host of the show, and via kinescopes of *The Texaco Star Theater* distributed throughout the United States, he was soon a national phenomenon. In November the Berle show recorded the highest rating ever recorded by the prestigious C. E. Hooper company, a rating equal to 86.7 percent of all TV households, and a share equivalent to 97.4 percent of all sets actually in use. Granted, live network TV reached only a handful of cities and there was not much on television in 1948 to rival the glamour offered by Berle and his gang. But these were impressive numbers in any context. And a year later he was still attracting formidable audiences: for example, in Washington, D.C., he commanded a 64.5 rating with a 98 share.

Berle offered a loud, aggressive, physical comedic style with plenty of laughs and action. He wore elaborate evening gowns, had pies and powdered pillows thrown in his face, dropped his trousers, made pratfalls, and mugged excessively before his audience. His jokes were riddled with puns and comic jabs at the audience. "I have on a marriage girdle—I'm just itching to get out of it," declared Berle, wearing a blond wig and dressed in a satin wedding gown on the program of May 29, 1951. And he continued with marriage jokes, among them: "I wanna tell you, marriage helps the sale of Texaco. It really does, 'cause when you're married you wind up taking gas"; plus, "Here's a guy that got married in a garage and he couldn't back out."

Berle did for TV what Freeman Gosden and Charles Correll as Amos 'n' Andy had done twenty years earlier for commercial network radio: the popularity of his program took a fledgling entertainment medium and made it a national necessity. As well as the automotive products peddled by his sponsor, the success of Milton Berle sold TV sets, comedy, stage entertainment, and the very notion that television should be an integral part of civilization in the United States.

To counter the popularity of NBC and its vaudeo comics, CBS and to a lesser degree ABC staked their futures on situation comedy.[11] TV sitcoms differed from comedy-variety shows in two major ways: sitcoms were conceptually different, and they were usually produced on film instead of live. Situation comedies focused primarily on the levity inherent in the family or quasi-family unit. Each week brought a return to a recurring situation (a home, restaurant, office, and the like) filled with regular characters. Predicaments were recognizable ones, inevitably resolved after a half hour of funny misunderstandings, misadventures, and conflicts between personality types. The humor here was more slowly paced than in comedy-variety, and viewers approached such programs as a weekly visit with likable people who confronted not-too-serious problems with lightheartedness and interpersonal trust. Jackie Gleason—whose credits included both vaudeo (Cavalcade of Stars and The Jackie Gleason Show) and sitcom (The Life of Riley and The Honeymooners)—compared aspects of the two forms. "Situation comedy is based on honesty," he observed. "On the other hand, the monologue is predicated chiefly on a succession of lies. You can bet that the 'honesty' factor will win out with the audience in the long run."[12]

Unlike the exaggerated nonsense of the slapstick and clownish vaudeo, the sitcom offered the commonplace as the context for leisurely levity. Affability counted more than gags in this comedy form. There may have been fewer laughs per minute with the sitcom, but domesticity was its strength, since it related directly to most Americans sitting at home with the family watching television.

In terms of network business, situation comedy was a more profitable investment. Unlike one-shot live productions, most sitcoms were filmed and packaged as a weekly series totaling thirty-nine episodes per season. The networks immediately realized the benefits of filmed programs; they could fill the thirteen weeks of summer hiatus with reruns of selected episodes. Moreover, once a series appeared for several seasons, it was possible to repackage it for sale to individual stations in each of more than two hundred TV market areas. At every step in the equation, there was money to be made.

Certainly, NBC did not reject the attractiveness of situation comedies. Among the early offerings of NBC television were *The Aldrich Family*, *The Life of Riley* with Jackie Gleason and then William Bendix, *I Married Joan* featuring Joan Davis and Jim Backus, *The Dennis Day Show*, and Wally Cox's low-keyed *Mr. Peepers*. But NBC had been the home of the most popular comedy-variety shows on radio, and it was a tradition maintained by the network in early television.

Conversely, CBS did not totally avoid comedy-variety. Among the few exceptions to its sitcom rule were programs featuring Ed Wynn, Ken Murray, Red Buttons, and Jack Benny. However, Benny's vaudeo program increasingly took on the situation comedy style favored by the network, and only Jackie Gleason, beginning in 1952, and Red Skelton, beginning in 1953, enjoyed prolonged success in the comedy-variety format. Ironically, the most successful vaudeville-inspired program at CBS was hosted by a noncomedic personality, Ed Sullivan, whose Sunday evening variety showcase lasted twenty-three years.

The development of sitcoms by CBS was methodical. The network moved quickly to bring idealized families to TV comedy in programs such as *The Goldbergs* (1949) and *Mama* (1949). Other shows, such as *The George Burns and Gracie Allen Show* (1950) and *Amos 'n' Andy* (1951), tied the network's efforts to some of the most popular comedians in the nation. By the mid-1950s, moreover, new comedies nurtured on CBS radio now moved to television, among them *I Love Lucy* (1951), *My Friend Irma* (1952), *Our Miss Brooks* (1952), *Life with Luigi* (1952), and *Meet Millie* (1952). The effectiveness of long-range CBS planning appeared inevitably in the ratings: in the four seasons 1950–54, NBC had a total of thirteen comedy programs in the top ten, while CBS had only five; during the next four seasons, 1954–58, only four NBC comedies reached the top ten, while CBS placed fifteen comedies.

At ABC the commitment to situation comedy was driven primarily by economics. Elaborate comedy-variety programs were expensive undertakings. For this junior network with few hit programs and a financially uncertain future, sitcoms seemed more appropriate. Such shows were produced by independent companies, thus demanding little capital outlay by the network. The network was not unfamiliar with sitcoms. Although not committed as much as CBS to their development, the most popular comedy on ABC radio, *The Adventures of Ozzie and Harriet*, eventually became the longest-running situation comedy in video history.

While ABC had limited success with domestic comedies such as *The Ruggles* (1949–52) and *A Date with Judy* (1952–53)—and even less impact with *The Jerry Colonna Show,* one of its few comedy-variety showcases—with series such as *Beulah* for three years, Danny Thomas's *Make Room for Daddy* for four seasons, *The Stu Erwin Show* for five years, *The Adventures of Ozzie and Harriet* for fourteen seasons, and beginning in 1958, *The Donna Reed Show* for eight years, ABC proved more successful than wealthy NBC in scheduling sitcoms during the first decade of the medium. As Table 3.1 reveals, during the 1950s lowly ABC televised several of the longest-running comedy series.

TABLE 3.1

longest-running situation comedies from the 1950s

	TITLE	YEARS	EPISODES	ORIGINAL NETWORK
1.	THE ADVENTURES OF OZZIE AND HARRIET	1952—66	435	ABC
2.	THE JACK BENNY SHOW	1950—65	343	CBS
3.	MAKE ROOM FOR DADDY	1953—64	336	ABC
4.	THE DONNA REED SHOW	1958—66	274	ABC
5.	THE BURNS AND ALLEN SHOW	1950—58	239	CBS
6.	THE LIFE OF RILEY	1949—50 1953—58	238	NBC
7.	LEAVE IT TO BEAVER	1957—63	234	CBS
8.	THE REAL McCoys	1957—63	224	ABC
9.	FATHER KNOWS BEST	1954—62	191	CBS
10.	I LOVE LUCY	1951—57	179	CBS

It was not a foregone conclusion that television would be accepted.[13] It had failed once before, when Americans rejected the sales efforts of NBC in the years preceding World War II. A decade later, nothing less than the commercial and cultural viability of TV was at stake. However, if the CBS comedy series *I Love Lucy* was an indication of the attitude of most Americans toward television, the medium was clearly a winner. This show made an indelible mark on TV programming as well as on U.S. popular culture. In terms of impact and popularity, *I Love Lucy* surpassed the achievements of Milton Berle. It was the top-rated show in the nation for four of its six full seasons (1952–53, 1953–54, 1954–55, and 1956–57). In its initial season (1951–52) it was ranked third behind the programs of Berle and Arthur Godfrey. And in 1955–56 it was second only to the faddish quiz program *The $64,000 Question.* As testimony to the appeal of the series, when CBS in December 1955 reran vintage *I Love Lucy* programs on Saturday nights while airing new episodes on Mondays, the first-run shows were rated number two in the nation while the reruns were ranked tenth.

Although Lucille Ball and Desi Arnaz were inspired by the techniques of physical stage comedy so prevalent on early video, in many ways *I Love Lucy* was the opposite of the vaudeville tradition. Its half-hour, filmed format contrasted with the generally hour-long live or kinescoped productions on NBC. Ball used the clownish costumes and mugging techniques of the vaudeo funnymen, but *I Love Lucy* offered recurring characters and a consistent image of family interaction and human vulnerability that was alien to the vaudeo showcases. Lucy and Ricky Ricardo —plus their well-meaning neighbors Fred and Ethel Mertz—confused, complicated, and contorted most everyday situations. With them a vacation trip, lunch at a restaurant, watching television, the purchase of a new dress, or an approaching birthday led inexorably to mayhem and hilarity, ultimately resolved through the understanding and love basic to the Ricardos' relationship.

Family-oriented situation comedy drew viewers into the homes and problems of average-looking Americans. Vaudeo was live performance that placed viewers in a theater seat to watch people performing onstage. Sitcom depended on affable characters contending with everyday matters. In comedy-variety shows the hosts were impresarios, each week introducing series regulars and greeting new guest performers. These productions succeeded because they were lavish and compelling; situation comedies were cozy and familiar—as sparse as Ralph and Alice Kramden's kitchen on *The Honeymooners,* as middle-class as the living room of Ozzie and Harriet Nelson, or as modest as the apartment of Ricky and Lucy Ricardo.

Ironically, for all their popularity neither situation comedies nor vaudeo innovatively exploited the capabilities of television. Only Ernie Kovacs consistently demonstrated that the visual alone could bring laughter. Certainly he used spoken words with such characters as his fey astigmatic poet Percy Dovetonsils and his German disc jockey Wolfgang Sauerbraten. But Kovacs was at his most inventive when he operated without spoken words. In his short blackouts Kovacs relied on visual absurdity: a bodyless arm rising from a sudsy bathtub to scrub the back of a bathing woman; a workman apparently sitting at a level desk having his lunch, only to have his food roll rapidly to the left and onto the floor; three marching men, one of whom falls into a hole so quickly the others march on without noticing his disappearance. As George Schlatter, later the producer of *Rowan & Martin's Laugh-In* and *Real People,* described his good friend, "Ernie was just weird. He did some great things, but you never really knew when they were over. He had a certain disdain for his audience. It gave him individuality, it gave him charm, and it gave him a unique appeal." [14]

But invention in commercial TV does not guarantee large audiences, and Kovacs was not popular with the average viewer. A close associate described him and his humor as "like olives and martinis—people either hated him or loved him or couldn't care less. His comedy was way over their heads, so that they [NBC] really didn't know what the hell to do with him." [15] But fifteen years after Kovacs died in an automobile accident, a comedian of the new generation understood the significance. "Ernie Kovacs was a video innovator," wrote Chevy Chase in 1977. "He knew that there was an intrinsic magic about television itself that should be explored." Chase continued, "What is memorable about Ernie was his inclination to stay away from the familiar. He chose to break precedents whenever possible." [16]

Already by the mid-1950s there were indications that TV comedy was losing its mass appeal. Among the vaudeo shows, the reason was twofold. First, the long-term profitability of filmed series rendered live programs expensive and inefficient. There were more revenues for everyone—networks, distributors, production personnel, performers—in rerunning filmed series than in a live show that would never be repeated. Eventually, too, audiences tired of vaudeo. Berle's jokes and physical antics lost their freshness, and even someone as inventive as Sid Caesar exhausted his talent. Writing about Sid Caesar in late 1950, a Chicago TV critic predicted the demise of this form of humor. "He is a great comedian," suggested Jack Mabley, "but how long before the now regular viewers of the ninety-minute Saturday night shindig will reach the saturation point of Caesar comedy? Caesar is building greatness doing once a week what Chaplin, the Marx Brothers, Weber and Fields, and Harold Lloyd used to do once a year." [17]

Viewer rejection of the genre became apparent in the cancellation of the comedy-variety format. *Your Show of Shows* was dropped in June 1954, and its less spectacular successor, *Caesar's Hour,* survived until 1957. Milton Berle left television in 1956. After one successful season, 1952–53, Red Buttons rapidly faded, even adopting a sitcom format before departing from TV in 1955. *The George Gobel Show* was rated eighth for the 1954–55 season and fifteenth the following year; but during its remaining four years on TV the program was never again listed among the top twenty-five. And beginning in early 1953 the seminal showcase *The Colgate Comedy Hour* began to dilute its comedic offerings with musicals, special events, holiday salutes, and scenes from upcoming Paramount feature films; now renamed *The Colgate Variety Hour,* it was canceled in December 1955.

By mid-decade, moreover, comedians such as Bob Hope, Jack Benny, Dean Martin and Jerry Lewis, and Jimmy Durante had cut back considerably on their video performances, some appearing only five times a season. Interestingly, Martha Raye tried to buck the trend. After several years of guest appearances and comedy specials, she hosted her own comedy-variety hour in 1955–56. *The Martha Raye Show* did not survive its first season.

In 1956 Edgar Bergen touched on the plight of many fading comedy stars when he complained that "TV is not the nicest thing that ever happened to a performer" and that many comedians who had been headliners for a quarter-century had been "washed up in six months. Where are you going to get comics to replace them?" Bergen knew that his answer—that "No comedian should be on TV once a week; he shouldn't be on more than once a month"—was commercially unrealistic. With his dummies Charlie McCarthy, Mortimer Snerd, and Effie Klinker, ventriloquist Bergen that year hosted a weekly comedy-quiz program, *Do You Trust Your Wife?* He argued, however, that a weekly comedy show may be "good for the sponsor but not for the comedian" and that advertising agencies and the networks "owe it to the performers who have sacrificed their careers by serving as guinea pigs to TV" to provide them with employment in radio. He added, however, that "the sponsors just aren't buying radio today."[18]

Comedy writer Budd Grossman faulted his fellow writers for the collapse of TV humor. According to the man who composed for *December Bride* and other programs, "Most comedy writers today are just trying to write as many scripts as they can and get residuals for their old age." He suggested in 1957, "The days of the top comedy writers are no more. The field is easier to break into—for newcomers—than it ever has been before. That's because the average producer is not interested in top writing. He is satisfied to get a happy medium and get the film in the can in time." Grossman blamed the decline of good writing on the nature of TV scripting. "There are many rewrites involved, and then the director often demands a rewrite," he explained. "Many scripts are changed in rehearsals by stars, bit players, and script girls, although a competent writer did the original script. And after all these changes, if it comes out bad, they blame the writer; if it somehow is good, they take the credit."[19]

A few stage comedians managed to maintain a weekly TV presence, among them Jackie Gleason, Steve Allen, and Red Skelton. Of these, only Skelton enjoyed consistently high ratings.

Skelton endured because he and his writers understood well the limitations of TV exposure. Unlike many gag comedy shows at the time, his program lasted only a half hour. Further, Skelton portrayed a variety of humorous characters—among them the corrupt politician San Fernando Red; the punch-drunken boxer Cauliflower McPugg; a stupid country boy, Clem Kadiddlehopper; Willie Lump Lump, a drunk; a henpecked husband in George Appleby; a loudmouthed Western lawman named Sheriff Deadeye; plus J. Newton Numbskull; Bolivar Shagnasty; and Junior, "the mean widdle kid." Although these characters emerged from Skelton's highly rated radio program of the 1940s, his hobo character Freddy the Freeloader was a pantomime character, a visual clown produced for television.

Skelton built diversity into his show. *Variety* termed Skelton "eight TV comics rolled into one" and suggested that since each telecast was given over almost entirely to one skit, *The Red Skelton Show* was essentially a situation comedy augumented by an opening monologue, a dance corps, and guest stars.[20] And he needed that adaptability. Skelton once admitted that during his first year on TV "I used up a hundred and sixty-five routines. Some of it was stuff I'd spent years putting together."[21]

As the popularity of other great stage comedians withered, Red Skelton survived in grand style. He lasted two decades on

TV—including his first two seasons and his last season at NBC, and the remainder at CBS. He flourished particularly at Columbia. In the period 1955–70 his programs were always among the top twenty shows on television. Withstanding all new programming trends and social fads, Skelton actually peaked in the latter half of the 1960s, when in an hour format he ranked second only to *Bonanza* during the 1966–67 season.

Except for *The Red Skelton Show*, by the late 1950s audiences looked to other TV formats for entertainment. Given the copycat methodology of programmers, the medium soon was filled with replicas of successful noncomedy series. There was a sudden rush to live quiz shows precipitated by the amazing popularity in 1955–56 of *The $64,000 Question*. New business arrangements with Hollywood film studios such as Warner Brothers and 20th Century-Fox increased the supply of action-adventure, detective, and dramatic anthology series. The most successful challenge to comedy came from the Western.

A Golden Age marked by live and lavish video spectacle ended as, increasingly, Americans embraced episodic series and newer formats. Nothing better epitomized the demise of this era of the great TV clowns than Milton Berle's inglorious mixing of worn-out jokes and gutter balls when he hosted *Jackpot Bowling* on NBC in 1960–61.

golden age of television drama

If one promise of TV had been a "theater in your home," in the first half of the 1950s it was impressively realized in weekly showcases such as *The Kraft Television Theater, Robert Montgomery Presents, Studio One,* and *The Philco TV Playhouse. TV Guide*, the national television magazine introduced in April 1953, even printed a separate listing for the live dramas of the week.

In their early seasons TV dramas and comedies offered employment for stars from screen and stage, but more often such shows were testing grounds for emerging young talents. Typically, *The Kraft Television Theater* on January 25, 1950, offered "Kelly," a romantic comedy with newcomers Anne Francis and E. G. Marshall and starring veteran actor George Reeves, one year before *The Adventures of Superman* would make him a household favorite as the extraterrestrial fighting his never-ending battle for truth, justice, and the American way. Almost two years before his Academy Award performance in the film *Cyrano de Bergerac*, José Ferrer appeared as Cyrano on *The Philco TV Play-*

house on January 9, 1949. And on June 22, 1949, unknowns Jack Lemmon and Eva Marie Saint starred with the well-known actress Glenda Farrell in "June Moon," an early production on *Studio One*.

The aesthetics of live programming tied television to the theatrical tradition of intimacy with the audience. Some called it the "two seats on the aisle" theory, in which the viewer was approached as a member of a large theater audience. Others subscribed to the idea that programs needed to unfold as if there were four viewers in the audience.[22] Compared to the distancing qualities of motion pictures, either theory projected a sense of proximity and immediacy intended to lure viewers. Even when live performances were telecast as kinescope recordings—and in the early 1950s most dramatic showcases were so filmed and distributed—the sense of theatrical presence was communicated. As explained in 1949 by Marc Daniels, a director for *The Ford Theater* —and later director of the first season of *I Love Lucy*—"Legitimate drama in television is basically theater. It is true that we use the camera techniques of moving pictures and the time element of radio, but all the other factors of production most closely resemble the theater."[23]

Television in the late 1940s and early 1950s was a new medium with vitality and uncharted potentialities. For many involved with the industry, these were exciting and creative times. This was particularly true for the directors, writers, and producers mounting weekly dramatic plays. Here were young directors such as George Schaefer, Sidney Lumet, John Frankenheimer, Yul Brynner, Daniel Petrie, and George Roy Hill. Many had come to television with experience in theater. Unlike their counterparts in film, who could rely on multiple takes, intricate editing techniques, and large budgets, these first TV directors had to handle large casts in live shows that were staged with no room for mistakes and completed within restricted periods of time—often with lowly paid neophyte actors.

The medium was also a creative experience for a generation of postwar American playwrights. Television was open to young writers such as Paddy Chayefsky, Rod Serling, Robert Alan Aurthur, Horton Foote, Gore Vidal, and Tad Mosel. Even book publishers recognized the artistry of these times, periodically printing anthologies of their TV scripts.[24] "For the writer, television is a godsend," wrote dramatist David Shaw in 1954, "for here at last is a medium which will give him a chance." He continued, "Television is the greatest school for writers ever devised, and I don't doubt but that some of the better writers of the future will get their start and their encouragement from the great new medium."[25]

Despite the importance of actors, directors, and writers, from the beginning the producer was the most vital element in the nascent industry. There was no handbook explaining how to become a TV producer. As Herb Brodkin remembered it thirty-five years after arriving in television, "I became a producer almost out of self-defense. We had to get a show out every week and nobody really knew how to do that, so we just did it."[26] To the medium came energetic young producers such as Brodkin (*The Plymouth Playhouse*), David Susskind (*The Kraft Television Theater*), Martin Ritt (*Starlight Theater*), and Worthington Miner (*Studio One*). Responsible for everything from accepting scripts and hiring a cast to arguing with meddlesome sponsors and advertising agencies, the producer quickly emerged, in the words of Paddy Chayefsky, as "the brains of TV." In describing one of his favorites, Fred Coe of *The Goodyear Playhouse*, Chayefsky illustrated the controls that producers exercised over what was seen on television:

I worked with Fred Coe and—oh, my—what a fine producer he is! Coe got more freedom for the writer than most television producers, but he fought for every inch of it. His programs were a success, so he enjoyed the confidence of the networks and the advertising agencies. I really don't know much about the backdoor fighting in the TV world because when you worked with Fred you were never troubled by anyone—not the networks, not the agencies. If he said "sounds like a good idea, go ahead and write it," that was the deal. I wrote about ten or eleven scripts for Fred. The third was Marty.[27]

Because early video nurtured talents such as Coe, Chayefsky, Lumet, and Lemmon, it is incorrect to assume that TV programming was always an artistic triumph. For every memorable dramatic success, the medium offered hundreds—many hundreds—of shows that were average at best. Turned out according to familiar formulas of boy-meets-girl, good-triumphant-over-evil, love-conquers-all, and the like, these productions filled the great showcases as well as the filmed half-hour programs that thrived. During the 1954–55 season, for example, the eight network series offering live dramas staged 343 plays. And the ten filmed anthology series used about 400 scripts. Such productions came from sources as varied as respected dramatists and unknown writers submitting unsolicited scripts. Furthermore, the financial reward for such creativity was not impressive: in 1955 fees for hour-long dramas extended from $500 to $750 on *Robert Montgomery Presents* to $1,000 on *The Kraft Television Theater* and $2,500 to $3,000 on *Studio One*.[28]

In a Golden Age of well-remembered theatrical giants, however, there were many creative pygmies at work. With an enormous appetite for mass-appeal programs and with myriad influences from unartistic, self-interested sources, network TV necessarily accepted much that was mediocre. For Mrs. A. Scott Bullitt, president of the King Broadcasting Company in Seattle, the dynamics of such shows could be reduced to a simple recipe. Speaking in 1952 before a group of educators and industry officials, she shared her "recipe for an average program":

Take 1 cup of Sponsor's Requirements and sift gently, next
  2 tablespoons of Agency Ideas, carefully chilled, add
  ½ dozen Staff Suggestions, well-beaten. However fresh and flavorful, they will curdle when combined with Agency Ideas, so they must be beaten until stiff.
Stir together in a smoke-filled room and sprinkle generously with Salesmen's Gimmicks.
Cover the mixture with a tight lid so that no Imagination can get in and no Gimmicks can get out, and let stand while the costs increase.
Then take 1 jigger of Talent, domestic will do.
Flavor with Production Problems
  A pinch of Doubt
  And, if you have any, a dash of Hope.
Fold these ingredients carefully together so they can get into a small studio. This requires a very light touch as the slightest jolt will sour the results.
Be sure to line the pan with Union Regulations otherwise the mixture will stick.
Place in the oven with your fingers crossed.
Sometimes it comes out a tasty delicacy, and
Sometimes, it's just cooked.[29]

Lest the playwrights of fledgling television—even the quality writers—forget they were creating for a mass medium with its roots in commerce, they inevitably confronted limitations on what they could say and show, especially when their dramas treated controversial issues. Whether the impetus came from sponsors and their agencies anxious about taking sides, or networks and local stations fearful of the reaction of viewers and advertisers, pressures toward blandness were powerful. Interference could be petty, such as the insistence of Alcoa (the Aluminum Company of America) that a lynching in "Tragedy in a Temporary Town" on *The Alcoa Hour* in 1956 could not be set in a trailer camp because most mobile homes were constructed of aluminum. Writer Reginald Rose had to substitute wooden shacks for aluminum trailers.

Advertiser involvement could also involve political issues. Describing why he could not write a TV drama about the civil rights controversy demanding national attention in the late 1950s, Paddy Chayefsky claimed that "you can't write the Little Rock thing because they can't sell the sets down South . . . or you can't sell the aluminum paper down South."[30] Reginald Rose described how in 1954 he was compelled to alter his play "Thunder on Sycamore Street"—a drama about a black family beset by white racists—because it "was unpalatable to the networks since many of their stations are situated in southern states, and it was felt that viewers might be appalled at the sight of a Negro as the beleaguered hero of a television drama."[31] Although writer Gore Vidal could maintain that "TV is a wonderful place to experiment. A writer can tackle anything if he learns how to dodge around the 'forbidden subjects,' "[32] Rod Serling was more convinced that censorship was "the big problem." As he told an interviewer in 1957, "I've found censorship always begins with the network. Then it spreads to the advertising agency. Then the sponsor. Among them, when they get through, there isn't very much left."[33]

shaping a

national

culture

Regardless of the relative strengths and achievements of NBC, CBS, and ABC, whenever their programming became available in a TV market it quickly conquered the audience and crushed local video production. First, the network fare usually was more glamorous and attractive; and second, since there were few genuinely independent stations in the United States, most stations were network-affiliated and eager to push aside costly locally produced fare in favor of highly rated national programs.

This pattern is noticeable by a comparison of leading programs in New York City, where the four networks flourished, and in Chicago before the coaxial cable in 1949 brought that city into direct contact with network shows. As seen in Table 4.1, Telepulse ratings from early January 1949 indicate that while New Yorkers were watching shows originating from the networks in New York City, only one national series, *The Philco TV Playhouse*, was among the top ten choices in Chicago.

The difference in Chicago TV viewing is noticeable in statistics from a later date. Once opened to direct telecasts of network features, stations gradually introduced national programs and canceled many local productions. As indicated in Table 4.2, the ratings in October–November 1950, Chicago was solidly integrated into an American audience.

National programming made its easiest conquests in those markets where there were few stations and a shortage of money and facilities for local creativity. San Francisco was such a city. By 1950 there were three stations serving the San Francisco-Oakland Bay Area, all of them network affiliates. Locally originated programming was scarce. Instead, KRON-TV, KPIX, and KGO-TV received their shows from New York, Chicago, and even Los Angeles. As did much of the nation, viewers in San Francisco watched network films: filmed series and movies made of shows when they originated live in the East. Table 4.3, listing

TABLE **4.1**

comparative telepulse ratings, january 1949[1]

NEW YORK CITY	CHICAGO
1. THE TEXACO STAR THEATER	1. WRESTLING (THURSDAY)
2. ARTHUR GODFREY AND HIS FRIENDS	2. SUPER CIRCUS
3. ARTHUR GODFREY'S TALENT SCOUTS	3. FEATURE FILM (FRIDAY)
4. THE TOAST OF THE TOWN	4. VAUDEO VARIETIES
5. THE KRAFT TELEVISION THEATER	5. FEATURE FILM (HENRY VIII)
6. THE ORIGINAL AMATEUR HOUR	6. WRESTLING (WEDNESDAY)
7. WE, THE PEOPLE	7. HOCKEY (SUNDAY)
8. THE ARROW SHOW	8. WRESTLING (MONDAY)
9. THE BIGELOW SHOW	9. THE PHILCO TV PLAYHOUSE*
10. THE GULF SHOW	10. FEATURE FILM (TUESDAY)

* NONLOCAL ORIGINATION

the leading programs in San Francisco in October–November 1950, illustrates the decisiveness with which that market was consumed in the national picture.

Although the transcontinental connection between the West Coast and the rest of the nation was achieved in September 1951, until cable capacities were enlarged and supplemented by more radio relay facilities, much of the nation continued to view network offerings on 16mm film. Via Railway Express, air freight, or the U.S. mail, filmed series such as *I Love Lucy, Big Town,* and *The Gene Autry Show* were distributed to stations not directly linked with the networks, or to localities where limited cable capacities or a scarcity of stations made it impossible to carry all the programs aired by the four networks.

For those situations where live shows could not be seen as they were being televised, by mid-1948 the kinescope process was used to record performances for future broadcasts. Kinescopes were 16mm motion pictures shot directly off the screen of a tele-

TABLE 4.2

comparative telepulse ratings, october 29– november 17, 1950[2]

NEW YORK CITY	CHICAGO
1. THE TOAST OF THE TOWN	1. THE TEXACO STAR THEATER
2. FOUR STAR REVUE	2. PRESIDENT TRUMAN SPEECH
3. THE PHILCO TV PLAYHOUSE	3. THE TOAST OF THE TOWN
4. PRESIDENT TRUMAN SPEECH	4. FIRESIDE THEATER
5. THE COLGATE COMEDY HOUR	5. ARTHUR GODFREY'S TALENT SCOUTS
6. YOUR SHOW OF SHOWS	6. YOUR SHOW OF SHOWS
7. THE TOAST OF THE TOWN	7. COMMUNITY THEATER *
8. STUDIO ONE	8. THE FRED WARING SHOW
9. FIRESIDE THEATER	9. THE KRAFT TELEVISION THEATER
10. THE CHILDREN'S HOUR *	10. THE SACHS AMATEUR HOUR *

* NON-NETWORK/LOCAL ORIGINATION

vision set. This procedure produced an image with a grainy, flat quality; but for many years the most popular offerings on TV, such as *Your Show of Shows,* with Sid Caesar and Imogene Coca; Ed Sullivan's *The Toast of the Town;* and *The Colgate Comedy Hour,* with its various guest hosts, reached less accessible communities only as kinescopes.

There was resistance, however, to the usurpation of American television by the networks. Two scholars, Dallas Smyth and Donald Horton, argued in January 1951 that TV was already compromising its potential. In a typical week of television in New York City they found only 4 percent of the time dedicated to "informational" programs, while 55 percent was concerned with "Wild West drama, crime, drama, sport, quizzes, stunts, and contests." In prime time, they concluded, a clear majority of time was devoted to entertainment programs with relatively low or perhaps negative survival value for the individual viewer or for society."[4]

telepulse ratings, october 29–
november 17, 1950[3]

SAN FRANCISCO

1. THE TEXACO STAR THEATER
2. THE ORIGINAL AMATEUR HOUR
3. THE TOAST OF THE TOWN
4. THE GENE AUTRY SHOW
5. HOPALONG CASSIDY
6. THE RUGGLES
7. ARTHUR GODFREY AND HIS FRIENDS
8. PARTI-PAK THEATER (FEATURE FILM) *
9. STANFORD-USC FOOTBALL *
10. SUSPENSE

* NON-NETWORK/LOCAL ORIGINATION

Another critic, Senator William Benton of Connecticut, was concerned about the failure of TV to educate. His fear in mid-1951 was that the creative talents of commercial broadcasters "may be channeled, in television as in radio, into a limited number of stereotyped but salable program formats." He wondered, prophetically, "Can we afford to waste as much time and talent on trivia in television as we have in radio?"[5]

It was difficult, however, to resist national programming. First, network-owned and -operated stations, located in the largest cities and serving about one-quarter of the U.S. population, rarely preempted shows coming, after all, from corporate superiors in New York. Once local stations began a network series, they could not cancel the series on their own. Furthermore, an affiliate station in the 1950s was contractually obligated to option to its network as much as twelve hours of each broadcast day. This "option time" as well as other contractual agreements effectively turned the local station into a possession of a New York-based network.

Virtual ownership of local stations was critical to network advertising strategies. As Stan Opotowsky explained in his pioneering study of video history TV—The Big Picture, CBS and NBC in 1951 discovered that they could reach two-thirds of the U.S. population through stations in only seventy-seven cities.[6] They quickly affiliated with the fifty-five most important of these as their "basic" network. To this was added a second tier of fifty-three areas, "desirable" because of the consumer buying strength they represented. A third tier of eighty mostly small communities gave the network virtually complete national coverage.

With such a grand design fully in place by the late 1950s, a network could sell programs based on the number of consumers an advertiser wished to reach. CBS, for instance, carried *The Danny Thomas Show* on 202 stations because the sponsor wanted to saturate the nation with its commercials; but the sponsor of *Have Gun, Will Travel* opted for 163 stations—and a cheaper price tag—as sufficient coverage for its commercial messages.

For their part, however, local broadcasters relished national shows. They usually "cleared," or accepted, network programs because they attracted large audiences, and high ratings meant that individual stations could charge high rates to their own advertisers for the minutes—usually the time between programs—ceded to them by the networks. Besides, the networks paid their affiliates about 30 percent of their normal local rates to clear national programs.

Failure to accept the network programming was rare. When a local did fail to clear a show it was usually because the series was not highly rated and a syndicated program (usually on film) was more attractive. The most common reason, however, was that station managers judged the network show to be too controversial for local sensibilities. This was the common excuse in the 1950s when southern affiliates preempted national shows in which African-American performers were favorably presented. Failure to clear a national program, however, opened a station to stiff competition from local network rivals and to great pressure from corporate officials in New York.

From the beginnings of the medium, syndicated series offered local programmers an alternative and a supplement to network fare. For independent stations they were the lifeblood of scheduling, since local production was never sufficient to fill a full broadcast day. Network affiliates and owned-and-operated outlets needed syndicated shows to fill the morning, afternoon, and late-night hours not covered by network fare, and local stations needed the attractive series provided by syndicators.

Syndicators handled both first-run and off-network reruns, distributing their series to individual stations in each TV market. The first-run programs came from scores of small and large studios, which, like Guild Films *(Liberace)*, Ziv Television Productions *(The Cisco Kid)*, and the Columbia Pictures subsidiary Screen Gems *(Jungle Jim)*, produced shows that rivaled network entertainment. Many memorable efforts in video history—from *Seahunt* and *The Adventures of Superman* in the 1950s, to *Hee Haw* since the 1970s, to *Fame* in the 1980s—were first-run syndicated series.

Although there was always a risk scheduling a new first-run program, reruns of network series were known commodities. Often such programs were syndicated by the film sales divisions of the networks on which they originally appeared. Nonetheless, whatever the alternatives to national programming, the networks still controlled most of what Americans saw on television. By 1955 programs from ABC, CBS, and NBC filled 78.2 percent of their affiliates' prime time.[7]

Local TV could resist standardization only in time periods where the national shows were scarce. Until the mid-1950s, when the networks were able to fill the daytime hours, many affiliates televised their own morning and afternoon features. Although these productions were built often around film—syndicated series, old movies, travelogues, B Westerns, varied syndicated shorts—they attracted advertisers and generated revenue for the fledgling outlets.

Attracting advertisers was the most vital function of any station. There were several ways in which this could be accomplished. Inheriting the fiscal arrangements developed by radio, the networks relied heavily on large corporations to underwrite entire programs. In this way, a major company such as Procter & Gamble or General Foods would sponsor complete shows, with production matters—including creation of TV commercials— handled through its advertising agency. In this manner Colgate-Palmolive Peet had its *Colgate Comedy Hour;* others included *The Texaco Star Theater, The Voice of Firestone, The Gillette Cavalcade of Sports, The Ford Show Starring Tennessee Ernie Ford,* and *The Schlitz Playhouse of Stars.* Even the NBC evening news was called *The Camel News Caravan.* Many sponsors were content to pay for programs without a corporate relationship in the title; for example, Chesterfield cigarettes with *Dragnet* and Maxwell House coffee with *Mama.*

As production costs mounted, corporations by the mid-1950s began to share their programs. This usually meant that sponsors alternated their underwriting of a single show. In this way, for example, the dramatic showcase *Robert Montgomery Presents Your Lucky Strike Theater* alternated with *Robert Montgomery Presents The Johnson's Wax Program,* and during the summer, *Robert Montgomery Presents The Richard Hudnet Summer Theater.* Sometimes arrangements consisted of alternating series from different production units, as did *The United States Steel Hour* with *The Motorola Television Hour* in 1953–54 and *The Elgin Hour* in 1954–55.

Individual stations relied less on single sponsors than on participating advertisers who placed their commercials in specific shows, or on general advertisers who allowed station programmers to insert their ads periodically throughout the day. A popular alternative to these arrangements was barter syndication. Here, programs were given or sold inexpensively to local outlets; in exchange, the syndicator retained several commercial minutes in the show and then sold them to national advertisers seeking to place their spots in local markets.

Whatever their origin, be it network TV or first-run syndication, this was mass programming meant for the cumulative U.S. marketplace. To resist the imposition of this homogeneous national culture, a locality needed money and independent facilities. It is not surprising that the market that most successfully withstood network encroachment was Los Angeles. Here, in the fourth-largest U.S. population center, there was ample capital as well as production expertise. Furthermore, television in Los Angeles was flourishing even while the networks in the East and Midwest were being organized. By 1949 there were seven stations operating in the city. Importantly, three of them had no network affiliation: KTLA, KFI-TV (later KHJ-TV), and KLAC-TV. These independents found sufficient means to lease or create competitive shows.

This was especially true of KTLA, which was owned by the television subsidiary of Paramount Pictures. By mid-1949 KTLA was nationally syndicating kinescopes of its own series, such as *Time for Beany; Armchair Detective; Pantomime Quiz;* and *The Spade Cooley Show*, a country and western musical variety hour featuring "your fiddlin' friend" Spade Cooley and his orchestra. As Table 4.4 suggests, before the opening of the coaxial link, viewers in Southern California preferred local live programs, mostly sporting events and musical programs, over network films and kinescopes.

Even with coast-to-coast linkage, network TV had to wage a strong battle to win Los Angeles viewers. By the summer of 1952 national favorites such as *Arthur Godfrey's Talent Scouts*, which ranked fourth in New York City and second in Chicago, Boston, and Philadelphia, was not in the top fifteen in Los Angeles. And Lawrence Welk's non-network program was seventh in the Los Angeles ratings, while a local country and western revue such as *Hometown Jamboree* decisively defeated *The Jackie Gleason Show*.[8]

TABLE 4.4

telepulse ratings, october 29– november 17, 1950[9]

Los Angeles

1. *Hopalong Cassidy* *
2. *The Alan Young Show* (local and live, but CBS)
3. *The Movies* (Sunday) *
4. *UCLA-Oregon football* *
5. *Harry Owens Royal Hawaiians* *
6. *The Spade Cooley Show* *
7. *Rams-49ers pro football* *
8. *The Texaco Star Theater*
9. *Ina Rae Hutton Orchestra* *
10. *The Lone Ranger*

* Non-network/local origination

For years the networks were hampered by residual local tastes, which as late as October 1953 placed three independent productions—the live musical programs of Lawrence Welk and Ina Rae Hutton and her All-Girl Orchestra (both on KTLA), plus disc jockey Peter Potter's musical panel show *Juke Box Jury* (on CBS-owned KNXT)—among the leading shows in Los Angeles.

National TV programming was hampered in Southern California by two technical problems. The difference of three time zones meant that shows originating in the East at 9:00 P.M. would be telecast inconveniently at 6:00 P.M. on the West Coast. On the other hand, kinescopes had a fuzzy picture quality, and they were days old—sometimes weeks old—before they were screened. This made kinescopes less attractive than live or filmed alternatives for, as *TV Guide* reported, "in some cities viewers apparently prefer to watch even a bad live show rather than a good show on kinescope." [10] As Table 4.5 demonstrates, even six months after the transcontinental connection, highly rated live productions from New York City often performed miserably in Los Angeles.

Still, Southern California viewers would not resist forever the attractions of national television. In some cases local hit shows were purchased by the networks, then brought to the national audience. In the fall of 1953, for example, ABC aired *Juke Box Jury*, and in the summer of 1955 the network introduced *The*

TABLE 4.5

comparative ratings, march 1952[11]

LIVE 9:00 P.M. EST/

LIVE 6:00 P.M. PST

PROGRAM	LOS ANGELES	NEW YORK	NATION
THE FRED WARING SHOW	4.2	9.2	13.5
THE GOODYEAR/ PHILCO PLAYHOUSE	6.7	21.3	31.4
STRIKE IT RICH	5.8	21.0	27.0

LIVE 8:00 P.M. OR 9:00 P.M. EST/
KINESCOPE 8:00 P.M. OR 9:00 P.M.
PST

PROGRAM	LOS ANGELES	NEW YORK	NATION
THE KEN MURRAY SHOW	10.2	25.8	26.5
THE BIG STORY	10.7	21.4	27.5
THE COLGATE COMEDY HOUR	19.6	28.9	36.1

Lawrence Welk Show. Further, as the networks turned increasingly to filmed series, the curtailment of live productions alleviated problems in scheduling and the quality of kinescopes. By the end of the decade the use of videotape and advancements in transmission eliminated almost totally the broadcast difficulties of a society extending across four different time zones.

A show business veteran as savvy as Groucho Marx understood early, however, that in terms of consistent, high-quality entertainment, local video could not compete for long against the elaborate capabilities of the networks. As he explained it with droll frankness in 1949:

We get lots of live TV out here in Hollywood, but it consists mostly of girls talking through dummies; animals pretending they're people; round table discussions by squareheads; hordes of stunted-looking professional kids; amateur boxing by professionals; and farm reports by a local Titus Moody. But the big-league stuff is all kinescope.[12]

Despite the triumph of national television fare, preceptible local tastes would endure throughout the United States. In those localities with surviving independent outlets, there would continue to be small ratings for programming other than that coming from the networks. Stations such as WGN in Chicago—which lost its CBS and DuMont affiliations by the mid-1950s—and WOR-TV in New York City—which abandoned hope of being the flagship station of a stillborn Mutual television network—would play prominent roles in their respective communities, eventually becoming national "superstations" thanks to satellite technology in the 1980s.

Mass programming plastered over the differences inherent in the diverse U.S. populace. There always would be ratings differences based on age and gender as children gravitated to shows not usually favored by men or women who, themselves, often demonstrated divergence in terms of time spent with TV and program favorites. Ratings from 1958 reveal that divergent viewing patterns resulted from scheduling differences and community tastes. The soap opera *The Brighter Day* earned a 17.8 rating in Pittsburgh at 4:00 P.M., when 32 percent of the TV homes watched television, but the rating dropped to 1.9 in San Francisco, where it was broadcast at 1:00 P.M., when only 13 percent of TV homes were viewing. Whereas *Gunsmoke* had a rating of 49.9 in Boston, it gained only a 17.0 rating in Milwaukee. And market size seemed immaterial, too, as *The Lawrence Welk Show* ranked seventh in Los Angeles but only sixteenth in more populated Philadelphia.[13]

The victory of national entertainment was striking not only in its destruction of local initiative but also in its influence on the way viewers lived and thought. Even in its earliest years, TV was more than a device for home diversion and enlightenment; it also was a persuasive conduit for the propaganda of mass marketing. The obvious commercial impact of the new medium was demonstrated in 1955 by an NBC study of the coming of television to Fort Wayne, Indiana. Until November 1953, when a local station began operations, residents with TV sets needed elaborate roof antennas to receive weak transmissions from stations in Chicago, Toledo, Cleveland, and surrounding markets. But with the opening of its own outlet, an NBC affiliate, Fort Wayne wholeheartedly entered the television age.

A survey of almost 7,500 households before, and six months after, the arrival of local video illustrates the pervasive impact of video advertising on viewers. According to the report, after a home received TV the new medium quickly became the chief source of advertising impressions, attracting viewers for 173 minutes per day—compared to 94 minutes spent daily with radio, magazines, and newspapers combined. The NBC report concluded, too, that video shaped consumer attitudes, firmly implanting sponsors' brands and messages in the minds of viewers, creating familiarity and respectful feelings toward advertised brands, and undermining sales of unadvertised brands.[14]

Although network fare could quickly make viewers respect nationally advertised products, the messages communicated on commercial TV still had to mesh with popular attitudes. But television was pictures as well as words in the private home, and as such it was more likely than the movies, print, or radio to clash with local mores. In those instances where resistance was large and vocal, video was compelled to adapt. Still, like local TV production, local values were ill-equipped for long-term resistance to the national medium. This was apparent early in the record of American television as it confronted controversial issues such as racial discrimination, violence, and sociosexual attitudes.

television and race

There were preliminary indications that TV would counteract the racial prejudice and pejorative stereotyping that had characterized print, film, and radio. Emerging in a postwar period of liberal reevaluation of chronic racial animosity, television seemed to promise, in the words of *Ebony* magazine in mid-1950, a color-blind medium "free of racial barriers."[15] African-American singers and dancers appeared often on early network TV. By 1950 jazz pianists Hazel Scott on DuMont and Bob Howard on CBS had their own programs, and *Sugar Hill Times* was an attempt by CBS in 1949 to offer an hour-long musical variety show featuring only black talent. While these were unsponsored, sustaining productions, in the fall of 1952 *The Billy Daniels Show* on ABC became the first sponsored network musical show hosted by an African-American.

But deeply rooted social patterns as well as the economics of video soon quashed reformist hopes. Whites were the main consumers of TV programming and of the corporate advertisers' products, and by the early 1950s ratings illustrated that white Americans preferred shows with blacks in traditional stereotypic roles. This was especially true for situation comedies. Whereas pop vocalist Billy Daniels lasted thirteen weeks, *The Amos 'n' Andy Show* endured for two years on CBS and then thirteen years in syndication. For three seasons *Beulah* featured the familiar "mammy" characterization of the stout black maid benignly dealing with the domestic problems of her white, middle-class employers. Similarly, the doltish but lovable "coon" character— stupid, scared of ghosts, barely able to speak in coherent sentences—was portrayed well by Willie Best in *My Little Margie, Waterfront,* and particularly *The Stu Erwin Show.* Other stereotyped black characters soon familiar on early TV comedy ranged from the sassy valet Rochester on *The Jack Benny Program* to subordinate natives on the syndicated *Ramar of the Jungle,* to those pickaninnies Farina, Stymie, and Buckwheat seen in vintage *Our Gang* comedies from the 1920s and 1930s that appeared on early TV as *The Little Rascals.*

Further, once the FCC freeze was lifted and TV spread beyond the West Coast, Midwest, and Northeast, networks and advertisers became increasingly sensitive to regional racial attitudes. Although it was not alone with its powerful racist prejudices, the white South was especially influential as a force for segregation, asserting its own world view and demanding the acquiescence of national video.

The networks could afford to be relatively liberal toward African-Americans when, as in December 1949, only 4.5 percent of all TV receivers were in the South. But with the national expansion of video, the fear of boycotts and other adverse reactions by white southern consumers—as well as by many white Northerners and Westerners who less overtly shared the white southern perspective on race—were realities quickly accommodated by advertising agencies and sponsors, as well as by writers, producers, and station and network executives. In practical terms this meant moderating or eliminating images of racial equality in TV dramas, lobbying against "overexposure" by black guest stars on network shows, nonsupport for programs hosted by Afro-Americans, and respecting Jim Crow state laws prohibiting black and white athletes from competing together.

There were exceptions to this pattern. But it took the personal intervention of white men as successful as Steve Allen and Ed Sullivan to keep African-American entertainers appearing on their prime-time variety programs—especially as the civil rights movement became a heated social reality. And the networks were willing to televise racially mixed boxing matches and baseball, football, and basketball games as long as the actual events took place within states permitting such athletic competition.

By the mid-1950s racial attitudes were not particularly egalitarian anywhere in the United States, and the potential for adverse white reaction in the South conveniently masked exclusion and stereotyping elsewhere in the nation. It is significant that even outside the South there were few black men or women starring in detective or Western series, announcing or participating in sporting events, gathering the news, hosting quiz programs, appearing in soap operas or spy series, heading comedy-variety shows or situation comedies, or acting in any of the great live theatrical productions that later characterized this period as a Golden Age of TV drama.

Like Latinos, Asians, Native Americans, and other racial minorities, African-Americans generally were excluded from television except in those derisive representations created by whites that trivialized, belittled, and otherwise condemned them to an inferior social status and then justified such treatment in terms of the unflattering characters blacks portrayed. Although NBC could proclaim in 1951 that "Defamatory statements or derogatory references, expressed or implied, toward an individual nationality, race, group, trade, profession, industry, or institution are not permitted,"[16] the reality reported by *Variety* in 1956 was that pressure from advertisers with southern markets was "setting back by many years the advancement made in television toward providing equal job opportunities regardless of race, creed, or color. At one major agency the word has gone out: 'No Negro performers allowed.' "[17]

television and violence

While national TV ran roughshod over minorities expecting respectful and equitable treatment, it clashed also with those who felt its reliance on violent imagery was equally destructive of private dignity and social order. Most Americans liked violence in their entertainment, especially when it was packaged in morality tales of police and private eyes.

Murder was the preferred form. It was in literature and motion pictures, and it was on the air. One critic of radio crime estimated that in 1945 there were 1,642 mystery and detective shows on the air—and each show averaged 10 million listeners.[18] By 1949 another writer deduced that radio was broadcasting 50 murders a week—2,400 killings a year—the majority of such deaths occurring in detective programs.[19]

One reason for the popularity of detective programs in TV

was their relatively inexpensive cost. Many were half-hour programs aired live with a small cast, a few cameras, and fewer sets.
Filmed series were more expensive to produce. *The Cases of Eddie
Drake*, for example, cost $7,500 per episode when filmed in late
1948. While that figure compared to the costs for mounting lavish
live comedy-variety series (*The Texaco Star Theater* budgeted at
$8,000 to $10,000 per show and *Toast of the Town* at $6,000) and
dramatic showcases (*The Kraft Television Theater* estimated at
$4,000 weekly), anticipating reruns and future residuals, the pro-
ducers of filmed programs did not need to recoup all their costs
during the first run of their series.[20]

Although they basically preached the moral that crime did not
pay, crime shows raised serious criticism. From the beginning,
powerful individuals and social groups assailed crime shows for
their fundamental violence. As was the case with crime fiction in
other media, critics alleged that there were causal links between
crime programming on TV and juvenile delinquency, social violence, and a general undermining of moral conduct in the United
States.

As early as 1949 the Southern California Association for Better Radio and Television found video violence unacceptable.
During one week of TV in Los Angeles the group reported ninety-
one murders, seven stagecoach holdups, three kidnappings, ten
thefts, four burglaries, two cases of arson, two suicides, one instance of blackmail, and cases of assault and battery "too numerous to tabulate." The organization protested in letters to local
stations that "TV comes into the home and many children are
looking at these programs. We believe without too much effort
your station could substitute acceptable programs which would be
suitable for family viewing."[21]

By 1951 anthropologist Ernest A. Hooten of Harvard University could claim that television in general, and crime shows particularly, were detrimental to the survival of humanity. He blasted
TV for presenting "an easy correspondence course in crime, a
visual education in how to do wrong." He continued, "Such vi-
cious programs result from the ignorance and venality of movie,
radio, and TV producers." Hooten concluded that the new medium was undermining humanity. "Just as our legs have shrunk
from using motor cars, our minds and our ability to read have
deteriorated because television offers, for the most part, foolish,
harmful material which stultifies audiences."[22]

In basic harmony with Hooten was Dr. Frederic Wertheim, a
controversial psychiatrist who precipitated a crusade against
comic books in the early 1950s. Although he was convinced that

comic books were the greatest cultural force directing children toward a life of crime, he widened his moral critique in 1952 to include television. To Wertheim, TV had great educational potential, but as presently used—with an overemphasis on "blood and thunder" and a glorification of crime that suggested that "crime is not so bad after all" [23]—he felt television to be socially damaging.

Particularly vocal in the critique of early television were leaders in the Roman Catholic Church who objected not only to televised violence but also to the sexual content of programming brought directly into American homes by the medium. In 1950 the National Council of Catholic Men (NCCM) urged broadcasters to establish a code of standards that would bar programs "detrimental to the best moral interests of televiewers, especially the family group and the children of the family." [24] By 1951 the NCCM was organizing a system of Church censorship that would rate TV shows for Catholics on matters such as responsibility to children; advancement of education and culture; program material; and decency, religion, and the handling of news and controversial problems. [25]

A year later, Archbishop Richard J. Cushing of Boston complained openly that "some television programs have sunk to a new low in breaking the laws of morality and decency." [26] The religious argument was direct: TV comes into the home, where it is violating family values and the moral guidance of the Church. As the Reverend Timothy J. Flynn of New York observed in 1955, "Television has been sold to the American public as an item for the living room, and, hence, the industry must keep in mind the essentially domestic nature of its audience. There is no closed-circuit system for adults, and, I am afraid, nine o'clock is only theoretically an adult viewing hour." The priest was quick to add, however, that the moral health of children was not his only concern. "Of course, morally offensive presentations are objectionable at any hour, and the prompt and effective protests of the public in various areas of the country indicate that public opinion will quickly censor objectionable material when the industry fails to do so." [27]

The television industry was not unresponsive. In 1951 the National Association of Radio and Television Broadcasters adopted a new Television Code establishing guidelines for program content and addressing the concerns of social critics. With respect to the crime programming, the Code promised that "criminality shall be treated as undesirable and unsympathetic," that "presentation of techniques of crime in such detail as to invite imitation shall be avoided," and that "brutality or physical agony by sight or by sound are not permissible." The Code also pledged that "law enforcement shall be upheld," that "murder or revenge as a motive for murder shall not be presented as justifiable," and that "the exposition of sex crimes will be avoided."[28]

That the standards in the Television Code were not fully followed is obvious. Protests against program content continued, and as early as 1952 the U.S. government began to study the impact of TV on social values. That year a House Commerce Committee subcommittee chaired by Oren Harris investigated "offensive" and "immoral" TV programs. The inquiry touched on a wide range of topics—from beer commercials telecast into a TV market that remained prohibitionist, to vulgarity, to dramas depicting suicide.

This was a new and ambiguous area for lawmakers and programmers. There was only a thin boundary between enforced good taste and official censorship. Still, there were those who demanded protection from the messages, direct and implied, offered in the new medium. As one member of the subcommittee, Representative Arthur G. Klein, concluded, "I've come to the viewpoint that someone must take the responsibility for policing the good taste of radio and TV programs that come into the home. The industry should do it, but if they don't, someone else should."[29]

Indeed, the United States in 1952 was well used to quiet censorship in the name of civic good. Official censorship boards existed in many states (Ohio, New York, Virginia, Massachusetts, Pennsylvania, Kansas, and Maryland), and in large cities (Chicago; Detroit; Atlanta; Memphis; and Portland, Oregon, among others). Often these boards of review were associated with police establishments. Their function was to ensure that within their jurisdictions no movies or books contained "obscene, indecent, immoral, or inhuman scenes, or . . . [were] of such character that their exhibition would tend to corrupt morals or incite to crime."[30]

The banning of controversial books in Boston was so familiar that the phrase "banned in Boston" became part of American argot. Censors in the South excised positive movie presentations of African-Americans, since such imagery was subversive to the ideology underlying Jim Crow social and legal arrangements. Chicago officials in 1950 banned the 20th Century-Fox feature film *No Way Out*, which treated racial hatred and dramatized a race riot that was won by blacks. The chronic sensitivity of Ohio censors to scenes of brutality compelled filmmakers to reduce the number of punches in fight scenes. To have their films distributed locally, Hollywood studios in many instances had to make special "protection" prints containing unique edits or revised scenes tailored to meet the requirements of particular state or city censorship boards.

Localism was a vital part of life in the United States at mid-century. Decisions to proscribe books, films, and other cultural products arose from a tradition of community self-protection. This entailed protecting the community against the morality of commercial industries insensitive to sectional and local peculiarities. In a society as historically and demographically diverse as the United States, creating cultural products for a national audience lead easily to confrontations with forces of parochialism and tradition.

Violence on television was a contentious matter that went to the heart of this issue. The fact that the federal government never resolved the problem only exacerbated the displeasure of offended groups. In 1954 the U.S. Senate through its Subcommittee to Investigate Juvenile Delinquency conducted public hearings on TV violence. Chaired by Estes Kefauver—the senator whose hearings on organized crime in 1951 had been widely followed after he allowed live TV coverage of the proceedings—the subcommittee began a long governmental quest to discover substantive evidence that TV violence actually caused juvenile delinquency.

During the next four decades hearings followed at irregular intervals, and social critics conducted rigorous research to prove the causal relationship between entertainment and crime. But the efforts produced ambiguous results. New crusaders, such as Senators Thomas Dodd and John Pastore, and Representatives Torbert MacDonald and Timothy Wirth, appeared over the years to castigate the TV industry. Yet Congress avoided creating specific rules to govern what could or could not be shown on TV. Calls for industry self-censorship never were effective, and discussion of governmental regulation always raised questions of artistic freedom and free speech.

Even the federal agency charged with broadcast regulation, the Federal Communications Commission, retreated from decisive action on the matter of TV violence. When Paul A. Walker retired in 1953 as chairman of the commission, his statement epitomized the chronic FCC attitude, both before and after Walker. "One side thinks we haven't gone far enough in controlling programming. The other side is just as firmly convinced that we are determined to establish federal censorship," he remarked. "I like to think that this conflict of opinion shows that we have been steering a fairly straight course down the middle of the regulatory road." [31]

Of course, steering to the center of the road meant allowing network programmers to broadcast their value system to the nation. The networks had their own censors, men and women who reviewed scripts and finished products before they were telecast. But the fact remained that day after day this seductive new mechanism was delivering a common message, laden with social and moral implications, directly into the homes and privacy of millions of Americans. Glamorous and trendy and delivered with the authority of truth, never had such a persuasive message been so pervasively communicated in the United States.

This was no subversion of the majority by a cunning minority. It represented, instead, the propagation of orthodoxy, the commonly held or consensus viewpoint, at the expense of minority attitudes. Rural values yielded to urban values; attitudes popular in the nineteenth century were replaced by modern perspectives; as laws changed, cultural orthodoxy adjusted. No counterculture here; this was the American Way of Life that was on television.

As for the citizenry, it came gradually to accept the TV version of moral life. Words and images and gestures strongly contested in the early years would become acceptable and routine in the following decades. In the early 1950s it was taboo on television to deal with unwed motherhood or drug addiction. At one time Arthur Miller's celebrated play *Death of a Salesman* could not be produced on TV, nor could the motion picture version of it be shown, because the plot involved suicide. As late as 1966, ABC rejected the teen film *Beach Blanket Bingo* because its standards and practices bureau forbade the showing of bare female navels.

sex and profanity on tv

In television the dominant point of view prevailed and influenced the nation. As long as most Americans were unwilling to redress intolerance, attitudes of social and economic justice for oppressed racial groups rarely entered the nation's video culture. If audiences kept violent series popular, then no amount of governmental regulation, short of outright censorship, would keep shootings, fistfights, and other forms of mayhem off the TV screen. The same was true for sex and profanity.

Sold to sponsors as a family medium, TV usually handled problems of language, dress, and body in terms suited to "family viewing." However, in the early 1950s the plunging necklines of female performers such as Dagmar on *Broadway Open House* and Faye Emerson on her own CBS show, as well as Roberta Quinlan, Lena Horne, and Dinah Shore, triggered considerable controversy. A Cleveland councilman was so perturbed by what he saw on television in 1951 that he urged the city council to pass a resolution asking the networks to stop plunging necklines.[32] Others in Cleveland charged that "plunging necklines replace talent," that such imagery "tempts incompetent people seeking publicity" and that it "puts a negative value on the nice, clean cotton-housedress type girl."[33]

That these female performers were wearing fashionable evening gowns acceptable in most social circumstances made no difference to the Chicago woman who assailed the plunging neckline as "one of the most horrible eyesores of television, and it corrupts the minds of teenagers, the future citizens of America."[34] To protect its reputation, the DuMont network in 1950 maintained bouquets of flowers for those emergency situations when a female star or guest arrived at the studio with too much cleavage exposed. In such cases the network ordered the woman to use one of the bouquets as a corsage to cover her bosom.[35]

While sexual imagery may have been tolerated in motion picture theaters, TV entered the privacy of the home, where it could confront unsuspecting viewers. Moreover, video programs could not always be supervised by parents concerned about their children's sensibilities. Because the ultimate goal of TV programs was to sell commercial products, few advertisers were willing to spend large sums of money underwriting shows that might offend large numbers of viewers.

There were other moral confrontations. When Arthur Godfrey in 1950 uttered the words "damn" and "hell" on one of his live national programs, he was roundly criticized by viewers, affiliate stations, and CBS officials. Popular songs with "questionable" lyrics—from Lena Horne's recording of "I Love to Love," to "Go to Sleep, Go to Sleep, Go to Sleep" by Arthur Godfrey and Mary Martin, and "The Song of the Sewer" by Art Carney —were banned from network TV even though Horne recorded for RCA and the Godfrey/Martin and Carney discs were recorded by a CBS company, Columbia Records. Even local productions encountered problems. When Houston station KPRC-TV in 1951 prepared a bedding commercial that would depict a husband and wife in a double bed, public criticism prompted the station to cancel the spot before it was ever aired.[36]

As a mass medium that assaulted the values of individuals and groups, TV invited a wide range of criticism and censorship.

In 1952 ABC censors previewed 6,750 films and rejected 186 as unsuitable for broadcasting because of "violence, sacrilege, children's standards, or characters prejudicial to minority groups."[37] Outrage from local Roman Catholics prompted WGN-TV in late 1956 to cancel a showing of *Luther*, a motion-picture biography of the catalyst for the Protestant Reformation and founder of the Lutheran religion. The networks were consistently attacked by interest groups—such as businessmen, intellectuals, and other professionals; racial and religious minorities; those opposing the sale of alcohol, the mistreatment of animals, and the like—that were concerned with the way they or their interests were depicted on TV.

Many Americans recognized the power of television to form public perceptions that were at once moral and opinion-making. To many it was critical to form interest groups to protect or promote particular viewpoints against the standardized interpretations propagated by the networks. City police establishments cooperated in the filming of police series such as *Dragnet* (Los Angeles P.D.) and *The Lineup* (San Francisco P.D.). Medical associations and facilities assisted producers of programs such as *Medic*. The U.S. Department of Defense was especially active in promoting the armed forces, providing stock footage, equipment, and personnel for cooperative producers.

Most anxious to propagandize their products, of course, were advertisers and their agencies. They prepared lists of do's and don'ts describing the proper way to treat their products. General Mills through the Dancer-Fitzgerald, Sample advertising agency issued a twenty-two-point edict demanding that "bulk American middle-class morals" be demonstrated in their commercials. For Coca-Cola, the McCann-Erickson agency even directed that "One does not serve 'Cokes' or 'Coca-Cola.' One serves 'bottles of Coke.' " The agency even explained how bottles of the soft drink should be poured: "When pouring Coca-Cola into glass, both bottle and glass should be tilted rim-to-rim, as in pouring beer. Ice should always be in the glass."

Not only were advertisers intent on shaping their images in TV commercials, they also sought to mold the programs themselves. Liggett & Myers through McCann-Erickson demanded "No portrayal of pipe or cigar smoking or chewing. Avoid shots of messy ashtrays crammed with cigarette butts. Use king-size Chesterfields only. Take cellophane off pack." As sponsors of *Circus Boy*, the adventures of a young boy traveling with a circus in the late nineteenth century, the Mars candy company announced that it was "very sensitive to the use of ice cream, soft drinks, cookies, competitive candy, or any other item that might be considered competitive to candy." And the Ted Bates agency for Miles Laboratories, manufacturers of a range of over-the-counter pharmaceuticals, prescribed that on its show *The Flint-stones* "There should be no reference to headache, upset stomach, or the taking of remedies to relieve same. There should be no statement or situation in conflict with One-a-Day Multiple Vita-mins. There should be no taking of bromides or sedatives for which Nervine might be used. . . . There should be no represen-tation of doctors, dentists, druggists (or drug remedies) in a derog-atory manner, or in situations embarrassing to them as a group."[38]

Still, it was sexual expression that most aroused moralists threatened by the intrusive new medium. Typically, a Roman Catholic bishop in Michigan praised TV in 1951 as "one of the great achievements of our age," then blasted it as a "sex-promoter" that popularized "sex artists whose stock in trade is to make sex didoes before innocent children in their homes." Ac-cording to the Church official, despite its technological brilliance television was "doing the work of the devil by bootlegging into homes foulness and obscenity."[39]

One of the bolder public moves against video imagery and language occurred in Chicago in mid-1950 when the weekly magazine *TV Forecast* spearheaded the creation of the National Television Review Board. The purpose of this panel of promi-nent citizens was to rate programs in terms of their effect on family life. Soon the Board publicly condemned shows it felt objectionable, among them *Howdy Doody* ("loud . . . confused . . . senseless . . . clown's role too feminine"), *Juvenile Jury* ("bad taste . . . smart-aleck kids should be spanked instead of applauded"), wrestling ("phony contest . . . unsportsmanlike tactics . . . glorifies sadism"), and *Leave It to the Girls* ("gowns cut too low . . . ridicules marriage . . . excessive frivolity con-cerning family authority and customs").[40] By early 1952 the Board issued its "Citizens' Television Code," complete with a twelve-point guide to "what shall be deemed objectionable":

1 IMMORAL, LEWD, AND SUGGESTIVE WORDS AND ACTIONS, AS WELL AS INDECENCY IN DRESS.

2 A DELIBERATE PRESENTATION OF VULGAR AND SORDID SIT-UATIONS.

3 IRREVERENCE TOWARD RELIGION OR PATRIOTIC SYMBOLS WHERE IT IS NOT ESSENTIAL TO A DRAMATIC SITUATION.

4 EXCESSIVE BAD TASTE IN WORDS AND ACTIONS, DELIBER-
ATELY PROJECTED FOR THEIR OWN EFFECT.

5 EXCESSIVE FRIVOLITY CONCERNING ESTABLISHED TRADI-
TIONS OF FAMILY AUTHORITY AND CUSTOMS.

6 MALICIOUS DERISION OF RACIAL OR NATIONAL GROUPS.

7 UNDUE GLORIFICATION OF CRIMINALS AND UNDESIRABLES.

8 EXCESSIVE BLOODSHED, VIOLENCE, AND CRUELTY.

9 EXCESSIVE NOISE, CONFUSION, AND TUMULT TO A POINT
WHERE IT DISRUPTS NORMAL FAMILY RELATIONS.

10 ANY IDEAS, SITUATIONS, OR PRESENTATIONS THAT ESSEN-
TIALLY INJURE THE DIGNITY OF GOD AND MANKIND AND THE
INALIENABLE RIGHT OF HUMAN INTEGRITY.

11 SHOWS THAT TEND TO GLAMORIZE FALSE VALUES.

12 DISLOYAL OR SUBVERSIVE SENTIMENTS THAT MIGHT IN-
JURE THE UNITED STATES.[41]

TV was under attack early and on many fronts as its programs conflicted with personal standards and tastes. From the proper attitudes with which to advertise laxatives or women's under-wear, to scripts with sexual overtones or violent imagery, even to questions of the patriotism and political loyalty of individual per-formers and writers, early video clashed frequently with individ-uals and groups abused by what they saw. The result was increasing pressure on broadcasters to establish industrywide boundaries for programming content. Network loyalty oaths and blacklisting were offered as guarantees that no Communists or Fascists were working in the industry. And in late 1951 the Tele-vision Code issued by the NAB reiterated the traditional commit-ment of commercial video to education, culture, and taste.

Facing possible FCC involvement in the controversy, the net-works and most stations quickly adhered to the NAB Code. The Code spoke of decency and decorum in production as well as in advertising. In the opening paragraph of its preamble, the Code defined the place of TV in American social life:

Television is seen and heard in every type of American home. These homes include children and adults of all ages, embrace all races and all varieties of religious faith, and reach those of every educational background. It is the responsibility of television to bear constantly in mind that the audience is primarily a home audience, and consequently that television's relationship to the viewers is that between guest and host.[42]

Broadcasters were aware of their potential for upsetting the moral standards of some viewers. The DuMont network, for example, sought to be as inoffensive as possible by reminding its staff and guests of the need for propriety. In 1950 the network posted three-foot by five-foot posters in all control rooms and studios, proclaiming its dedication to good taste. Signed by the network's president, Mortimer W. Loewi, and its program director, James L. Caddigan, these signs declared:

Attention, producer directors and talent: Your audience is the average American family—Mom and Dad—Junior and Sis—Grandma. You are a guest in their living-rooms. Any violation of this privilege through the use of material in bad taste, immoral business, situations, dialogue, lyrics, routines or costuming will not be tolerated by the DuMont Television Network.[43]

NBC was typical. In the 1950s, Stockton Helffrich operated as the continuity acceptance director—the censor—charged with overseeing the words and images broadcast on the network. Recalling the position of the American Civil Liberties Union that all industry codes necessarily infringed on free expression, he argued in 1956 that "the spirit of this attitude hits me as more well intended than practical. The industry has to have some rule of thumb for moving in on patently salacious material, racial stereotyping, ignorance toward the mentally and physically afflicted, etc." Helffrich continued, "The real problem in codes comes when they are used negatively to repress artistic expressions of reality and are followed after such uses with no alternative handling of any stature."[44]

5 CHAPTER

streamlining

How quickly it captivated the nation. In little more than a decade television became a necessity of life in the United States. By 1960 more than 87 percent of U.S. households possessed at least one set, and millions of new receivers were being assembled for future purchasers. And Americans watched. They spent **culture** more time with TV—a daily average of five hours, nineteen minutes per household—than with any other medium of mass communication.

Television also became very big business. Whereas gross revenues for TV totaled almost $106 million in 1950, a decade later the figure rose more than twelvefold, to almost $1.3 billion. By 1960 there were 559 stations on the air, 96 percent of them affiliated with the three surviving networks. The industry directly employed 40,800 workers, but indirectly countless others depended on it. **streamlining**

Significantly, this beguiling medium of sight and sound also had become a persuasive vehicle for teaching a point of view, a consensus "All-American perspective" that was at once cultural, economic, political, social, and moral. "All television is educational television," wrote Commissioner Nicholas Johnson of the FCC in 1967. "It may not teach the truth. It may preach violence rather than love. It may give more emphasis to the quality of acquisition than to the quality of use. It may produce more mental illness than **industry** health. But it teaches. Endlessly."[1]

Detective programs constantly affirmed that crime did not pay. Daytime soap operas reiterated the inevitable triumph of those who endured unjust suffering. Westerns showed the national forefathers bravely conquering their enemies in the name of individualism, property rights, technological superiority, and divine will. Quiz shows confirmed the Horatio Alger myth of material achievement through the personal enterprise of the common citizen. In situation comedies, medical series, lawyer series, children's adventure programs, sports, and the like, television proclaimed moral standards fit for all the nation.

Even TV news reflected this perspective, displaying and explaining the world ethnocentrically. U.S. social and political values were universal goods toward which the rest of the world strived. American mistakes stemmed from human fallibility, not systemic determinants, although the reverse was true for captive Communist nations. The rest of the world was often dangerous, but there were always good foreigners desiring to bring their societies into harmony with American ideals.

At a time when political and economic power were becoming increasingly centralized, conceded to be handled best by elites and ever-narrowing circles of *cognoscenti*, broadcasting centralized American culture by disseminating a single cultural viewpoint to the nation. Although people in Maine, Mississippi, and Montana had dissimilar histories and cultural perspectives, TV gave them only the same shows with the same standards. While these viewers shared certain values basic to U.S. citizenship, there was no room in national programming for the qualities that made them different from one another, nothing that exploited regional or historical or individual differences.

This was not new to television. The nature of a commercial popular culture had already been spawned by other media, such as magazines, phonograph recordings, broadcast radio, and motion pictures. But TV maximized the national cultural experience. Viewers encountered its perspective effortlessly, conveniently, inexpensively, and frequently.

TV programming was not propaganda in the sense that it was manufactured by state bureaucrats intent on shaping the minds of a nation. But it was propagandistic. It took stands. It offered an interpretation—indeed, a popular one—as the truth. And it adhered to the ideological premises of American political and social organization. No Communist or socialist points of view here: this was the mind-set of capitalism inherent in the drama and wit being televised. No fascism in this viewpoint, either, for middle-class democratic values always triumphed. No authentic rural representation, no authentic blue-collar ethic, no religious or racial minorities projected either: this culture was middle-class, capitalistic, urban, and white—and it was rapidly molding the streamlined national standard.

In a study of political blacklisting completed in 1956 for the Fund for the Republic, representatives of many of the leading corporate sponsors of TV programs demonstrated clearly that they understood the medium in propagandistic terms.[2] A policy statement at Procter & Gamble declared, "We would never knowingly engage anyone who aids either directly or indirectly the Communist cause." According to the president of Dow Chemical Company, "We would certainly look with disfavor on the appearance on a Dow program of any person so controversial as to place us in a questionable light by association." The head of American Tobacco Company went farther, stating, "We would disapprove of employing an artist whose conduct in any respect, 'political' or otherwise, has made him or is likely to make him distasteful to the public." Perhaps the frankest statement, however, came from an executive of Westinghouse Electric Corporation, who summarized the relationship between video entertainment and propagation of the All-American perspective. "We buy *Studio One* as a package from CBS through our agency, McCann-Erickson," he wrote. "These two businesses, as well as all of us at Westinghouse, have a great stake in our capitalistic society. It is therefore in our own best interests never to engage in any activities that would jeopardize the free-enterprise system."

The supplanting of local orientations by the networks assured the dominance of the official point of view and an erosion of nonconformism. No doubt, earlier developments in transportation, communication, and education played a part in amalgamating and homogenizing American society, but there had never been a medium as persuasive, desirable, and available as television. Except to turn off the TV set, a dissatisfied viewer had no choice but to select from network products and confront constantly the propagation of the popular, from entertainment genres to political philosophies.

Most persuasive in presenting consensus interpretations were TV commercials. More than sixty- or thirty-second preachments in favor of specific products, commercials propounded an ideology, a declaration of plenty based on middle-class, capitalistic values of affluence and the gratification of material wants. The advent of television occurred in the most economically bountiful period in the history of the United States. After decades scarred by the Great Depression, global warfare, and peacetime dislocation, the nation experienced in the 1950s social and economic expansion manifested in a housing boom, low unemployment, rising salaries, and a consumerist splurge. There were more things to buy, more people had more money, and more wants could be gratified than ever. Television commercials proposed a simple formula: wanting + spending = satisfaction and acceptance.

American TV was punctuated by a barrage of commercials

with their acquisitive messages. During a typical week in 1957, for example, the average viewer encountered 420 commercials totaling five hours, eight minutes.[3] Television sold Fords by showing how the automobile met the physical and psychological needs of the family. The chant "A whistle, a wink, and Wildroot will get her every time" assured men of sexual conquest if they used the right brand of hair tonic. From dancing Old Gold packs to cowboys inhaling Marlboros while an orchestra played manly music in the background, cigarette manufacturers blended American myth with song and dance to epitomize the satisfaction inherent in their products.

Viewers encountered and soon became familiar with cartooned national icons such as Speedy Alka-Seltzer; Kellogg's Tony the Tiger; the Cheerios Kid; Bucky Beaver for Ipana toothpaste; and Sharpie the Parrot, who hawked Gillette razors and assorted shaving paraphernalia. There were other inducements to buy. A visual gimmick such as an "invisible shield" demonstrating the protective qualities of Colgate toothpaste with "Gardol" simplified scientific studies about dental hygiene; memorable clichés such as "Which twin has the Toni?" for Toni home permanent, and "Better things for better living through chemistry" for DuPont products substituted catchy phrases for informed shopping.

The command to "See the U.S.A. in your Chevrolet" had no offensive character when sung by Dinah Shore. Proper grammar was never an impediment to pithy salesmanship, as advertisers freely bent the rules of syntax to proclaim that "Winston tastes good like a cigarette should." And then, to tweak critics of its incorrect English, the same advertiser asked, "What do you want, good grammar or good taste?"

Potent, too, were those commercials featuring celebrity endorsements, such as former heavyweight boxing champion Jack Dempsey for Bull Dog beer, baseball player Yogi Berra for Puss 'n' Boots cat food, golfer Sam Snead for Lucky Strike cigarettes, and rodeo star Casey Tibbs for Wheaties breakfast cereal. Even federal politics were affected by TV hucksterism. Beginning in the campaign of 1952, nominees for the presidency of the United States turned to television commercials to sell themselves, in the process employing established advertising agencies to merchandise their candidacies.

From its beginnings, television played a convincing role in its relationship with the American public. As an electronic billboard it was welcomed warmly into the homes and private lives of almost every person in the nation. Although it was a source of

constant commercial propaganda, it was embraced by most viewers as a prized possession, hailed as a wonderful wellspring for
learning and escape. Americans accepted its one-way communication of material plenty, in the process helping to create what
advertising executive Leo Burnett in 1957 called the "commercial
culture in this vital country of ours where selling things and services and ideas to each other is part and parcel of our accepted,
respected, and dynamic way of life."[4]

The social message was obvious in the abundance sold via
television: after great deprivations the United States now possessed a corporate economic system capable of immense production that was responsive to consumer wants. Less obvious was the
political concomitant of this TV message: such plenty could come
only from the existing capitalist arrangement within its present
level of representative democracy and political activism. In a
period of Cold War rivalry with socialism and communism, this
was strategic propaganda for those people and enterprises committed to conserving the system.

Increasingly, network TV disseminated the national culture
from an industry that was rational and cost-efficient. In its earliest
years television retained much of the legacy of its radio background. Comedians from radio gravitated to video, as did dramatic actors and production personnel; live programs were the
network rule; networks carefully watched their programs for offensive words and ideas that might assault the family audience;
and major U.S. corporations sponsored programs, often caring
more about the public image of the company than stuffing its
program with product commercials.

But there was a rival entertainment philosophy that engulfed
TV in the late 1950s. Motion-picture exhibition was considerably
different from radio. Here the emphasis was on exploitation of
audiences. Movies for youngsters needed certain emphases; adult
films could be violent and sexy and generate much less criticism
than the equivalent on radio. Seeing a movie was an act of voli-
tion, the customer consciously deciding to buy a ticket to see a
film about which there existed a certain amount of public information. For the exhibitor the challenge was to lure that customer
into the theater. The clash of these approaches is best illustrated
in a consideration of two separate developments: the failure of
NBC daytime programming as conceived by Sylvester "Pat"
Weaver, and the refashioning of ABC by United Paramount Theaters under Leonard H. Goldenson.

network daytime programming

If the intent of the networks had been to develop profitable daytime schedules, by the end of 1954 the goal had been realized —at least at CBS and NBC. By that date 35.2 percent of CBS television revenues came from daytime advertising. At NBC the total was 25.7 percent. The figure was considerably lower at ABC, which did not launch a full daytime schedule until September 1958. And at DuMont, a network sliding toward economic collapse, daytime shows and billings were slight.

While the rivalry between CBS and NBC might appear to be close, in terms of soap operas CBS held an overwhelming advantage. In fact, throughout the 1950s NBC was unable to develop successful soaps. Between a few early years with *Hawkins Falls* —its first daytime serial—and *The Doctors* (1963–82) and *Another World* (1964–present), NBC broadcast a string of highly forgettable daytime dramas. While CBS in the first half of the 1950s was televising popular, long-lasting shows such as *Search for Tomorrow*, *The Guiding Light*, and *Love of Life*, its chief rival offered disasters such as *Miss Susan*, *First Love*, *Three Steps to Heaven*, and *Follow Your Heart*.

CBS developed a few unpopular programs, such as *The Egg and I*, *Woman with a Past*, *Portia Faces Life* (later called *The Inner Flame*), and *The Seeking Heart*. But if Nielsen ratings are an indication of network accomplishment, the CBS record was formidable. Among the top four soap operas in each of the fifteen TV seasons from the fall of 1952 to the spring of 1967, CBS programs held every position except one: *Hawkins Falls* was rated third in 1952–53. Not until the 1978–79 season, when the ABC serial *All My Children* became the most watched soap, did CBS relinquish the top ranking. And no NBC serial has ever been rated number one.[5]

Ironically, for many years NBC radio soap operas had been overwhelmingly popular. *Ma Perkins*, *Pepper Young's Family*, *Life Can Be Beautiful*, *Stella Dallas*, *Just Plain Bill*, and *Road of Life*, all among the most successful serials in the history of daytime broadcasting, were heard on NBC. NBC radio was strongly committed to the genre: in the fall of 1948 NBC aired nineteen different quarter-hour daytime dramas, while CBS offered only sixteen such shows. That NBC television never was competitive within the genre seems to have been a consequence of the programming philosophy of Sylvester "Pat" Weaver, the network's vice president for television in 1949–53, and its president from December 1953 to December 1955.

Weaver envisioned television as something more than sight radio. He espoused the noble notion that the medium would be the conduit for social betterment, an "enlightenment machine" that would create "an all-people elite."[6] Weaver speculated in 1951, "Television will become the chief instrument accelerating self-realization in our viewers. It is this broad job and the fact that devices can be used to give people things that they do not really want—this is part of the television impact for the future."[7] Influenced by the long-form programming on NBC's prime-time schedule, particularly its sixty- and ninety-minute comedy-variety shows, he sought to fill large daytime segments with lengthy shows in what *Variety* in 1951 termed NBC's "Think Big" concept.[8]

Weaver favored the magazine format, which he employed successfully to cover two hours in the early morning with *Today*, which premiered in January 1952. And he blocked out 105 minutes in the late evening, which debuted as *Tonight!* (later called *The Tonight Show*), hosted by Steve Allen in the fall of 1954.

But long-form, conversational shows seemed to work well only in fringe viewing hours. This became evident with his attempt to fill the later morning and afternoon. Weaver produced *Home*, a one-hour weekday magazine feature hosted by "Editor in Chief" Arlene Francis and staffed by "contributing editors" with specialties in fields such as food, home decoration, and family affairs. Although it ran from early 1953 until mid-1957, *Home* never generated the ratings NBC anticipated.

In a similar fashion, Weaver sought an antidote to soap operas with *Matinee Theater*, an hour-long afternoon showcase offering live plays five days week. The productions were often restagings with new casts of plays that had appeared on evening dramatic series such as *The Kraft Television Theater* and *Robert Montgomery Presents*. Although relatively few viewers owned color TV receivers (there were 37.8 million sets in U.S. homes by the end of 1955; that year only 50,000 color sets were purchased), the daytime versions were enhanced by being telecast in RCA-compatible color. *Matinee Theater* televised about 650 plays in its run from October 1955 until June 1958, but it was an expensive program, costing $100,000 per week to produce (the quarter-hour *Search for Tomorrow* cost about $9,800 per week), and it failed to attract large audiences.

While Weaver was busy structuring daytime TV to match his programming philosophy, NBC in the 1950s was doing little with the soap opera. There were a few false starts, such as the premieres of seven soaps in 1954 and four in 1958, but the network failed to nurture its dramas, canceling four serials in 1954, seven in 1955, and three in 1958. At one point in 1957 NBC televised only one daytime serial (compared to eight at CBS), *Modern Romances*, an anthology program that each week told a complete story in five quarter-hour installments.

When it was not blocs of time for its longer shows, NBC was placing its daytime faith in quiz and audience-participation offerings such as *Concentration, The Price Is Right*, and *Queen for a Day*. At times these were among the most popular programs on morning/afternoon TV. But the backbone of daytime video remained the dramatic serial. The soap opera tended to capture viewers' imaginations and hold them through years of loyal attention. And chronically popular soaps enhanced the ratings of the quiz and audience-participation shows on the network schedule. This point was driven home in early 1954 when Procter & Gamble shifted two of its audience-participation shows—worth $8.8 million annually in advertising—to CBS reportedly as "a repudiation" of NBC for failing to support soap operas.[9]

Conversely, William S. Paley and Frank Stanton held no lofty notions about daytime network TV. They understood the importance of soaps, as did Procter & Gamble, which reported that by mid-1954 the audience for the genre was now larger on television than on radio. By the late 1950s, while NBC was still seeking the formula for daytime success, CBS had a special unit, headed by a former executive from Procter & Gamble, strictly concerned with the development of soap operas.

Even CBS audience-participation shows reflected the sentimentality of the soaps. *The Verdict Is Yours* offered serialized courtroom trials intended to draw viewers into emotional cases that would test their sense of justice and ensure their loyalty to CBS.[10] The network also brought melodrama to quiz shows. On *The Big Payoff*, male contestants who best described the deserving women in their lives were given the opportunity to reward feminine selflessness by winning furs, vacations, jewelry, and other valuable prizes for their women. On *Strike It Rich* from May 1951 to January 1958, needy contestants with sad personal problems competed as much for public sentiment as for dollars. In a case of life imitating art, however, many less fortunate people came to New York City in hopes of being selected to appear on *Strike It Rich*. Social service agencies blasted the program as a heartless exploitation of human misery, as many of the migrating would-be contestants soon turned to city, state, and private welfare for assistance.[11]

"live cats" versus "dead cats"

While nobility found little reward in TV, efficiency did. This was particularly so once a network surrendered to the most cost-effective vehicle possible: the filmed program. In the tradition of network radio, which eschewed recorded shows, early TV programs were usually broadcast live. But live shows were expensive and inefficient. Variety programs such as *The Texaco Star Theater* and *The Colgate Comedy Hour* were headlined by highly paid performers, plus an array of guest stars, musicians, dancers, and production personnel who substantially added to costs—and the programs were designed to air only one time. Similarly, plays seen weekly on the great showcases of the Golden Age were costly undertakings intended to appear once.

Although national television was primarily a medium for live entertainment, it had always been open to filmed series. Early network Westerns such as *The Lone Ranger* and syndicated offerings such as *The Cisco Kid* demonstrated the mass acceptability of filmed programs from the outset. Because of its merger with United Paramount Theaters, the American Broadcasting Company had a strategic relationship with men who understood film better than most broadcasters did. Once the FCC approved the merger in early 1953, ABC became the leading network televiser of filmed programming. Under the leadership of Leonard H. Goldenson—with a cadre of eager devotees who included President Robert Kintner of the network and Vice-Presidents Oliver Treyz and James T. Aubrey—ABC turned first to the Walt Disney studio, which debuted its *Disneyland* in 1954. The following year the network invited Warner Brothers to enter TV with *Warner Brothers Presents*, and eventually *Cheyenne, Maverick, 77 Sunset Strip*, and *Bourbon Street Beat*, among others. As Richard Bunce has pointed out, ABC fortunes soared—gross billings leaping 68 percent between 1954 and 1955—once its commitment to film was anchored in arrangements with Disney and Warner Brothers.[12]

Film was not new to ABC. By 1953 almost 48 percent of its weekly schedule was on film. At CBS the figure was little more than 13 percent, and at NBC it was 18 percent. Only at the DuMont network was programming 100 percent live.[13] Seven years later, however, DuMont was out of business, filmed shows filled 83 percent of all network prime time, and *Variety* predicted that the 1960–61 season would "go down in the books as the year the networks wrote off live television as a force in weekly prime-time programming."[14]

Important to the transition to film was the migration of ABC executives to the other networks. In 1957 Kintner came to NBC-TV, where the following year he became president of the network. Aubrey, who had left CBS to become vice-president for programming at ABC, returned in 1960 as president of CBS-TV. In both cases the officials came as disciples of schedules relying heavily on film. By late 1960, with Treyz now president of ABC-TV, the three networks were headed by Goldenson protégés.

The ascendency of filmed shows constituted the triumph of industry economics over television aesthetics. This result was ensured when major Hollywood studios in the mid-1950s abandoned their inital reluctance to produce for the new medium. Whereas subsidiaries of the smaller studios such as Screen Gems (Columbia), Interstate Television (Allied Artists), General Teleradio (RKO), Revue Studios (MCA), United World Films (Universal), and Hollywood Television Services (Republic) had supplied programs since the early 1950s, the ascendency of film was not finalized until mid-decade when, as well as Disney and Warner Brothers, prestigious film giants such as 20th Century-Fox, Metro-Goldwyn-Mayer, and United Artists (through its purchase of the successful independent TV producer Ziv) began producing video series. As film historian Thomas Schatz has illustrated, this was no casual decision by the major Hollywood studios, since revenues from these TV series soon were used to stabilize their operations and offset the rising costs of making feature films.[15]

When these were added to those sizable independent companies already filming for television—in particular, Desilu and Four Star—the fate of live TV was sealed. Sealed, too, was the destiny of hundreds of small production houses that had supplied early TV. Whereas there were 331 such companies listed in the 1956 edition of *Television Factbook*, that figure was halved in three years.

While the networks were becoming more efficiently organized to program and advertise to the nation, the movement to film catalyzed the centralization of TV production. Large companies either bought or drove out of business most of the small operations. By late 1963 one of the biggest winners, MCA, was employing 5,300 actors and technicians for its Revue productions, while two-thirds of the earnings of members of the Screen Actors Guild came from work in television films.[16] At that time *Fortune* magazine estimated that MCA had a financial interest in "no less than 45 percent of all TV evening hours."[17]

Still, in phrases coined by producer Martin Manulis, there were those "live cats" who favored live television production and opposed the movement of the "dead cats" toward greater utilization of film. As a "live cat," David Sarnoff was an early critic of the trend to motion pictures, asserting in 1956 that "the true function of TV will have failed if the film programming snowballs [so] as to become the dominant appeal." [18] The following year producer David Susskind predicted that "audiences will demand a return to live because they will be overwhelmed by the mediocrity of film this season." For him the problem was in the contrast between the "dynamic, creative programming" produced live in New York City and the "trite and cheap imitations" filmed in Hollywood, where the major concern was "how to make a fast buck." [19] For producer Martin Stone the case for live television involved aesthetic matters such as immediacy, the nature of communication, and transporting of the viewer. He contended, "Film in abundance on television is the equivalent of the home movie in continuous performance. Live television is magic of its own." [20]

Filmed programs, however, were too profitable to resist. Produced quickly and inexpensively, such series could continue to make money in syndication long after they premiered. Individual episodes of a series could be rerun to supplement the thirty-nine-week regular schedule. The life cycle of a filmed show depended only on its popularity. When a popular network series ended, it could be edited down to allow for more commercial minutes, then rented for nonnetwork use. Here it could continue to attract viewers and advertisers indefinitely. Such a series might also reappear on network stations but outside prime-time hours, or in a few instances, such as with *I Love Lucy* during 1955–56 and *Gunsmoke* during 1961–64, reruns could be offered as a network series on one evening while new episodes aired on another night.

Further, filmed programs could be leased to television in foreign countries. Action-adventure and Western series that were long on action and short on dialogue and complexity were particularly easy to prepare for export. With vocal dubbing or subtitles, these programs could become entertainment staples in many countries now entering the television age. "Talk about jumping from camel to jet plane," remarked an official of the United States Information Agency who was excited in 1956 about the Cold War advantages that would accrue from the penetration of foreign cultures through American TV, "this is jumping from papyrus scroll to television." [21]

What had occurred in American TV by the early 1960s was little more than the conquest of a new medium by an old medium. During the 39 weeks of the 1958–59 season the networks broadcast enough filmed programs in prime time to make 936 feature movies. By this date Desilu, Revue, and Screen Gems grossed an estimated $100 million by selling programs to television. And by the fall of 1959 Warner Brothers was filming seven series for ABC, which constituted 30 percent of the network's evening schedule.[22]

As well as creating filmed series for TV, the movie studios also began to lease their vintage motion pictures to network and local stations. Slowly at first came lesser movies: in the late 1940s and early 1950s B Westerns from PRC, Monogram, Grand National, and similar studios were prevalent; also available were British films from J. Arthur Rank, low-budget movie series featuring the likes of the Eastside Kids (The Bowery Boys) from Monogram and Sherlock Holmes from Universal, plus packages of several hundred cartoons from Warner Brothers, Universal, and Columbia.

The marriage of film to television was consummated in 1955. With the traditional studio system of integrated production, distribution, and exhibition in collapse for various reasons, and with rising costs in all facets of moviemaking, the lure of video proved irresistible. In that year RKO released 740 feature films to TV, while Columbia released 104, J. Arthur Rank 165, Paramount 35, Selznick 11, and Universal-International 8—plus 192 Westerns from Columbia and Universal and 123 Gene Autry/Roy Rogers cowboy films from Republic. In the area of short subjects, the figures, too, were impressive: Paramount released 1,600 shorts, RKO 1,000, 20th Century-Fox 600, and Paul Terry's animated Terrytoons nearly 1,100. This development led one commentator to suggest that "apart from an actual wholesale release to video of all the properties in all the vaults of all the majors, there isn't very much more that the studios could do to make themselves more strongly felt in the video field."[23] By 1961 there were 12,209 feature films available to television; 2,651 made after 1948, and only 10 percent of them were Westerns.[24]

With the inundation of TV by film companies came the triumph of Hollywood over all other video production centers. In the early years of television New York City was the premier site for origination; here the spirit of Broadway was notable in the great live comedy-variety and dramatic fare on network TV. Chicago also contributed to the live network schedule with series such as *Kukla, Fran, and Ollie;* Dave Garroway's variety offering *Garroway at Large;* and a one-hour weekly circus, *Super Circus.* But with reliance on motion pictures, the networks turned to the reservoir of movie talent situated in Southern California.

Through motion pictures and network radio, Hollywood already possessed a production stranglehold on U.S. popular culture. It seems inconceivable that TV would have withstood the lure of California any longer than necessary. By the mid-1950s the networks originated from lavish new West Coast production facilities, and in the fall of 1957 more than 71 percent of all network prime-time offerings came from Hollywood, and a substantial number of live network shows were also broadcast from Southern California. Coincidental with the move, network live programming dwindled from 80 percent in 1953 to 33 percent by 1960.[25]

quantity and quality on television

The prominence of filmed shows by the late 1950s exacerbated a problem inherent in American popular culture and broadcasting: how to create and maintain productions of quality while satisfying the hunger of television for products in quantity. It is not coincidental that low-budget motion pictures, the so-called B movies, disappeared when Hollywood studios turned their attention to churning out quick TV films, as many as thirty-nine episodes per season per series.

On filmed anthology series such as *Ford Theater* and *The Loretta Young Show* as well as in the surviving live playhouses, formulaic stories overwhelmed originality and flair. In Westerns, crime dramas, spy series, medical dramas, and the like, familiar predicaments with predictable consequences were told and retold, while old plot lines were repackaged as "new" shows and mediocrity threatened to overwhelm the medium.

It was difficult to attract and hold quality writers when they found their creativity affected by sponsors, ad agencies, network officials, and ratings. Considerations of "proper" language, the prejudices of the majority population, the intellectual parameters presumed acceptable to the mass audience, and a multitude of social and religious taboos drove many talented playwrights to the stage and motion pictures.

It was also difficult for writers to produce satisfying material when the demands on them were so heavy—and the audience usually preferred the formulaic to the inventive. As writers Richard Levinson and William Link described this quandary on *60 Minutes* in the early 1980s, TV writers were trapped by the nature of the medium and the culture. The result was mediocre television.

Levinson: *It is mediocre because you're programming 18 hours a day, 365 days a year. And the average household has a television set on six or seven hours. Nothing that goes on for six or seven* *hours a day can avoid being mediocre. A noted playwright will write a play every three or four years. Many television writers write what is analogous to three or four plays a season. And the system forces people against their best intentions to do work that is not their best work. And I think finally, the audience does not always support quality when it is aired.*

Link: *And then when a really good show goes off the air, again the creative community says, "Why should we come up with something new, something unique? Why should we really go in and try to sell something which might open a new door and might be pioneering, when all the good things—or most of the good things—that go on the air don't make it?"* [26]

American television was primarily a business. While Robert Sarnoff, the president of NBC, could argue in 1956 that a network was constructed around three major service functions—to the public, to affiliated stations, and to advertisers—it was increasingly obvious that making a profit and satisfying shareholders were the prepossessing foci of industry management.

The networks filled hundreds of hours with their programming each week, and affiliates supplemented network shows to fill broadcast days lasting as long as twenty-four hours. To discover if their programs, and therefore their commercials, were being watched, measurement statistics from the A. C. Nielsen Company, Arbitron, Pulse, and other research companies became critical objective factors in American TV culture. If its ratings were low, a series was failing its principal goal of drawing large audiences for advertisers. Cancellation from the network schedule was justified as sound business. Even though several million viewers were fans of the series, a program needed enough millions to survive.

Even if a sponsor were willing to continue underwriting a poorly rated series, it would be shifted or canceled by the network on the grounds that it was detracting from the remainder of the network's evening schedule. In 1957 this was made aware to the sponsor of an hour-long showcase of live drama, *The Kaiser Aluminum Hour*. As a representative of Kaiser explained to an FCC committee two years later, the corporation was pleased with the quality audience it was reaching even though it was being beaten decisively in the ratings by *The $64,000 Question* and *The Red Skelton Show* on CBS. "However, NBC took the position that it could not afford to continue such a low-rated program in that time period because of its effect on the NBC audience for the balance of the evening. This is the concept of the 'audience flow.' In other words, it was NBC's position that the large shift of audience to CBS occasioned by *The $64,000 Question* adversely affected the total audience that NBC could deliver for the balance of the evening."[27] Rather than shift to a less visible time period, Kaiser took its $4 million investment in the show and left NBC—ending up soon on ABC sponsoring the popular Western *Maverick*.

Emerging from this dynamic was a pattern of massive program mortality. The cancellation rate for network shows during the period 1953–56 was 68 percent. By mid-1957 only 23 network series had been on the air for five or more years, and several of these were daytime soap operas.[28] Significantly, of the 763 prime-time network series scheduled between the fall of 1950 and the end of 1964, a total of 660 were canceled, and 42 of the survivors had been on the air for less than four months.[29]

Television programming evidenced the cyclical, trendy qualities more familiar to movies than to broadcasting. By the 1960s TV already had lived through the early dominance of comedy-variety shows, followed by the primacy of filmed situation comedies led by *I Love Lucy*, flowing then to a rage for quiz shows precipitated by *The $64,000 Question*, and then to a preponderance of Westerns catalyzed by series such as *Gunsmoke* and *The Life and Legend of Wyatt Earp*. There was a simple mechanism at work here: a newly successful program prompted the creation of more and more "duplicate" series having similar attributes; these programs continued to appear until the ratings suggested viewer boredom, or until a new hit show spawned another faddish wave of replication.

Such recombinance was the mark of an industry concerned less with risk-taking than with marketing the proven. As media sociologist Todd Gitlin has explained it, the practice may have come to TV early, but it was not new. "Cultural recombinance is not simply a convenient if self-defeating way of concocting shows to exploit established tastes," he wrote. "It is part of the ground rhythm of modern culture. . . . Consumers want novelty but take only so many chances; manufacturers, especially oligopolists, want to deploy their repertory of the tried-and-true in such a way as to generate novelty without risk. The fusion of these pressures is what produces the recombinant style, which collects the old in new packages and hopes for a magical synthesis."

For Oliver Treyz, president of ABC-TV, pleasing average people was what American television was all about. "In trying to satisfy most of the people most of the time," he wrote in 1960, "we are merely clinging to a time-honored show business tradition that projected a P. T. Barnum, a David Belasco, a D. W. Griffith, and a Cecil B. DeMille into preeminence." He concluded on a bizarre note of self-congratulation: "From Shakespeare to Barnum to Belasco to ABC—nothing's changed."[30]

Treyz was less than candid. The record of program failures suggests that more than viewer interest or popular taste was at work in network TV. Like lemmings headed for inevitable disaster, the networks and production studios followed failed shows with more series of the same sort—often produced by the writers, directors, producers, and stars of those programs that had been canceled.

The idea was not to offer a wide range of shows and thereby please most people, it was to make the TV business more efficient and profitable by limiting the variety and increasing the similarity of productions. Network programming placed great demands on the film industry, hundreds of hours per month of new programs; the equivalent of hundreds of feature films churned out each season for first-run screening from September to June.

This could be done only by maximizing the use of production facilities and personnel. Sets used on one series could easily be utilized for another, particularly if the two were the same genre of entertainment. Stars could be shuttled from one series to another. The formula of one success could be cloned and moved to a similar program or into another genre. Thus *Riverboat* was conceived by NBC as *Wagon Train* in a different historical context; and the success of *The Real McCoys* in the late 1950s sparked a rush to rural situation comedies such as *The Andy Griffith Show* and *The Beverly Hillbillies* in the early 1960s.

At Warner Brothers, recombinance was paramount. Writers admitted freely borrowing story lines from John Steinbeck, William Shakespeare, Mary Shelley, Oliver Goldsmith, and other celebrated authors. The formula made famous by the popular private-detective series *77 Sunset Strip*—one detective middle-aged and sensible; another detective handsome and younger; and an assistant, still younger, who appealed to teenage viewers—was replicated in many other Warner Brothers series: *Hawaiian Eye, Bourbon Street Beat, Surfside 6, The Roaring Twenties*. This was efficiency and cost-effectiveness.

There was no scramble to discover new styles and inventive genres. If anything, program diversity diminished. The respected documentary series *See It Now*, with newsman Edward R. Murrow and producer Fred W. Friendly, was canceled by CBS in 1958, replaced by *Do You Trust Your Wife?* with ventriloquist Edgar Bergen and his three dummies. Live sports were greatly diminished, as were the great dramatic showcases of the Golden Age, all to make way for filmed Westerns, detective programs, and the other series coming from Hollywood. Classical music left network prime time, as did news discussion series, children's fare, and religious shows.

Nothing less than the rationalization of a new industry was occurring in the late 1950s. Standardization of product, reliance on familiar formulas, use of mass production techniques by the film studios and networks: national TV, like national culture, was emerging as an efficient, streamlined reality that existed to please the majority, a majority that in great part it had helped to create. Programmers were bringing regularity and controllability to their fare. No surprises here, with regularized genres, regularized plots, and regularized characterization. Everything was being brought under control so advertisers could be enticed to spend billions of dollars in a safe and predictable medium.[31]

The rationalization of the television business was most obvious in the glut of Westerns that inundated American TV in the late 1950s. Granted, series such as *Gunsmoke* and *Bonanza* were excellently realized and lasted for many years; granted, too, that Westerns had a valid place in American popular culture and that they had appeared in moderation on TV since the late 1940s. But by the fall of 1959 there were twenty-eight Western series on network prime time, almost one-quarter of the evening programming. Westerns were well received, too. At their height, sixty million viewers each evening watched them. By March 1959, eight of the top ten shows were Westerns.

The reason for the flood appears to lie less with a gargantuan demand by Americans for that many formulaic programs, and more with industry inexperience with filmed series. As Hubbell Robinson, formerly CBS vice-president for programming, described the relationship between the Western and TV, it was "the easy solution for every programmer who couldn't think of anything else to do."[32]

Clearly, the business of television was affecting American culture. Actor Guy Madison has reported on the rapidity with which *The Adventures of Wild Bill Hickok* was turned out for a cost of $12,000 per episode in the early 1950s. "We couldn't waste any time in TV," Madison revealed. "We made a half-hour show in two and one-half days. That included dialogue, action, and everything. At one point we knocked off seven films in seventeen days."[33] It was this kind of efficiency and cultural product that came to network TV once the total commitment to filmed programming was made.

Increasingly these Westerns relied on sex and violence to

attract viewers. Handsome leading men, often shown bare-chested in manly endeavors, brought audiences to series such as *Cheyenne,* while shoot-outs and murder scenes permeated the genre. This formula for mass culture success was well understood by Robert Kintner, the erstwhile head of ABC-TV, who learned from Leonard H. Goldenson and the motion picture distributors who took over the network in 1953. Kintner brought the formula to NBC programming when he became network president in 1958. He immediately met—and overcame—resistance from those clinging to older notions about TV and social responsibilities.

This is revealed in one of the frankest network documents in the public record. Like most American corporations, NBC does not usually make its private records—at least not the confrontational, potentially embarrassing ones—open for public scrutiny. But in a seventy-four-page letter written July 13, 1961, to NBC's board chairman, Robert W. Sarnoff, the outgoing vice-president for TV programs and talent, David Levy, revealed fascinating details about the inner workings of NBC management. Seeking to justify himself after being relieved of his programming duties by Kintner, Levy assembled old letters and memos to buttress his defense.

Levy had a long and distinguished career before coming to NBC in 1960. For most of a quarter-century he was a writer/director/producer/executive with Young & Rubicam advertising agency. As such, he was responsible for the appearance of distinguished series such as *Father Knows Best, Our Miss Brooks, Arthur Godfrey's Talent Scouts, Wagon Train,* and *The Twilight Zone.*

Levy wrote of his own commitment to "programs of substance and quality in drama, music, special events, and in the area of social documents and wholesome entertainment." But part of the Levy letter explains the way in which Kintner brought a new philosophy to NBC programming. Levy expressed dismay that he and his department had been "confronted with another philosophy which to be perfectly frank was espoused largely by one man. It is more a formula than a philosophy—a point of view that lays heavy stress on programs of mass appeal, programs strenuously and systematically developed to broaden acceptance through exploitation of 'sex and violence.' " Levy continued:

This counter-philosophy originated and fostered at ABC when Mr. Robert Kintner was President of that network, undeniably has a proven commercial record and a powerful appeal to the masses. Mr. Kintner was the great champion at NBC of this latter formula although he took great pains both inside the company and publicly never to permit his name to be associated with this policy. It is my duty to report that Program Board minutes were prepared under his specific instructions to eliminate all comments made by the President urging or supporting sex and violence. . . . I will venture to prophesy that by 1963, the date to which I am contracted, the short-range hopes of those broadcasters who live by a Kintner formula will have evaporated from the TV screens.[34]

The studios and networks filled the nights of the late 1950s with the "adult Westerns," in which characterization (costing less to film) was emphasized over action and chase scenes (being more expensive to produce). Certainly, many became hit programs, and deservedly so. But many also failed, canceled in a season or two—sometimes even less. They were usually replaced by other Westerns, not because there was a certainty that the new series was culturally correct for this moment or that it would succeed, but because of complex commitments to advertisers, production companies, distributors, and to a marketing notion that dictated manipulating a buying trend by flooding the market with trendy, similar products until that spree abated and a new one was created.

The Westerns glut was also the result of the newness of the alliance between Hollywood and the TV networks. This was an excessive first attempt by the movie industry at last geared up fully to turn out B films for television, and a miscalculation by network programmers who overindulged the public taste with Western films now easily available. They had learned the formula: handsome people in violent or potentially violent situations, moral dilemmas easily comprehended and resolved, a physical setting that gratified the audience, characterization that invited viewer identification, and memorable mannerisms that carried over from episode to episode. Inadvertently, however, Hollywood and the networks had allowed regularization to become monotony. When the Western began its decline by 1960, it collapsed rapidly and definitively. No Western series introduced since the late 1960s has earned high ratings.

With the fiscal regeneration of ABC, there existed three formidable national programmers. But there was little difference between them. Call it monopoly, oligopoly, or triopoly, the fact was that three similarly structured, similarly operated corporations controlled what the United States saw as television each day.

Government did little to curb such power. Investigations by the House of Representatives, the Senate, and the FCC in the late 1950s concluded that the power of the networks was monopolistic. It was clear, for instance, that option-time provisions in network-affiliate contracts extended the influence of the networks far beyond the five VHF stations allowed by the FCC. It was obvious, too, that affiliate obligations to televised network programs stifled not only local and syndicated programming but also interfered with free competition. As a House committee reported in 1958, "If network survival depends upon curtailment of competition—if networks must be insulated from normal market rivalry—that is a clear admission that competition in television broadcasting cannot be an adequate regulator." [35]

Despite such concentration of power, the FCC took only weak action. Concluding that option time was "reasonably necessary for successful network operations and is in the public interest," the commission in 1960 ordered minimal changes in the practice. The FCC divided the broadcast day into four different time elements, then decreed that no more than two and one-half hours per segment could be time-optioned by the networks. This meant that affiliates needed only to accept ten instead of twelve hours daily from their respective networks. Stations were free, however, to clear network offerings beyond the minimum time requirements.

The irony of the network video monopoly, however, was that most Americans enjoyed TV as it existed. In mass entertainment values, it was the most prolific and successful operation in the world. Occasionally, TV programs and series pleased even the snobbiest of critics. But the fatal flaw in U.S. video was not the mediocrity of its programs; network TV failed the nation because of its fixation on popularity. It paid insufficient attention to the qualities that made Americans interestingly different, and to the potential of the medium to enlighten the society it served. The networks never allowed television to be all it might have been.

The most glaring deficiency in American TV was a consistent commitment to intellectual programming. Of course, there were outstanding series, such as *Omnibus*, with its impressive mix of fine dramas and musical productions, and *The Voice of Firestone*, which blended music from grand opera with musical favorites from Broadway and Hollywood. But many, like *Omnibus*, were shunted to Sunday afternoons in the "cultural ghetto"; and classical music programs such as *The Voice of Firestone* survived in prime time with poor ratings only as long as corporations such as

129

Firestone Tire & Rubber Company paid the bill, and networks such as ABC were willing to lose money for the sake of prestige. In the case of the Firestone musical feature—on network radio beginning in 1928, and a TV staple since 1949—time ran out in 1959. Its half hour on Monday nights was occupied by the first half of *Bourbon Street Beat*, a formulaic private-eye series from Warner Brothers that lasted one season.

Such developments led informed observers to bitter assessments. In 1957 historian Arthur Schlesinger, Jr., was succinct: "I cannot repress my feelings that, in the main, television has been a bust."[36] The following year a critic in *Fortune* magazine described TV as filled with "pap" and "mediocrity." He argued that "By and large the 1958–59 season is compounded of bathos from Boot Hill, counterfeit celebration via quiz shows, barbarism from the police blotter, inanity from outer space, monstriphilia from Hollywood's celluloid closet."[37] Similarly stinging in his appraisal was Robert M. Hutchins, former president of the University of Chicago, who decried the condition of the medium in 1961:

We have triumphantly invented, perfected, and distributed to the humblest cottage throughout the land one of the greatest technical marvels in history, television, and have used it for what? To bring Coney Island into every home. It is as though movable type had been devoted exclusively since Gutenberg's time to the publication of comic books.[38]

Inherent in such disapproval was recognition of the largest void in U.S. television: its lack of educational purpose, even though station licenses were committed in theory to public service. When the FCC decided in 1952 to allocate 250 channels —no more than one per market area—for noncommercial telecasting, Educational Television (ETV) was launched with a high purpose. But it had no money.

Its first operations, in 1953, were KUHT at the University of Houston and KTHE in Los Angeles, both UHF stations that few people could receive; and in 1954 at WQED in Pittsburgh and KQED in San Francisco, the first VHF educational channels. Although the Ford Foundation and other national and community philanthropies offered funding, by mid-1955 there were only 12 ETV stations on the air—the majority of them on the obscure UHF spectrum.

Essentially a federation of noncommercial stations, by 1961 ETV still consisted of only 52 outlets, compared to 527 commercial stations. To meet programming demands and save on costs, ETV stations rotated their kinescopes and films. Production and distribution were coordinated through the National Educational Television and Radio Center in Ann Arbor, Michigan, and later in New York City.

Typically, these stations transmitted for only a few hours weekly. Their schedules might consist of cultural programs such as an imported British series, *Arts and Artists,* hosted in 1956 by Kenneth Clark; *The Written Word,* in which Dr. Frank Baxter of the University of Southern California traced "the story of the human record from the pictograph to the photograph"; and *The Challenge,* an interview series hosted by Hugh Downs and produced by WTTW in Chicago.

ETV also gave evidence early of a commitment to uplifting children's programming. WGBH in Boston created *Discovery* in 1957 to observe natural phenomena through explorations such as "Webs and Their Weavers" and "The Edge of the Sea." At the same time KECT-TV in St. Louis developed *The Finder,* which treated topics such as the history of riverboats on the Mississippi River and the story of printing.

This programming was neither compelling nor popular, but it addressed one of the original purposes of broadcasting in the United States, to educate the public. Importantly, it laid the groundwork for the more sophisticated National Educational Television (NET), which was formed in 1963, and its successor in 1969, the Public Broadcasting Service (PBS). Not surprisingly, public educational TV made it easier for the networks to reduce production of documentaries, discussion programs, public-service features, and whatever educational commitment remained in commercial broadcasting.

For all the early failures to realize fully its public promise, it would be simplistic to condemn video as trashy or irrelevant. Throughout the 1950s the networks broadcast series and specials that were well crafted, inspiring, exciting, and enlightening. Technological innovations such as color, UHF, and the introduction of videotape in 1956 augured well for the future of the medium.

Another indication of the growth of TV was the emergence of Community Antenna Television (CATV) or cable TV in the early 1950s. Established originally to provide clear video images to those living in areas inaccessible to broadcast TV transmissions, cable slowly brought isolated Americans into the mainstream of the national video culture. Whereas in 1952 there were 70 cable systems servicing 14,000 subscribers (0.1 percent of all TV homes), by 1958 there were still only 525 systems with 450,000 subscribers (1.1 percent of all TV homes).[39]

Cable brought closer to reality, however, the concept of "pay TV" as an alternative to "free" network television. Cable constituted a potential delivery system of diverse programming, a medium by which to transmit special entertainment for which subscribers would pay a direct fee. Although by the end of the 1950s cable remained in an incubative form, the commercial networks seemed terrified by its possibilities. In 1958 CBS purchased a two-page advertisement in *TV Guide* so its president, Frank Stanton, could warn the public:

> *Free television as we know it cannot survive alongside pay television. . . . If only a small fraction of the 42 million families who now enjoy television free were to agree to pay for what they see, the huge funds thus available would enable proprietors of pay television to pre-empt the best talent and the best television programs for their own subscribers. The rest of us would gradually be forced to ride second-class.*[40]

Nevertheless, a majority of Americans enjoyed TV exactly as it existed. In swelling numbers, viewers rated video as their preferred source of both diversion and information; increasingly, too, they expressed their trust in the messages television delivered. In 1959 a Roper poll indicated that 57 percent of the public felt TV stations were doing a "good to excellent" job. When asked which of the mass media they would most want to save, 42 percent of the respondents selected television; the closest competition came from newspapers, with 32 percent, and radio, with 19 percent.[41] In little more than a decade video had wrested from the older media the allegiance of mass America.

The discrepancy between intellectual expectations and popular acceptance was wide. The situation was all the more perplexing because respected people within the industry agreed with its critics. After a decade of TV, Edward R. Murrow concluded in 1958 that Americans must recognize "that television in the main is being used to distract, delude, amuse, and insulate us."[42] The following year his colleague at CBS Eric Sevareid lamented, "The most intimate and powerful medium for human instruction and inspiration science ever devised has failed to claim its own birthright."[43]

To advertising executive John P. Cunningham the problem was that advertisers and broadcasters in their selfish search for increased profits were destroying the appeal of TV with boredom and mediocrity. "We must never forget," he told a convention of advertisers in 1957, "that the airwaves do not belong to the advertisers—nor to the networks—nor to the FCC—nor to the federal government. They belong to the people of the United States."[44] Perhaps Allen B. DuMont expressed this perspective best. "How can 47,000,000 television sets be tuned to this kind of [trivia] five hours and more a day?" he wondered in 1961. "My reaction has been that of the creator of a Frankenstein. . . . Rather than honored, perhaps I should instead be censured."[45]

As historian James Baughman has recently suggested, the basis of much of this criticism lies in the disappointment of liberal intellectuals with the reality that was commercial television after its first decade. To them, TV was to have been the great enlightener, the means of uplifting and educating and ennobling. Certainly, there was to have been entertainment, but the electronic marvel was to have been the vehicle through which the goodness of American social life was to be improved.

In Baughman's view, the liberal economic prescription had cured the *quantitative* problems of the Great Depression; by the end of the 1950s the United States had become fat and wealthy, an affluent society replete with labor-saving devices, rising life spans, early retirements, and expanded leisure time. Now it was time to focus on the *qualitative* needs of mass society, to improve the style and intelligence and quality of American civilization.[46]

The condition of TV by 1960, however, spoke to another mentality, one not fully anticipated by the architects of the new popular culture. The fact was that most Americans did not demand the qualitative fullness intended for them. To the mass audience, television was an escapist utility, not a pedagogic device. As a simple way to transcend the complications of daily living, most Americans preferred programming that was trivial or facile or silly. Liberal dreamers since the birth of the republic apparently had been wrong: satisfied with the triumphs of quantity, the general population seemed unconcerned with the urgency of quality. As sociologist Edward C. Shils wrote in 1957, "Universal education, the alleviation of physical misery, the drift of equality have not brought with them that deepening and enrichment of the mind to which liberals and revolutionaries alike aspired." Instead, "the silliness of television" seems to have satisfied the masses.[47]

The acceptance of an imperfect national TV system, however, did not result necessarily from the conscious plans of either broadcasters or viewers. The attitude of the mass audience toward television was a function of myriad factors, among them the reluctance of the networks to schedule low-rated educational programs at popular hours; the uses to which most Americans put their receivers; the easy attractiveness of much that was on commercial TV; the lack of coordination between national video and the nation's educational system; the lack of any realistic regulatory system to direct national TV toward social enlightenment; and, above all, the organization of this powerful resource as a private business enterprise, monopolized by three profit-seeking networks that restricted the program choices available to the mass audience. Americans had become conditioned to radio and then television as relaxing diversions; education was incidental, confined for the most part to slim news programs and occasional documentaries.

# of scandal

and power Although video had failed to satisfy the expectations of many of its early idealistic supporters, it had still become a powerful and influential force in American life. In his poignant satire of the broadcast industry, *Network*, screenwriter Paddy Chayefsky in 1974 described television as "the most awesome goddamn propaganda force in the whole godless world."

Yet, in only its first decade, TV had demonstrated its awesome ability to persuade. When Joan Weber's song "Let Me Go, Lover" was used as background music on a *Studio One* drama in 1954, the exposure led to national popularity, and within a week her recording of the song was on the *Billboard* record charts, where it soon reached the top position.

The managers of Elvis Presley understood the persuasive potential of TV, establishing their client's presence on twelve national telecasts between January 1956 and January 1957—six appearances on *Stage Show* hosted by Tommy and Jimmy Dorsey, then two appearances on *The Milton Berle Show*, one on *The Steve Allen Show*, and finally three on *The Ed Sullivan Show*—then abandoning video (except for an appearance in May 1960 on *The Frank Sinatra Show*) for more than a decade while the King of Rock and Roll flourished as a recording and motion-picture star.

Those with the most faith in the persuasive power of the medium were the chief propagandists of television, the advertisers who spent billions of dollars annually to win customers for their products. Of course, where there was no real niche for a product to fill—as in the case of the Edsel automobile, introduced in the mid-1950s—TV advertising could not be effective. But where a potential market existed, the medium could be potent, especially when it was associated with a program high in the ratings.

Those companies underwriting the quiz show boom of the 1950s, for example, found video advertising rewarding. Net profits from Geritol sales were $10.5 million in 1956, but after Geritol began sponsoring *Twenty-One* on NBC, profits reached $14 million in 1957 and $12.4 million the following year. Revlon, which underwrote *The $64,000 Question*, was even more successful. Between 1950 and 1954, the cosmetics firm made an average annual profit of $1.2 million; but after buying *The $64,000 Question*, profits for 1955 through 1958 averaged $7.68 million, and for 1959 and 1960 they averaged $11.1 million.[1]

As a vestige of radio production procedures, early TV programs frequently were produced by advertising agencies on behalf of their corporate clients. Broadcasters did little more than stage and/or televise a packaged product. That the agencies were influential was obvious in the case of Young & Rubicam, which on one evening in early 1954 placed for several clients seven shows touching every evening time slot. *Variety* termed Sunday, March 28, "Y&R Night on TV" as the agency began at six-thirty with *The Roy Rogers Show* for General Foods, and finished at ten-thirty with *What's My Line?* for Remington-Rand.[2]

While the television networks could sell Remington electric shavers and Geritol vitamin supplements, their greatest selling accomplishment was in selling their realization of television to the American people. It had begun with radio, when these programmers established high-caliber entertainment and a reliable flow of information as national broadcast standards. The selling continued in the early years of video as ABC, CBS, and NBC sought to convince the audience of their capability to telecast as well as they had radiobroadcast. Left in the hands of the networks, TV programming—which in other nations was often dull and pedantic and scarce—was a shining stage in the United States.

But the relationship between networks and audience was built on trust: the latter having surrendered its precious airwaves, the former in return presenting authentic, credible entertainment. It was, however, a spiritual relationship sorely tested by a program scandal of the late 1950s that shook the new industry and challenged the networks to reestablish a trust betrayed.

the quiz show scandals

The temptation of advertisers and their agencies to exploit network television reached a peak in the quiz show craze of the late 1950s. Quizzers had been popular in radio a decade earlier, but TV had been reluctant to venture deeply into the genre until the U.S. Supreme Court in 1954 invalidated an FCC rule that restricted giveaway programs and treated the quiz shows as a form of lottery.

The first program to emerge following this ruling was *The $64,000 Question*, a half-hour show that premiered in June 1955. Its concept was taken from a radio quiz show popular throughout the 1940s, *Take It or Leave It* (later renamed *The $64 Question*), where contestants started with $1 and doubled their winnings by answering questions until reaching the top prize, "the $64 question." Television simply increased the jackpot a thousandfold. There had never been a success like this TV show: within a few weeks the CBS quizzer was the leading show on television, and it stayed there during the 1955–56 season, falling to number four the next season and to number twenty in 1957–58.

The program employed a seductive set featuring an eye-catching category board, a modernistic isolation booth in which competitors stood (ostensibly to prevent them from overhearing answers offered from the audience) to answer the big-money questions, plus engaging contestants, attractive women such as actress Barbara Britton for the Revlon cosmetics commercials, and a glib host in Hal March. Contestants apparently relied on their own expertise in topics as diverse as Shakespeare, boxing, opera, the Bible, and art.

Importantly, *The $64,000 Question* was not produced by CBS; it was packaged by an independent company that worked closely with a single sponsor who, as was customary, had considerable input into the direction of its show. CBS did little more than sell a half hour of weekly prime time to the advertising agency representing Revlon, and then televise the finished product. It is impossible to explain fully the popular appeal of *The $64,000 Question*. Be it the vicarious lure of sudden wealth, the challenge to answer esoteric questions, happiness at seeing other people achieving financial success, whatever in the program touched the American psyche at midcentury, this was stunning TV.

Predictably, imitations soon followed in prime time and daytime with offerings such as *Haggis Baggis, High Finance, The $64,000 Challenge, The $100,000 Big Surprise, Do You Trust Your Wife? High-Low, Twenty-One, Tic Tac Dough,* and *Dotto*. By the end of the 1957–58 season there were twenty-two network quiz shows, and 18 percent of NBC's programming consisted of quizzers that filled forty-seven half-hour segments per week. Such programs were cheap to produce, and to build advertiser name recognition they allowed a sponsor to affix his name and/or logo to a wall, podium, or other stage prop, where it hung visibly throughout the entire show.

They also earned wonderful ratings, especially when a popular champion and a challenger competed for many weeks for an increasingly higher cash prize. On the NBC program *Twenty-One*, college professor Charles Van Doren and Vivienne Nearing battled over several months until in March 1957 Van Doren lost. That final program earned NBC a 34.7 rating/51.5 share, beating *I Love Lucy*—the number one program that season—by a safe distance (26.1 rating/38.7 share). The Van Doren–Nearing showdown buried its opposition on ABC, *Life Is Worth Living,* with Bishop Fulton J. Sheen, which garnered a lowly 3.6 rating.[3]

Unfortunately for many associated with such programming, these shows also were usually fixed. Martin Revson, executive vice-president of Revlon, Inc., sponsor of both *The $64,000 Question* and its clone *The $64,000 Challenge,* made it clear at weekly meetings which contestants he personally wanted to win.[4] To Revson, this was legitimate criticism, not intended as direct orders; but to the producers of the shows, the critique was understood as a command to allow contestants with good viewer ratings to win, while causing unattractive competitors to lose quickly. Jack Barry, the coproducer of *Twenty-One, High-Low,* and *Tic Tac Dough,* explained in 1984 that the motive for rigging the shows was purely commercial. "In the first few weeks we didn't resort to this practice. But after the third or fourth week, we had a couple of contestants who missed almost every question," he recalled. "It was painful. The sponsor and the advertising agency called and said, 'Don't ever let that happen again.' "[5]

The rigging took several forms. Competitors were often told the answers or given entire scripts in advance. When ratings sagged, current champions were ordered to lose and attractive new winners replaced them; questions were tailored to the strengths of popular competitors; designated winners were also coached on how to give their answers more suspensefully. In the confusion caused by such high finance and fraud, some producers even accepted bribes from people wanting to appear on a show.

There were several big winners who performed legitimately, although questions were tailored to match their intellectual strengths. Ten-year-old Robert Strom won $192,000 on *The $64,000 Question,* and Teddy Nadler appeared 38 times on *The $64,000 Challenge,* earning a total of $252,000. But many names and careers were tarnished by a New York grand jury investigation, and by congressional hearings in 1959.

Among the biggest losers was Lewis Cowan, who developed *The $64,000 Question* and parlayed its success into the presidency of CBS; he was forced in 1960 to resign his network position. Charles Van Doren was a distinguished university professor and winner of $129,000 on *Twenty-One;* he not only lost public trust, but NBC also relieved him of his anchor position on the *Today* show when he admitted that he had participated in the fraud. Jack Barry and his coproducer, Dan Enright, were banished from network TV for more than a decade. And contestant Elfrida Von Nardroff, who won $220,500 on *Twenty-One*, joined seventeen other winners in 1961–62 in pleading guilty to committing perjury before a state grand jury more than two years earlier; they received suspended sentences.

As it affected American television, the quiz show scandal was disconcerting for the networks. NBC and CBS in particular were upset by threats of greater FCC regulation, possible antitrust action against network television, investigation of tax violations in broadcasting quiz shows, and the possibility that federal law had already been violated. To cooperate with an investigation by the House Subcommittee on Legislative Oversight, NBC demanded notarized depositions from all its broadcast executives, demanding to know, "Did you at any time learn or know, or do you know now of the following:

1 SECRETLY GIVING CONTESTANTS IN QUIZ, PANEL, OR AUDIENCE PARTICIPATION OR CONTEST PROGRAMS QUESTIONS OR ANSWERS OR ANY OTHER INDIVIDUAL ASSISTANCE TO HELP THEM WIN (YES OR NO).

2 GIVING A WINNING CONTESTANT IN SUCH PROGRAMS LESS THAN THE FULL PRIZE WHICH THE PROGRAM ANNOUNCED HE WON (YES OR NO).

3 RECEIPT BY ANYONE CONNECTED WITH SUCH A PROGRAM OF ANYTHING OF ANY VALUE FROM A CONTESTANT ON THE PROGRAM (YES OR NO).

4 CHARGES BY CONTESTANTS OR ANY OTHER PERSON CONNECTED WITH SUCH PROGRAMS, RELATIVE TO ANY OF THE FOREGOING POINTS (YES OR NO).[6]

The presidents of NBC and CBS did not relish having to testify publicly before the House subcommittee. Robert W. Kintner pleaded that at NBC "We were just as much a victim of the quiz show frauds as the public." Frank Stanton told the committee of his ignorance of program irregularities until "gossip" came to his attention at CBS in late 1958. "We believe that legislation is no cure-all for these ills and that the primary responsibility lies with the broadcasting industry itself," he stated defensively.

William Paley has recalled in his memoirs that Stanton publicly accepted responsibility for CBS mistakes, and the network soon adopted practices to authenticate future programs that included creation of a Program Practices Department to ensure that the rules were followed, and insertion where appropriate of announcements such as "This program was prerecorded" and "Participants in this program were selected and interviewed in advance."[7]

Overly cautious, Stanton went so far as to cancel Edward R. Murrow's popular *Person to Person* series of live interviews. For six seasons Murrow had interviewed celebrities in their homes through a remote hookup while he remained in a CBS studio in New York City. Guests ranged from the Duke and Duchess of Windsor and Duke Ellington to Groucho and Harpo Marx and Marilyn Monroe. But Murrow's questions were discussed with the guests ahead of airtime, and network technicians had to plan in advance the routes they would take, laying transmission cables and moving bulky cameras around the interviewee's residence. In this period of authenticity, however, the "rehearsed" qualities of *Person to Person* were no longer tolerable. The series returned in the fall, but it was no longer a live show, and it no longer was hosted by Murrow.

Stanton was taking no chances in stemming the tide of possible government intervention in the business of broadcasting. He knew, as he told a broadcast audience in December 1959, that the scandal could have onerous consequences for network television. In a direct acknowledgment of public criticism directed against what the networks had done to the public airwaves, the CBS president enumerated the areas in which his industry was vulnerable. "Millions of Americans think that TV programming can and should be improved—that there are too many Westerns and crime shows, too much violence; that the range of programs available during prime time evening hours is too limited . . . there is too much advertiser control; that in meeting the demands of advertisers for the largest possible audience, our programs too often appeal to the lowest common denominator of entertainment."[8] It was a concise summary not only of past criticism but also of public condemnation of the networks in the future.

These were unnerving times, made all the more uncertain because Congress was also investigating a payola scandal affecting prominent radio disc jockeys. Accusations of fraud peppered the broadcast industry, some critics charging that there also was fraudulent misrepresentation in many TV commercials, others (even Frank Stanton for a while) contending that laugh tracks on network situation comedies were unacceptable deceptions.

One U.S. senator even claimed that politicians were being

of scandal and power

dishonest when they appeared on television wearing makeup and relying on prompting devices. "No one who has followed political campaigns in America in recent years can help but be concerned over the tendency to substitute playacting for reality," wrote Senator Richard L. Neuberger in late 1959. "This may be all right for the theater. It is not all right when it comes to selecting individuals to govern the United States." Neuberger added, "If George Gobel and Red Skelton now have to be honest, what of programs which seek to elect a president, senator, or governor?"[9]

changes in the industry

The quiz show scandal presented network television with a difficult task that it would face again in the future: how to recover from serious blows against the existing industry while increasing popularity and profits. In part it was accomplished with new popular shows—curtailing the overabundance of Westerns and emphasizing benign situation comedies; mature, even intelligent dramatic series; and turning to a staple of American pop culture, the detective/police series. Since it would take time to adjust season schedules, most of this upgraded programming would occur in the following decade.

But the most important weapon in the network arsenal could be employed immediately. The monopoly that was national television was shaken but not broken by the scandal. A sound scolding by Congress was foreboding, but as long as nothing altered the fundamental structure of national television, the American public could be expected to get over any residual pique.

The first and most permanent result of the scandal was manifest in TV advertising. If regularity and controllability had been goals of network streamlining in the late 1950s, the quiz show affair demonstrated network deficiency in the sponsorship of programs. Seeking the most palatable way of blunting governmental and network confusion, the networks worked with the leading agencies to reform the relationship between advertisers and programs. No longer would single sponsors be strongly identified with individual series, as had been the practice during the halcyon days of radio and in the first decade of TV. The agencies accepted a "magazine" approach in which several companies would buy commercial time on a single program or series. Charges for such commercial time would be set by the networks in accordance with ratings figures gathered during measurement periods scheduled throughout the year.

But the scandal only catalyzed changes in network advertising that had been evolving for several years. Rising costs of program production and airtime made cooperative sponsorship inevitable. There was a limit to how much advertisers could afford. By one estimate, 88 percent of the television advertisers in 1964 would have been priced out of the TV market were they underwriting a series alone.[10] Further, since there was a finite number of hours in a broadcast day, the sale of a full half hour or hour to one sponsor appeared increasingly inefficient to the networks. This was especially true because there were scores of would-be advertisers desiring access to the enormous market serviced by national video.

As early as January 1954 *Television* magazine published the opinions of ten leaders of the advertising community on the question of television advertising. Several discussed the need for arrangements that would open national TV to new clients who could not afford to sponsor complete programs, and to clients who had only periodic need to advertise on television. To Leo Burnett a pressing concern was for "networks and stations to find a way to accommodate the seasonal needs of certain major advertisers. . . . if TV is to serve business, and be supported by business, it must realistically recognize the varying conditions of business."

William R. Baker, Jr., the chairman of Benton & Bowles, suggested that "another avenue open to the small advertiser to participate in a low-cost yet effective and practical manner in television is through the use of what has been termed the 'magazine' concept of TV sponsorship."

Fairfax M. Cone of Foote, Cone & Belding was most direct. Declaring that "I see no reason why a little group of companies should own all the best time," Cone saw the solution years before the network made it canon. "I believe there is an answer that has to come: the magazine concept of telecasting. Under this plan . . . stations and networks would select and produce all programs" while advertisers and agencies would concentrate on making commercials. "Just as a newspaper or magazine editor selects the editorial content of his publications, station and network producers would build their programs," Cone noted. "But it is most important in such a plan for the networks to rotate commercial messages, just as magazine publishers rotate their pages of advertising, to give all their advertisers a fair break."[11]

CBS advertised as early as 1953 that it was building "new flexibility" into TV with innovative advertising options: alternate-week sponsorship with cross-referencing of advertisers; division and sale of daytime programming in segments of five minutes; and a participation plan "whereby the cost of some of the biggest shows may be assumed by as many as three or four sponsors on an equal basis."[12]

While CBS proposed, ABC disposed. As the distant number three network, ABC required bolder strategies to compete—indeed, to survive in its first years. The merger of ABC with United Paramount Theaters in 1953 brought to the leadership of the network Leonard Goldenson—a film man, not a broadcaster. One of his first steps was to rid ABC of its sponsored half hours and hours and turn, instead, to the advertising agencies to sell time on programs selected by the ABC management. He also moved aggressively into the area of film, signing Walt Disney studios to produce *Disneyland,* and then Warner Brothers to introduce *Cheyenne, Maverick,* and many other Western and private-eye series by the end of the 1950s. M-G-M and 20th Century-Fox also debuted series on ABC.

Importantly, Goldenson sold advertising time on *Disneyland* to several sponsors, and the same was true for most other ABC series. In this way, for example, the *Disneyland* telecast on February 29, 1956, contained two generic commercials from the American Dairy Association (one for milk and one for butter), an advertisement for Swift canned meats, and two commercials from American Motors for its 1956 Rambler automobiles.

"We made up our minds we would not wait for the advertisers to come to ABC," explained Goldenson. "They brought us only their poor programs. They took their best ones to the other two networks, and when a good one developed at ABC, they took that away, too. So we simply took control of the programs."[13] The ABC model worked, elevating the network in terms of viewership, program quality, and profits. Soon CBS and NBC began to adopt the ABC style.

As *Business Week* magazine reported in late 1959, the ending of one sponsor/one program arrangements freed advertisers and their agencies from any compunction to prevent overcommercialization on TV. "When the advertiser was sponsor, it behoved him to be sensitive to the frequency and length of his program interruptions," noted the magazine. "As a buyer of minute packages which disperse his message over an assortment of programs on various nights of the week, he is unburdened of that aesthetic decency as well as other responsibilities."[14]

More than ever, according to journalist Les Brown, advertisers came to influence American television by their patterns of spending. "When by consensus advertisers determine that Saturday morning is a cheaper and more efficient way to reach young children than by investing in early prime time," Brown wrote in

1971 in his perceptive critique *Televi$ion: The Business Behind the Box,* "the juvenile-slanted shows vanish from 7:30 P.M., which had been the children's hour since the start of television." He continued:

> *When the advertiser's need is to set his fall budgets six or seven months ahead of the season, the networks adjust their fall planning accordingly. When advertisers manifest an interest in sports, they proliferate on the home screen; an aversion to original plays, they evaporate. And when the advertisers spurn the viewers who are past the age of fifty and assert a preference for young married couples, the networks obediently disenfranchise the older audience and go full tilt in pursuit of the young.*[15]

The quiz scandals were a turning point in TV history. Certainly, quizzers with big prizes would return to television, especially as daytime entertainment. But the clear victors in this scandal were the networks. A mild federal law against TV fraud was a minuscule price to pay for control over advertising and programming. Where elected officials did not favor, and public opinion did not want, government control of programming, the networks eagerly filled the void. Already they had enormous wealth and power, which they used to shape U.S. television. Now they would control the pricing and placement schedules for airtime. Frank Stanton explained the new arrangement with candor: "From now on we will decide not only what is to appear, but how."[16]

Oliver Treyz has dated the decline of commercial television as beginning with the decision by network executives to assume total control of their industry. "In the old days when the advertising agencies did the programming, there was more competition, more creative people, more thought going into programming," revealed the former president of ABC-TV. "The minute a network assumed the programming power, the industry lost its diversity and fired most of the creative people and the power gravitated to a few."[17]

By the early 1960s the networks had moved deeply into all aspects of the industry. As CBS management told its stockholders less than four years after the scandal, they could count on the "continuing participation of the Network's programming officials at every stage of the creative process from the initial script to the final broadcast."[18] This meant planning, production, exhibition, and distribution, creating what one industry analyst described as "a vertically integrated medium."[19]

The networks profited at every turn. Ostensibly the filmed programming that filled national TV was the creation of Hollywood moviemakers, but with only ABC, CBS, and NBC to sell to, the flat-rate prices for filmed series stayed low and production houses actually went into debt creating new series for television. Hollywood producers did not start to profit until their series went into off-network syndication, where they could be stripped (aired two or more times per week) as reruns and sold in each market separately. But to provide enough shows for a normal twenty-six-week rerun commitment, a production company needed to complete a hundred programs—and that took from three to five years on national television, especially as the networks steadily decreased their first-run annual commitments from fifty-two or thirty-nine episodes in the early 1950s, to twenty-eight installments in the 1960s, to twenty-two or less by the 1970s.

And if a series did become a national hit, running sufficiently to accumulate enough episodes for syndication, the networks invariably owned a sizable percentage of the syndication action. By putting up some (up to about $50,000) of the seed money needed to produce a pilot episode, a network often demanded ownership of as much as 50 percent of the series. Further, it could demand syndication rights up to 35 percent of future revenues as part of the price for televising the series in the first place. Even merchandising rights—a percentage of the T-shirt and decal trade—went to the networks. According to an FCC report in 1970, the networks had contracts guaranteeing them a portion of the nonnetwork income of 98 percent of their prime-time series.[20]

The broadcasters needed only to sit back like great emperors and await the arrival of vassal production companies come to peddle programs. Then the broadcasters could invite advertisers to buy sixty-second commercial openings on the shows selected for airing, selling six minutes each hour (plus two minutes per hour for the local stations), or 21 minutes per prime-time day to corporations seeking access to a nation of consumers. The actual rates, of course, varied, depending on the ratings and other factors. In no case, however, was time cheap. And though network radio had a long history of sustaining series—programs without commercial sponsorship that were broadcast for prestige value, often for many years—modern TV did not broadcast sustaining series. In his penetrating analysis of the great media empires, *The Powers That Be,* David Halberstam described the condition of CBS and network television as it entered the 1960s:

So it was not good enough to succeed, to put on a good program that was sponsored, and make a profit, now there had to be a dominance of the ratings, a super-profit. . . . Nielsen was the new god of television; his truths were not truths, they were commandments; what was rated high was good; what was rated low was bad. There was room for nothing else, no other value systems, no sense of what was right and what was wrong. The stakes were too great, and became greater every year.[21]

By 1960 television had become a mature and streamlined business, a great "cash cow." The focus now shifted from invention to convention, from carving out an acceptable social role for itself to counting the rewards of investment, planning, and monopoly. This is not to say that U.S. television atrophied. Often the networks offered exhilarating and engrossing programs; occasionally these productions deserved and received critical acclaim for their entertainment qualities, or less frequently, their educational values.

But the exciting early spirit of video had dissipated. TV was no longer a novelty; there were fewer niches to find and fill. Clearly, the years of experimentation had passed, as bold programming ventures yielded to the process of homogenization. Much of what the networks now offered was bland old wine poured into new bottles: filmed formulaic dramas with little lasting importance, silly situation comedies featuring gimmicks borrowed from stage humor a half-century old, sports competition increasingly shaped to fit the needs of TV advertisers, violence and sex substituted for well-crafted suspense and mystery.

Already the voice of aggrieved criticism was to be heard. Writing in early 1962, the noted Canadian film director Norman Jewison criticized network decision-making that "leaves us with a congestion of dull, unimaginative shows. . . . This is not reasonable, intelligent, and hardly understandable." According to the man who later directed such films as *The Cincinnati Kid*, *In the Heat of the Night*, and *Fiddler on the Roof*:

Video programming can improve if it caters to the selective viewer, the one who wants a representative grouping of programs on his TV screen. Why must we have a plethora of Westerns one year, detective shows the next, and so on? There should be a versatility of shows, whether it be variety, Western, private eye, or animated cartoon. There shouldn't be a sudden rash of copyists of one successful formula, for all they do is cancel their own efforts in the long run.[22]

The Years of Plenty

the 1960s and 1970s

PART

3

appearance

CHAPTER 7

Television had come of age by
the 1960s. Almost every American had access to TV, and for a
growing number it was in living color, too. Manufacturers continued to churn out new receivers for eager buyers: 5.7 million sets
in 1960, 11.4 million in 1968. With

and reality

the average household using TV
five to six hours every day, only sleeping occupied more human
time.

Television was as lucrative as it was popular. The three networks and 565 stations in 1963 realized $1.8 billion in total reve-
nues. Leading the pack, CBS that year earned $555 million—a
rise of 700 percent over revenues in 1948. Moreover, CBS in 1963
pulled in 39 percent of all network business, compared to 35 percent at NBC and 26 percent at ABC. Such individual success
within a fabulously profitable industry prompted *Forbes* magazine
in 1964 to dub William S. Paley's network "the money tree of
Madison Avenue."[1]

There was little in U.S. society that television did not touch.
From politics and mass consumption to entertainment, fashion,
and morality, TV was the common carrier of the national standard. Touching so much of the American experience, it is no
wonder that the distinguished writer Leo Rosten in 1961 described the omnipresent medium as "this marvelous, exciting,
depressing, promising, wonderful, deplorable miracle."[2]

Nothing better summarized the significant maturing of television than the first of the four "great debates" between John F.
Kennedy and Richard M. Nixon in the fall of 1960. The strengths
and weaknesses of the medium were encapsulated in the first
rhetorical confrontation—held September 26 in Chicago—between the Democratic and Republican candidates for the presidency of the United States.

Truly, TV had arrived. Here were contenders for the most
powerful job on Earth appearing live on camera to compare their
views for the benefit of the common citizen. It was a historical
first. Television was at its communicative best, providing the na-

tion with the opportunity to make crucial democratic decisions in the privacy of the home. The medium had become what its pioneers had predicted, a national political forum, and no politician thereafter could run effectively for office until deciding how to handle its intrusive existence.

But the debate was not wholly what it appeared to be; it had limitations emanating from the fact that it was on television. First, it was not really a debate. Sensing the power of TV to magnify a momentary mistake—a flash of anger, a slip of the tongue, a raised eyebrow, an appearance of arrogance or humiliation—the candidates agreed not to argue directly with one another. Instead, the format resembled a dual press conference, with soft questions lobbed by participating journalists. Anticipating such queries, moreover, the candidates were well coached on what to say and how to say it.

Viewers did not receive a profound comparison of ideas or prospective policies. Television seldom offered much more than the superficial. Instead, the audience that evening was the first to confront the critical importance of glamour in modern politics, the first to assess a candidate's capacity to lead the nation and the Free World based on how well he looked and performed on TV.

Nixon was gaunt and needed a shave. His light-colored suit blended with the light backdrop, and he started to perspire midway through the hour-long program. Kennedy was suntanned and worked without makeup. His dark clothing contrasted flatteringly with the surroundings, adding a note of savoir-faire to his demeanor. What the two men said was much less important than how they looked. Radio listeners actually voted Nixon the winner; TV viewers chose JFK.

A year earlier the senator from Massachusetts wrote in *TV Guide* of the importance of physical appearance in the age of video. He hailed the "new breed of candidates" that was successful because of a "particular reliance on TV appeal." Most of the breed were young men, for youth, according to Kennedy, "is definitely an asset in creating a television image people like and (most difficult of all) remember." He continued:

Honesty, vigor, compassion, intelligence—the presence or lack of these and other qualities make up what is called the candidate's "image." While some intellectuals and politicians may scoff at these "images"—and while they may in fact be based only on a candidate's TV impression, ignoring his record, views, and other appearances—my own conviction is that these images or impressions are likely to be uncannily correct.[3]

The pattern of social success masking inherent shortcomings that was apparent in the Kennedy-Nixon debate persisted in network television during the next two decades. On the one hand there were impressive accomplishments; on the other there were festering problems that could not be resolved by television as then structured. National TV was firmly in place, and for the next twenty years its principal concern was the battle between three corporate giants struggling from rivalrous season to rivalrous season for ratings supremacy. Still, the angry and the dismayed criticized it for the impact it was having on American society—and for the impact they felt it should be having. It may have pleased many, even most Americans, but there were countless citizens who felt abused and disenfranchised by a national utility that seemingly ignored their protestations.

This was an enormously profitable time, however, well worth the periodic struggle against critics and would-be reformers. The business of TV settled into a routine of making money, as industry profits rose from a gross of $1.3 billion in 1962, to $1.9 billion in 1965, and to $2.5 billion by 1968. Significantly, about half of this money went to the three networks and their fifteen owned-and-operated VHF stations.

Statistics confirm the overwhelming control of television exercised by ABC, CBS, and NBC. As Chairman E. William Henry of the FCC phrased it in the mid-1960s, the three networks dominated "virtually all programming which the American public sees during their prime evening hours." That dominance had grown rapidly and definitively. In 1957 the three national program services owned (29 percent) or had some proprietary rights (38 percent) in two-thirds of their prime-time programming. In 1964 the figure reached 93 percent; only 7 percent of the nation's TV fare came from producers with no network ties. Moreover, by the early 1960s CBS was the second-largest producer of network filmed programs, trailing only MCA.

Network control did not end with first-run TV. Packaged reruns of old network series dominated the syndication market. The programs were familiar to audiences and usually had more attractive production values than first-run syndicated series. And with the limited non-network marketplace for filmed series, it was risky for Hollywood studios to gamble on first-run programs. According to Henry, in 1956 there were twenty-nine first-run series released to syndication; a decade later there was one such series.[4]

By far the most successful operation was at CBS, where President James T. Aubrey charmed the American people by emphasizing soap operas in the afternoon and sitcoms in the evening. Especially popular in prime time were rural comedies such as *The*

Andy Griffith Show, The Beverly Hillbillies, Hee Haw, and *Green Acres,* which reprised the "rube" humor of turn-of-the-century vaudeville. Rube humor generated high ratings that enticed advertisers. Whereas advertisers in 1964 could buy a prime-time minute on NBC for $41,000 and on ABC for $45,000, champion CBS demanded $50,000, a figure that translated into $1 million every night.

Stockholders may have rejoiced along with most network executives that CBS—and network television, for that matter—had achieved what William S. Paley later described as "that elusive, fragile, ideal mixture of programming that caters to some of the more specialized, more refined tastes and yet pleases a large part of the mass audience most of the time."[5] But others felt it regrettable that the scarce public airwaves were being manipulated so unabashedly to make greater and greater amounts of money.

The broadcasting business had become the corporatized communications industry, a Wall Street/*Fortune* 500 operation with profitability as its principal goal. Edward R. Murrow was disappointed, declaring as early as 1958 that although "we have in this country a free enterprise system of radio and television. . . . I find nothing in the Bill of Rights or the Communications Act which says that they [the networks] must increase their net profits each year lest the republic collapse."[6] To Fred W. Friendly, it was all quite simple: "The people from Harvard Business School taught the networks how to institutionalize their greed."

David Halberstam sketched the corporate fever that gripped TV by the early 1960s. "Companies like CBS became increasingly dominated by a new generation of bright young men who knew systems, how to take an existing structure and make it far more profitable," wrote Halberstam, "cutting quality here, adding a minute or two of advertising there, little changes which, when carried through for an entire year, might mean millions and millions of dollars. Their loyalty was to the bottom line."[7]

Network officials usually responded to such criticism with statements about performing public good and providing the viewing public with what it wanted. But one eminent TV writer was more direct. David Karp noted in 1965, "TV is not an art form or a cultural channel; it is an advertising medium." Thus "it seems a bit churlish and un-American of people who watch television to complain that their shows are so lousy. They are not supposed to be any good. They are supposed to make money." And not without a touch of irony, Karp added, "The ugly truth about television is that the 'quality' of television programming has nothing to do with its 'success.' In fact, 'quality' may be not merely irrelevant, but a distraction."[8]

The debate was intense and honest, but the fact remained that, inherently, if television were either good or bad, it was that way because of decisions made by men with vested interests. As distinguished professor Herman S. Hettinger of the Wharton School at the University of Pennsylvania had suggested at the dawn of the television era, TV was among those new electronic inventions that were changing American communications, but "these inventions are amoral; they are agencies for good or evil, depending upon how men choose to use them." Then he posed questions that still demand answers:

> *Will they make us less reasoning, more given to catchwords and the oversimplification of issues, more prone to follow the attractively presented shibboleth, swaying from one extreme to another? Will these new arts add further to the pressure of speed, which is the enemy of reflection, and the mass of detail, which impairs assimilation? Will they provide increasing escape in passive entertainment? Or will the increasing supply of knowledge, attractively presented, open up new vistas to the average citizen, lay the basis for a growing discrimination in enjoyment and in the judgment of issues, and eventually develop a more wide-awake and civically conscious public?* [9]

As with the layered meaning of the Kennedy-Nixon debate, the response to Hettinger's questions must be ambiguous, for they are answerable partially in the affirmative, partially in the negative. This is made clear by a consideration of U.S. television in terms of its political, cultural, and economic significance in its years of plenty.

political implications

Most Americans embraced TV as a parlor device for personal and family diversion. As demonstrated in an exhaustive survey of the audience completed in 1960, the vast majority of viewers did not deliberately rely on video as a source of information. "He would like TV to be more informative and educational but certainly not at the expense of entertainment," concluded Gary A. Steiner about the average video user. "Aside from the day's news and weather—which he watches regularly—he rarely uses the set as a deliberate source of information, and he is extremely unlikely to turn on serious and informative public affairs presentations, even if he is watching while they are on the air." [10]

It is ironic that while most viewers avoided informational programs, by the 1960s television was the window through which much of the U.S. citizenry came to see and understand national and world realities. It had been the dream of the early developers of TV that it should one day become a significant source of mass enlightenment. But no pioneer adequately anticipated the social implications of the accelerated enlightening and politicalization of millions accomplished via television.

TV in the 1960s was the nation's primary source of information. The introduction of new electronic equipment such as videotape and lightweight portable cameras only expanded news coverage, while the communications satellite Telstar, successfully launched in July 1962, internationalized the scope of American television. Although news generated ratings far below those of prime-time programs, NBC and CBS increased production of documentaries, expanded the size of their news staffs nationally and locally, and in September 1963 doubled the length of their evening newscasts to a half hour.

In reporting on such matters as the struggle for civil rights, the Vietnam War and domestic protests against it, the emerging ecological and women's movements, and emerging alternative life-styles, TV gave flesh to social developments that remained relatively cerebral when reported by other media. Certainly, newspapers offered deeper coverage, but television was better at personalizing and capturing the drama in the events of the day. Radio may have been instantaneous in reporting the news, but through its words and images video offered audiences a fuller vantage from which to observe.

By what it did and did not televise, national video framed the events of a turbulent era and offered them to a nation seeking to understand their meaning. What William Small, CBS News director in Washington, D.C., noted about the relationship between video and the civil rights movement could apply to the coverage of most major social movements as they reached TV. In contrast to a half century in which whites were ignorant of or indifferent toward the lynching of more than 4,500 black citizens, "television coverage that grew in the 60s served as companion to demonstrations. Unlike those of other years, attention was now paid. With success, the demonstrations grew, the coverage increased, and the Revolution spun on with frenzied momentum." [11]

TV was not the prime mover in these events, but it did affect them. In some cases the presence of video equipment actually triggered manifestations of discontent intended to influence audiences at home. In other instances, the need for attractive images affected decisions on what to report. But those reports set the sociopolitical agenda for the nation.

As millions watched, the nightly newscast expanded awareness and compelled viewers to confront urgent problems. Many felt that television was shaping American politics unfairly, deciding what the truth was, telling viewers what to think. Images of U.S. Marines burning Vietnam villages, for example, prompted charges of giving aid and comfort to the enemy. A CBS documentary on hunger in the United States raised protests from government officials charged with distributing surplus food; it also prompted Congress and the FBI to investigate the network. When Senator Robert F. Kennedy was assassinated, President Lyndon B. Johnson wondered aloud if violence on TV had not played a contributory role. And many attributed the defeat of presidential candidate Hubert H. Humphrey in 1968 on network coverage of the police repression of massive street demonstrations held outside the Democratic National Convention that summer in Chicago.

Television is a medium of communication, and politics is about communicating. Politics, naturally, flourished on television. Even electoral affairs were affected by the medium. From the great debates to the perfecting of the "media event"—that speech, gesture, or otherwise routine event planned by a candidate solely to create attractive pictures for TV news—TV molded modern politics. Add to this the live press conference, the well-covered domestic or foreign visit, the political commercial, and telegenic candidates—all meant to manipulate for partisan ends.

In this politicized atmosphere, reality soon touched fantasy. Advancements in the civil rights movement were reflected in the growing number of black actors appearing as guests, regular supporting characters, and even stars of their own shows. In fact, the appearance of African-American stars and stories on U.S. television became an informal means by which to measure the effectiveness of civil rights efforts.

This trend reached its apogee in the late 1960s during a relative Golden Age for African-American imagery that included the first black newscasters on network TV, plus series such as *Julia*, *I Spy*, *The Bill Cosby Show*, *The Mod Squad*, *The Outcasts*, and *Room 222*. By the fall of 1968 at least one black regular character appeared in twenty-one of the fifty-six nighttime dramatic series, and one black writer exclaimed, "Black people are hot! You could almost go roller skating in the street and they'd put you on television!"[12]

Even a breath of the 1960s counterculture wafted into national programs. Although the networks were always inhospitable to sharp criticism of the U.S. system of government and its established authority—especially when criticism was directed against the federal government, which held regulatory power over the networks—*That Was the Week That Was* in 1964–65, and later *The Smothers Brothers Comedy Hour* satirically prodded the powerful. More good-naturedly, *Rowan & Martin's Laugh-In* from 1968 to 1973 also blended politics and humor, touching on social issues with more burlesque and less censorship than its predecessors.

But there were the structural shortcomings, flaws that blunted the potential of television to communicate as fully and accurately as possible. TV news did sketch the world, but it did so in short-hand fashion. Although NBC and CBS doubled the length of their nightly news in 1963—and ABC joined them early in 1967—network newscasts compressed U.S. and foreign developments into less than thirty minutes. Compounding the illusion of thoroughness, the networks reported more or less the same stories with the same techniques and with essentially the same point of view. Local coverage was less sophisticated. It was concerned mostly with fires, shootings, demonstrations, accidents, and human-interest events that could be readily filmed or videotaped. The one actuality form having depth, the documentary, tapered off to insignificance by the late 1960s. But even when they did look at issues, broadcast journalists usually avoided profound analysis, statistics, economic dynamics, and ideological matters. TV required pictures, story, and personality; facts and figures, it was felt, only drove the mass audience to rival stations.

Certainly, national television played a role in discouraging the popular will to wage war in Vietnam. The relentless flow of information about the military engagement provided data with which increasing numbers of Americans decided the effort was futile. On the other hand, TV had contributed considerably in creating the will to fight in a nation with a long history of isolationism, through a decade or more of aggressive entertainment (spy series, military documentaries and sitcoms, war dramas, Westerns) and a relentlessly anti-Communist perspective on news events. Moreover, if national television undermined the war effort, as some have alleged, it took many years to accomplish that result—from 1965, when the U.S. military buildup began in earnest, to early 1973, when American involvement ended.

The civil rights movement, too, profited from TV coverage. The moral dynamism of the movement galvanized many African-Americans, turning indifference into activism. The movement on television also shattered white-middle-class complacency; it compelled whites to reevaluate personal feelings, social institutions, and national myths.

The movement and the enthusiasm of television for it constituted only a temporary engagement. The racism of centuries could not be overcome in ten or twelve years. Soon video interest, along with much of white public opinion, shifted to other matters as the movement collapsed under political, economic, and social pressure. Actress Ruby Dee was close to the truth when she remarked in late 1968, at a time when black actors at last were entering national culture as stars of their own dignified series, "We're in the most commodity-conscious nation in the world, and the black man is the commodity this year. If black people sell, they'll be back. If they don't, they won't." [13]

That those in government understood the political implications of national television was made obvious by two events during the decade: critical speeches delivered by Chairman Newton Minow of the FCC in 1961 and Vice-President Spiro Agnew in 1969. From differing perspectives, these attacks on TV opened and closed the decade on a note of official consternation. In both cases, influential executives assailed broadcasting because they felt it was distorting what the citizenry saw and understood of reality.

talking back to tv: newton minow

Minow came to the FCC after an era of considerable scandal. This had been a time of alcoholic commissioners and bribe-taking, of padded expense accounts, influence-peddling, and collaboration with the businesses supposedly being regulated. According to maverick Chicago broadcaster Sterling "Red" Quinlan, "What Minow saw when he came to Washington literally gave him heartburn. The real Whorehouse Era of the FCC had largely passed . . . but there was still much that Minow did not like." [14]

After fifteen years of FCC drift, Newton Minow embodied a return to the activist spirit of the early 1940s. The new chairman moved beyond the quantitative arguments of James Lawrence Fly, who had championed increased competition and diversity. Minow was in the tradition of Paul Porter, who felt the commission had a role to play in improving the quality of programming.

Appearing at the annual convention of the National Association of Broadcasters on May 9, the chairman declared provocatively, "I am not convinced that the people's taste is as low as you assume." And in one of those phrases for eternity, he summarized American television as "a vast wasteland." This was Minow the chief regulator of broadcasting, Minow the lawyer and intellectual point man for a new Kennedy administration that prided itself on prestigious university educations and, although the president kept abreast of the latest developments in TV programming, an appreciation of high culture.

Therefore, there was concern in the industry when Minow told executives that by watching their own stations they would encounter an arid and monotonous "procession of game shows, violence, audience-participation shows, formula comedies about totally unbelievable families, blood and thunder, mayhem, violence, sadism, murder, western badmen, western good men, private eyes, gangsters, more violence, and cartoons. And, endlessly, commercials—many screaming, cajoling, and offending. And most of all, boredom."

The FCC chairman directed much of his scorn toward operators of local stations. He was direct, asking them "to make a conscientious, good-faith effort to serve the public interest" by recognizing that "Every one of you serves a community in which the people would benefit by educational, religious, instructive, or other public-service programming. Every one of you serves an area which has local needs." The root of the problem, according to Minow, was in the "concentration of power in the hands of the networks," which caused "too many local stations [to] operate with one hand on the network switch, and the other hand on a projector loaded with old movies."

This was a lecture like none ever delivered by the FCC to U.S. broadcasters—biting, sarcastic, and on-target. And it struck at the core feature of American television: network domination and its stultifying effect on public broadcasting and American culture. Minow recognized the limiting results of network indifference toward the diversity of tastes and needs of the national audience. He wanted television that gave the people not only what they wanted, but also what they needed. "We all know that people would more often prefer to be entertained than stimulated or informed," he noted.

> But your obligations are not satisfied if you look only to popularity as the test of what to broadcast. You are not only in show business; you are free to communicate ideas as well as relaxation. You must provide a wider range of choices, more diversity, more alternatives. It is not enough to cater to the nation's whims—you must also serve the nation's needs.[15]

To many it was elitist to think that popular culture could be shaped by symphony-lovers and those desiring educational uplift from the medium. To others it was time to rescue television from mediocrity and waste. A collection of critical essays about television published in 1962 as *The Eighth Art* captured the debate into which Minow had moved. Leo Rosten, for example, argued that "Most intellectuals do not seem to understand, or are unwilling to admit, that the mass media are meant for the masses, not for the intellectuals." [16] And Marya Mannes warned, "It is time, then, that the intellectuals learned a little humility; at least enough to recognize that a five-minute talk by a man like [Eric] Sevareid or [Chet] Huntley or Howard K. Smith or [David] Brinkley might do more to inform the American people than six issues of 'little reviews' or a fifty-page thesis." [17]

On the other hand, the well-known British anthropologist Ashley Montagu rebuked the programmers: "Too often the television audience has been treated as if it were some conglomerate mass of low intelligence and of even lower taste, incapable of appreciating the best that is being said and done in the world." He continued, "Without putting too fine a point upon it, those who will guide the future development of television should understand that it is not so much what the public wants as what the people 'need' that should be considered, and what the people 'want' is not incompatible with what they need." [18]

One of the more telling arguments against Minow came from producer Roy B. Huggins in a perceptive article published in *Television Quarterly* a year after the speech. Here Huggins dealt with one of the most troubling implications of the liberal agenda for TV. While conceding that the Communications Act was irritatingly ambiguous in defining FCC functions and that the industry still needed federal regulation in certain problem areas, Huggins argued that the logical result of Minow's policy would be to turn the FCC into an office of censorship. Certainly, the chairman had not proposed such a development, but to deny a license renewal on the grounds of poor program performance was to cede to government the power to decide indirectly what was televised. As Huggins phrased it, "denial of a license on programming grounds must mean that the licensee broadcast too many programs aimed at tastes different from those of a majority of a seven-man regulatory agency of government." His conclusion was forthright: "If television is to remain free to be good, it must remain free to be bad." [19]

Minow had little area in which to maneuver. He could call for hearings, and he did; he could further condemn video violence, the lack of children's programs, and the banality of many shows, and he did; he could even threaten to say and do more to improve U.S. video. But he could not operate effectively unless both the president and Congress were supportive of him.

Although he enjoyed the strong support of JFK, who abetted Minow's crusade with other liberal appointments, the reformers on the FCC, even though they formed a majority coalition, could not overcome impediments placed in their way by Congress. As James L. Baughman has noted, these included laws passed decades earlier that "provided broadcasters so many guarantees against swift and arbitrary justice that the commission had difficulty deciding anything quickly, if at all. The resulting regulatory lag normally served the status quo, while weakening the resolve of those favoring punitive measures against a violator-licensee." The moderate-to-conservative Congresses of the early 1960s repeatedly embarrassed the commission, refusing to reform the old laws that impeded speedy, effective action, even passing a resolution rebuking FCC efforts to curb the number of commercials on TV.[20]

Broadcasters were not relieved, however, when Newton Minow resigned from the FCC in June 1963. His successor as chairman, E. William Henry, was already on record in his beliefs that a broadcaster was "not free to maximize profits at the expense of the public interest" and that "the essence of the Communications Act's public-interest mandate is that broadcasting must be more than a business."[21] Speaking to the National Association of Broadcasters four years after the "great wasteland" speech, Henry proclaimed his agreement with Minow's assessment of TV as imitative and barren, overemphasizing amusement and relaxation while neglecting stimulation, ideas, and information. Chairman Henry also let the broadcasters know that he was pleased with neither the many entertainment shows nor the few public-service offerings they were televising:

Television entertainment has changed very little. . . . Still present in daytime schedules are the same vast bulk of movies and cartoons, repeats from former network seasons, sob stories, and game shows. They still sell the same vast bulk of soap, peanut butter, and pain-killers. Late afternoon is still the Children's Hour—still dominated by cartoons, slapstick, and adventure serials. In prime evening hours, feature movies have won a larger and larger place. Situation comedies have taken over from action-adventure shows; untouchable mobsters have given way to unwashed monsters; and the newest innovation—the spicy nighttime soap opera—has top priority on Hollywood's drawing boards. . . . Entertainment "specials" bring some rare and wonderful moments . . . [but] the overall size of network public service has remained static or declined. Using the Nielsen rating service and its definition of public-service programs [which excludes hard news] in the 1963–64 season, only 210 network hours made the grade. Thus the so-called barren season of 1960–61 had 22 percent more network public-service hours than the season just past. In all the years from 1961 to 1965 the proportion of total network time devoted to public-service programs . . . has remained about 4 percent.[22]

This was potentially devastating criticism. But the broadcasters were used to the bluster of occasional FCC idealism. Given the political nature of the commission and its historic reluctance to become involved in matters of program quality—even though an outspoken chairman or commissioner might publicly call for improvement—Henry's zeal, like that of Minow, led nowhere.

But Henry had even more difficulty than his predecessor in waging the crusade. Whereas Kennedy suported Minow, Lyndon B. Johnson—involved through his wife in the ownership of an Austin television station—was reluctant to battle station owners and network chiefs. LBJ needed the allegiance of broadcasters to help him on the broader issues: the Vietnam War, civil rights legislation, the War on Poverty, and the Great Society. Of the six appointments he made during his presidency, all but one—the aggressive young reformer Nicholas Johnson, whom LBJ soon regretted appointing—opposed the activism represented by Minow and Henry.

Proof of Henry's isolation from the White House could be recognized early. At the same NAB convention where he shared his disgust with contemporary televison, Vice-President Hubert H. Humphrey addressed the group with praise for the industry. "I'm no snob, I like television," Humphrey announced, adding that U.S. television was "the greatest single achievement in communication that anybody or any area of the world has ever known." And Humphrey assured the broadcasters that his boss also liked TV. "Government doesn't own you, government is not your master," he said. "Government is here to help you serve. President Johnson made it clear, he does not believe in government by scare or threat."[23]

If national programming did not change it was because the networks had no reason to change it. Commercial TV would never become a vehicle for education and social uplift because not enough millions wanted to see this type of TV fare. The oligopoly that was national television could always rally around the argument so concisely put by Frank Stanton in 1960: "We cannot force people to like what they don't like or want what they don't want."[24] Of course, the networks could have broadcast informational shows, if only for the few million viewers who would watch such productions. But in the United States, television was a private business, and channel scarcity was a tool for maximizing profit.

Unlike FCC chairmen, moreover, television networks were social fixtures. Critics urging upgraded programming would last at best a term or two on the commission. That is one reason why the legacy of Minow and Henry lies in speculation about what broadcasting could be, rather than in any profound reshaping of its reality.

talking back to tv: spiro agnew

More than eight years after Minow officially brought exciting criticism to governmental regulation, Vice-President Spiro Agnew moved on another front. This time the assault was political and partisan as the vice-president renewed a critique not heard since the days of Franklin D. Roosevelt's New Deal: that national broadcasting was politically biased, and newsmen, specifically, were skewing the truth to which viewers were entitled.

Speaking for the conservative Republican presidency of Richard M. Nixon, Agnew blasted the way political news and events were handled on TV. He decried the fact that network news was prepared by "a handful of men responsible only to their corporate employers . . . and a handful of commentators who admit to their own set of biases." He assailed the commentators who dissected Nixon's speeches as soon as the chief executive finished a televised address to the nation. The "President of the United States has a right to communicate directly with the people that elected him," Agnew asserted, "and the people of this country have the right to make up their own minds and form their own opinions about a presidential address without having a president's words and thoughts characterized through the prejudices of hostile critics before they can even be digested."

Written by White House aide Patrick Buchanan, Agnew's

162

speech was one of the first shots fired against established broadcasting by the New Right political movement. But beyond the partisan agenda he was articulating, the vice president raised fundamental questions about the appropriateness of vital information being filtered through a few people in fewer networks. Whatever their protestations of journalistic professionalism and political fairness, Agnew was correct to say that "no more than a dozen anchormen, commentators, and executive producers" were the ones who decided "what forty or fifty million Americans will learn of the day's events in the nation and the world."[25]

Agnew's tirade went to the core of a national television and national culture that were controlled by three like-thinking corporations. Granted, Agnew was politically motivated, but his critique had implications beyond conservative Republicanism. His was the anger of the disenfranchised, the frustration of the minority without a place on popular TV. Agnew argued that the medium needed to serve more people; that it needed alternatives to the homogenized viewpoint developed in New York City and then presented to a richly variegated nation as the single truth.

Like Minow and Henry, Agnew received little support within the industry, many feeling that he, too, was about to assume the mantle of "cultural czar." That he received considerable popular acclaim, however, raises questions about TV and the depth of its public support. Within two months of his speech, for example, a Gallup poll rated Agnew the third most admired man in the nation, behind only Richard Nixon and Billy Graham. While much of Agnew's acclaim can be adduced to partisan political feelings, the fact remained that many millions of viewers were upset enough about what the networks offered that they found Agnew's critique valid.

Despite the misgivings of Minow and Agnew, national television would continue to play an informational role in American life. No matter that the evening "news" was little more than headlines and a few short "in-depth" stories; this was the network news service that mesmerized millions nightly. And a poll in 1971 revealed that Americans preferred TV to newspapers as the source of "most of your news"—and by a margin of 40 percent for TV to 20 percent for newspapers, they found television the "most believable" medium for news.[26]

No matter that the documentary was never a prominent part of the national schedule; network documentary units such as *ABC News Close-up*, *CBS Reports*, and *NBC White Paper* continued to produce long-form analyses—some of them stunning in their artistry and candor—and millions watched. It was not purely intellectual commitment, however. At NBC, for example, motivation for increased documentary production, according to one executive, emanated from a desire to exploit the rising popularity of newscasters Chet Huntley and David Brinkley, and the need "to placate critics in the trade and government who did not think television was designed as an opiate and an outlet for 'sex and violence.' "[27] Such flexibility, however, led to a renaissance of the documentary—rising from 178 programs in 1958 to 336 in 1961, 447 the following year, and 396 in 1963. However, with the death of President Kennedy, the crisis passed, and output dropped precipitously, to 290 in 1966 and 251 by 1968.[28]

There was, however, National Educational Television and eventually the Public Broadcasting Service. By the end of the 1960s ETV/PBS, with 185 stations (compared to 160 for ABC, 193 for CBS, and 215 for NBC), constituted a virtual fourth network, albeit lowly viewed and relegated in great part to UHF channels. Public stations also were cash-poor. Proscribed from accepting paid commercials, the stations were dependent on donations solicited from viewers plus stipends received from the Corporation for Public Broadcasting, a nonprofit, private organization created in 1967 to oversee noncommercial broadcasting. As the entity that established PBS in 1969, CPB would receive partial funding from Congress but remain greatly dependent on sizable donations from major U.S. corporations.

Nevertheless, in an age of inner-city rebellions and lunar explorations, political assassinations, youthful alienation, international warfare, and domestic confrontation, the ability of television to cover important events live was appreciated by the American audience. Not only did several million people view documentaries about contemporary problems and issues, but also, as revealed in Table 7.1, the citizenry overwhelmingly used television to participate in the most compelling events of the times.

sports and television

Sports events on TV resemble news programming in that they are actualities reported as they happen. But the networks put much more energy into the development of the games Americans play than the pursuit of current events. Since many of the highest-rated programs on national radio in the 1930s were sports specials—the baseball World Series, college football games, championship boxing involving heavyweight Joe Louis—it was

TABLE 7.1

top special events of the 1960s[29]

1960 KENNEDY-NIXON ELECTION RESULTS: VIEWED IN 91.8 PERCENT OF TV HOMES; AVERAGE: FOUR HOURS, THIRTY MINUTES

1961 KENNEDY INAUGURAL ADDRESS: IN 59.5 PERCENT OF TV HOMES

1962 JOHN GLENN'S SUBORBITAL FLIGHT: IN 81.4 PERCENT OF TV HOMES; AVERAGE: FIVE HOURS, FIFTEEN MINUTES

1963 KENNEDY ASSASSINATION/FUNERAL COVERAGE: IN 96.1 PERCENT OF TV HOMES; AVERAGE THIRTY-ONE HOURS, THIRTY-EIGHT MINUTES

1964 JOHNSON-GOLDWATER ELECTION RESULTS: IN 90.6 PERCENT OF TV HOMES; AVERAGE TWO HOURS, FIFTY-ONE MINUTES

1965 GEMINI-TITAN IV LAUNCH: IN 92.1 PERCENT OF TV HOMES; AVERAGE: FOUR HOURS, FORTY-SEVEN MINUTES

1966 CONGRESSIONAL ELECTION RESULTS: IN 84.4 PERCENT OF TV HOMES; AVERAGE: SIX HOURS, TEN MINUTES

1967 JOHNSON'S STATE OF THE UNION ADDRESS: IN 59.6 PERCENT OF TV HOMES; AVERAGE: ONE HOUR

1968 DEMOCRATIC NATIONAL CONVENTION IN CHICAGO: IN 90.1 PERCENT OF TV HOMES; AVERAGE: NINE HOURS, TWENTY-EIGHT MINUTES

1969 APOLLO XI MOON LANDING: IN 93.9 PERCENT OF TV HOMES; AVERAGE: FIFTEEN HOURS, THIRTY-FIVE MINUTES

inevitable that athletics would be a concern of developmental television.

TV sports was born through a procession of technical "firsts" produced in 1939. On May 17, NBC, via W2XBS, aired the first baseball game, a remote broadcast pitting Ivy League university teams from Columbia and Princeton in a contest in New York City. The announcer was premier radio sportscaster Bill Stern, who appeared three days later on NBC commenting live from a marathon bicycle race in Madison Square Garden.

On June 1 heavyweight boxing contenders Max Baer and Lou Nova fought in Yankee Stadium on live TV. More important than the result of the fight (Nova won by a technical knockout in the eleventh round), it was the first remote telecast of a boxing match. On August 9 Stern returned to television, this time to cover the first TV tennis match—the Eastern Grass Courts Championship from Rye, New York. Other sports firsts followed precipitously: on August 26, the first professional baseball game, matching Cincinnati against Brooklyn; then the first college football game as Fordham University clobbered Waynesburg College, 34–7; followed by the first professional football game as the Brooklyn Dodgers defeated the Philadelphia Eagles, 23–14. And in 1940 came more breakthroughs, with remote telecasts of professional hockey, basketball, and track.[30]

One of the chief appeals of sports to broadcasters was cost-effectiveness. Sports required little to produce, and games could be easily scheduled for unproductive network hours—particularly on weekend afternoons. Independent stations found it profitable, too, to program sports attractions that the national networks—because of the demands of weekday and prime-time schedules—did not fully exploit. In this way a network could offer the nation one baseball game per weekend, but a local station could build its entire spring and summer schedules around home games of the local professional team—day and night contests, plus many, if not all, games played on the road.

Sports was also a good buy for TV advertisers. Although ad rates were high in terms of the number of viewers delivered for each dollar spent, a major segment of the audience for televised sports comprised middle-class males, a demographic entity not necessarily guaranteed by other programming forms. This made sports especially attractive for manufacturers of beer, tobacco products, automobiles, shaving equipment, gasoline, and tires. Although CBS by 1967 was charging advertisers up to $75,000 for a minute of time on its National Football League telecasts, the network had little trouble attracting clients.

After the domination of roller derby, wrestling, and boxing, these staples of the 1950s yielded to a greater variety in televised sports. By 1962 the three networks had committed $80 million for sports programming, one-quarter of it for college and professional football on CBS, another quarter for baseball on NBC. Added to that were pro hockey and basketball, plus special events such as the Kentucky Derby and the Masters golf tournament. Less popular competition such as tennis, track, bowling, automobile racing, skiing, and swimming appeared, too, often packaged under umbrella titles such as *CBS Sunday Sports Spectacular* or *ABC's Wide World of Sports*.

But commercial television was not content simply to televise sports as they happened: in the name of offering "a good show" the networks shaped American sports for the video age. Engineering advances such as instant replay and slow-motion video were developed for sports coverage, in part to liven up lulls in action. After the launch of Telstar and other communications satellites in the early 1960s, transmission from foreign continents became possible. This was made obvious in the Olympic Games of 1964. While the Winter Games competition in Innsbruck, Austria, were seen in the United States via videotape flown overnight to ABC in New York City, the two-hour opening ceremony of the Summer Games in Tokyo was transmitted live from Japan via the Syncom III satellite. Due to a time-zone difference of fourteen hours—the live telecast from Tokyo was seen on the U.S. East Coast at 1:00 A.M.—the remainder of the Summer Olympics was covered via videotape flown to NBC in Seattle.

With the orbiting of the Early Bird satellite in 1965, live telecasts between Europe and the United States became commonplace. In the first year of Early Bird operation, NBC televised the World Cup soccer championships while ABC aired eight sports events—including the Le Mans Grand Prix road race from France, a championship boxing match from Frankfurt, the Irish Derby from Dublin, the British Open from Scotland, and a U.S.-U.S.S.R track meet from Kiev. With visions of complete live Olympics coverage of the 1968 Winter Games from Grenoble and the Summer Games from Mexico City, the executive producer of ABC Sports, Roone Arledge, predicted confidently in mid-1966 that "we are approaching an era when live coverage of a sports event in Frankfurt will be no more unusual than live coverage of a game show in a New York City studio." [31]

Athletics meant great profits for TV. The gross revenues of network sports during the 1968–69 season approached $180 million. Writing in *Variety* a year earlier, Murray Horowitz aptly summarized the impetus for this boom: "TV has made 14 carat gold out of posts, putts, pucks, bats, and balls," he noted. "Now, there is not a major sports event in the United States that does not have some tie with TV. The reason is simple: money." [32]

But television demanded a price: in return for cash and exposure, it received a direct hand in shaping sports to fit TV needs. When Bert Bell, the commissioner of the National Football

League, decreed in 1957 that referees could call time-outs for TV commercials during the first and third quarters of sponsored games, he opened the door for the restructuring of any sport selling itself to TV.[33] Three years earlier, celebrated sports journalist Grantland Rice bemoaned the deleterious effects TV was having on boxing, football, and baseball. "Whatever future these sports follow, they will be very much changed by television," lamented Rice. "TV itself has no answers to the many problems that it poses. It's too young to answer questions. It came up with the roar and the rush of a tidal wave."[34]

The impact of video on sports was manifest in many ways. Following decades of baggy uniforms, major league baseball adopted tighter-fitting, sexier clothing. In baseball, football, and basketball there was an increase in the number of night games because sports in prime time drew larger audiences and networks could charge higher advertising rates.

Once a phenomenon of weekend afternoons, professional football expanded eventually into Monday and Sunday evenings—and sometimes Thursday and Friday nights. The World Series increasingly took place under the lights. College basketball teams found themselves playing on Sundays because the networks needed Sunday programs. From the sponsorship of major sporting events by corporations seeking advertising and tax write-offs, to pressure for the racial integration of televised competition, video affected sports.

Above all, televised sports linked Americans in a web of professional and college leagues competing before the national audience. Whereas once video existed to cover athletics, sports now existed to entertain TV viewers. Spreading from sea to shining sea, sports franchises became tickets to riches as local and network broadcasters were eager to sign up the advertisers and go on the air. And where city size could not justify a professional team, there were university teams to fill the void. One historian has concluded that while "television contributed to the nationalization of American sports," it also "trivialized and diluted the traditional sporting experience." Benjamin G. Rader has contended that "television and the large sums of money that seemed to invariably accompany the medium led to the demise of amateur sports in America."[35]

When TV wanted a sport such as college football or college basketball, money flowed, and college amateurism became semiprofessionalism. When TV was basically disinterested in a college sport—such as baseball, tennis, swimming, gymnastics, and most women's sports—traditional amateur qualities endured. Many major U.S. universities used proceeds from men's basketball and football to support the rest of their sports program. But nowhere was the influence of television on sports more obvious than in the restructuring of professional football that occurred in the 1960s.

Pro football expanded in size and profitability during the decade because one network held a virtual monopoly over telecasts of NFL games and the other networks desired to fill their weekend schedules with pro football. To counter the stranglehold CBS had on the sport, ABC and then NBC began televising the games of the upstart but economically weak American Football League. Importantly, network money for the faltering AFL not only rescued the nascent league, it also precipitated a costly competition among the networks seeking to lease broadcast rights from the leagues. Whereas CBS had payed $1.5 million to televise a season of NFL games in 1960, with new network competition the fee rose to $4.5 million in 1962, $14 million in 1964, and $18.5 million in 1966. For rights to televise AFL games on Sunday afternoons, NBC in 1964 outbid ABC by fivefold, agreeing to spend $42 million over a five-year period.

Recoiling from such expensive rivalry, the networks applauded the merger of the leagues negotiated in 1966. The motivation was profitability: the leagues and networks expected to make more money playing each other rather than programming against one another.[36] From that monopolistic agreement came the ultimate in marketable sports events, the Super Bowl, the annual championship game, which, promoted as "Super Sunday," became a national ritual—and among the highest-rated programs in video history.[37]

programming trends in the 1960s

Sports and news shows notwithstanding, viewers in the 1960s watched television principally for the entertainment series and specials in prime time. This programming was marked by familiar patterns of shifting public tastes, most noticeable in the slippage of the Western from dominance at the opening of the decade to irrelevance in the 1970s. With programs such as *Gilligan's Island*, *Get Smart*, and *The Carol Burnett Show*, the varieties of comedy reappeared—on film and videotape, but seldom live—as the most popular form of video fare. Other trends of note included a decline in the popularity of police and detective crime shows; the limited success—in offerings such as *Combat*, *12 O'Clock High*, and *The Rat Patrol*—of action dramas set in World War II; and the commercial boom sparked in 1966 by the campy comedy-adventure series *Batman*.

Critics have tended to assess TV programming in the 1960s as esssentially facile. To prove the point, they describe an excess of fantasy-comedies featuring bizarre characters that included a talking Palomino, a domesticated witch, a Martian, a cornpone southern sheriff, a nun who could fly, and two ghoulish but lovable families. The irony, of course, is that this was American popular culture, not sprung from a consensus among viewers but because its offbeat characters appealed to the most important demographic entity in the TV audience during the decade: the children of the postwar "baby boom," predominantly middle-class and white, who were now entering adolescence and early adulthood. By attracting sizable numbers of youngsters and their families through *Mr. Ed, My Favorite Martian, The Addams Family,* and the like, ABC, CBS, and NBC sold their advertisers access to a large and lucrative market. In U.S. television, commercial mandate begat national culture.

TV in the 1960s exposed what music listeners already knew, that mass culture in the United States was being created by the desires and pocketbooks of youngsters. From their musical tastes to their rejection of "establishment" standards, Americans born in the years after World War II exerted their influence. By 1965 almost 41 percent of the U.S. population was nineteen years old or younger, and children watched TV more than adults, especially in the early evening hours.

Not only were they numerous, but juvenile viewers also had money and a high propensity to spend it. Even the preteen market in 1965 generated sales of $50 billion. As critic Les Brown noted in *Variety* that year, "For the first time in history, popular culture is not being handed down to the younger generation but handed up by it."[38]

But youth represented not only a cultural force. Many young people in the 1960s proclaimed their political separateness. This was expressed in the civil rights movement, the antiwar movement, environmental protest, and demonstrations against a desensitized mass society—Hippies, peaceniks, free-love advocates, radicals—whatever their cause, whatever their label, those coming of age in the decade exerted enormous influence. The older generation—the one that owned and operated television—may not have understood or agreed with the purpose of its offspring, but the adults showed it and pandered to it on TV.

Network television helped to nurture a national sense of generation, a spirituality that linked, if not united, youths in the decade. There was communion in the dances shared by *American Bandstand, Shindig,* and *Hullabaloo.* Seeing their peers emerge triumphant on *The Adventures of Ozzie and Harriet, The Many Loves of Dobie Gillis,* or *Leave It to Beaver* fed a sense of generational superiority. Viewing their naive value system flattered in countless "Good always defeats Evil" dramas reaffirmed the untested moral code that motivated much of their support of Truth against Falsity.

In many ways television was the font from which the younger generation drew understanding and inspiration. This was a theme touched by noted Swedish sociologist and economist Gunnar Myrdal when he asserted in the mid-1960s that "television is a big factor in what has been going on." For Myrdal it was "tremendously important" that through TV "all the dreadful things that happen are brought into our living rooms," for here was the vivid classroom where American youth learned of the world.

Every child knows about the physical horrors of the Vietnam War. This is not fiction. Real people are killed. We see them lying dead. The effect is that youth discovers the credibility gap. It sees the horrible reality of the war. It feels that it is being talked to by liars. To young people this is serious. This is what has roused the generation. This is what has given us the present period of protest and demonstration.[39]

Among the significant developments in the 1960s was the emergence of the socially relevant program. Whereas social criticism appeared rarely in the early dramatic showcases, now entire series were fashioned around pressing issues. The most successful of these offerings was *The Defenders*, which featured E. G. Marshall and Robert Reed as a father-son team of lawyers involved in cases touching on civil rights and civil liberties. Among the topics treated in *The Defenders* were capital punishment, censorship, military justice, abortion, and political blacklisting.

The NBC series attracted major playwrights such as Reginald Rose, Ernest Kinoy, and Howard Fast, and prominent directors such as Buzz Kulik, Lamont Johnson, and Franklin J. Schaffner. During the years it was on the air, 1961–65, *The Defenders* earned thirteen Emmy awards. Importantly, its record suggested—in many cases, erroneously—that other series with mature political themes might find popular acceptance.

Among the laudable failures to replicate such success were *Channing*, which treated university life in the early 1960s; *Slattery's People*, focusing on issues confronting state government; and *East Side, West Side*, which probed urban racial and social problems. History also received short shrift: with its dramas of human achievements in the building of America, *The Great Adventure* found no great audience and even the death of President John F. Kennedy could not make a hit of *Profiles in Courage,* with its stories inspired by Kennedy's Pulitzer Prize-winning book of the same title.

But there were familiar genres that offered stories of substance. There was sensitive medical theater in *Ben Casey* and *Dr. Kildare,* suspense in *The Alfred Hitchcock Hour,* and mature science fiction on *The Twilight Zone* and *Star Trek.* Soap opera came to prime time with *Peyton Place,* and *The Fugitive* offered compelling action-adventure entertainment. In fact, when telecast on August 29, 1967, the final episode of this two-season search for justice was the highest-rated broadcast—earning a 45.9 rating and a 72.0 share—of the decade.[40]

In offering relatively sophisticated filmed series, network TV was reacting to criticism of the late 1950s and early 1960s. The fact that many of these dramatic series lasted no longer than one season was not as important as the fact that government criticism could persuade the networks to upgrade their product. As critic Richard Schickel explained it in *TV Guide* in 1964:

> *Live TV drama was pronounced dead, after a lingering illness, three years ago, just as the industry was getting its hardest buffeting in the aftermath of the quiz scandals. Coincidentally, there was a shift in national mood toward deeper concern over social issues and the national purpose. The New Frontier was possibly the product of that mood and certainly the focus of it. It remained only for the former Federal Communications Commission Chairman Newton Minow to point out, as he did in the Wasteland speech, that there was a certain variance between this mood and the actual content of television programming. Forthwith, things began to take a turn for the miserable on the dramatic series.*[41]

The network shift toward dramas of increased complexity and social relevance demonstrated the political sensibility basic to broadcasting in the United States. Not only because they are subject to governmental regulation, the networks are structurally political. As powerful corporate enterprises rooted in the status quo, they are by nature self-protective, conservative, and woven profitably into the institutional fabric of the nation.

In general, the networks support the established, and in turn receive support. Joseph Turow has detailed how the networks cooperated with one establishment institution, the American Medical Association, to offer only a flattering image of physicians in TV drama.[42] Since the first doctor series, *Medic,* which premiered on NBC in 1954, the AMA cooperated to make medical personnel and facilities available to filmmakers; it also reviewed scripts for negative connotations, and advised, pressured, and otherwise labored to make certain its favorable picture of doctors, as well as its own positions on controversial medical issues, were communicated to the audience.

In this way, television drama seldom focused negatively on doctors. And were a program to spotlight an unethical or inept physician, his depiction would be strongly countered by good doctors and by a central, heroic figure whose respect for the profession was boundless. Similarly, a script that seemed sympathetic to government medical insurance programs or regulation of the profession—strategically labeled "socialized medicine" by the AMA—would not appear on commercial TV.

But the AMA was only one of many entities consulted by the makers of TV dramas. No matter that such relationships could turn drama into propaganda, producers and networks sought assistance from other medical organizations as well as local, state, and federal law enforcement groups. An eager participant was the Federal Bureau of Investigation, which considered the series *The FBI* to be effective public relations during its run on ABC in 1965–74. Writing in 1972, Director J. Edgar Hoover of the FBI praised the series for winning "additional friends and admirers for the Bureau" and helping "to give millions of persons here and abroad (*The FBI* has been seen in more than fifty other countries, requiring sound tracks in nine languages.) a better understanding of the caliber of public service which the FBI strives to provide."[43] It was a wonderful endorsement from the nation's top G-man.

Through the nine seasons of *The FBI,* the Bureau maintained control over its scripts, casting, and even its sponsorship. According to biographer Richard Gid Powers, "Hoover watched over television's FBI as closely as he did the real Bureau." He assigned an agent in Hollywood to oversee the filming. Hoover even appeared on-camera each fall to introduce the new season of *The FBI.* As Powers noted, the video FBI was for Hoover an idealized Bureau—"the FBI of his dreams: unfailingly polite, white, male, middle-class agents to whom the FBI was family, men protecting a public that responded with gratitude and respect."[44]

Cooperation between Quinn Martin Productions and the Bureau gave writers and producers access to records, equipment, facilities, and personnel. Because it was cleared by the FBI, it ensured, too, that powerful governmental and social agencies would not criticize the final product. For the FBI, such an arrangement guaranteed that television would avoid embarrassing realities—incidents of corruption among local police, illegal burglaries or wiretappings, ideological narrowness, discrimination within Bureau units, investigatory activities that violated civil liberties—in its portrayal of the law enforcement officers.

Although the FBI sought favorable publicity by cooperating with Hollywood, its efforts were minor compared to the U.S. military. To shape its own image in the public mind, the Department of Defense actually produced its own programs for free distribution throughout the nation. *The Big Picture,* a weekly U.S. Army filmed series, ran from 1951 to 1970 and totaled more than eight hundred half-hour episodes. The Pentagon also lent advisers to other TV series, made stock film footage available to cooperative producers, offered military bases and equipment to approved filmmakers, and even lent troops to be used as extras in war dramas requiring large military forces.[45]

Such cooperation was part of the massive propaganda campaign by the Department of Defense to create and maintain popular approval of the U.S. military. In his revealing study *The Pentagon Propaganda Machine,* former senator J. William Fulbright in 1970 described the process by which the Pentagon retained final approval rights over any film made with its assistance:

> *When shooting is finished and the film put together, the filmmaker is then required to submit the completed production to the Assistant Secretary for Public Affairs for an official review . . . so that changes can be made if necessary. This review ostensibly is to ensure accuracy and check for violations of security. Even if a filmmaker does not require physical assistance and the Department of Defense involvement entails only the sale of stock footage, the review process is supposed to be followed.*[46]

For all their flaws and vulnerability, the networks maintained their hegemony over U.S. television and profited enormously therefrom. As long as nothing drastically altered network-affiliate arrangements or the basic structure of VHF/UHF broadcasting in the United States, ABC, CBS, and NBC would remain robust financial operations. Even if challenged with restrictions on their business operations and their access to the national audience, they had flexibility enough to maintain profits and audiences, ensuring in the process that this would remain one nation under network television.

the networks

CHAPTER 8

It is tempting to consider the national culture propagated via television as a timely reflection of popular thought in the United States. In such a view, programs were on TV because they spoke to verities of social life at the

at home time they were popular. They enjoyed success because the audience recognized—subconsciously, perhaps—their articulation of relevant attitudes and values. While such interpretation has the veneer of credibility, it overlooks the process of programming in network TV.

Decisions to telecast series are not made by scholarly researchers shaping shows to mesh with their assessments of public opinion and cultural trends. Ultimately, the choice of programs rests with upper management, after ideas have risen through lay-, ers of subalterns hired to develop and evaluate concepts. In a

and abroad lengthy memorandum to his subordinate Felix Jackson in the NBC Programming Department, David Levy offered insights into the decision-making process of national TV. Written in April 1961— and reprinted in Levy's lengthy letter to Robert Sarnoff three months later—the memo suggests that programming had become the preserve of business managers operating with one eye on the ratings and another on the contractual arrangements between the network and other commercial entities within the video industry.

Levy wrote at a time when NBC trailed CBS and ABC in the ratings; the letter analyzed prime-time scheduling for the summer of 1961. The following excerpt, with several bracketed annotations, indicates clearly that commerce and not cultural sensibilities ultimately determined the NBC lineup:

On Sunday, we scheduled THIS IS YOUR LIFE at 10:30 because we had a firm commitment for two years with Ralph Edwards [host and producer of the series] and because P&G [Procter & Gamble] felt that their program judgment was correct in insisting on scheduling PETER AND MARY [Peter Loves Mary] at 10:00 on

175

Wednesday. As you know, the Program Department objected to this move, but we either had to make it or lose the business without any further consideration of the fact that THIS IS YOUR LIFE has been the No. 1 show in its time period, and scheduling it at 10:30 opposite a program with similar appeal, but deeply entrenched [What's My Line *on CBS*], *was certain to place it at least second.*

BARBARA STANWYCK [The Barbara Stanwyck Show], *whose show was scheduled at 10:30 Sunday, was scheduled in a 10:00 time period because Alberto Culver [sponsor] made that a condition of their order which originally covered LAWLESS YEARS* [The Lawless Years] *at 10:30 Thursday as well as other business. The only place where STANWYCK could be scheduled as early as 10:00 was on Monday.*

As you know, we could not clear stations on Thursday and had to give up the LAWLESS YEARS despite the fact that it had been winning its time period due in large measure to its scheduling following THE UNTOUCHABLES on ABC. The positioning of STANWYCK at 10:00 made it mandatory to find a new time period for NBC Specials. Regrettably, the only period which was saleable and available was 10:00 Tuesday. I would like to point out that the Program Department was vigorously opposed to the scheduling of STANWYCK at 10:00 Monday because (1) we felt that the Specials would do poorly against GARRY MOORE [The Garry Moore Show *on CBS*], *and (2) we felt that STANWYCK would be on third place on Monday. Incidentally, in all of these positions that the Program Department took with respect to STANWYCK, Specials, and PETER AND MARY, we were supported by the Research Department. I might also add that many members of the network Management felt the same way, but these business accommodations were vital to making sales. As a result of the STANWYCK move, we had a weak 10:30 period available on Monday and business considerations alone prompted us to accept the BERLE BOWLING show* [Jackpot Bowling]—*never considered a winner by anybody at NBC.*

In addition, we accommodated BELL TELEPHONE [The Bell Telephone Hour] *by giving them 9:00 on Friday since they flatly refused any later time period. This, of course, made the MICHAEL SHAYNE spot of questionable value as far as being a winner in its time period. Finally, it was decided to continue with THE NATION'S FUTURE on Saturday which effectively killed Saturday from 9:30. I might add that the Program Department as well as the Research Department vigorously opposed the scheduling of DEPUTY* [The Deputy] *on Saturday, but here again business considerations prompted our acceptance of this admittedly weak Western. The scheduling of PEOPLE ARE FUNNY repeats at 6:30, hardly an ideal show to lead into SHIRLEY TEMPLE* [Shirley Temple's Storybook], *was also prompted by a business opportunity for revenue.*[1]

Although the networks extracted part of the profits of the series they aired, responsibility for most of the filmed TV series rested with the major movie studios that had gravitated to the medium. Here were motion-picture giants such as M-G-M, MCA/Universal, 20th Century-Fox, and Paramount (which purchased Desilu in 1967)—as well as powerful independents such as Bing Crosby Productions and Quinn Martin Productions. Many smaller studios had gone out of business, however, as filming for television became costly. By 1968 a ninety-minute series such as *The Name of the Game* or *The Virginian* cost $275,00 per episode—or $7.15 million for the twenty-six episodes broadcast during a normal season. Comparable budgets were needed for hour programs such as *Mission: Impossible* (at least $180,000 per episode) and half-hour situation comedies such as *Hogan's Heroes* ($80,000 or more per installment).

Moreover, production of a series was far from a guarantee of success. Network programming was a highly inefficient operation. According to the ratings standards by which ABC, CBS, and NBC operated, much on TV was rejected by the public. Of the 379 new series introduced in the ten-year period 1966–76, a total of 60 percent disappeared after one season; 17 percent lasted a second season; 14 percent lasted for three or four seasons. Only 9 percent remained on the air for five years, the number of years usually conceded to be required for profitable rerun syndication.[2]

As illustrated in Table 8.1, between 1960 and 1970 the per-season failure rate for fall prime-time series averaged 38 percent. Although figures suggest greater efficiency by the end of the decade, these smaller totals actually reflect network reconsiderations of what constituted audience acceptance. Whereas cancellation usually awaited shows failing to garner at least a 30

TABLE 8.1

prime-time cancellation rate, fall 1960–fall 1970[3]

SEASON BEGINS	FALL SHOWS	SHOWS CANCELED	PERCENT CANCELED
1960	107	49	46
1961	101	45	45
1962	95	43	45
1963	87	37	43
1964	92	36	39
1965	97	45	46
1966	89	40	45
1967	82	37	33
1968	82	22	29
1969	81	26	32

percent share of those viewing TV, changes in programming philosophy, a preference for shows lasting sixty minutes or longer, and greater care in shaping series to fit audience specifications meant by 1970 that the networks retained weaker programs longer. Nonetheless, mortality figures never became negligible. During the years 1984–86, for example, the networks canceled 146 prime-time series.[4]

Despite its failures, however, commercial TV continued to be profitable. Between 1960 and 1977 gross advertising revenues for the industry rose from $1.62 billion (13 percent of all U.S. advertising) to $7.5 billion (20 percent). While the network share of this total actually dropped from 50.4 to 44.2 percent, network gross income rose from $820 million to $3.3 billion.[5]

But there were other revenue sources for the networks. These ranged from domestic off-network syndication to leasing network studios to independent producers contractually bound by the networks to use those facilities. As it affected their economic power, however, the most promising source of additional revenues came from the international dealings of the American networks. By the late 1960s, ABC, CBS, and NBC were at the forefront of the movement toward the economic rearrangement of the world along multinational corporate lines. Forging for themselves preeminent roles in the globalization of electronic mass communications, the three American networks were fast becoming TV programmers for the world.

global strategies

With their substantial profits, the networks were able to think beyond U.S. television. This was the time to diversify, and in the early 1960s they began to buy outside the telecommunications field. CBS led the way, purchasing companies as varied as the New York Yankees baseball team, the cartoon filmmaker Terrytoons, the Steinway piano company, the toy manufacturer Creative Playthings, and several magazine and book publishers. Through RCA, its parent company, NBC spent its massive profits on such businesses as the Hertz automobile-rental company, a carpet manufacturer, a real-estate-management operation, and a venture into computer manufacturing.

More significant, however, was their involvement in international broadcasting. At a time when major corporations in Europe, Japan, and the United States were moving beyond their national borders to establish dominance in other nations, the American television networks were the most attractive communications corporations in the world.

ABC, CBS, and NBC had been thinking globally for a long time. With distribution rights to thousands of hours of episodic filmed series, U.S. networks since the 1950s had profited from leasing their programs abroad. And there were many outlets for the American products. By 1959 there were 435 stations and 23.2 million sets in non-Communist foreign countries; there was also a great demand for prepackaged filmed programming.

Erik Barnouw has shown how American exports undermined local creativity. When the networks and other American distributors leased their films cheaply to Australia, Canada, and other countries, they often gained dominating positions that allowed them to thwart native film industries unable to match the low prices offered by the Americans. Throughout the Cold War, moreover, foreign aid was tied to the import of American-made products by recipient countries. Among the products urged on them were transmitters, studio equipment, and supplies for television facilities. "In the mid-1950s," wrote Barnouw, "television, like missionary expeditions of another era, seemed to serve as an advance herald of empire. Implicit in its arrival was a web of relationships involving cultural, economic, and military aspects, and forming the basis of a new kind of empire. All this was not entirely unplanned."[6]

American TV, with its cultural values and social assumptions, became global in the 1950s and 1960s. The *International Television*

Almanac for 1962 gives indication of this penetration, describing aspects of the world market as follows:

Argentina: "Programs consist mainly of American TV serials, and strong resistance has already resulted from this circumstance."

Australia: "Despite agitation by Actors Equity, the bulk of material on TV—certainly, the most popular programs—are American filmed shows."

Brazil: "Transmissions comprise all kinds of programs, musicals, humor, sports, interviews, live theater, etc., including lately also filmed serials, which had been thought of as impossible due to their being mostly in English language with Portuguese subtitles."

Italy: "Best programs are still unabashedly modeled on American shows. For three years the equivalent of *The $64,000 Question* was the leader here. Now it has been supplanted by *Twenty-One* and *Name That Tune*. Some American kinescopes have been shown here (either dubbed or with a superimposed spoken commentary) to great success."

Peru: "Programming depends greatly on Westerns and mystery (detective) shows from the United States that have been Spanish-dubbed in Mexico. . . . Film programs are preferred to live because of the cost factor."

Sweden: "An ordinary TV week in Stockholm sees about fourteen hours of 'live' programs and six hours of film: Swedish, French, American (U.S.A.), British, and Soviet pictures have been shown on TV, and serials like *Perry Mason, The Perry Como Show, Hitchcock Presents, Gunsmoke, Disneyland, Robin Hood* (British), and *Colonel Flack*."[7]

The U.S. networks were heavily committed to overseas business activities. By the early 1960s ABC was billing itself "the world's largest buyer of programs for telecasting outside the United States," while CBS claimed it was "the world's largest exporter of films produced for television," and NBC reported sales in 110 markets in 60 countries.[8] Exporters of U.S. television programs in 1968 anticipated a foreign gross of $70 million to $80 million.[9] And one observer estimated that in 1969 approximately 80 percent of the current programs in Latin America—shows such as *The Flintstones, I Love Lucy, Bonanza, That Girl,* and *Route 66* —were produced in the United States.[10]

The networks created other affiliations with foreign operations. NBC became a partner in managing the Nigerian federal TV system, and by 1965 had direct minority investments in thirteen foreign stations in eight nations. Moreover, through NBC

International, the corporation by 1968 was selling its programs in eighty-two foreign countries. Although CBS was less active in foreign dealings in the 1960s, it was involved in cable TV in six countries; it held minority positions in broadcast outlets in five countries in Latin America and the Caribbean; it had production companies in Argentina, Peru, and Venezuela; and CBS had technical-advisory arrangements with TV outlets on five continents.[11]

By far the most successful foreign operations were the Worldvision enterprises of ABC International. Founded in 1959 by the perennially third-ranked U.S. network, Worldvision soon catapulted ABC into the premier position in international telecommunications. In Venezuela, for instance, ABC was part owner of three of the nation's fourteen stations, and it managed programming for eight others. Only three Venezuelan outlets were free of direct Worldvision input. ABC International also advanced funds to create the Central American Television Network (CATVN)—an arrangement among ABC-supported stations in Costa Rica, Nicaragua, Guatemala, Honduras, and El Salvador—principally to broadcast filmed programs supplied by ABC.

By 1968 ABC International/Worldvision operated in sixteen Latin American countries and eleven other nations outside the Western Hemisphere. ABC was also tied to the Arab Middle East Network involving Syria, Lebanon, Jordan, Kuwait, and Iraq; and the Latin American International Network Organization (LATINO), which contained Mexico, Uruguay, Chile, Ecuador, Argentina, and Venezuela. Through its 64 TV transmitters Worldvision in the late 1960s reached 20 million television households, fully 60 percent of the TV homes in foreign countries with commercial TV. Importantly, by the end of its first decade ABC was distributing almost nine hundred filmed programs to more than ninety countries.[12]

Such expansion was not without impact on international communications. Cheap U.S. films stifled film production in those countries committed to American TV products and corporations. The import of American cultural values through the programs often clashed with national culture. Significantly, American influence in foreign markets upset plans for noncommercial television in the state-run style of most European video. This was especially true in less-affluent developing countries, where the influx of private U.S. capital first brought television to the citizenry. In Latin America, for example, the alternative public TV was undermined by the pressure tactics and popularity of American-style commercial broadcasting.

Globalization also spread American capitalism in the postwar era. With the hardware and software came American advertising agencies ready to devise commercials for U.S. products, whose manufacturers soon followed. This formidable video package of transmitters/programs/advertisers influenced many countries in terms of patterns of mass consumption and domestic economic growth.

Even sophisticated Great Britain was affected by the power of American video and commerce. As Barnouw has shown, by helping to persuade Parliament to sanction the first British commercial broadcaster—the Independent Television Corporation, which debuted in September 1955—the J. Walter Thompson agency played a major role in breaking the video monopoly of the sponsor-free British Broadcasting Corporation. Whereas U.S. advertisers used to beam commercials at British consumers from studios in Radio Luxembourg, the opening of ITC opened the British market to television spots transmitted from British soil.[13]

American-made programming was also strategic to waging the Cold War. The U.S. Information Agency, the foreign propaganda operation of the federal government, worked closely with the networks to place American-made shows on world TV. The USIA lobbied abroad for U.S. video interests, collaborated with corporations such as NBC to produce informational telefilms for foreign distribution, and even urged U.S. networks and producers to put out positive images of American life.

The USIA helped to distribute American entertainment, ranging from semiclassical music on *The Voice of Firestone* to anti-Communist espionage dramatics on *I Led 3 Lives*. As early as 1959 *TV Guide*, a strong supporter of U.S. television series as Cold War propaganda, urged "intelligent cooperation between the USIA and the producers" in the effort "to see to it that American shows reflect our country in a favorable light when they are presented to foreign audiences."[14]

There were occasional problems, however, with U.S. video exports. Cultural differences could generate suspicion and distrust. References to Jews—a child studying Hebrew on *Room 222*, the Star of David sewn to the boxing trunks of 1930s heavyweight champ Max Baer on *Greatest Fights of the Century*, a son named Israel on *Daniel Boone*, Libyan insistence that Ben Casey, like the Israeli leader David Ben-Gurion, was obviously Zionist —compromised series in anti-Zionist Arab states. Many British and Australian veterans, who had fought Nazis in North Africa long before the United States entered World War II, resented the glorified image of Americans as seen in the war series *The Rat Patrol*. The Swedes canceled *Gentle Ben* because they did not want their children becoming friendly with the bears that were plentiful and dangerous in their well-forested country.

Although these examples illustrate the way individual series conflicted with national characteristics and social values abroad, the import of any U.S. television series necessarily brought with it a foreign value system. At a time of intense nationalism, especially in the disintegrating white empires in Africa and Asia, the propagation of the values inherent in U.S. video often was received with disdain. As early as 1961, when foreign sales reached an estimated $35 million, correspondent Murray Horowitz reported in *Variety* that the "expanding foreign market is astir with problems. From Rio to Sydney, rising tides of nationalism are seeking to stem the influx of American shows, mainly vidfilm series." [15] According to Horowitz, the most telling accusation was that American-made series were often too violent and sadistic.

But TV-generated anti-Americanism was not limited to neophyte nation-states. A Canadian critic in 1967 bemoaned the domination of his country by U.S. video products. According to Henry Comor, president of the Association of Canadian Television and Radio Artists, "American television has damaged, almost irreparably, the Canadian television industry. It has made it impossible for Canadian performers and writers to earn a living in Canada. . . . our writers and our performers have now found their way to Hollywood." Arguing that the appeal and abundance of U.S. television—much of it received in Canada from American stations broadcasting across the border—subverted the interests of his country, Comor continued:

American television has made the development of a Canadian cultural identity almost impossible. American television has distorted the values of Canadians about the realities of their own lives and their own history. Through its own faulty development, American television has negatively influenced the development of a worthy native television in Canada. American television has destroyed television as an art. Canadians are often told that their potential enemies are Russia and China. In my view, the United States is a much more dangerous enemy. Our armed forces should be there to protect us against the United States. Canadian guns should be trained on New York and Los Angeles and not on Moscow and Peking. I am serious when I say this. Partly serious. [16]

The globalization of American pop culture was irresistible. Herbert I. Schiller, one of the first scholars to discuss this phenomenon, described it as "a global American electronic invasion" and an "electronic siege" of the rest of the world.[17] Some nations such as Great Britain and Canada tried to defend themselves with quotas limiting the amount of U.S. entertainment acceptable on their TV screens—14 percent of airtime in the case of Britain, 45 percent for Canada.

In the 1970s, however, the fortunes of international distribution abruptly ended for the networks. FCC rulings and judicial decrees confined network activity in this area to only those programs wholly produced by the networks. This effectively limited ABC, CBS, and NBC to news and documentary programming. Major producer/distributors such as Paramount, Warner Brothers, and MCA/Universal eagerly filled the void.

While problems of program content and intent persisted, demand for American series also dipped because nations such as Japan and Great Britain developed their own TV industries and entered the global syndication market. Although in the readjustment years 1970–72 the gross figures dropped 15 percent to $85 million, by the end of the decade TV sales abroad totaled about 20 percent of gross revenues earned by U.S. television producers. In 1988 the major market for American TV was Europe, where syndicators earned $630 million.[18]

limitations on monopoly

It is ironic that at the moment of their greatest global power, the three networks confronted one of those rare occurrences when the interests of the FCC, Congress, and the White House converged to make forceful regulation a reality. This resulted in a series of rulings adversely affecting network profits, yet never threatening to destroy the "cash cow" that was national broadcasting by the early 1970s. The rulings were several—including passage of the Prime-Time-Access Rule, institution of the Financial Interest and Syndication Rules, restrictions placed on network production, and a ban on cigarette advertising.

They materialized from an unlikely convergence of interests that included FCC idealism left over from the 1960s, the desire by the White House to dilute the political influence of the networks, pressure from consumer interest groups, and medical advice from the Federal Trade Commission and the Office of the Surgeon General. The rulings that materialized in the early 1970s constituted the most serious adjustments of network monopoly practices since the days of Chairmen Fly and Porter.

the prime-time-access rule: By the mid-1960s there was essentially no such commodity as an independently made first-run TV series. Whereas they had been a rich part of the TV mix during the 1950s, when network prime time was from 8:00 P.M. to 10:30 P.M. (EST), the expansion of local news and network news plus the widening of prime time from 7:30 PM. to 11 P.M. by the early 1960s effectively destroyed this market. FCC and congressional study of this development culminated in 1965 in an FCC report documenting how the network monopoly had suffocated the free-enterprise efforts of affiliate stations and independent programmers. In response to its findings, the FCC in April 1970 enacted the Prime-Time-Access Rule (PTAR).

Effective in September 1971, the rule limited network programming to three prime-time hours per night in the fifty largest markets. The move took from them a total of 10.5 fringe hours weekly, although a later modification excluding Sunday evening lowered the total to nine hours. In unison, ABC, CBS, and NBC passed to their member stations the first half hour—and least profitable time segment—of prime time (7:30 P.M. to 8:00 P.M. EST). Moreover, since the networks found it unprofitable to program for scores of smaller markets, the decision regarding the top fifty markets affected all their affiliates.

Although the FCC's chairman, Dean Burch, newly appointed by President Richard M. Nixon, protested this regulatory action, a majority of the commission, led by Nicholas Johnson and Kenneth A. Cox, was convinced by the 1965 study that TV needed to be more competitive. In passing the rule, the commission admitted its purpose was to rectify a situation in which three national program services "for all practical purposes control the entire network television production process from idea through exhibition."[19] The FCC foresaw that the extra half hour would afford local stations the chance to air programs of community interest, but its principal desire was that the move would enhance advertising revenues at local stations and increase the business of independent producers, who had seen their share of network programming slip from 33 percent in 1958 to 5 percent in 1968.

the financial interest and syndication rules: In the same action creating the PTAR, the commission ordered the networks to surrender all financial interest and syndication rights in any series they did not produce totally. The Financial Interest and Syndication Rules (FISR—sometimes called "fin-syn") constituted the most damaging attack against the network TV monopoly in FCC history.

YEARS OF PLENTY: THE 1960s AND 1970s

Although the networks produced little except their own news programs, by 1970 they held financial and syndication concessions in about 98 percent of all their programming.[20] In some cases—especially those involving independent producers without sufficient financial reserves—this was justified on the grounds that the network had advanced seed money to programs during their development stages. But the networks demanded a financial interest in programming, sometimes as much as 50 percent, even if it was produced by a major film studio not needing start-up funds. The networks argued that by airing a series nationally, they were contributing to its value and therefore they merited a financial interest in its present success and in its future syndication.

When it knocked down the financial-interest aspect of such arrangements, the FCC also ended network syndication prerogatives. No longer could ABC, CBS, or NBC distribute series domestically, and they were prevented from syndicating shows abroad unless they had fully financed and produced those programs. This aspect of FISR placed domestic and foreign syndication rights in the hands of the studios actually producing the programming.

FISR cut deeply into network syndication operations, relegating them to news and public affairs programs, which constituted about 9 percent of foreign sales. And to seal the new arrangement, the networks were given one year to divest themselves of their syndication companies. From this in 1972 came the creation of a new company, Viacom International, to distribute CBS films; and the melding of NBC properties into National Telefilm Associates, and ABC interests into the now-independent distributor Worldvision.

restricted network production: In supplementary action taken in 1975, the Department of Justice settled a protracted legal proceeding against monopolistic practices at NBC by limiting the number of hours a network could fill even with its own productions. By this consent agreement, which was not effective until accepted by CBS and ABC, the networks were limited to a weekly total of two and one-half hours of prime-time entertainment shows—sliding to five hours by the late 1980s—and eight hours of daytime shows.[21] Unlike the FISR and the PTAR, this agreement was to last ten years. It is scheduled to expire in November 1990.

Clearly, this latter action avoided a permanent curtailment of the monopolistic controls exercised by the networks. In fact, *Variety* termed it a "coup" for NBC.[22] Nevertheless, relative to the self-policing usually recommended by federal regulators, even this mild prohibition was a striking development. But unlike the earlier FCC rulings, this agreement appears to have been more political than reformist.

Although the Department of Justice had been investigating antitrust patterns in U.S. broadcasting for years, the decision to press the case against network television came from the Nixon White House. After initial hesitancy, adviser John Ehrlichman urged President Nixon in 1971 to give the go-ahead for the lawsuits—but only after a public-relations game plan was devised. In a private memo to Nixon in September, he wrote, "We have to anticipate that the television media will counterattack vigorously and it is necessary for us to have mobilized the film industry, the print media, and others to set forth our side of the case." Nixon agreed in an annotation that it was "vitally important to plan P.R. aspects" before instituting the lawsuit.[23]

The antitrust prosecution was but another blow by the White House against a perceived political enemy. But it was not a purposeless campaign: from the beginning the administration understood what it wished to accomplish, and the speech by Spiro Agnew in November 1969 had been only the first shot in a virtual war against the networks.

The White House goal vis-à-vis national television was well delineated by Patrick Buchanan, who wrote to the president in late 1972 that "The Nixon White House and the national liberal media are as cobra and mongoose—the situation extends beyond the traditional conflict between democratic government and free press." For the "New Right" Nixon adviser who three years earlier had penned Agnew's attack on TV news, nothing less than the future of the nation depended on the destruction of network power:

A small, ideological clique has managed to acquire monopoly control of the most powerful medium of communication known to man; and they regularly use that unrivaled and untrammeled power to politically assault the president and his administration. This is not a question of free speech, or free press—it is a basic question of power. Shall we acquiesce forever in left-wing control of communications media from which 50 percent to 70 percent of the American people derive their information and ideas about their national government? The interests of this country and the furtherance of the policies and ideas in which we believe demand that this monopoly,

187

this ideological cartel, be broken up. . . . again, this must be viewed as a question of "power." . . . We should move against it the way TR moved against the financial monopolies. Our timing should be right, but we should be unapologetic about what we are doing.[24]

ban on cigarette advertising: When Congress voted to ban cigarette advertising from TV and radio, the issue clearly seemed to be about improving the health of the nation, and particularly discouraging the addiction of young people to nicotine. Interestingly, this action was suggested as early as 1964 after the surgeon general announced the causal relationship between cigarette smoking and cancer. But it required years of political wrangling before Congress enacted legislation banning cigarette advertising on television, commencing January 2, 1971. In a cynical final gesture, however, New Year's Day 1971 was avoided, since the football bowl games that day allowed broadcasters one last lucrative opportunity to sell airtime to the cigarette makers.

As with most regulatory decisions in U.S. broadcasting, this ban derived not from social concern as much as from hard political decisions. To many senators and representatives the issue was a medical problem as well as a budgetary question, since a rising number of cancer cases represented a drain on public health funding. There was also pressure for congressional action from consumer groups and professional medical associations. Perhaps most decisively, however, when a federal court ruled that under the fairness doctrine TV stations had to provide free airtime for anti-smoking groups to answer protobacco propaganda, TV stations and manufacturers reluctantly agreed that a ban would be preferable.

Still, the ban was upsetting to the TV industry, since broadcasters earned about $250 million yearly (about 20 percent of annual billings) peddling tobacco. Moreover, the reliability of tobacco accounts was strategic by 1970 because network advertising in general was in decline as the U.S. economy entered a recession.

The networks were nothing if not flexible, however, and except for a short-run dip in annual revenues, the restrictive rulings of the early 1970s did no lasting damage to broadcasting. The networks still dominated national TV, and national video still dominated the leisure time of the American public. For advertisers wanting access to the broadest possible audience there was still no alternative to national television. And there were such advertisers, hundreds of them, waiting to buy time if the price were right.

Led by CBS, the networks in December 1970 adjusted their advertising schedules to the new realities: commercial rates were raised by establishing the thirty-second commercial rather than the one-minute spot as the standard unit. In this way companies unable to afford a minute on NBC's *The Flip Wilson Show* at $65,000 or *Ironside* for $60,000 could now purchase a half minute from the network for $40,000 and $38,500, respectively.[25]

The strategy worked. Whereas pretax profits at CBS had fallen dramatically, from $92.7 million in 1969 to $50 million in 1970 and to $53 million in 1971, by 1972 the network was again booming, making almost $111 million and more than double that figure in 1974. Even lowly ABC did well, company pretax profits exploding from about $25 million in 1975 to more than $200 million four years later. Advertising billings for the entire industry demonstrated similar rejuvenation, moving from $3.6 billion in 1970 to $4.1 billion in 1972 and to $7.5 billion by 1977.[26]

Above all, the networks could rebound because the American audience continued to choose their programming. Daily HUT (homes using television) figures averaged a record-high 62.1 percent during the 1969–70 TV season. As early as November 1963 —only two months after CBS and NBC expanded their evening newscasts to thirty minutes—TV for the first time overtook newspapers as a Roper poll indicated that by 36 percent to 24 percent Americans found TV a more reliable news source than print. Even after the turmoil of inner-city rebellions that marked a collapsing civil rights movement, and years of dissent over the U.S. involvement in the Vietnam War, the differential between video and newspapers spread to 44 to 21 percent in 1969 and to 48 to 21 percent in 1973. Also in 1973, by a margin of five to one Americans even judged commercials as "a fair price to pay for being able to view the programs."[27]

In a span of two decades, the American public had come to rely on television. While popularity was not synonymous with profundity or adequacy, the medium occupied a position of great social authority. One person urging the industry to exert its influence more responsibly was Lou Harris, whose polling organization was a respected gauge of public opinion. For Harris, having the trust of the nation required those in television to exercise social leadership by facing and reporting the truth. Speaking in late 1970, he argued that "what the American people want more than anything else today is leadership which will not back off the hard truth." In a statement with ramifications for developments that

would confront the industry in the early 1970s, Harris asserted
that TV

> *must be willing to stick its neck out by a willingness to take these
> major substantive areas and to report them, research them, explain
> them, and even take stands on where we ought to go to solve them,
> albeit giving wide open access to all those who disagree. Leadership
> is not simply to reflect, but to be prepared to go that step beyond the
> present and to spell out the implications, the costs, and the sacrifice
> and pain involved in going through the crucible of genuine better-
> ment of mankind.*[28]

the politics

# of television

On July 21, 1969, astronaut Neil Armstrong took mankind's first step on the surface of the moon. As technologically brilliant as was this feat, similarly astounding was the fact that millions of Americans—indeed, much of humankind back home on Earth—watched the event as it happened: it was on network TV. If a goal of the developers of video was to produce a medium through which to improve citizen awareness, coverage of the lunar adventure suggested that the goal was achievable. While a picture live from the moon was only a technical achievement, it symbolized the new sophistication and importance of television for Americans.

As coverage of the lunar landing suggested, national TV was by this time integral to life in the United States. It consumed a sizable percentage of the average citizen's leisure time, even to the point, many alleged, of undermining the national educational system. In the process of entertaining and informing, TV imposed a shorthand guidebook for living. Its dramas offered lessons on morality; its commercials spoke to economic affairs; and its news programming played a vital role in raising and shaping popular awareness and in setting the national agenda. Yet nowhere was it more influential than as a medium of politics, for by the time Neil Armstrong stepped on the moon's surface, television was already the principal vehicle through which most Americans understood the political direction of their nation.

Government had anticipated and feared the overt manipulation possible in mass communication. Buried in the Communications Act of 1934, Section 315 stipulated that candidates for election must be given "equal time" should an opponent use the air without charge. Section 315 also mandated that if a candidate purchased airtime for politicking, opponents must be allowed to buy a similar amount of airtime at the same cost. To these "equal time" provisions, the FCC in 1949 added the "fairness doctrine." Here, at the dawn of the television era, the commission ruled that all sides on controversial issues should be treated equitably in news and commentary; indeed, broadcasters were obliged to seek out and present all sides when covering controversy.

Although later amendments shifted slightly the wording of Section 315 and the fairness doctrine, they continue to restrain the overt manipulation of American politics by broadcasters. Industry leaders such as Frank Stanton, however, saw them as restraints on broadcast journalism. He called Section 315 a "straitjacket" that "strips broadcast journalism of both the right and the responsibility of news judgment." In his disgust for such control, Stanton even blamed the equal-time requirement for the failure of television as an instrument of mass education. In his words, by 1960 the "use of television as education for democratic living and, indeed, for democratic survival is plagued and choked."[1]

Of course, the implementation of equal time and the fairness doctrine often led to adjudication when the opposing viewpoints came from radical fringes of the American political spectrum; but Section 315 worked well in its primary purpose, preventing Democrats or Republicans from dominating the airwaves. Although no party could dominate the medium, American politicians readily integrated television into their strategies. Spending for TV in presidential campaigns, for example, increased from $6.6 million in 1956 to $10 million in 1960 and to $27 million in 1968.[2]

By the 1970s, television was the principal medium of political communication. The overt propaganda of the "paid political announcement" in election campaigns was supplemented by televised speeches, press conferences, and events staged expressly for the cameras. Advisers, pollsters, and advertising consultants —what one scholar has called the "media managers"[3]—became a force in TV from election campaigns to the exercise of power.

Most affected by television were presidential campaigns. What was revolutionary in 1960, the "great debates" between the two major candidates, was revived in the campaign of 1976 and made almost mandatory thereafter. Preconvention state primaries, minimal until the advent of television, proliferated now, principally because candidates and parties desired the TV exposure afforded by these electoral tests. In many ways the success in 1980 of Ronald Reagan, a former actor with motion-picture and video skills, suggested that the talents crucial to entertainment could be politically profitable in the age of audiovisual communication.

But television was a double-edged instrument of revelation. While it could be manipulated to show a political leader in a flattering guise, the medium also could be unforgiving toward those it exposed as flawed, and such exposure did not happen necessarily during political campaigns. The Watergate scandal of 1972–74 demonstrated this aspect of its social influence. Perhaps David Sarnoff was too enthusiastic in 1953 when he predicted that viewers eventually would be able to use two-way video to vote on important political matters.[4] But the investigation, near-impeachment, and resignation of President Richard M. Nixon were an approximation of Sarnoff's forecast.

The discrediting of Nixon and his eventual surrender of the presidency constituted a protracted national calamity in which television played a vital role. It began in June 1972 with a break-in at the offices of the Democratic National Committee in the Watergate hotel and apartment complex in Washington, D.C. Although the investigative energy in the unfolding scandal came primarily from newspapers—most notably, the *Washington Post* and the *New York Times*—it was through network TV that most citizens learned how President Nixon participated in, even orchestrated, a conspiracy to obstruct the FBI investigation of that break-in committed by White House aides and members of Nixon's reelection committee.

Newspapers carried detailed accounts of the break-in throughout the last half of 1972, a point not lost on TV critics at the time.[5] And media scholar Marilyn A. Lashner may be correct to point out in her study of television and Watergate, *The Chilling Effect in TV News*, that "there are no laurels due for television in its Watergate commentary, which was at best pale and thin."[6] Nevertheless, not until early 1973, when network TV began reporting in earnest, did Watergate become a pressing national issue.

Then, in evening newscasts, special reports, weekend interview forums like *Face the Nation* and *Issues and Answers*, and live coverage of relevant events, video operated as a national press to deliver the latest details in this sordid story. Especially influential was the role of the networks in bringing the public directly into two strategic investigations conducted by congressional committees. On live TV in the summer of 1973 hearings conducted by the Senate Select Committee on Presidential Campaign Activities, chaired by Senator Sam Ervin, revealed the seriousness of the accusations against the president and his cohorts. The following summer live telecasts of impeachment hearings conducted by the House Judiciary Committee, headed by Congressman Peter Rodino, carefully uncovered the president's involvement not only in the Watergate affair but in an extensive campaign of illegal domestic surveillance conducted against people considered "enemies" of the White House.

The information communicated via the national medium of

news was devastating to the president. Nixon himself had attempted to use TV to win his case, holding press conferences, staging photo opportunities, making speeches, and otherwise seeking to persuade the public of his innocence. But a stream of revelations, instantly related to the public via television, made the president's departure inescapable.

The unprotested acceptance of Nixon's resignation on August 9, 1974, represented an enormous shift in public opinion. Before Watergate, the public esteem for Richard Nixon was high. This was the leader who in his first term boldly visited China and the Soviet Union, and then ended U.S. involvement in the Vietnam War. In 1972 he was reelected by the largest plurality and the second-highest electoral vote in U.S. history. Although impeachment had been anticipated by the framers of the Constitution, the removal of a president from office was unprecedented and its ramifications were unknown. Further, the resignation meant that for the first time the United States would have a chief executive who was not elected to the presidency or vice-presidency, because a year earlier Nixon had appointed, and Congress confirmed, Congressman Gerald Ford as vice-president of the United States. Ford replaced a discredited Spiro T. Agnew, who resigned the vice-presidency because of his involvement in accepting bribes while he was governor of Maryland.

In covering the Watergate scandal, however, network television reached the limits to which it could go as a conduit of news. Its function was to inform a citizenry which had opted through its laws to receive information unfettered by government controls. But Watergate shook the foundations of the republic. That it occurred was one matter, but its prolonged and detailed public exposure, especially on television, challenged the validity of the System. Coming so quickly after Nixon's reelection, the resignation compromised the national electoral process. Callous abuse of power by the White House may have undermined the credibility of the presidency, but the replacement of Nixon by Gerald Ford was nothing less than a *coup d'état* made possible, acceptable, and necessary through the popularizing effect of TV news.

Certainly, Watergate legitimated the role of the free press, and especially broadcast journalism as a social watchdog. But freedom of the press was a notion conceived in an age of newspapers with small distribution patterns. In the age of broadcasting, with the ability to inform millions instantly and sometimes superficially, the power of the press was considerably enhanced. Watergate raised questions about how much society needed to know, about the responsibility of journalists to act discreetly, about whether or not the United States could afford informational openness. While some, like ABC president Elton Rule, could proclaim at the time that "all of us are living through journalism's finest hours," and that to ignore Watergate "would have been an abdication of the truth,"[7] questions remain: How many Watergates could the System withstand? Would TV journalism have pressed for a full investigation had President Ford been involved in such a scandal? Was there a limit to the number of Watergates the networks would report? Was Watergate a trend? Or was it a glorious moment for American journalism, but one that must never happen again?

At the crux of the issue, too, was the ambiguous relationship between the free press and the structural realities of U.S. society. While TV does not consider itself a medium for government propaganda, it often broadcasts such propaganda. Although networks do not report the news as a branch of American big business, they are tied to multibillion-dollar corporations which themselves are integrally woven into what President Dwight D. Eisenhower once termed "the military-industrial complex."

As Bill Greeley clearly demonstrated in *Variety*, there is a rich and chronic relationship between government and corporations owning TV networks, as well as between TV and businesses sponsoring national programs. In fiscal 1971, for example, one of the largest TV sponsors, American Telephone & Telegraph, had Defense Department contracts worth $1.2 billion; and three corporations with TV holdings, General Electric, Westinghouse, and RCA, had Pentagon contracts totaling $1 billion, $437 million, and $250 million, respectively. General Tire & Rubber, the parent company of RKO-General, manufactured rocket warheads, cluster bombs, and mine and bomb dispensers. And CBS Laboratories contracted to develop improved laser detectors— so-called sniffers—used by the U.S. military to detect the whereabouts of humans and other animal life in the jungles of Southeast Asia.[8]

Importantly, Watergate unfolded before a national audience accustomed to moral and political themes as normal fare. For a decade the medium reported on such matters as civil rights, the Vietnam War, women's rights, and the environmental crisis in terms of right and wrong. The heroes of TV entertainment also were flawless types who resolved moral dilemmas with style, teaching viewers in the process the value of honesty and integrity.

Programmers could go too far in their preachments. Americans would not accept smarmy moralists. Whereas Vice-President

Marvin Antonowsky of ABC could suggest in September 1970 that "we should meet our obligations to the American public to give them entertainment of substance and broad appeal that is relevant, timely, entertaining, and exciting, and that can hope-fully help to ameliorate the deepening divisions in our country,"[9] he was speaking on the eve of the most disastrous fall season in TV history.

Within three months overt social relevancy was rejected by the audience, and the networks scrambled for replacement pro-grams. Gone quickly were sentimentally liberal shows such as *The Storefront Lawyers* (liberal white lawyers working in a ghetto) and *Barefoot in the Park* (upscale, kissy black couple in a romantic comedy set in Manhattan). Gone, too, were offerings with prom-inent black characters liberally melded into familiar genres: the medical drama *The Interns*, the police series *The Silent Force*, the medical drama *Matt Lincoln*.

Indicative of the unctuous liberalism rejected by the public was the following exchange in *The Young Rebels* telecast of December 27, 1970. Ostensibly the story of two white men and one black man fighting together for freedom during the Revolution-ary War, this conversation ended an episode in which a slave named Pompey assisted the young rebels in destroying a British munitions depot. Together with their mentor, the Marquis de Lafayette, the rebels decided that Pompey had earned his free-dom—and the right to a last name.

Led by black rebel Isak Poole, the conversation turned quickly from Pompey's surname to poetry and human freedom.

Pompey: *Thank you, General. But if it's all the same to you, I think I'll keep my own name. Just to remind me that no men are free unless all men are free.*

Poole: *Pompey, can you read?*

Pompey: *Can I read? What do you want me to read, boy?*

Poole: *A poem. Henry gave it to me when I was feeling kinda like you do right now.*

Pompey (reading):
Oh, come the time
And haste the day,
When man shall man no longer crush;
When reason shall enforce her sway,
Nor these fair . . .

Poole (completing the poem):
Nor these fair regions raise our blush;
Where still the African complains,
And mourns his yet unbroken chains.

Pompey: *Yeah. You write this, Henry?*

Henry: *No. A poet of the Revolution, Philip Freneau.*

Lafayette: *I thought it sounded French.*

Pompey: *Sounded black to me. (laughs)*

Third Rebel: *Sounds like maybe someday it won't matter.*
(music swells)

Announcer: *In 1777 a slave named Pompey was instrumental in capturing the key British fort at Stoney Point, New York, giving the Americans control of the Hudson River. He was only one of ten thousand black men who served gallantly in the Revolutionary War.*

Rejected in do-gooder dramas, liberal political views did find a home in situation comedy, where they emerged judiciously from the satire, sarcasm, and cynicism of topical humor. *The Mary Tyler Moore Show* may have delivered consistently nice, happy endings, but Mary Richards—single, tenacious, careerist—became a role model for the growing ranks of women struggling to survive economically and emotionally in the American patriarchy. Whereas it remained controversial to criticize the Vietnam War in a drama or documentary, *M*A*S*H* was a lightly camouflaged critique of the war; but because it was set in the Korean conflict, the series avoided direct confrontation with the controversies emanating from the war in Southeast Asia. As "the silent majority" turned national politics away from the civil rights concerns of the 1960s, *Chico and the Man* offered its own perspective on the condition of racial minorities in the United States. And in *Barney Miller* lessons in urban sociology were woven cleverly through the jailhouse humor that made the series popular.

The pacesetting programs in this political-comedy trend were those produced by Norman Lear and Bud Yorkin—*All in the Family, Good Times, The Jeffersons, Sanford and Son*, and *Maude*. They deftly mixed humor with bold satirical attacks on contemporary social issues such as bigotry, the Vietnam War, and the Nixon administration. Maude Findlay was a consummate liberal whose sensitivities toward the downtrodden emerged through a comedic persona that was pompous and brash. Amid the discordant interplay between old Fred Sanford and his strongly willed adult son Lamont there were flashes of racial pride and rebelliousness, jabs at white insincerity and racism that were often cheered by the sympathetic studio audience. George Jefferson gave the nation its first lovable Afro-American bigot, but *The Jeffersons* also offered a perspective on the black middle class that was alien to network television. And on *Good Times* it was the Evans family, black and cohesive, trapped in Chicago's stark Cabrini-Green housing project while struggling to find the good life in a world of disadvantage and racial bias.

Still, no Lear-Yorkin program delivered its political messages with more punch than *All in the Family.* Anticipating viewer antipathy to the controversial humor of the series, CBS began the first several episodes with an announcement, written and spoken, cautioning that *All in the Family* was being offered as humorous entertainment intended to vent some of the prejudices and misconceptions in contemporary society: "The program you are about to see is *All in the Family.* It seeks to throw a humorous spotlight on our frailties, prejudices, and concerns. By making them a source of laughter, we hope to show—in a mature fashion —just how absurd they are." [10]

The show soon hit its mark. Although there were critics who panned it as "wretched" and "a minstrel show," those on target included Cleveland Amory in *TV Guide,* who called it "The best show on commercial television;" [11] and *Variety,* which hailed it as "the best TV comedy since the original *The Honeymooners.* It's the best casting since Sgt. Bilko's squad. It should be the biggest hit since *Laugh-In,* or the Nielsen sample is in need of severe revision." [12] Within a year *All in the Family* was the top-rated program on television.

Through seven and a half TV seasons and 206 episodes, *All in the Family* confronted every pressing social and political matter of the decade. From anti-Semitism, homosexuality, patriotism, and Vietnam to racism, rape, gun control, and presidential politics, it used laughter to explore the implications of contemporary problems. This was not roundtable discussion, but given the unwillingness of the networks to offer public-affairs programs in prime time, it was perhaps the best that commercial television could have produced—and that the American audience would have accepted.

Those responsible for the program have claimed that *All in the Family* was an innocent attempt to deflate the rancor and intensity existing in public debate by the 1970s. But it cannot be denied that the series was a liberal vehicle that associated narrow-minded Archie Bunker with the reactionary/conservative side of public issues. If anything, *All in the Family* contributed to national debate. Minority groups protested its racial satire as too subtle for mass entertainment. Those with a solemn commitment to particular issues invariably found the show irreverent or insensitive. In 1972 and 1976 unsanctioned "Archie Bunker for President" campaigns reflected many who found in Archie an articulation of their political sense.

All in the Family, like most Lear-Yorkin comedies, was paradoxical. At a time when social relevancy was dead in drama, it led the Nielsens for five consecutive seasons, the only series with such distinction in TV history. It also was a program with great meaning for the 1970s, but it was crafted each week by writers, directors, and producers who had developed their skills in the 1950s working for the live comedy programs of Sid Caesar, George Gobel, Jack Benny, Red Skelton, Garry Moore, Danny Thomas, and others. Some even had credits dating to the 1940s and radio gagsters, such as Eddie Cantor, Fred Allen, and Jimmy Durante. To Norman Lear, the answer was simple: his programs were adult television offered within an industry too long used to innocuous entertainment. Maude's decision to have an abortion; venereal disease discussed on *Good Times;* Mike Stivic's sexual impotency on *All in the Family:* in Lear's view these were adult themes "for which the American people have always been ready. We in television simply weren't trusting the people . . . to accept or reject as they saw fit." [13]

The paradox of *All in the Family* and similarly structured comedies was the acceptability of a liberal moral tone in an era of burgeoning social and political conservatism. From Nixon to Gerald Ford to Jimmy Carter to Ronald Reagan, Americans preferred conservative leadership to the reformist agenda of the previous decade. Whatever its motivation—racial reaction to the civil rights movement, the failed U.S. effort in Vietnam, economic dislocation, a perception of national moral disintegration—this was a decade of defeat for progressives. Instead, the decade was marked by the rise to national influence of fundamentalist Protestantism; rejection of the feminist movement; demands for tougher law enforcement; the sanctification of "family values" as guideposts for social and moral living; intensified anticommunism; and after a short-lived era of détente early in the decade, a rekindling of Cold War rivalry. In this atmosphere, the staggering success of the Lear and Yorkin shows suggests that liberal social messages remained acceptable, but only if they were in well-written programs that allowed viewers to judge for themselves on matters of social and political import.

program trends and accomplishments

Whatever the political stripe of the program, the bottom line in television remained profitability. If anything, the networks had proven their ability to thrive no matter what the political atmosphere. Even when government seemed to be restricting their enormous power, the networks could prosper. Despite blows against the network monopoly that were the Prime-Time-Access Rule, the Financial Interest and Syndication Rules, limitations on network production, and the loss of tobacco revenues, as long as the foundations of the monopoly—the scarcity of channels and the financial strength of multistation national organization—remained unscathed, actions such as these would create only superficial and momentary adversity.

Indeed, by the late 1970s the national programmers were more profitable than ever. Whereas the networks in 1960 had programmed a total of 434 half-hour segments weekly and almost 493.5 half hours in late 1971, their grip on the broadcast day increased despite rollbacks required by the Prime-Time-Access Rule. By 1976 they offered 540 weekly half hours that were cleared by almost all their affiliates.[14]

Further, throughout the 1970s an average of 57 percent of all receivers in the United States were tuned daily to the prime-time offerings of the three networks. This was essentially the same rate of usage enjoyed by national video since 1959. Even as a new decade approached, the networks remained popular, for 91 percent of those watching prime-time TV during the seasons 1978–80 were viewing either ABC, CBS, or NBC.[15]

In monetary accomplishments, the networks were equally impressive. As economist Barry Russell Litman has shown, the three national programmers accounted for 46 percent of all television time sales in the period 1970–76. There may have been as many as 710 commercial stations operating during the decade, but the networks—together with the owned and operated outlets —accounted for 40 percent of the total income of the industry.

That was a prodigious income. In 1976 the networks earned $295.6 million on their combined depreciated stock of tangible capital equipment, a rate of return of more than 221 percent. In that year their fifteen owned and operated stations also generated profits: $159 million on a rate base of $41.9 million, a return of more than 379 percent. Combining these figures, the rate of return on investment for the networks in 1976 was 258.8 percent.[16]

American TV by the 1970s was a smoothly running operation. Rivalries among networks continued, sometimes fiercely. But given the similarity of their offerings, the crucial ratings edge usually went to the best scheduler. Each network tried to create attractive programming flows for prime time. Among the possibilities, a network might opt for a run of four half-hour sitcoms capped by a one-hour drama, or a night of crime and adventure shows, or one with programs oriented more toward women than men. If the evening began with a popular program or two—*60 Minutes* on CBS on Sundays, or *Happy Days* and *Laverne and Shirley* on ABC on Tuesdays—audiences tended to stick with the fortunate network and bring decent ratings to the programs that followed.

The networks also counterprogrammed, slating blockbuster films, series, or totally different genres of entertainment intentionally scheduled to disrupt the prime-time flow of a rival. In the fall of 1978, for example, NBC offered the police series *CHiPs* at 8:00 P.M. opposite two half-hour comedies on both CBS and ABC; and opposite *Monday Night Football* on ABC, CBS usually ran programs with known appeal to women viewers, such as *Lou Grant*, *M*A*S*H*, *Maude*, and *One Day at a Time*.

As for the content of those series, by the 1970s national TV was heavily influenced by two philosophies: the practices of least objectionable program (LOP), and segmented audience scheduling. LOP was the procedure by which a network sought viewers by airing shows less likely to offend viewers than those appearing simultaneously on the rival networks. As NBC program chief Paul Klein explained it, this was best accomplished by avoiding the "tricks" guaranteed to alienate the mass audience. "Thought, that's tune-out, education, tune-out. Melodrama's good, you know, a little tear here and there, a little morality tale, that's good. Positive. That's least objectionable."[17]

A supplement to LOP was segmented audience scheduling. Brought to TV and perfected by ABC, this scheme borrowed greatly from theatrical exhibition techniques as well as target marketing strategies of TV advertising. The idea here was to forget large, undifferentiated audiences in favor of reaching large demographic groups whose needs and income predisposed them toward a spectrum of particular products. For advertising agencies, target marketing meant targeting commercials at specific audiences—commercials for luxury automobiles on news and finance programs; spots for household cleaners and baby-care products on daytime TV; ads for African-American beauty products, or ads simply starring black actors, on shows known to be popular with black viewers.

As programming philosophy, it meant courting specific audiences with shows crafted to their tastes. In the 1970s, ABC skewed much of its programming toward young people. The result was a flood of youthful situation comedies produced by Garry Marshall—series such as *Happy Days, Laverne and Shirley, Mork and Mindy,* and *Angie*—through which ABC rode the demographics of the baby boom to the leadership of prime-time TV. To offset that success, NBC sought to appeal to the older end of the ABC audience, siphoning off some of the young viewers with more sophisticated shows while appealing to adult viewers who had no interest in the ABC schedule. Although series in the fall of 1978 such as *Dick Clark's Live Wednesday* and *Project UFO* did not dent the ABC appeal, Paul Klein defended the NBC calculus as an attempt "to skim the top off the audience scale":

Now, we're not going to succeed even one-third of the time. But if we do 20 or 30 percent of the time, we will have one fantastic year, and we will do a job on ABC, enough to lower their rating points, and pick up the most salable part of their audience. That's what I'm looking to do, targeting the programs to do that, and it's not easy.[18]

Clearly the battle in network TV was internecine, a war of any one network against its two rivals. With general viewership remaining at more than 90 percent, as it had for two decades, fluctuations in audience loyalties were discernible only in the relative ratings of ABC, CBS, and NBC.

Changes in network popularity during the 1970s generally followed the career moves of one executive, Fred Silverman. As CBS vice president for programming in the early 1970s, Silverman followed his hunches and maintained that network in first place for five consecutive seasons. Then, as president of ABC entertainment, he led that network in 1976–77 to the leadership of national TV for the first time. With shows such as *Charlie's Angels, The Love Boat, Soap,* and the Garry Marshall sitcoms, ABC retained the lead for three seasons—even after Silverman left in early 1978 to accept the presidency of NBC. Here, however, he ran out of luck when his celebrated "golden gut" failed to divine a winning lineup. With financial and ratings disasters such as *Supertrain* in 1979, NBC soon trailed ABC and CBS by a considerable distance. So misdirected was NBC leadership that during Silverman's first two seasons he failed to land an NBC series in the top thirteen. The highest-rated NBC program in 1981–82 was *Real People,* and it finished twenty-first. In fact, in the five TV seasons between 1978 and 1983, no NBC series ever finished higher than tenth—and that happened only twice.

But these were the machinations of network rivalry, and coming in last among the three networks just meant less profits. No one really lost; everyone made millions in network broadcasting. National television was a rationalized business where standardization made everything more or less the same. The same producers supplied the three networks, the same themes were found in their programs, the same attitudes and procedures shaped their corporate leadership. As Laurence Bergreen has pointed out, "Only in an era when all networks shared the same values could Silverman become the first individual to program in turn for CBS, ABC, and NBC." [19]

No matter the outlet, the success of national programming had always been network ability to discern and exploit, and even precipitate, movements in audience tastes. Whatever their source—changes in the sociopolitical-economic realities of the citizenry, the dynamics of faddist U.S. popular culture, mass marketing breakthroughs, or the attraction of glamour and personality—TV could capitalize on social concerns and make profitable entertainment.

The concern about rising crime rates and a general perception of lawlessness drove national television toward crime series in the 1970s. Police, private eyes, lawyers, and vigilantes who solve crimes returned to prime time with vengeance on their minds. From plodding police procedure on *The Streets of San Francisco* to sexy investigation by private eyes on *Charlie's Angels,* TV went to war against crime—amid tropical beauty on *Hawaii Five-O,* with liberated femininity on *Police Woman,* via former hippies on *The Mod Squad,* and with militaristic police efficiency on *S.W.A.T.*

The respect for tradition inherent in the crime series appeared also in a return to the nuclear family. Often with a nostalgia for things forever lost, *Family* and *Eight Is Enough* focused on contemporary home life, and the megahits of the decade—*Little House on the Prairie, The Waltons, Happy Days,* and the two *Roots* miniseries—filled entertainment with lessons in familial love, respect, and cooperation.

If program content relied heavily on nostalgia and traditional themes, the greatest newness in TV appeared in program structure. The made-for-TV movie and the miniseries came of age in the 1970s. Born of the need for fresh feature films for TV and the desire of the networks to gain a profitable foothold in the motion-picture business, the telefeature first appeared in the mid-1960s. Only sixty such productions, however, were broadcast in that decade. The miniseries did not premiere until 1973.

The principal chronicler of these forms, Alvin H. Marill, has argued that during the 1970s—when the networks offered 1,010 different made-for-television movies and 35 miniseries—the tele-feature was a quality product. According to Marill, "within its restricted time limits and on a quarter of the budget [it became] the equal of what is done for the big screen. On the high end, quality that represents television at its best; at the low end, bread-and-butter fare generally several notches above standard series episodes as contemporary counterparts of the fondly recalled the-atrical 'B' movie."[20]

Whether or not "B" movies should be recalled with fondness remains a matter of opinion, but made-for-TV films in the 1970s certainly ranged from "high end" horror in *The Night Stalker* (January 11, 1972) and historical drama in *Eleanor and Franklin: The White House Years* (March 13, 1977) to "low end" triviality in *How to Pick Up Girls!* (November 3, 1978). Occasionally the form at-tracted major actors, writers, and directors; more often, produc-tion budgets and time requirements mitigated against the quality of the finished products.

The miniseries format may have been anticipated by Walt Disney's three-part *Davy Crockett* series in the mid-1950s and the protracted serial drama *Peyton Place* in the 1960s, but it was not a production reality until the mid-1970s. It was a risky format, committing a network to multiple evenings that could be a ratings disaster if the series did not appeal to viewers. A popular mini-series, however, could generate compelling TV drama and sizable ratings maintained over several days. Among the most successful series of the decade were *Rich Man, Poor Man* (1976), *Holocaust* (1977), *Centennial* (1978), *Pearl* (1978), and *Backstairs at the White House* (1979).

No miniseries were more striking, however, than the two *Roots* productions on ABC: *Roots* (January 23–30, 1977) and its sequel *Roots: The Next Generations* (February 18–23, 1979). The story concerned an African-American family that started with a young Gambian husband and father, Kunta Kinte, who was cap-tured and then shipped to Colonial America to become a slave. It culminated in the emotional return of author Alex Haley to the West African village from which his progenitor had been kid-napped more than two centuries earlier. The process took two miniseries totaling twenty-six hours distributed over eight nights in 1977 and six nights in 1979.

Before it ended, 140 million Americans saw at least part of *Roots I* and 110 million watched at least a portion of *Roots II*. And the reward for innovation was impressive: the second series averaged a 30.2 rating/45 share; the original averaged a 44.9 rating/66 share, still the highest-rated miniseries in TV history. The first series' final episode, moreover, with a 53.3 rating/76 share, remains the third-highest-rated program in the 1960–89 period, and six of its eight installments were ranked among the top thirty telecasts of the period. *Roots* also won eight of the thirty-seven Emmy awards for which it was nominated.

But the two *Roots* productions, like all network miniseries and made-for-TV films, resulted from business calculations, financial gambles that these commodities would attract advertisers because they would attract viewers. The networks even promised their advertisers a minimum audience size; if that viewership failed to materialize, they were committed to make good by providing those advertisers with free commercial time at a later date.

Operating at such a level, there was little room for public service or loss leaders. This was evident in children's programming. Children's TV realized its most influential achievement with the debut in late 1969 of *Sesame Street*. A creation of the Children's Television Workshop, *Sesame Street* was a concerted, daily attempt to entertain and instruct preschool youngsters. But it was on public television. There had been significant educational programs on network TV, among them *Ding Dong School* on NBC in the 1950s and *Captain Kangaroo* on CBS for three decades. But *Sesame Street* employed sophisticated video techniques and efficient editing to deliver its lessons with the visual intensity of a powerful TV commercial.

The acclaim and popularity of *Sesame Street* helped nudge ABC, CBS, and NBC toward upgrading their children's fare. The networks were also pushed by developments within the industry. From the FCC, the surgeon general, Congress, and many public-interest organizations the networks confronted a steady barrage of criticism concerning their children's programming that, for the most part, was now relegated to Saturday mornings. Many assailed the excessive violence in network "kidvid"; others pointed to the lack of minorities and the stereotypical depiction of women. Another point of contention was exploitive commercialism in Saturday morning network programming.

The most impressive strategy to address such criticism occurred at CBS, where *Fat Albert and the Cosby Kids* became the

pattern after which the network redesigned Saturday programming. Debuting in the fall of 1972, *Fat Albert* was the product of
TV star Bill Cosby. It was based on his childhood memories of
growing up in Philadelphia, and with Cosby in front of and behind
the camera, it became a vehicle for educational ideas refined
while Cosby was earning a doctoral degree in education at the
University of Massachusetts.

By 1974 the Cosby formula of blending entertainment with
themes of social responsibility and ethics became CBS philosophy. In a closed-circuit message to network affiliates, CBS-TV's
president, Robert Wood—a champion of topical programming—
explained that beginning in the fall his children's shows would be
more socially responsible than ever. *Valley of the Dinosaurs*, he
noted, would place a modern family in prehistoric times, thereby
dealing with recognizable people having to live harmoniously with
totally different human beings. *Shazam* would have Captain Marvel helping to resolve youthful problems such as going along with
the crowd; suffering the consequences for wrongdoing; respecting
others; and making value decisions affecting peers, parents, and
the community. Wood explained that other series that fall—*The
Hudson Brothers Razzle Dazzle Comedy Show*, *The U.S. of Archie*,
and *The Harlem Globetrotters Popcorn Machine*—also would act
responsibly, emphasizing themes of brotherhood, environmental
concern, sportsmanship, and the like.[21]

It was a noble gesture. But poor ratings, the resignation of
Wood in early 1976, and the importance of Saturday mornings as
a network profit center destroyed the effort. According to Sonny
Fox, who in 1977 brought similar shows to NBC as its vice president for children's programming, the educational purposes of
such diversion eroded considerably after the mid-1970s. "Today's
programming shows a total abdication of responsibility and I
know why," he stated. "It's strictly a matter of dollars and cents.
And unless the networks or the stations believe that they have
government pressure, or they'll lose their licenses, it isn't going
to improve."[22]

dynamics of video competition

With the emphasis on profitability at all levels of broadcasting, commercial TV in the 1970s drifted farther from the idealized
potential many of its pioneers had recognized. Television was a
national informant, but it was far too shallow and ephemeral in
its coverage of the news. But when the networks proposed an
extension of their evening newscasts to one hour, the affiliates

balked. They argued that it would cost them money if the networks preempted an extra half hour of local evening programming.

When the FCC in 1972 instituted the PTAR, it had hoped that local stations would produce community-oriented programs to fill part of the void. Most broadcasters, however, saw the extra time as thirty more minutes to make money with high-power, attractive strips. Instead of investing in productions that were local and original, they turned five nights a week to syndicated game shows, gossip, and audience-participation programs; or they extended lucrative local newscasts that were already too long, too repetitive, and too superficial. But whatever the format, they organized the extra thirty minutes optimally to accommodate clients seeking advertising airtime.

Given the realities of the business and of the nation, it was quixotic to anticipate anything less than such developments. Yet those wanting an improvement in the quality of TV programming continued to urge reform. And when the FCC, Congress, CBS, and the National Association of Broadcasters collaborated in the spring of 1975 to create the family viewing hour, idealism seemed triumphant. The ruling establishing the family viewing hour required that from 7:00 P.M. to 9:00 P.M. EST (6:00 P.M. to 8:00 P.M. in the Central time zone) stations telecast only shows that were appropriate for viewing by a general family audience. The move was taken in reaction to mounting governmental and citizen complaints about sex and violence on early-evening television.

Support for the decision was less than unanimous. Vested interests within the business quickly challenged the rule in court. To the operators of independent stations it was an infringement of a newly found profit center: non-network stations were attracting large audiences and new revenues airing *The Untouchables, The Mod Squad,* and other sex-and-violence series opposite the game shows and talk programs now filling the access half hours of many local affiliates.

For the politically liberal community in Hollywood—producers/writers/directors such as Norman Lear, Larry Gelbart, and Danny Arnold; actors such as Carroll O'Connor, Alan Alda, and Mary Tyler Moore; as well as industry labor unions such as the Screen Actors' Guild, the Writers' Guild, and the Directors' Guild —establishment of the family viewing hour was tantamount to government censorship. They considered it to be an infringement of civil liberties. As writer David Rintels explained it, "A policy directed against sex and violence has in practice turned out to be something very different, a crusade against ideas."[23]

In November 1976 a federal court overturned the family

viewing hour as a violation of free speech. Although the court would allow the networks to adopt the family viewing hour voluntarily and without FCC threats or NAB coordination, the offer was never seriously considered. Victorious in the courts, Rintels was uncertain about the consequences. "Does our victory in the family [viewing] hour case open the floodgates to vulgarity and violence?" he wondered in a speech shortly after the court decision. "I pray it does not. I don't think it will. But there are only three people in the world who can answer that question, and they are the men who run the networks." But Rintels held out hope:

> If they, or any one of them, succumb to the need to hype their ratings, to make more money, we could again be swallowed up by the gratuitous excesses. If they think that now, because of victory in the lawsuit, they are immune from government constraint and can be reckless with matters affecting taste and sensibility, it would be a disaster for all of us. If they choose not to see that you and we are all deeply, personally committed to seeing better, freer, more responsible television, then it could be that we have won our lawsuit and lost our last, best chance for better television. But I can't believe that any of that will happen.[24]

There was no sudden rush to sex and violence in network TV. But, certainly, ABC, CBS, and NBC retained that right, which they exercised occasionally in specials and theatrical movies such as *Death Wish, Ritual of Evil, Murder Once Removed,* and *Operation: Cobra,* which began during the first hour of prime time. The transition period was slow but inexorable. By the early 1980s it was complete. In the fall of 1983 network series beginning at 8:00 P.M. Eastern/7:00 P.M. Central included *Knight Rider; The A-Team; The Dukes of Hazzard; Magnum, P.I.; Scarecrow and Mrs. King; T. J. Hooker; Hardcastle and McCormick;* and *The Fall Guy.*

The reemphasis on sex and violence was not so much the result of network crassness as it was predetermined by the program limitations the networks placed on themselves. Sex and violence may have been criticized, but they were chronic winners. And by the late 1970s there was little attempt to program anything except those genres and forms that survived the decades.

The narrow, repetitive nature of such entertainment was not coincidental; it was a function of the organization and dynamics of American commercial video. In the three-headed monopoly that was national television, program diversification threatened audience flow, made audience size less predictable, and destabilized advertiser expectations. There was really no need for costly experimentation or programming for smaller demographic units, since the three networks were already handsomely profitable, and financial uncertainty developed when programmers strayed too far from the expected. Invention was basically counterproductive; conventionality was the monopolistic way.

Fiscal success lay in mutual reinforcement of that limited menu popularly accepted as network TV. And the networks ensured that their narrowly ranged fare would be widely consumed because what they offered was all there was to see.

The degree to which ABC, CBS, and NBC winnowed choice is noticeable in a comparison of two TV seasons: the fall of 1953, with 155 programs on four networks; and the fall of 1979, with 70 offerings on three networks. The prime-time schedule, relatively full in the early years of the medium, was streamlined to a few entertainment genres that had been worked and reworked for more than thirty years. Gone were network shows devoted to religion, current events, science, and the general edification of viewers; absent, too, were musical features, comedy-variety productions, Westerns, quiz programs, and talent shows. As indicated in Table 9.1, whereas comedy formats occupied 21.3 percent of the 1953 schedule, they constituted 45.7 percent in 1979. When crime shows are added to the latter figure, the total demonstrates that by the end of the 1970s almost 63 percent of the network evening schedule was either comedy or crime.

The audience was not unaffected by the repetitive quality of U.S. television. After decades of loyalty and forbearance, viewer ardor for TV was in decline by the late 1970s. This was detected in the research of Robert T. Bower. Continuing the academic task begun in 1960 by the late Gary A. Steiner, Bower compared audience attitudes toward the medium in 1960, 1970, and 1980. His conclusion, that "there appears to be a definitive fading of enthusiasm, but one that stops far short of rejection," was proven by data gathered from about two thousand respondents in each of these years.

Bower found Americans sliding toward middle-ground neutrality in their assessment of television. Scoring from 0 for the least favorable attitude to 5 for the most positive attitude, respondents were asked to assess the quality of TV in seven judgmental categories: exciting–dull; important–unimportant; generally excellent–generally bad; in good taste–in bad taste; interesting–uninteresting; wonderful–terrible; for me–not for me. With a possible range of 35 for the superfan to 0 for someone who de-

TABLE 9.1

program diversity, fall 1953 vs. fall 1979[25]

PROGRAM TYPES	1953 SHOWS	%1953 SEASON	1979 SHOWS	%1979 SEASON
SITUATION COMEDY	24	15.5	26	37.1
DRAMAS	23	14.8	11	15.7
MUSIC	20	12.9	—	—
QUIZ	17	11.0	—	—
NEWS (NON-NEWSCAST)	12	7.7	3	4.3
SPORTS	12	7.7	1	1.4
CRIME	11	7.1	12	17.1
COMEDY-VARIETY	9	5.8	—	—
TALENT SHOW	6	3.9	—	—
RELIGIOUS	3	1.9	—	—
SCIENCE FICTION	3	1.9	1	1.4
TESTIMONIAL	3	1.9	—	—
WESTERN	3	1.9	—	—
SCIENCE	2	1.3	—	—
AUDIENCE PARTICIPATION	2	1.3	1	1.4
DISCUSSION (NON-NEWS)	2	1.3	—	—
U.S. MILITARY	1	0.6	—	—
TRAVELOGUE	1	0.6	—	—
VARIED	—	—	2	2.9
OTHER COMEDY	—	—	6	8.6
MOVIES	—	—	7	8.6

spised the medium—with 17.5 as the neutral middle ground—the average attitude score dropped from 24.3 in 1960 to 22.3 in 1970 and to 20.9 in 1980. More significantly, Bower discovered a decline of 40 to 50 percent in the ranks of the video superfan, the supporter who felt TV was relaxing, interesting, excellent, exciting, important, and getting better.[26]

More negative in its conclusions was a *TV Guide* poll in the spring of 1979. It indicated that 44 percent of the American people now were unhappy with what they found on their screens. Dissatisfaction was strongest among better-educated and more affluent viewers; conversely, the medium was most acceptable to young adults as well as blue-collar workers and the poorer sectors of society. But across the board, a total of 75 percent of those surveyed felt the quality of programming was getting worse (33 percent) or was unchanged (42 percent); only 22 percent felt television was improving. And when asked to grade the medium in terms of the program choices offered, 56 percent rated TV poor (16 percent) or fair (40 percent); 41 percent considered it good or excellent.

The writer for *TV Guide* understood these figures as reflecting an audience of great diversity compelled to watch a medium dedicated to homogenized programming. There was no single "audience" for TV, suggested Myles Callum, "there is only a diverse, demanding, fascinating galaxy of demographic groups and subgroups, in short, many audiences, each with its own profile, passions, and peeves."[27]

What Callum touched on went to the core of network broadcasting. How could three similarly programmed national video services ever satisfy a citizenry as varied as that of the United States? How unfair was it to the nation when the networks homogenize cultural and intellectual diversity in the name of economic profitability? How artificial, even destructive, was a TV system that turned a national asset into a monopoly whose first duty was to corporate shareholders, not to the citizenry who "owned" the airwaves and expected so much from them?

After decades of sameness, Americans were growing disenchanted with TV. Whereas once giants of American show business such as Skelton, Ball, Gleason, and Sullivan helped to realize the early video promise, the medium was dominated now by lesser lights. Whereas once most Americans devoured it nightly, television by the end of the 1970s was repetitive; recombinant; cautious; and to millions of viewers, boring. Although Nielsen figures still showed a rise in the minutes viewers spent daily with television, the *TV Guide* poll reported that 49 percent of the respondents were watching television less than they did a few years earlier.

From the beginning the secret to network success had been popular faith that commercial television was the best that could be achieved, and that in serving a people as diversified as the U.S. population, the networks were satisfying most of the people most of the time. But after thirty years of the same genres and forms it became increasingly difficult to convince viewers that television was the best it could be.

increased public debate

Despite occasionally successful series, films, and miniseries— perhaps because such productions illustrated the potential of TV as entertainer and educator—network TV generated considerable debate in the 1970s. Particularly devastating were those critics inside the industry. One of the most stinging rebukes came from Commissioner Nicholas Johnson of the FCC, who concluded in 1970 that television had been a failure. In the qualitative tradition of Newton Minow, Johnson felt enormous disappointment in comparing the potential and the reality of television in American society. "Not only has it failed to make us a better race of men, it has actually made us worse than we were before," he stated. "Not only does television not exercise its power to turn us on as individuals, it is so busy getting us to turn it on that it educates us away from life." Johnson continued:

> One of the most vicious of television's predatory habits is its stalk-ing of the poor. The affluent have nothing to lose but their money and control over their own lives and personalities. The poor are not so lucky. They must sit there, without even the depressing knowl-edge that money can't buy happiness, and be constantly told that their lack of material possessions is a badge of social ostracism in a nation that puts higher stress on monetary values than moral values. . . . That television—as it is presently run—is the enemy should be obvious to all.[28]

Johnson's was not a voice in the wilderness. Other prominent detractors were upset at the condition of television in the United States. For Fred Silverman in 1977, TV was performing poorly in its role as social leader, televising pap instead of insights into the problems of society.[29] For Leonard Grossman, the president of PBS, the controlling ethic of TV had become greed. "Greed is in charge of TV, fear is what runs TV," he proclaimed in 1978. "The struggle for corporate power dulls creativity, kills experimenta-tion, makes everyone follow the leader." Grossman also attacked the FCC, alleging that "the government is responsible for the state of TV today. . . . If TV did not do what the government really wants, the FCC would move in on it."[30]

In a three-part series in *TV Guide* in 1978, Neil Hickey fo-cused on the intense rivalry for ratings and profits among the networks, suggesting that this frantic maneuvering was a prelude to more serious convulsions. In agreement with Hickey, producer Aaron Spelling wondered, "How in the hell do we stop this net-work mania?" Norman Lear called network rivalry "the most destructive force in television today." And Frank Price, the president of Universal Television, argued that if "the heavy emphasis on ratings" and the urge "to acquire greater and greater profits" were lessened, the networks might "feel a little more free to put on something they thought was good."[31]

One of the most blistering attacks on national television came from Ted Turner, a millionaire broadcaster not without professional motives for bashing the networks. Distressed by the violent imagery on network video, Turner spoke forcefully before a subcommittee of the House of Representatives in 1981. He was unequivocal when declaring, "A large portion of our population is sick and the major culprits are the tremendous television networks and the motion picture companies that make the horrible movies and TV programs that are turning our young people into a society of lawbreakers, murderers, drug addicts, and perverts." Turner continued his assault on national television:

> They glorify violence, illicit sex, reckless driving, materialism, and just plain stupidity. Their entertainment programs make a mockery of all our institutions that have made our Nation the greatest, freest, best governed, most prosperous, and most generous the world has ever seen. For at least the last 10 years their programming has become antifamily, antireligion, antilaw, antieducation, antibusiness, and antigovernment. They have sold us down the river to fatten their pocketbooks. They were given their use of the public's airwaves with a promise and understanding that they would use our airwaves to serve the public interest. . . . they have done just the opposite.[32]

Network TV, however, was not without prominent defenders. As early as 1967, distinguished CBS journalist Eric Sevareid, reacting to a series of rebukes of the medium published in *TV Guide*, chided the critics for their snobbism and lack of common sense. Seeking to praise the medium while acknowledging its imperfection, Sevareid referred to television as a "medium for amusement, information, enlightenment, inspiration, boredom, irritation, and anxiety." He concluded with support, arguing that TV "is already imbedded in the warp and woof of America, is going to be with us permanently, often reflects the mediocre in our society, rarely the worst and sometimes the finest."[33]

ABC's president, James Duffy, was a staunch defender of network prerogatives. "We have nothing to be ashamed of . . . nothing to be defensive about . . . simply because we're a giant.

It's always been the fashion to kick giants," he told fellow broadcasters in 1970.[34] But two years later he was ready to become defensive. "The broadcast medium—radio and television—has allowed itself to become a pawn that has been pushed around too freely by powerful pressures," he declared. "Our American system of broadcasting remains, despite its critics, the most varied, balanced, representative, and responsive in the world. Let us begin to be more vigilant—and more militant—in our defense of it."[35]

NBC's president, Herbert S. Schlosser, addressed those who felt that network TV was creating instead of solving national problems. Blaming TV for social disharmony, he claimed, was a disservice because it "diverts attention from the real causes of these problems." To Schlosser, "Many studies have shown that poverty, drug addiction, and urban decay are most responsible for the nation's rising crime rate. Television did not create these conditions. On the contrary, it has been a prime instrument in focusing public attention on them with great impact." And on the question of the service delivered by TV, Schlosser was similarly supportive. According to him, the system of broadcasting that existed in the United States "reflects and fits the diversity of our democratic society."[36]

The clash of insider opinion suggested that the industry lacked not only a clear understanding of what it was doing to U.S. society but also agreement on its proper function within that society. Such divisiveness was only aggravated by the swelling condemnation of the medium from organizations and individuals outside the industry. There had always been criticism of the medium. Any institution as pervasive and influential as broadcast TV would invariably provoke contention. And as Kathryn C. Montgomery has illustrated well in her book *Target: Prime Time*, public argumentation was often constructive, sometimes prompting TV executives to adjust their product to ameliorate problems.[37]

This was the time, for instance, of "jiggle" television, where successful shows such as *Three's Company* and *Charlie's Angels* exploited braless women and sexual innuendo to rise to the top of the ratings. Such obvious breaks with the essential prudery of broadcasting offended many who felt that the networks were encouraging moral reevaluation. Politically, coverage of the last years of the Vietnam War rankled liberals and conservatives in U.S. politics, both sides feeling that TV was deleterious to their perspectives of the conflict. Minority groups, often with support from governmental committees and commissions, organized to demand more on-screen and behind-the-scene representation for

214

African-Americans, Latinos, Asian-Americans, and women. And groups concerned with the welfare of children frequently assailed network TV for its manipulation of youngsters through an over-abundance of commercials, sexual content, and gratuitous violence.

More than ever, social groups and individuals challenged what was on the networks and what they felt the networks should be programming. Since networks were not licensed entities, the most direct tactic in confronting remiss broadcasters was to petition the FCC not to renew the licenses of individual stations. In a significant case decided in 1964 and confirmed by litigation in 1966, licensees operating WLBT, an NBC and ABC affiliate in Jackson, Mississippi, had their renewal challenged by the Office of Communications of the United Church of Christ and a group of local citizens. The challengers successfully argued that the station owners had failed to serve Afro-American viewers, who composed 45 percent of the Jackson population, and therefore had not met the public-service obligations of a broadcast licensee. Before the WLBT case, only other station owners claiming electrical interference or economic injury could petition the FCC to deny renewal.

It was not an easy victory. The case began in 1964 with the FCC denying standing to the challengers. In 1966 a federal Court of Appeals ordered the commission to consider citizen protest in renewal cases; but even then the FCC renewed the license. Only in 1969, after the Court of Appeals overruled that FCC decision, was the WLBT license ceded to a new operator.

With success in Jackson, however, the doors to citizen protest before the commission were opened. As *Broadcasting* magazine understood its significance, "The case did more than establish the right of the public to participate in a station's license-renewal hearing. It did even more than encourage minority groups around the country to assert themselves in broadcast matters," the magazine noted. "It provided practical lessons in how pressure could be brought, in how the broadcast establishment could be challenged."[38]

Results came quickly. Whereas only 2 petitions to deny renewal—affecting 2 stations—were filed in 1967, there were 50 petitions affecting 150 outlets filed in 1973.[39] And in a ringing victory for civic action, the FCC in January 1975 refused to renew the licenses of eight TV stations of the Alabama Educational Television Commission. Although this was a public television operation, a chronic record of racial discrimination was sufficient to strip the broadcaster of his license.

Among the more prominent protesters, the Office of Communications of the United Church of Christ annually published statistics showing patterns of bias against racial minorities on TV. Other prominent action groups included Action for Children's Television, which lobbied the networks, the FCC, Congress, and the NAB to obtain beneficial programming for children; the Black Media Coalition, which represented black interests in programming and employment; and the Parent-Teacher Association, which published a periodic *Program Review Guide*, rating programs from "most commendable" (e.g., *Little House on the Prairie, Eight Is Enough, The Waltons, Donny and Marie*) to "least quality" (e.g., *Soap, Maude, Kojak, Three's Company*).

Another grass-roots protest group, the National Federation of Decency, established in 1977 by a Mississippi minister, Donald Wildmon, was a forerunner of the mix of conservative politics and Protestant fundamentalism so influential in the 1980s. In February 1977 Wildmon organized—in great part because TV news coverage took his local appeal to the nation—a national "Turn Off TV Week." And as late as the summer of 1989, he launched a national crusade against network programming. The focus of such Old Testament wrath was the violence and sexual permissiveness Wildmon detected on network TV.

The condemnation of television practices reached new levels of popularity in the 1970s. For TV writers Richard Levinson and William Link, such protests from grass-roots organizations exercised a salutary influence. In their view, people in broadcasting "do not have any particular purchase on the truth," and pressure groups functioned as "a necessary goad." They suggested, "Without their complaints, strident or otherwise, the television community would perhaps fall victim to its own parochial interests."[40]

But industry officials were less understanding. They often greeted organized criticism with irritation. Typically, Robert Wood of CBS warned in 1973 that television needed to be on guard against "a small, vocal, and, at times, highly organized minority" wishing to decide what would appear on TV.[41] The theme was reiterated by NBC's board chairman, Julian Goodman, who urged network affiliates the following year to be more aggressive in representing their interests. According to Goodman, "Broadcasters have a responsibility to speak out—publicly, forcefully, and persistently—on the direct and indirect attacks made on our service."[42]

By the late 1970s a widening estrangement between national television and segments of its audience had developed. The top-rated program on television in the 1979–80 season was *60 Min-*

utes, with an average rating of 28.4 percent, but that suggested that 71.6 percent of the nation did not watch the program. Where HUT (homes using television) figures in 1977 reached 62.1 percent, it meant that on a given evening 37.9 percent of the American people were not using their TV sets.

Robert Mulholland, the president of NBC, recognized the problem when he noted in 1978 that "only about 28 percent of new series last from one September to the next."[43] Similarly, writer-producer Hal Kanter raised the theme when he criticized the planners of the 1978–79 season for "the woeful lack of gut-felt, intuitive showmanship and the gamblers' instincts that established American entertainment as a major world commodity." Upset at an increasing reliance by network programmers on the methods of social science to discern audience tastes, Kanter added, "The development of scientific approaches to prejudging audience acceptance has burgeoned to the point where it has become a crutch, not a tool."[44]

More foreboding than citizen and industry criticism, however, were reform activities from the federal government. Here the most persistent complaint was against violence in programs seen by children. The interest was not new to the decade. As early as 1954 the Senate Subcommittee to Investigate Juvenile Delinquency focused on the linkage between TV and juvenile crime.

The discussion was reinvigorated during the Kennedy administration. Senator Thomas Dodd was especially upset at the mayhem popularized by shows such as *The Untouchables.* He spearheaded several years of hearings and open criticism of broadcasting for its failure to curb violence. Beginning in the late 1960s, Congressman Torbert MacDonald and Senator John O. Pastore took up the fight once more, holding new hearings and helping to form the Surgeon General's Advisory Committee on Television and Social Behavior to investigate the link between violent imagery and juvenile crime. When that committee reported its findings in 1972, it concluded that there did exist a causal relationship between TV violence and aggressiveness in children mimicking what they see on TV, and particularly in children predisposed toward violence.[45]

Importantly, the report was only the first shot fired in a decade-long attack on network violence. Augmented by findings of academic researchers such as Dr. George Gerbner of the Annenberg School of Communications at the University of Pennsylvania and Drs. Bradley S. Greenberg and Charles Atkin of Michigan State University, government critics offered statistical evidence that the networks were failing to curb violence and that children were being bombarded weekly by as many as three hundred acts of physical aggression. Although issued in a minority dissenting report in 1977, the frustration of elected officials with national TV was evident in the comments subscribed to by Representatives Barbara Mikulski, Timothy Wirth, and John Murphy:

> From time to time the networks promise that they will reduce the level of violence—usually in response to a public outcry or a congressional inquiry. But they rarely do; and when they do, they soon relapse. The industry has never been able by self-regulation to lower the violence quotient. And so we now think that the time has come to take a hard and fundamental look at the basic institutional structure of American television: to find ways of diffusing the control of the networks and to open the structure to alternative sources of programming.[46]

Such criticism from citizens, industry, and government illustrated the impossibility of establishing the harmony between broadcaster and public desired by the pioneers of television. But if decades of protest and critique could yield little diminution in the power of national programmers, structural developments were under way that threatened to do what no regulation or critic had ever accomplished: loosen the grip of monopoly television on the nation.

The challenge came from emerging new electronic technologies. They were the powerful rival over which the networks had minimal influence. While the president of the National Association of Broadcasters, Vincent T. Wasilewski, could argue in 1979 that "technological advances could prove the industry's boon rather than its bane,"[47] even by this time developments in program delivery and reception were striking directly at the heart of the structural arrangements that made network video popular.

Although the challenge began to take form in the late 1970s, its most serious ramifications would be felt in the following decade. At exactly the moment American video was realizing its greatest financial achievements and weathering its most intense and broad-based criticism, it was rapidly losing control over its future. And by the beginning of the 1990s network TV was in decline—still profitable but well beyond its prime, weakened, and unable to contain disruptive forces that had subverted the old order and were redefining national television in the United States.

TOWARD A NEW VIDEO ORDER

the 1980s

P@RT 4

the decline

# of network

Robert Sarnoff explained it well. Speaking at an NBC affiliates gathering in December 1961, he reiterated the credo of commercial broadcasting, the belief that TV in the United States was what the American people wanted it to be. "It is a mistake to assume that viewing can take place without the consent of the viewers—that a mass audience will just sit there and watch, regardless of what is on the screen," he asserted. "The ultimate decisions on what the public sees can come only from the public itself, as long as it is free to watch or not to watch as it pleases."[1]

television

Like most self-serving philosophies, Sarnoff's witness before his NBC kindred was only partially true. Certainly, the networks were providing the entertainment fare desired by a large segment of the potential audience—in many cases, a majority of the population. The comedies, action-adventures, dramatics, and feature films that filled the air night and day were popular with most viewers. Granted, TV programs were formulaic and predictable, but they were occasionally excellent, and TV served a civilization conditioned by broadcasting since the 1920s to accept quality with heavy doses of mediocrity.

But there were fatal flaws in U.S. video. At every step television served interests seeking to amalgamate Americans. Audiences were to be as large as possible, shows as popular as possible, and program content was to be as common as necessary to attract viewers. Little appealed to parochial interests. Like so much else in U.S. commerce—from automobiles to shopping malls to franchised hamburger stands—national TV offered the same products to everyone everywhere: everything worked, looked, and tasted the same. The United States may have been the most pluralistic civilization on Earth, but network monpolistic practices confined the population to sameness.

In the 1980s, however, the fragile foundation on which U.S. television had been constructed began to disintegrate. Developments that were technological, political, and economic began to undermine network hegemony and liberate the American audience. Much as radio had changed decades earlier from *broadcast*ing (programming for undifferentiated, broad audiences) to *narrow*casting (programming for specific, or narrow audiences), TV now began to deliver many more channels and greater choice.

network tv and the new technology

National television had never offered viewers what they wanted; it offered what audiences most accepted. And as network officials discerned the most popular program types they streamlined their business, canceling "unpopular" ones and extending the running time of surviving types. In the fall of 1950 there were 177 network prime-time series in a variety of formats, most running 15 or 30 minutes. By the fall of 1986 there were only 74 network evening programs, most running one hour. The pluralistic potential in the American population was forced to select from the standardized products of the mass culture industry.

As a result, there were entertainment genres that never appeared in prime time. Among the forgotten forms were foreign-language shows, literary programs, intellectual shows, uninterrupted feature films, all-news formats, racially and regionally oriented programs, sexually explicit entertainment, and business information. Also missing, except in peripheral viewing hours, was a consistent commitment to educational, children's, and fine-arts programming, to public-service shows, roundtable discussions, and documentaries. Except for *ABC Monday Night Football*, even sports programming—a proven winner with male audiences —was excluded from prime time.

As long as nothing new or uncontrollable entered U.S. television, network TV flourished according to guidelines established decades earlier. But technological innovations emergent in the 1980s mounted the greatest challenge to commercial broadcasting since the Wagner-Hatfield amendment in the 1930s. Above all, affordable and available advances in electronic machinery made it possible for viewers to find the wide range of choices never there in broadcast TV.

The videocassette recorder (VCR), widely available in the decade, made it possible to play prerecorded features that were neither interrupted by unwanted commercials nor shortened to fit the time requirements of a TV scheduler. The most popular use for the VCR, however, was in time shifting, taping off the air and watching the resultant recording when convenient for the viewer.

Growth of the VCR was phenomenal, rising from 4 percent of all TV households in 1982 to 60 percent in early 1988. By this date, too, 21 percent of all TV homes contained at least two recorders. In large cities the penetration figures were high: in Los Angeles and San Francisco, 64 percent of the homes had VCR's; for New York City and Chicago the figure was 62 percent; and in Washington, D.C., and Dallas–Fort Worth it was 60 percent.[2]

And owners used their machines. According to Nielsen figures for the first quarter of 1988, each month the average VCR household made 14.1 recordings and watched 16.9 recordings. During an average week the average household watched recordings for 296 minutes and taped for 179 minutes. Further, VCR owners also rented an average of 2.3 videocassettes per month, and 41 percent had purchased at least one prerecorded videocassette during the previous year.[3]

If the VCR turned viewers into programmers, the electronic remote control device gave Americans even greater control over what they chose to watch. The remote control unit that was standard equipment with VCR's allowed a user "to zap," or fast-forward, through intrusive advertisements. And those with similar devices for their TV sets were able "to zip" or "to graze," jumping from channel to channel to avoid commercials or to follow more than one show at a time.

Other electronic technologies were threatening network control. Videodiscs delivered inexpensive feature films with remarkable clarity. The camcorder (camera and recorder) turned the domestic TV set into a playback monitor for "home movies." Video games converted receivers into amusement centers. And those with home computers sometimes used their sets as monitors.

On a higher plane, orbiting satellites served as space stations off which to bounce a TV signal and send it from anywhere in the world to anywhere else in the world. As transmission equipment became more portable and affordable, it became possible for programmers with enough product to create their own networks. In private homes, satellite ground dishes receiving these signals brought to their owners a vast array of shows: programs from foreign countries, movies, distant domestic stations, closed-circuit network feeds, and other transmissions not intended for public viewing.

A problem in this new programming approach was how to deliver those signals to millions of consumers, few of whom owned a ground dish. The solution was through coaxial cable wired directly into the home. The result was a boom in the business of cable television.

Other alternatives to conventional network broadcasting had

appeared periodically since the early years of TV. One of the first proposals, in the 1950s, was by film studios and theater owners who wanted to wire movie theaters and then charge customers to see Milton Berle, Sid Caesar, sports and dramatic attractions, and the like. By the end of the decade the enemy was over-the-air "pay TV" in the home. Although broadcasters had beaten back these proposals, they could not eliminate cable TV totally, because it was a necessity to millions of viewers.

When it first appeared in 1949, cable (Community Antenna Television, or CATV) was intended to bring local and network transmissions to those rural or mountainous areas where over-the-air signals could not be received clearly. The technology was simple: a large antenna perched on a high local mountain pulled in the signals; coaxial cable from the antenna was fed to amplifiers; the amplified signals were then delivered to subscriber homes by more cable. Without such technology, millions of Americans would not have had TV service.

Inexorably, however, cable operators expanded their technical and fiscal horizons. With the spread of microwave transmissions—point-to-point, line-of-sight emissions at high frequencies—local cable companies could supplement their original fare by adding stations from distant locations. They even envisioned the eventual delivery of programming exclusive to cable.

By the 1960s cable was being fought by several entities in the broadcast TV industry. Fearing that cable programming would dilute their audience size, especially in the three-station markets that were the norm at the time, local station owners and the networks worked in the courts and in Washington, D.C., to arrest its spread. Syndicators, too, worked against cable. They were upset because operators were pulling station transmissions out of the air and distributing them to subscribers without paying rental fees for the programs being aired. The FCC, too, was upset about cable. The commission wanted to protect the broadcasting industry, and especially its greatest disappointment, the UHF station. The FCC feared cable would crush all hopes that UHF would someday become a real competitor to VHF and network domination of television.

After considerable litigation and political lobbying at the FCC and in Congress, the U.S. Supreme Court in 1966 upheld the authority of the FCC to regulate cable. The Court stipulated that cable operators in the top one hundred markets had to apply to the commission for the right to carry distant transmissions. Flooded soon with applications, the FCC took a familiar course of action: in 1968 it issued a freeze on the issuance of licenses, a condition that lasted until 1972.

Even with the lifting of the freeze, cable had technical problems that inhibited its growth. To expand, cable operators had hoped to attract subscribers—especially those in the big cities and suburbs where, unfortunately, there was no broadcast reception problem—by delivering original programming nationwide. But national distribution via land-based microwave relay stations was cumbersome and expensive. The answer, however, was in the stars. By bouncing signals off orbiting communications satellites, then receiving them on the ground in satellite "dishes," cable operators could offer attractive program service that would compete with the networks in drawing audiences.

The missing element in the equation, the financial support for a long-range commitment to satellite transmission, was provided by Home Box Office, a new pay-TV venture owned by Time, Inc. In September 30, 1975, HBO launched regular satellite transmission with the heavyweight boxing championship bout between Joe Frazier and Muhammad Ali. Transmitted live from the Philippines via the RCA Satcom I satellite, this was the "thrilla in Manila."

Only two Florida cable systems bought the live feed to sell to their subscribers. And competitors were slow to follow: Turner Broadcasting's WTBS went satellite in December 1976, and the Showtime pay-cable network did not link up until March 1978. But the precedent was set. By the 1980s, cable was delivering via satellite a multiplicity of program signals from origination points throughout the United States and the world. And this diversity was not limited to exurbia and rural America; cable TV was moving into the big cities and their suburbs.

Cable offered new local and regional channels plus new national networks devoted to specific interests such as news of the day, popular music, religion, financial matters, sports, Congress and national politics, travel, home shopping, and weather. With these specialties, cable could appeal more effectively to narrower interests such as those of African-Americans, children, country and western music fans, nostalgia buffs, fundamentalist Christians, Roman Catholics, and speakers of languages ranging from Spanish to Polish to Korean.

Cable systems throughout North and Central America also delivered "superstations"—WTBS from Atlanta, WGN-TV from Chicago, and WWOR-TV from New York City—as these local stations became national, even international, thanks to innovations in telecommunications technology. For several dollars beyond the price of basic cable, subscribers also could receive pay cable channels such as HBO, Showtime, Cinemax, and The Movie Channel, which presented recent Hollywood films—uninterrupted by commercials and uncensored by sensitive network officials—as well as exclusive comedy, music, and variety specials. Pay-cable networks with more specialized fare offered old movies (American Movie Classics), foreign feature films (Bravo), sexually provocative programs (The Playboy Channel), and children's shows (The Disney Channel).

Because cable TV was also pay TV, the profit potential of this new video reality quickly attracted leading U.S. communications industries. The most successful programmers—and a few of the programming services in which they held equity interest—included Time, Inc. (HBO and Cinemax), Viacom (Showtime, The Movie Channel, Nickelodeon, MTV: Music Television, and VH-1: Video Hits One), the Hearst Corporation (Arts & Entertainment), Warner Communications (Turner Broadcasting System, Movietime, Cable Value Network), and Walt Disney Productions (The Disney Channel). Opportunities in cable also nurtured the growth of powerful new corporations. These media companies—and a few of their equity holdings—included Tele-Communications, Inc. (Turner Broadcasting System, American Movie Classics, The Discovery Channel), and Cablevision (American Movie Classics, Turner Broadcasting System, Sports Channel America).

Other corporations moved into the hardware of cable, accumulating many local cable systems and creating in the process a new video entity, the multiple system operator (MSO). And in many cases programmers were also MSO's. Time, Inc., owned one of the largest MSO's in the nation, American Television and Communications Corporation (ranked second in 1989), and Viacom operated Viacom Cable (ranked twelfth). Warner Brothers became involved in cable television as an MSO through Warner Cable Communications, and as a program supplier via Warner Satellite Entertainment Company. Among the MSO's owned by newspaper-based corporations were those of Scripps-Howard, Post-Newsweek Cable, and Times Mirror Cable TV. Other cable names familiar to communications enterprises were Cox, Newhouse, RCA, and Westinghouse.

The cable threat may have been imposing, but it was only the most obvious aspect of a multifaceted technological assault on the network TV empire. In mid-1982 the J. Walter Thompson advertising agency painted a bleak picture of the future of broadcast television. According to an agency report, even more challengers to national broadcasting were about to appear as "Interactive cable is here, pay-per-view looms as the next big money-maker, cost of dishes and transponders is coming down, MDS [multidirectional signal] could develop into a multichannel delivery system, STV [satellite television] has been deregulated, and DBS [direct broadcast signal] has just been given the green light by the FCC."[4]

Of all these new technologies, pay-per-view (PPV) was potentially the most damaging to the old television order. PPV is a system under which a wired household receives special programs —a first-run film, a championship sports attraction, a special dramatic or musical performance—by paying an extra fee to the cable company. As an addition to the distribution continuum of American commercial culture, it constituted one more level of exploitative exposure. Now a Hollywood motion picture could follow a lengthy and lucrative route: from first-run theatrical release, to PPV, to home video sales and rental, to pay cable, to broadcast network, to syndication and/or basic cable lease.

Quickly, PPV became a familiar part of cable service, reaching about one-fifth of all wired households by 1989. By this date, too, cable subscribers no longer had to schedule PPV purchases days in advance: through improved telephone technology it was now possible for last-second impulse buyers to phone for automatic connection and billing.

More than any other technical innovation, PPV has the potential to revolutionize video and the popular culture industries in the United States and the world. The billions of dollars realizable by appealing to those willing and able to purchase television creates possibilities still unforeseen for the construction of commercial audiovisual products.

Robert Wright, the president of NBC, well understood the direction in which TV was going. In mid-1989 he told a group of business journalists that the future of all television is pay. As he contemplated the billions already being generated by forty thousand home video stores and twenty-three major nationally distributed or internationally distributed cable networks, as well as PPV, Wright concluded, "We're going from a period in the late seventies where there was an insignificant amount of total dollars, contributing to or driven by television, to the so-called Golden Age of television in terms of actual cash paid by consumers." The days of "free TV" are limited, he suggested. "You just can't make it" with advertiser support alone in the new communications order. Wright felt confident that audiences would pay for TV, and revenue raised this way would finance even better programs and technical services.[5]

But French political scientist and telecommunications authority Jacques W. Oppenheim has raised profound social and moral questions about pay TV in general and PPV in particular. In his recent book *Code: télévision à la carte,* he indicated that the nature of video entertainment was already being altered by pay TV. Instead of remaining a mass medium serving an audience of equals, he recognized this new *à la carte* television as a parasitic development, basically unnecessary, but flourishing halfway between films and classic video. Success in this context, according to Oppenheim, turned television into an elitist instrument; a pay-TV subscription became a symbol of higher social standing, an emblem of class. "Through the scrambled images and the subscription, there is a secret aspiration toward 'cultivated' culture," he wrote of pay TV. "The decoder permits consumption 'with discretion,' day and night, a cineaste culture of exclusive and specific programs that the masses of televiewers cannot receive free of charge. Such is the contractual substance of the business of pay television. In this it meshes perfectly with the cult of difference and distinction that holds together the society of consumption."[6]

Statistics illustrate that the onrush of new electronic technologies in the 1980s was dramatic and sudden. Whereas in 1964 only 8 percent of television households in the United States could receive nine or more channels, that figure reached 71 percent by the fall of 1987. Figures for cable penetration—the number of households subscribing to basic cable service—were likewise impressive, rising from 17.1 percent in early 1978 to 57.1 percent in late 1989, and projected by the cable industry to reach 70 percent by the early 1990s, when the largest American cities are to become more accessible to cable operators.[7]

Another indication of the changing environment was a dramatic downward trend in network viewing. Although network prime time averaged a 56.5 rating/90 share during the 1979–80 season, the figure fell precipitously, to 48.5/77 for 1984–85 and to 41.5/67 for 1988–89—a ratings drop-off of 26.5 percent and a share loss of 25.5 percent in less than a decade.[8] Although summer ratings are always lower than statistics from the previous season, in the last half of July 1989 the networks reached an all-time low of 55 percent share of the total TV audience. As an executive with Grey Advertising explained the figures, comparing network programming with the original programming on independent stations, cable, and the small Fox network, "All the networks do during the summer is air busted pilots. The American public is not stupid. Network thinking is, Why should I do original programming when the HUT [homes using television] levels are down? It's about the same kind of thinking Detroit used to have competing against the Japanese in the automobile market."[9]

Broadcast TV in the 1980s found it difficult to compete with pay television. After years of accepting variations on the same fundamental themes, viewers seemed ready to abandon the networks for the variety of choices now available. And cancellation rates for prime-time series suggest that officials at ABC, CBS, and NBC were unable to find series attractive enough to assure audience loyalty. Where the three networks together scheduled approximately one hundred series per calendar year, cancellation figures since the early 1980s reveal clearly that the networks were not pleasing viewers: [10]

TABLE 10.1

network program cancellations, 1982–89

Year	Programs Canceled
1982	40
1983	56
1984	50
1985	46
1986	48
1987	47
1988	47
1989	44

A Roper poll in 1989 demonstrated that network attrition was attributable, in great part, to viewer preference for cable programming. While respondents continued to express their preference for network news, by a spread of 47 percent to 26 percent they felt cable delivered "better entertainment programs." In other areas, too, cable performed better than "regular TV." Cable TV was considered "more educational" (47 to 28 percent); it provided better cultural shows (51 to 21 percent) and sports (61 to 17 percent); it offered better children's fare (39 to 31 percent); and it generally offered better program quality (37 to 32 percent). Cable also outperformed broadcast television in breaking taboos —offering more sex (71 to 6 percent), more violence (58 to 11 percent), and more profanity (69 to 7 percent).[11]

As well as rivalry generated by new electronic mechanisms, network television in the 1980s encountered substantial competition from two over-the-air competitors: local independent stations and the new Fox Broadcasting Company. If national programmers suffered disastrous seasons with scores of short-lived series such as *I Married Dora, Leg Work,* and *Peaceable Kingdom,* independent stations could fill their prime-time hours with proven hit shows. To counter weak network offerings, the syndication market provided the independents with reruns of the greatest series in broadcast TV—from *The Honeymooners* and *The Andy Griffith Show* to *All in the Family* and *The Cosby Show.*

Long-time anemic players in the broadcast industry, independent stations were revitalized also because production studios—themselves invigorated by the Financial Interest and Syndication Rules and the Prime-Time-Access Rule—found it profitable again to produce for first-run syndication. Such syndicated successes as *Wheel of Fortune, Donahue, The Oprah Winfrey Show, The People's Court,* and *Star Trek: The Next Generation* provided stiff competition for failing network stations—and even for cable outlets.

The result was a further decline for traditional broadcasting operations. In 1983 ABC, CBS, and NBC held 80 percent of the prime-time audience and 71 percent of the 24-hour viewing day; independent stations averaged only 14 percent of prime time and 20 percent of the complete TV day. But by late 1988 the slippage was stunning: the spread between the three networks and independents was now 68 percent to 20 percent in prime time and 60 percent to 23 percent over a full day.[12]

The inauguration of the Fox television network in April 1987 created something absent since the collapse of DuMont in 1955—a fourth broadcast network with a national presence. Although the challenge from Fox was not as decisive as that from the independent stations, even during its formative first years Fox programming detracted from the ratings generated by ABC, CBS, and NBC. During the first nine weeks of the 1989–90 season, for example, the average ratings for programs on the major networks (NBC at 15.2, ABC at 13.5, and CBS at 12.5) were clearly held down by the 6.6 rating averaged by Fox programs.

The new network was hindered, however, by formidable problems. Billions of dollars in debts were incurred by Rupert Murdoch in creating Fox from purchases of the small Metromedia television network and the 20th Century-Fox Film Corporation. Moreover, with a paucity of available VHF channels the new network had to build its national presence through affiliate contracts with less popular UHF stations. Because Fox Broadcasting, even by the end of 1989, continued to lack affiliates in all TV markets, less than 90 percent of the American audience had access to its offerings. Although weekly ratings figures usually showed Fox series at the bottom of the charts, it is significant that

after nine weeks of the 1989–90 season several of its programs—
Married . . . With Children (ranked fifty-fourth out of ninety-four
prime-time programs), *America's Most Wanted* (ranked sixty-fifth),
and *Totally Hidden Videos* (ranked seventy-fifth)—drew greater
ratings than many shows on the three major networks.

politics and national tv

In search of an explanation, some in broadcasting blamed the
decline on new measurement techniques and equipment, specifically the electronically advanced "People Meter," introduced by
the A. C. Nielsen Company in 1987 to replace its thirty-year-old
diary system. Others maintained that viewers were simply bored
because the same production companies had been producing the
bulk of prime-time entertainment for too many years. Another
explanation held that the networks did not provide enough exposure to their new series, that if a show did not deliver with a few
telecasts it was rudely bumped to another time slot or canceled
outright. The true culprit, however, was the changing reality of
U.S. telecommunications in the 1980s.

But this change was more than alternative distribution and
program services or millions of VCR's in private hands. Industry
upheaval was precipitated, too, by the politics of the decade. The
presidential victories of Ronald Reagan in 1980 and 1984 were
exhilarating experiences for the American political right. The
popular president espoused conservative values, and he soon took
steps to realize his ideological agenda.

In broadcasting this was evident in the movement toward
deregulation championed by Mark Fowler and Dennis Patrick,
the young and philosophical FCC chairmen appointed by Reagan. Like the president and conservatives in general, Fowler and
Patrick rejected the classical liberal belief that broadcasters, as
lessees of the public airwaves, had a special responsibility to serve
that public. Fowler enunciated his ideas in 1984 before an audience of radio and TV executives: "It was time to move away from
thinking about broadcasters as trustees," he declared. "It was
time to treat them the way almost everyone else in society does
—that is, as businesses." As he understood it, "Television is just
another appliance. It's a toaster with pictures." [13]

Broadcast deregulation was born of the laissez-faire principles
that guided conservative economic thought. Here was the classic
faith that good men will do good if unfettered by government:
specifically, less government involvement in business matters

would lead to enhanced competition, creating inevitably better service and increased profitability. Indeed, from this point of view TV was no more than a business. Fowler summarized his controversial philosophy in *Television Quarterly* in 1982:

> *One principle now guides the commission's efforts. It is the policy of "unregulation," and simply it means that we examine every regulation on the books and ask, "Is it really necessary?" If, in our judgment, it has outlived its usefulness, we must make every effort to get rid of it. This approach is in harmony with the concept that government should eliminate unnecessary regulation of business and society. Our ultimate aim in broadcast regulation is to operate as a traffic cop, not as Justice Frankfurter suggested, as a determiner of the traffic. We are calling on broadcasters to solve their own problems, and meet their needs, even insofar as engineering coordination is concerned, rather than devote commission resources to those tasks. . . . The end result should be a commercial broadcasting system where the marketplace rather than the myths of a trusteeship approach determines what programming the American people receive on radio and television and who provides it.*[14]

Deregulation unleashed the networks from many federal restrictions, freeing broadcasters to conduct their affairs as never before. The networks were given increased leverage within the industry when limitations on ownership of TV stations were increased from the ceiling of seven established in the late 1970s to as many as twelve (as long as their stations directly served no more than 25 percent of the national population)—plus interest in two more if these were controlled by minorities or women.

Instead of every three years, stations were now asked to renew their licenses every five years. Requirements that some broadcast time be devoted to community issues and reported annually to the FCC were dropped in favor of a vague provision urging broadcasters to address local matters. Freed from length-of-ownership restraints, investors could now buy and sell TV stations as if they were simple commodities.

One of the most disputed actions of the commission in the Reagan years involved revocation of the fairness doctrine. As an interpretative outgrowth of Section 315 of the Communications Act of 1934, the doctrine since 1949 was a commission policy requiring that broadcasters balance their presentations of controversial issues with reasonable opportunity for representation from all sides. But in the theoretical framework of deregulation, this proviso constituted government intrusion into the business affairs of station owners. When the doctrine was revoked late in Reagan's second administration, Democrats in Congress sought to resurrect the policy by making it a formal law. But the president vetoed the measure to which Congress had attached its fairness doctrine law as a rider. Early in his tenure, moreover, President George Bush pledged to follow Reagan's precedent should Congress attempt to pass a similar bill.

Deregulation reflected network weakness more than broadcast strength. The ability to own more stations did not ensure increased corporate power; it meant only that the networks could struggle to maintain their dominance and profitability in the face of formidable new competition. No longer the embodiment of American television, network TV now became just another free-market business—albeit strategically situated within the industry —and regulated only by the ethics of capitalistic enterprise.

If political conservatism affected the control of broadcasting, it influenced as well the content of television. In many regards this meant renewal of the ideological criticism so prevalent during the Nixon presidency. The centrist point of view traditional to broadcasting came under fire in the Reagan presidency. It was not that the networks had been uncooperative with government in the past. They all had been anti-Communist, patriotic, and supportive of and friendly with official Washington since the Truman presidency.

The networks had their loyalty oaths in the 1950s, and various executives and on-air performers cooperated with the Pentagon and other federal agencies. But these were basically consensus activities, harmonious with the philosophical direction of national government at the time. Thus network TV seemed sympathetic to the civil rights movement, much as the federal government had been since the early 1960s. Coverage of the Vietnam War seldom doubted presidential direction, and protesters were appropriately presented on TV as radicals or misguided people out of step with carefully planned national policies.

The challenge of the Reagan presidency came from a new and passionate style of political conservatism whose adherents since the mid-1960s had found in the Republican party an increasingly hospitable constituency for their understanding of the world. Fumblingly, this New Right had made its first moves against the communications industry during the Nixon years and failed. Tested and ready for power, conservatives by the 1980s were organized and dedicated in their hope to fill the ideological void left in politics by an American liberalism torn apart by issues of the past half century.

Until the 1980s the only prominent TV spokesman for this point of view had been William F. Buckley, Jr., an erudite conservative idealist whose talk show *Firing Line* began as a syndicated feature in 1966 and came to PBS during the Nixon presidency. There had been little network effort to supplement Buckley's lone voice. When ABC news anchorman Frank Reynolds and producer Blaine Littell were questioned in 1968 about political bias in network journalism, they summarized the problem confronting the New Right in its search for national legitimacy. On an NET documentary Reynolds and Littell were forthright:

Reynolds: *Ah, sure, I suppose maybe there is an Eastern Establishment, left-wing bias. But that just happens to be because the people who are in it feel that way. On our program, I know we have people who are hardly members of that Establishment. They make appearances as guest commentators.*

Questioner *(to Littell): Would you put a conservative on as often as you'll put a liberal on?*

Littell *(smiling): If you can find them, you bet.*

Questioner: *"If you can find them." Now, what does that mean?*

Littell: *There's a problem, but—*

Questioner: *How hard do you look?*

Littell: *We look very hard. And what seems to be true is that most people who write well and are in the arts and in the business of communicating, tend to be liberal. Conservatives tend to be businessmen, and businessmen do not tend to write well.*[15]

Network political thinking was evident when ABC News began a regular commentary feature on its evening newscast in mid-1968. ABC offered a narrow spectrum indeed. Although the network assembled twenty-six thinkers from academics, arts, politics, science, fashion, sports, and international affairs, the overwhelming majority were from the moderate-to-liberal middle ground. Few of the viewpoints ever matched the network promise of "commentary that will reflect the different schools of opinion in our society."

Robert Higgins in *TV Guide* studied 150 of the pronouncements and found only ten that were "hard, abrasive ideological opinions." Of these, only one came from the left, an angry statement on civil rights from actor Ossie Davis; two came from the conservative right, including James J. Kilpatrick's insight that the Poor Peoples' March and encampment at Resurrection City was "show biz. . . . Many of the abandoned shacks were a litter of beer cans. . . . Most of the residents were loafing in their bunks, drawing welfare checks." Unapproached by ABC were articulate spokesmen for the American left such as Herbert Marcuse, Abbie Hoffman, and Paul Krassner; and on the right the network failed to invite the opinions of prominent editors such as Arthur Krock and David Lawrence as well as writers such as John Chamberlain, Ralph de Toledano, and Victor Lasky.

After only eight months, the commentary notion was abandoned by ABC News. Blaine Littell admitted that the network had been "hugging the middle," going after "the common denominator. There are many vital issues that we won't go near. We censor ourselves." But a newsman at CBS was more pointed: "Nothing scares the networks more than the full spectrum of American political thought." [16]

Even during the Nixon presidency, White House operative Patrick Buchanan expressed the frustration of the New Right. Appearing on *The Dick Cavett Show* in March 1973, he was characteristically blunt as he denounced PBS for its failure to provide a balance between liberal and conservative points of view:

> . . . *if you look at public television, you will find you've got Sander Vanocur and Robert MacNeil, the first of whom, Sander Vanocur, is a notorious Kennedy sycophant, in my judgment, and Robert MacNeil, who is anti-administration. You have Elizabeth Drew . . . she personally is definitely not pro-administration; I would say anti-administration.* Washington Week in Review *is unbalanced against us . . . you have* Black Journal, *which is unbalanced against us . . . you have Bill Moyers, which is unbalanced against the administration. And then for a fig leaf, they throw in* William F. Buckley's program.[17]

In the 1980s, however, New Right commentators became familiar as panelists on political discussion shows. In the era of Ronald Reagan several even hosted their own programs. Among these were George Will on ABC, Patrick Buchanan and Robert Novak on CNN, and John McLaughlin on PBS and CNBC. One program, *Crossfire,* on CNN, actually turned the conservative-liberal dichotomy into a verbal wrestling match as controversial guests endured the rantings of Buchanan and his liberal political opponents, Tom Braden and later Michael Kinsley. Although such theatricality did little to advance understanding or consensus, it constituted a widening of the political spectrum, at least to the right, permissible on U.S. television. Although few authentic American leftists were ever invited as guests—and certainly no anticapitalist, socialist, laborite, Communist, or radical type ever hosted his or her own series on capitalistic American TV—this was a step toward expanding public debate so long absent from broadcasting.

The conservative push into public-service video was complemented by the appearance of politicized TV religion in the 1980s. In the early days of TV, religious leaders such as Bishop Fulton J. Sheen who sought wider electronic congregations relied on airtime donated by the networks and local stations. But in the 1950s revivalist preachers such as Oral Roberts and Rex Humbard discovered they could amass large religious followings—and sizable ministry fortunes—by leasing airtime on local stations from which they spread religious messages and solicited cash donations.

Broadened video capabilities by the 1980s energized a new generation of fundamentalist ministers eager to invest in satellite technology and the divine. Through modern technology, Protestant evangelists such as Jimmy Swaggart, James Robison, Pat Robertson, and Jerry Falwell could disseminate their programs to cable systems and local outlets throughout the country and even throughout the world.

But the more ambitious among the brethren need not settle for one station or one show. Jim and Tammy Faye Bakker supplemented their anchor program *The PTL Club* with religious productions from other preachers and formed the PTL Network. From his nationally syndicated program *The Old-Time Gospel Hour,* the Reverend Jerry Falwell initiated the influential Moral Majority in 1979 as an overtly political advocacy organization.

Pat Robertson best demonstrated the power of religion and video technology. To create the Christian Broadcasting Network (now called CBN The Family Channel), he used his politicized Christian talk show, *The 700 Club,* as a keystone, then added other religious shows as well as reruns of vintage network sitcoms and Westerns, plus family-oriented series imported from Australia. Robertson used his daily TV exposure and championing of conservative politics to launch a truly temporal career in politics, running unsuccessfully but formidably in state primaries in 1988 for the Republican nomination for president of the United States.[18]

Televangelism added the moral fervor of fundamentalist Christianity to conservative secularity. The potent New Christian Right melded biblical authority and partisan politics to create a compelling mandate for supporting the Reagan presidency. Many televangelists regularly addressed current political topics. On domestic issues they spoke out strongly against abortion, the Equal Rights Amendment, sex education in schools, girlie magazines, and homosexual rights. On international matters they usually recommended vigorous interventionism to resolve problems threatening U.S. interests, especially in terms of fighting communism and terrorism.

With increased visibility on public-affairs and religious programs, political conservatives sought also to influence network entertainment. The Reverend Donald Wildmon founded the National Federation for Decency in 1978 and merged it in 1981 with the efforts of the Moral Majority to create the Coalition for Better Television. Other advocacy groups with interest in TV imagery included The Eagle Forum headed by Phyllis Schlafly, the Clean-Up TV campaign of Reverend John Hurt, and Accuracy in Media headed by Reed Irvine.

Typically these groups voiced opinions critical of network shows. Their condemnations ranged from generic complaint against violence and graphic sexuality on TV to specific anger when one of their major issues—e.g., abortion, homosexuality, the Soviet Union—was shown in a tolerant light. The political implications of such criticism were overtly demonstrated in the wake of the ABC broadcast of *The Day After*, a two-hour, made-for-TV film concerning thermonuclear war between the United States and the Soviet Union.

Even before it aired in November 1983, conservative political groups charged that the series was propaganda for pacifism and pro-Soviet policies; they threatened chary sponsors with boycotts and demanded airtime to rebut the subversive values they detected in the film. Not only did ABC arrange for right-wing spokesmen to appear on a panel discussion following the telecast, but also the network eventually commissioned a major anti-Communist miniseries as counterprogramming. Ironically, although *The Day After* appeared with few advertisers, it garnered the largest audience (46 rating/62 share) of any made-for-TV movie in history, and it was the fifteenth-highest-rated telecast in the period 1960–89.[19]

In part to allay conservative suspicions about ABC, the network commissioned and in 1987 broadcast a seven-part, 14.5-hour miniseries *Amerika,* a fictional story depicting patriotic reactions to a Soviet military occupation of the United States. Even before it was aired there was nationwide controversy. This time, liberal protest ranged from picketing the ABC offices in New York City to an article in *TV Guide* in which celebrated journalist Harrison Salisbury asked and answered an obvious question: "Could it happen here? . . . I've spent forty years reporting on Moscow from the inside and the outside, and I'm afraid this rather murky script doesn't convince me. Too many holes in the concept."[20] Unfortunately for the network and the future of overt Soviet-bashing, *Amerika* averaged mediocre ratings (19 rating/29 share); moreover, it cost $41 million to produce and returned only $22 million. With little prospect for a lucrative appearance in reruns, *Variety* accurately termed the financial result "a big loss to swallow."[21]

The influx of conservative political values into U.S. television did not represent a crushing of the centrist consensus viewpoint familiar to viewers. Still, from the selling of Chrysler automobiles by displaying the U.S. flag, to the opening of the 1984 Olympic Summer Games as a musical salute to American political freedom, the essential spirituality of political conservatism was incorporated into national TV.

Nowhere was this more obvious than in children's programming. Between 1979 and 1983 network television abandoned children's fare as average time devoted to such programming dropped from 11.3 to 4.4 hours per week. Much of the decline resulted from cancellation of after-school productions in favor of money-making shows aimed at older viewers. Independent stations, however, quickly filled the void. Primarily through syndicated adventure cartoons they soon were engaging the nation's youth with an array of lethal superheroes equipped with technologically advanced weaponry, all fighting to impose American ideological values throughout the universe.

With *Rambo and His Force of Freedom,* totalitarian evil was thwarted routinely by all-American Rambo and his fellow soldiers of fortune. Good guys thwarted oppressors and rescued helpless innocents in futuristic shows such as *He-Man and the Masters of the Universe; She-Ra, Princess of Power; Voltron; M.A.S.K.; Defenders of the Earth; Jayce and the Wheeled Warriors;* and *Thundercats.* Even that senior militaristic series *G.I. Joe* made a triumphant return, waging war against the international terrorist activities of the evil COBRA. As one critic has described this onslaught of politicized juvenile champions, the cartooned heroes waged a battle that was decidedly moral and ideological:

*In this struggle between Good and Evil, light and darkness, blond-
ness versus purpleness (or sickly yellowness), blue-eyedness versus
glowing red-, purple-, or yellow-eyedness, what is at stake is nothing less than "the secrets of the universe" (He-Man), "the universe" (Voltron), "the destruction of the universe" (Jayce), "the
ultimate battle for survival" (Sectaurs), "the fate of the entire
world" (Robotech), "the ultimate doom" (Transformers). . . .*[22]

Ironically, the expansion of televised political dialogue by the
American right occurred as the popularity and boldness of network TV journalism declined. Throughout the 1980s the audience
for network TV newscasts atrophied, falling more than 22 percent
from a 76 share in 1979–80 to a 59 share in 1988–89.[23] Certainly
the maturation of CNN and other newscasts accounted for some
of this lost audience, but there were other factors. Perhaps because the Watergate scandal had illustrated the disconcerting potential of exposé at the highest level, viewers did not want to
know "the whole truth." Perhaps network management did not
wish to upset a citizenry that seemed pleased with Ronald Reagan
—after two decades of war and economic dislocation presided
over by a succession of one-term chief executives. Perhaps, too,
corporate interests came to influence the willingness of network
journalism to pursue divisive stories to their logical conclusions.
Whatever the root causes, network news failed to press controversial issues during the 1980s.

When the Reagan administration prevented the press from
observing the U.S. military invasion of Grenada in October 1983,
there was momentary protest by some network personnel, but the
government had its way, and most of the public approved. The
networks failed also to press the issue on corruption in the administration—in the Department of Housing and Urban Development, in the regulation of the savings and loan industry, and in
many other areas of executive responsibility—until Reagan was
out of office and the Bush administration and Congress started to
investigate the criminality. And the Iran-Contra scandal, although it convicted an eloquent Marine Corps colonel and a few
of his operatives, was not pursued by TV news to the highest
levels of responsibility.

The degeneration of television journalism is poignantly revealed in a comparison of network coverage of presidential elections two decades apart. An analysis of more than 280 daily
network newscasts aired between Labor Day and Election Day
in 1968 and 1988 illustrated that pithy "sound bites" and candidate commercials have come to dominate American political dis-

course of TV. As reported by Kiku Adatto of the Shorenstein Barone Center on the Press, Politics, and Public Policy at Harvard University, the average bloc of uninterrupted political speech on TV fell from 42.3 seconds in 1968 to 9.8 seconds in 1988. Whereas about half the sound bites in the 1968 campaign lasted at least 40 seconds, only 1 percent lasted that long in 1988. Most strikingly, while candidates in 1968 spoke for a minute without interruption in 21 percent of all newscasts, this never happened in 1988.

And as for political commercials fashioned by advertising professionals, Adatto noted that in 1968 excerpts from paid political announcements appeared in news stories only 3 times, but in 1988 it happened 125 times as commercials became the news. And in the latter case, reporters addressed the veracity of the claims in those commercials less than 8 percent of the time.[24]

Such acquiescence by TV news prompted Congressman David Obey of Wisconsin to tell PBS journalist Bill Moyers in late 1989, "I don't regard network news organizations as being serious news organizations. I regard them as a public affairs/entertainment division of a profit-making corporation." And Michael Deaver, the presidential adviser and mastermind of much of Ronald Reagan's political imagery, was equally blunt. When asked by Moyers if it was "hard to get the media to go along with you on the use of those visuals," he responded, "Not at all, because the media, while they won't admit it, are not in the news business, they're in the entertainment business."[25]

Even one of the industry's own journalistic pioneers, Sig Mickelson, who headed news operations at CBS Television during most of the 1950s, has drawn pessimistic conclusions about the relationship between TV and politics. According to Mickelson, "The promise that television would open up the electoral system, encourage candidates to be more candid with voters, increase the turnout at the polls, and create a more responsive democracy has collapsed in an era dominated by packaged campaigns and avoidance of issues."[26]

political and fiscal uncertainties

With the legitimization afforded by such cultural trends, some in conservative politics moved against the bête noire of the movement, the "liberal" news media. In many respects this was the revival of an old campaign against the moderate tradition in TV journalism. The latest crusade against perceived press bias was triggered by a *CBS Reports* documentary, "The Uncounted Enemy: A Vietnam Deception," aired January 23, 1982. In that ninety-minute broadcast, correspondent Mike Wallace and producer George Crile accused the former head of military operations in Vietnam, General William C. Westmoreland, of purposefully deceiving President Johnson in the mid-1960s by lowering estimates of enemy troop strength to ensure the president's commitment to prosecute the war.

The first important volley in the controversy created by the documentary was fired four months later in *TV Guide,* when authors Don Kowit and Sally Bedell published a lengthy list of "inaccuracies, distortions, and violations of journalistic standards" contained in the CBS program. Their conclusion spoke directly to conservative concerns: "Are the network news divisions, with their immense power to influence the public's ideas about politics and recent history, doing enough to keep their own houses in order? . . . television news' 'safeguards' for fairness and accuracy need tightening, if not wholesale revision."[27]

Motivated by regard for personal vindication rather than conservative ideology, Westmoreland filed a $120 million libel suit against CBS that fall. Nevertheless, the suit drove directly to the heart of right-wing complaints against national TV. During the trial the courtroom was filled with accusations of journalistic distortion, irresponsible editing techniques, and generalized liberal prejudice in video news. Although the suit was dropped by General Westmoreland before a final verdict could be rendered, CBS was forced during the proceedings to admit many shortcomings in its reportorial procedures.

The trial wounded CBS grievously. First, the corporation had to spend millions of dollars defending itself. The trial also hurt the public image of CBS, for to have been taken to court by one of the few military heroes of the Vietnam War did not win many friends for "the Tiffany network." CBS had been rendered vulnerable. By 1985 the advocacy group Accuracy in Media (AIM) and Senator Jesse Helms of North Carolina mounted an open campaign against network news operations, and specifically CBS and its news anchorman, Dan Rather. Instead of the familiar moral critique and righteous indignation, the conservatives tried a different approach: Helms and AIM urged wealthy supporters to buy CBS stock and, thereby, controlling interest in the corporation. Then it would be simply a matter of firing Rather—and others stained with liberal sin.

Recognizing the opportunity to increase his corporate position within the industry—and hoping to exploit the confusion created by the ideological attacks on CBS and Rather—cable broadcast magnate Ted Turner launched his own assault, a hostile bid to take over the network. Relying on junk bonds as capital, Turner offered to purchase a controlling 67 percent of CBS stock at a price nearly double its current selling price. Although CBS leadership felt the Turner bid had little chance of succeeding, to protect itself from a possible Turner triumph the network was compelled in July 1985 to borrow $954 million to buy back 20 percent of its own stock at an inflated price of $150 per share. Since the latter offer was made with cash and solid securities, it effectively quashed the Turner bid.[28]

It was an expensive battle, in some ways a Pyrrhic victory for CBS. Although the network now controlled its own destiny, it had tripled its debt (which rose to $1 billion) and depleted two-thirds of its equity (which fell from $1.5 billion to $519 million). Added to this was a string of financial losses in ancillary activities: millions of dollars wasted in overexpenditures in the purchase of twelve Ziff-Davis magazines; money lost in the acquisition of Ideal Toy Company; millions more squandered on the abortive fine-arts CBS Cable Network in 1981–82; the loss of $40 million in the corporation's Theatrical Film Division; and the forced sale of TriStar Pictures when conflicts arose between CBS and its partners in the venture, HBO and Columbia Pictures.

Before the financial hemorrhage ended, CBS endured personnel changes in its highest offices, divestiture of many of its subsidiaries, rationalization of its broadcast operations, and fiscal retrenchment. At its News Division alone, CBS in 1987 cut the budget by $30 million and discharged almost 230 employees. Significantly, for the first time in the history of U.S. television, CBS fell to third place among the networks. Moreover, during the November 1988 "TV sweeps"—one of the four months annually when audience ratings are used to establish local and national advertising rates for the coming quarter—CBS billings actually came in fourth behind NBC, ABC, and the cumulative total for independent stations.[29]

Regardless of financial specifics, the economic decline at CBS was only the most glaring example of the challenges facing network broadcasting in a decade of industry metamorphosis. In 1983 overall profits of the owned and operated stations of the three networks may have increased 30 percent over the previous year,[30] but two years later RCA and its NBC subsidiary were purchased by General Electric for $6.3 billion. In that same year Capital Cities, a small but successful group of TV stations, paid $3.5 billion to buy the ABC network. Add to this other economic crises such as a strike by the Writers Guild against ABC News in 1987; a more devastating Writers Guild strike, lasting twenty-two weeks, against the networks and production studios in 1988; the billions of dollars spent in 1985 by Rupert Murdoch to buy 20th Century-Fox and Metromedia; and the $94 million lost by Murdoch during the first two years of operations at the Fox television network.

Although there were financial peaks and valleys throughout the decade, the long-range vitality of deregulated national video was clouded. Reflecting the fundamental uncertainty of network economics, one prominent TV critic concluded in early 1988 that while "TV has definitely been getting better . . . soon, fearfully soon, it may be getting worse."[31]

To counter such foreboding, the president of NBC, Robert Wright, felt it necessary in the middle of the year to reassure the public that the broadcast networks "are in no immediate danger of collapse."[32] A few months earlier the chairman of Capital Cities/ABC also tried to describe the deteriorating situation in positive terms. According to Thomas S. Murphy:

> Change has become a central fact of life for the telecommunications industry. All three networks are deeply affected by a significant and permanent erosion of audience. . . . Network television, in short, is now a mature business, one which can no longer simply assume continued growth or expansion. This maturity makes us much like other American businesses, with each company's survival contingent on its ability to increase its market share and control its costs.[33]

11

broadcasting

Network television seems not to have fully comprehended the threat inherent in cable. When Home Box Office in 1975 requested from the FCC the right to bounce its TV signal off the orbiting Satcom I satellite, the commission announced a public hearing at which all dissenting parties would have the right to protest **versus** before a final decision was made. If ever there was a time to bring out the top executives and lobby the FCC for a rejection of the HBO proposal, this was it. Instead, the public hearing produced no network dissent. To compound the error, the satellite leased by HBO was owned by the Radio Corporation of America, parent company of NBC.

A biographer of HBO has summarized this development concisely. "Most of those opposed to pay television, such as movie studios, theater owners, and broadcast networks, **cable** clearly did not understand anything about the new technology and its implications," wrote George Mair. "Or if they did understand it, they didn't care, because they didn't think Home Box Office could make it work financially." He continued, "One of the three factors in the amazing success of Home Box Office was the stupidity of its competitors. This mute response to the FCC's invitation to protest HBO's request to go up on satellite is a classic illustration of that stupidity."[1]

The stupidity of the mid-1970s became consternation in the 1980s as broadcast and cable became locked in intense competition. The most obvious results in this contest for the heart and mind of the American viewer could be seen in the programming records of both delivery systems during the 1980s.

program rivalries: broadcast tv

In this time of confusion and erosion, network programming seemed more than ever reliant on definable demographic units rather than the broadest possible audience. Yet, having streamlined the shows to a few entertainment types, it was increasingly difficult for the networks to attract viewers by simply refashioning the comedy, crime, and conversation styles that survived the decades. By the 1980s, for example, TV had nurtured an entire generation of viewers without a taste for musical variety shows and Westerns. When they did schedule musical fare, there was insufficient viewer interest in *Barbara Mandrell and the Mandrell Sisters* (fifty-sixth its first season, sixty-sixth in its second season) or *Dolly* (fifty-ninth) to trigger a revival of the genre. Even more off-target were Westerns. They were essentially a dead TV form since the early 1970s, but the networks attempted periodically to resurrect Westerns and ended up broadcasting some of the worst-received series—*The Young Pioneers* (ninety-third), *Young Maverick* (eighty-eighth), *Wildside* (eighty-second), and *Paradise* (seventy-eighth)—of the season.[2]

In general, the first hour of prime time was surrendered to youngsters and parents looking for "family" shows to share with their offspring. Here was a domain of precocious children, understanding parents, cute people, angels, and cuddly toys that talked. With programs such as *Head of the Class*, *The Cosby Show*, *A Different World*, and *Growing Pains*, youthful viewers made hits out of series highlighting youngsters and their antics. From such shows emerged a galaxy of TV stars especially pleasing to young people, among them Michael J. Fox and Justine Bateman of *Family Ties*, Ricky Schroeder of *Silver Spoons*, Tony Danza in *Who's the Boss?* and Emmanuel Lewis in *Webster*.

But viewers of early prime time also accepted oldster Michael Landon as an angelic visitor and an extraterrestrial, Alf, as a visiting alien. Even in the violence-prone adventure shows shown at this time, audience favorites were confined to exaggerated, comic-book heroics in the likes of *Knight Rider*, *The A Team*, *Airwolf*, and *The Dukes of Hazzard*.

But television also served another audience segment: the aging viewer. Above all, the reality of a graying society was recognizable in a respect for the economic-strength attractiveness of older Americans. Whereas the advertising industry for years had sought eighteen-to-forty-nine-year-olds as its prized audience, the range was expanded in the 1980s to age fifty-four. Programs pitched at this group included tales of reinvigorated youth on *The Love Boat* and the achievement of lost dreams on *Fantasy Island*. On *The Golden Girls* it was three mature women, sexy and self-sufficient, and unwilling to retire to their rocking chairs.

Although the mature viewer may have developed a wide range of interests while passing through life, network TV did not program to those traits—advertisers would spend only so much money attracting the middle-aged and older. Instead, in another variation on the theme of lost youth, programmers exploited nostalgia by hiring vintage movie stars for guest appearances. Such casting had made *The Love Boat* and *Fantasy Island* popular, but the most successful manipulator of the technique was *Murder, She Wrote*, which specialized in stars of the 1940s and 1950s. In the 1987–88 season, for instance, this detective series featured film legends such as Janet Leigh, Eddie Albert, Dorothy Lamour, Ruth Roman, Gloria DeHaven, Kathryn Grayson, Claire Trevor, Julie Adams, and Gisele Mackenzie. That the star of the series, Angela Lansbury, began her adult film career in 1944 only reinforced the maturity reflected in its casting.

For those chronologically in middle age, situation comedies such as *Cheers* and *Taxi* offered no concessions to children. And via series such as *China Beach* and *Tour of Duty*, aimed at adults' memories of the Vietnam War, and *The Wonder Years* and *thirtysomething*, aimed at the memories of childhood and the realities of midlife, the networks sought the baby boomers, those born between 1946 and the mid-1960s who had transformed TV and civility while passing through youth, and who remained numerically large and financially influential as they now entered middle age.

The appeal to adult tastes was not confined to network prime time. Reality-based talk shows, particularly prevalent in first-run syndication, brought adult topicality to the weekday audience. Sometimes poignantly but more often in an exploitative and tawdry manner, long-standing video taboos against sexual frankness were broken on *The Oprah Winfrey Show*, *Donahue*, and *Geraldo*. TV with the gossipy values of supermarket tabloids appeared in *A Current Affair* on Fox and on the syndicated shows *Inside Edition* and *Entertainment Tonight*.

In a related format, the role of television as a promoter of constructive public debate also gave way to the hyperbole and bombast of show business. Adopting now the rhetorical style of wrestler Hulk Hogan, men with distinguished records in public service and journalism verbally lashed at one another on *The Capital Gang* on CNN, *The McLaughlin Group* on PBS, and the syndicated *Morton Downey, Jr., Show*.

In crime programming, too, new levels of theatrical directness were realized. In *America's Most Wanted* and *Unsolved Mysteries* viewers became involved in solving horrible crimes, and in the Fox actuality series *Cops*, audiences traveled with real police officers on evening patrols. Less flamboyant, but targeted nonetheless for adult segments, were "reality-based" legal series such as

246

The People's Court, Superior Court, Divorce Court, and *Arthur Miller's Court*, where viewers vicariously joined professionals in resolving legal issues and actual courtroom cases.

Programmers also found in the soap opera a mix of romantic melodrama, suspense, and lusty characterization that gripped prime-time audiences for more than a decade. The show that set the pace for the genre was *Dallas*, which premiered in 1978. Here millionaire oilman J. R. Ewing and his cohorts populated a grown-up world of tycoons, their sexy women, and intriguing adventure. In manipulating its stereotypical Texans made rich in the business of petroleum, *Dallas* exploited a powerful social ethos growing in the United States in the age of political conservatism. The narcissism and materialism that found fertile ground in the "me decade" and that achieved its full stature in the economic climate of the 1980s made the program a primer on attaining and maintaining success. To David Jacobs, the executive producer of *Knots Landing*, the stories of greed and glamour seemed to fit the times. As he noted at the end of the decade, "I think for a while during the Reagan years it was OK to be ostentatiously wealthy and glitzy."[3]

Dallas was the first adult serial to lead the prime-time ratings. But the attraction of the series proved impermanent. "I don't think of it as erosion of a genre. A show sometimes just gets old and tired," explained Jacobs. Table 11.1 demonstrates the familiar pattern of a programming fad: rising quickly, remaining popular through several seasons, then declining precipitously.

TABLE 11.1

rankings for *dallas*, 1979–89[4]

SEASON ENDING	POSITION	RATING
1979	39	18.4
1980	5	25.0
1981	1	31.8
1982	1	28.4
1983	2	24.6
1984	1	25.7
1985	2	24.7
1986	7	21.8
1987	11	21.3
1988	22	16.8
1989	31	15.4

As expected, the success of *Dallas* prompted imitation. By the mid-1980s there were several other evening soap operas with villains and purehearts struggling for wealth, power, and romance —and a decent share of the adult audience. Among this imitative second generation were *Knots Landing*, *Dynasty* and *Dynasty II— the Colbys*, *Flamingo Road*, *The Yellow Rose*, *Falcon Crest*, *From Here to Eternity*, and *Emerald Point*, *NAS*.

These soaps offered melodrama not seen regularly in prime time since *Peyton Place* had appeared two and three evenings a week in the 1960s. American adults, many nurtured on daytime soaps, now found the evening variety seductive. In the peak season for this type of programming, 1984–85, four evening serials—*Dynasty* (first), *Dallas* (second), *Knots Landing* (ninth), and *Falcon Crest* (tenth)—ended the year among the top ten.

In this decade of segmented scheduling, one of the more important developments was the renewed appeal by network TV to African-Americans. It was not the first time the entertainment industry had sought to arrest a downward spiral by approaching blacks. During the 1970s the boom in black exploitation feature films helped rescue a collapsing U.S. movie industry. The TV networks now turned to black viewers to bolster sagging prime-time ratings.

Broadcasting had always been comfortable with racial stereotyping, whether it was the abrasive representations so abundant in the 1950s or the subtler stylizations of the 1970s. Chronically missing from network TV was a consistently respectful and realistic depiction of African-Americans. Ironically, prime-time TV had a positive precedent to follow: by the 1970s daytime soap operas such as *All My Children* and *General Hospital* were involving black dramatic characters who were free from traditional stereotyping. Although the programmers faced criticism from whites uncomfortable with such imagery, the nature of the genre—plus the fact that black viewers constituted about one-quarter of the audience for soaps—stiffened the resolve to introduce African-Americans into popular daytime serials.

By the 1980s, however, blacks entered the heroic urban professions so familiar in prime time—police, doctors, lawyers— appearing as strong characters in dramas such as *Miami Vice, Hill Street Blues, St. Elsewhere*, and *L.A. Law*. But it was with *The Cosby Show* that network TV finally realized the potential of positive black imagery. Commencing in 1984, this situation comedy featured Bill Cosby as Dr. Cliff Huxtable, obstetrician, husband of a successful lawyer, and father of five distinctive children. The series demonstrated that successful programs need not recapitulate racist notions of how African-Americans acted, nor limit the number of blacks on-screen in order to sustain the myth that significant American life was lily-white.

There had been earlier examples of positive representation. All of the products with which Bill Cosby had been associated—*I Spy*, *The Bill Cosby Show*, *The New Bill Cosby Show*, *Cos*—eschewed racist stereotyping. *Benson* moved in this direction when Robert Guillaume was permitted in 1981 to trade his butler's position for that of state budget director. Still, *The Cosby Show* was unique. Here, for the first time, network TV offered a black nuclear family that was believably human—where parents nurtured their children, and children loved their mother and father and related with each other respectfully; where audiences laughed with the wittiness, not at the pejorative tomfoolery, of its leading characters. The long-overdue model worked, becoming the leading program throughout the last half of the decade, sparking a renaissance of the sitcom genre and precipitating a business turnaround that soon made NBC the premier operation in national television.

The Cosby Show fostered not only imitation but also enhancement of African-American imagery. By the second half of the decade, the networks presented distinguished depictions of blacks in comedies such as *Charlie & Co.*, *227*, *Amen!*, *A Different World*, *The Robert Guillaume Show*, and *Frank's Place*. More than simply placing black characters in "white-middle-class" situations, several of these series offered African-Americans operating within "black" contexts.

The people on *227* lived and interrelated in a working-class environment. Hal Williams as husband and father arrived home from work carrying the black lunch can familiar to laboring Americans. And he returned to an African-American universe: an apartment building filled with black neighbors offering no concessions to affirmative-action casting quotas and no demeaning presentation of its urban characters. Similarly unfamiliar was the environment of *Amen!* Its comedic cast operated in and about a church without whites. *Frank's Place* not only depicted the offbeat denizens of the Chez Louisiane restaurant, a New Orleans eatery owned by a black man, it also wove themes from African-American folk culture into its "dramedy"—partly drama, partly comedy—story lines.

These series were stereotypical only in that they were scarce and perpetuated the tradition of black comedians working to make white audiences laugh. But their appeal to black sensibilities was bolder than in the past. They were programs where whites were certainly welcomed, even desired, as viewers and vicarious participants; but these shows were not shaped to fit familiar projections of black life. Coming after years in the mid-1980s when Mr. T ran amok as B.A. (Bad Attitude) Baracus on *The A-Team,* such series offered an image of African-American humanity that was considerably more emulable and realistic.

Still, this was no projection of the authentic Afro-America, and, in fact, it may have been deleterious in the happy picture it projected of the black condition. In a stinging report issued in the summer of 1989, the National Commission for Working Women of Wider Opportunities for Women (WOW) concluded that "Real-world racism, which is pervasive, subtle, and blatant, is commonplace in America but virtually invisible on entertainment television." The commission found that more than 90 percent of the minorities on TV—almost all of them blacks—were middle-class and rich, and less than 10 percent were working-class or poor; and that 75 percent of all minority females were on comedies. Moreover, the TV world misleadingly projects racial harmony and an egalitarian workplace; here, too, injustice is always a matter of individual immorality, never the result of oppressive social structures.[5]

However limited, improved treatment of blacks on TV did not proceed from any moral conversion among the Caucasian males who dominated the executive leadership of network TV. In fact, the WOW report indicated that even on shows featuring blacks, 93 percent of the producers were white. Motivation for the new imagery existed overwhelmingly in the need to tap narrow segments of the audience.

Although blacks constituted less than 12 percent of the U.S. population, statistics proved that on a per capita basis they watched more TV than whites. And racial viewership patterns affected overall ratings. Nielsen reports in 1985 and 1986 substantiated that African-American households each day used video 40 percent more than other TV homes.[6] By early 1988 black households watched television an average of 10.6 hours daily, while others watched an average of 7.3 hours daily. African-Americans were also more loyal to the networks, viewing national shows at a rate 80 percent higher than other households in the daytime and 19 percent higher in prime time.[7]

Here was a marriage of needs that had been chronically resisted by the industry. With discernible tastes that did not always match those of the white viewership, black audiences responded well to shows featuring black characters. Advertisers also needed effective programs through which to reach the multi-billion-dollar African-American consumer market, a socioeconomic reality that in the 1980s was wealthier and more populated than most nation-states in the world. As illustrated in Table 11.2, black viewers definitely had their own tastes in programming.

TABLE 11.2

viewing differences by racial households, january–february 1986[8]

PROGRAM	BLACK RANK	OTHERS RANK
THE COSBY SHOW	1	1
227	4	16
FACTS OF LIFE	6	26
HUNTER	9	46
CHARLIE & CO.	12	75
MURDER, SHE WROTE	25	3
60 MINUTES	32	4
DALLAS	52	7
WHO'S THE BOSS?	54	9
NEWHART	59	12

But a large or a small black response could strongly affect a TV series in terms of its rating and relative rank, figures helpful in terms of present and future profitability. The statistics in Table 11.3 demonstrate how the fate of some programs in 1988 was reflected in their acceptance or rejection by the African-American audience.

TABLE 11.3

rating/ranking differences by racial households, january–february 1988[9]

PROGRAM	BLACK RATING/ RANK	OTHERS RATING/ RANK	FINAL RATING/RANK
A DIFFERENT WORLD	46.6/1	22.4/4	25.0/2
227	35.1/5	14.8/31	16.9/22
KNOTS LANDING	24.3/9	15.4/29	16.4/25
GROWING PAINS	21.0/17	22.9/3	22.7/5
MY TWO DADS	16.4/38	16.7/20	16.7/24

program rivalries: cable tv

Whatever the networks' success in programming for audience segments, the vitality of the networks was steadily eroded by new competitive realities within the industry. By the late 1980s, ABC, CBS, and NBC faced a collective crisis created by nothing less than a desertion of network broadcasting by much of the American public. The attrition has been dramatic. Average and median ratings cited in Table 11.4 reveal that between 1953 and 1988 there was a relentless decline in the popularity of top ten and top twenty programming. During that thirty-five-year period average ratings for the best TV had to offer plummeted 54 percent; median figures dropped by approximately the same amount.

Ominously, much of that collapse occurred in the 1980s. Ratings rose slightly in 1968–78, but during the following decade the collapse was startling: a 14 percent drop in the average rating for top ten series, and a 12 percent decline in the average rating for shows in the top twenty. Expectably, median figures also declined in that period, dropping 19.5 percent for top ten programs and 17.5 percent for top twenty shows.

TABLE 11.4

average and median ratings of top network series, 1953–88[10]

Season Ending	Top Ten Average	Top Twenty Average	Top Ten Median	Top Twenty Median
1953	47.7	46.3	42.7	40.4
1958	34.6	33.6	31.7	30.5
1963	29.9	29.8	27.3	26.6
1968	25.4	25.5	23.0	23.6
1973	25.3	24.2	23.6	23.4
1978	25.8	24.4	23.7	22.8
1983	23.0	23.1	21.7	20.9
1988	22.1	21.3	19.0	18.8

Viewers have begun to reject network TV as it existed through five decades—and electronic entertainment as it flourished since the late 1920s. With greater choice in what to watch and when to watch it, plus an incipient trend toward rejection of all TV programming, both broadcast and cable, the future of broadcasting in the United States has become uncertain. The most obvious catalyst in this development has been cable TV. The television universe was large, composed of 669 VHF stations (122 of them educational outlets) and 645 UHF stations (218 of them educational operations). But there existed what former FCC chairman Dennis Patrick described as "ferocious competition that was unimagined 10 years ago."[11] By November 1989 more than 57 percent of the nation's households were wired, and more than 29 percent were receiving pay cable channels as well. Moreover, there were 8,413 cable systems serving local subscribers with a mix drawn from 55 basic networks, 8 pay networks, and 6 pay-per-view operations.

And Americans were finding a broader choice in cable. By the end of 1988 some 64 percent of the households in the United States could receive at least fifteen channels, and 45 percent could pick up at least thirty channels. Significantly, most of this availability was in suburban and rural areas. Within the largest U.S. cities, where cable was unavailable or relatively new, the full impact of pay TV was yet to be determined.

Nonetheless, by the end of 1988 there were significant numbers of cabled households in big-city market areas such as New York City (47.8 percent), Los Angeles (46.5 percent), and Boston (63.5 percent). Among the twenty largest market areas, the highest cable penetration rate was in Pittsburgh (66.5 percent); the lowest penetration was in Chicago (40.7 percent.)[12]

Important for cable operators, additional households were waiting to receive cable. A survey of nonsubscribers in 1989 demonstrated that more than one-third were without cable because it was not yet available—and 22 percent felt it was too expensive. Only 24 percent rejected cable because of disinterest.[13]

While the principal attractiveness of cable has been its channel availability and diverse programming, for the most part the cable revolution has been accomplished through the attractiveness of off-network reruns. From the vintage Westerns that dominate weekends on CBN The Family Channel, to the women-centered series (e.g., *Cagney & Lacey, Partners in Crime, Lady Blue, Falcon Crest*, and *Kay O'Brien*) common to Lifetime, and the vintage child-oriented programs (e.g., *Dennis the Menace, Lassie, My Three Sons*, and *The Donna Reed Show*) on Nickelodeon, cable has relied on historical television to assure its future.

Several networks, however, have offered innovative programming: the two commerical-free channels of C-SPAN (Cable-Satellite Public Affairs Network) air not only the proceedings of the U.S. House of Representatives and Senate but also speeches, conferences, and major events affecting public policy. Many of the educational programs on The Discovery Channel and The Learning Channel have consisted of old films—often from Europe, Australia, or Canada—but they have been new to U.S. television. And the all-news formats on Turner Broadcasting System's two actualities outlets, Cable News Network (CNN) and Headline News, are unprecedented in U.S. video.

A major problem confronting cable in the 1990s, however, is the need for original entertainment programming to supplement the network reruns. Certainly the music video has not been exclusively a cable feature, but these filmlets produced to advertise performers and their record ablums have created two cable channels—MTV: Music Television and its VH-1: Video Hits-One offshoot—and they have been a prominent part of the program schedule on Black Entertainment Television, The USA Network, The Nashville Network, and others. Rising popular interest in stand-up comedy in the late 1980s not only spawned a rash of comedy specials and series such as *It's Gary Shandling's Show* on pay cable, but also the fad led to the creation in November 1989 of The Comedy Channel, an HBO-owned program service devoted solely to comedy, as well as *HA! The TV Comedy Network*, produced by MTV, which debuted in April 1990.

HBO also has spent considerable sums for exclusive coverage of boxing championships, new series and miniseries, and made-for-cable movies. Similarly, Showtime has invested in comedy specials, sitcom series, and stage plays. The move toward original productions has come more slowly to basic cable, yet The USA Network, Lifetime, CBN The Family Channel, and Turner Network Television (TNT) have shown first-run programs and specials.

Cable operators have found fresh programs to be an effective means to attract advertisers as well as audiences. As noted in 1989 by Farrell Reynolds, the president of broadcast sales for Turner Broadcasting, "Advertisers are attracted to original programming like moths to a flame." [14] With increasing popular interest in cable —the total cable share of the prime-time audience rose from 13 percent in 1985 to 22 percent in 1988—there are signs indicating a placement of advertiser money in cable. With the demographic precision offered by cable narrowcasting, plus the relatively low price of cable fee structures, the economy and target marketing potential of cable have attracted major advertisers in recent years, as demonstrated in Table 11.5.

Cable TV, with its dozens of commercial networks, still attracts far less revenue than the three major broadcasters. Esti-

TABLE 11.5

top cable network advertisers, 1987 and 1988[15]

RANK	COMPANY	1988 (MILLIONS)	1987 (MILLIONS)	% CHANGE
1.	PROCTER & GAMBLE	$30.2	$23.7	+27
2.	PHILIP MORRIS	$23.1	$20.6	+12
3.	ANHEUSER-BUSCH	$21.4	$22.9	− 7
4.	TIME, INC.	$21.1	$16.4	+29
5.	GENERAL MILLS	$20	$18.6	+ 8
6.	RJR NABISCO	$14.2	$14.7	− 3
7.	EASTMAN KODAK	$11	$ 2.5	+331
8.	CLOROX CO.	$10.1	$ 6.9	+47
9.	MARS, INC.	$10	$14.9	−33
10.	CHRYSLER CORP.	$ 9.5	$ 6.1	+55

mates for 1989, for example, placed total network advertising at $21.1 billion, a rise of 4.1 percent; cable advertising was expected to reach only $1.5 billion, but that would constitute a rise of 65 percent over the previous year.[16]

Though sparse, cable-originated programming has found respectability within the industry. Not only has cable honored its own productions via the annual Ace awards, presented by the National Cable Television Association, but also made-for-cable programming moved into the artistic mainstream in 1988 when shows from Turner, HBO, Showtime, and Disney were nominated for fifteen Emmy awards. This was the first time in the history of the National Academy of Television Arts and Sciences that cable products had been permitted to compete against broadcast TV. Importantly, the HBO production *Dear America: Letters Home from Vietnam* won two Emmy awards. It was chosen for outstanding informational special, while its writers William Couturie and Richard Dewhurst were selected for individual achievement in informational programming. The bittersweet documentary about young American combatants in the Vietnam War gained further acclaim when it was released abroad as a theatrical motion picture.

The most expansive commitment to cable-originated fare, however, has been in sports; and significantly, this is where the broadcast networks have taken their most expensive stand against the encroachment of cable. The relationship between network TV and sports has been long and profitable. Network video played an influential role in shaping American sports to fit the demands of show business. As it affected baseball, for example, the networks brought billions of dollars to the sport. Whereas the average major-league baseball salary was $24,909 in 1969, it leaped in 1979 to $113,558 after a decade of increased TV interest in the sport. The money needed to meet sizable team payrolls came from lucrative contracts negotiated by individual teams with stations desiring local coverage, plus arrangements between Major-League Baseball and network television for exclusive rights to a game of the week, plus the "jewel" events: the All-Star Game, the League Championship Series, and the World Series.

With the maturation of cable TV, professional baseball profited handsomely. By 1989 the average major-league player earned $485,000 annually. Moreover, there were 108 players—one-sixth of those in the major leagues—earning $1 million per year; and 21 of these were contracted for at least $2 million annually. And commercial television paid for most of it.

To sign Major-League Baseball to a four-year network contract, effective with the 1990 season, CBS agreed to pay $1.06 billion, a considerable sum for a network claiming financial difficulties. But the CBS deal could not blunt the appeal of cable. Baseball officials contracted with ESPN to televise 175 games each season—an average of six games per week, several preseason contests, and extra games on holidays—during the same four-year period. The cost to ESPN was $400 million.

As striking as these figures were, they were surpassed in local arrangements between individual baseball teams and cable operators. In Chicago and Atlanta, it was no coincidence that professional baseball teams—the Cubs and Braves, respectively—were the anchor attractions on two superstations, WGN and WTBS, outlets that otherwise were committed to rerunning old sitcoms and movies. The fact that the owners of the superstations—the *Chicago Tribune* and the Turner Broadcasting System, respectively—also own the Cubs and Braves reaffirms the symbiotic relationship between pro sports and commercial television. This vital linkage was made most apparent in 1989, when the Madison Square Garden Network—a regional cable operation that offers baseball, basketball, hockey, football, track and field, tennis, horse racing, boxing, and wrestling to more than 2.4 million subscribers in New York, New Jersey, and Connecticut—paid $500 million to the New York Yankees for twelve years of Yankee baseball games.

By the end of the 1980s, industry competition to televise the best college and professional attractions resulted in new heights of sports saturation and expense. In one decade, the commitment of ABC, CBS, and NBC to sports programs rose from 1,288 hours in 1979 to 1,490 in 1989 (excluding Olympic coverage), an increase of more than 15 percent. College basketball on network TV mushroomed from 34 events in 1980 to 74 in 1988—and on cable from 129 events in 1980 to 234 in 1988.

And with visibility came increased cost to the televiser. Commencing with the 1990 season, NBC agreed to pay the National Basketball Association $600 million over four years to air twenty to twenty-six regular games and as many as thirty playoff games. For the cable rights to NBA games, Turner Network Television paid $275 million for four seasons, triple the rate it paid for the last contract period. For rights to the Olympic Games, NBC paid $401 million for the 1992 Summer Games, while CBS agreed to $243 million for the 1992 Winter Games and $300 million for the 1994 Winter Games. CBS also spent $1 billion for exclusive rights beginning in 1991 to seven years of the college basketball championship tournament mounted each spring by the National Collegiate Athletic Association. As impressive as such figures may be, they were topped when the National Football League—"the gold standard in television entertainment programming," according to President Roger L. Werner of ESPN—negotiated a new TV contract in 1990. For rights to games in the four seasons from 1991 through 1995, ABC, CBS, NBC, Turner Broadcasting, and ESPN paid the NFL more than $3.7 billion. Its previous three-year arrangement with ABC, CBS, NBC, and ESPN totaled more than $1.4 billion.

Ironically, there is no guarantee that the networks will realize profits from such expenditures. ABC lost $64 million on the 1988 Winter Olympic Games, and the World Series of 1989 that pitted San Francisco and Oakland—a series of regional interest at best, but one that was interrupted for ten days by a deadly earthquake and ended unspectacularly by Oakland after four consecutive one-sided victories—brought ABC historically low ratings and a loss of $20 million. During the past decade popular interest in baseball actually declined on NBC's *Game of the Week*, dropping from a 7.6 rating/28 share in 1978 to a 5.6 rating/18 share for the 1988 season.

Motivation for the large expenditures is varied. Certainly, live sports are attractive to viewers and therefore to advertisers, but many TV executives understand sports in terms of enhanced prestige and reputation for a network and its stations. This is especially true for cable TV, where much of the lure for subscribers has been ESPN, Sports Channel, WTBS, WGN, and TNT. At CBS, however, sports have become the programming weapon of choice in an attempt to fight out of the network cellar. Here sports are expected to attract a sizable audience, but also to promote the entire CBS prime-time schedule. As Neal Pilson, president of CBS Sports, noted at the end of 1989, his massive expenditures on sports were "part of a much larger corporate strategy, a larger mosaic to recapture the No. 1 position in prime time. We will use sports as a weapon to do that." [17]

Cable and electronic TV accessories liberated American viewers from the limitations historically integral to U.S. broadcasting. In the medium dominated for decades by three similarly structured networks, the only commitment to diversity had been the underfunded Educational Television/Public Broadcasting Service. But even here there were exasperating limitations, as ETV/PBS stations—with their variety of stunning performances and informative public affairs and documentary programming, plus an abundance of dull educational series, nature films, cooking and gardening shows, British miniseries and comedies, and old feature films—were often buried inconveniently on the UHF spectrum. The TV order taking shape in the 1980s, however, was as close to narrowcasting as Americans had ever encountered. By the end of 1989 approximately half of American homes received thirty or more stations.

As new technologies made possible a multiplicity of channels and TV usages, the long-suppressed pluralism in popular tastes was manifest in the diffusion of the broadcast audience. While the United States remained a nation committed to television, it was a new type of medium. The future of American video was aptly demonstrated in 1987 in a survey of preteen viewing habits. The day before the survey was taken, 30 percent of the children had viewed a prerecorded cassette, and 70 percent had watched cable programming. Mothers of the respondents advised further that their children were turning from traditional broadcasting for many reasons, among them perceptions that afternoon cartoons were poorly made, that after-school programs were too similar, that there were too many reruns and outdated situations, and that too many daytime offerings were oriented toward boys. [18]

As if alternative video forms were not threatening enough, another incipient audience trend noticeable in the 1980s was a movement away from all forms of TV. As early as April 1983 a report commissioned by the National Association of Broadcasters indicated that Americans were becoming dissatisfied with the medium. Whereas 41 percent of the respondents in 1977 said television was important to their lives, the figure fell to 32 percent in 1983. During the same six-year span, belief that the medium was livelier and more realistic dropped from 72 to 59 percent, and the conviction that video was varied and better than in past seasons dipped from 65 to 52 percent.

Since the impacts of the VCR and cable TV were not widespread in 1983, reasons for this early disenchantment lie elsewhere. According to the NAB, network rejection was caused by adverse reactions to too much sex and violence, the lack of family programs, and "sillier and more juvenile" situation comedies. "From the mid-1970s and continuing into the present day, viewers have become increasingly evaluative, judgmental, and critical of programming offered them by the three commercial television networks," concluded an executive of the research company that developed the NAB study. Although network representatives attempted to dismiss the report as flawed, the research executive explained pointedly, "The hardest attitude for the television industry to overcome is the belief that the public out there loves them. But the industry needs to understand the dissatisfaction." [19]

What the NAB report detected in 1983 was confirmed by A. C. Nielsen statistics following the 1986–87 season. For the first time in the two decades Nielsen had recorded such figures, weekly TV viewing time declined in the average household—falling from fifty hours, sixteen minutes during the previous season to forty-nine hours, forty-eight minutes. The loss was noticeable among children as well as among adult women and men. Importantly, the pattern of diminished viewing continued into the 1987–88 season, declining by another forty-four minutes. [20]

One CBS executive blamed network disintegration on the new competitors. As he understood the situation by 1987, people were still watching the "megahits" on commercial television—although these were becoming more and more difficult to develop—but they were turning to recorded entertainment during those less attractive hours when in earlier decades viewers had little choice but to endure this "middle range" network programming. [21]

Spurred by the weakening of network control, many other communications corporations entered TV, eager to establish new interests or expand existing interests. This was no economic democracy, no opening in which small business and inventive entrepreneurs with new ideas were welcomed to compete. Major movie studios, wealthy film syndicators, large newspapers, and national magazines as well as ABC, CBS, and NBC themselves all jumped into the opening in search of profitability. The capitalistic ethic that had fashioned the network monopoly remained operative.

Todd Gitlin was correct to point out that cable stood a good chance of becoming a monopoly industry itself. When he wrote, statistics from 1981 showed that the top ten cable operators controlled 44 percent of all subscribers, the bulk of cable programming came from only a few distributors, and most cable executives had been nurtured in "the television-industrial complex" that shaped monopoly broadcasting. Today, similar patterns of dominance exist in cable. Government has expressed great interest in regulating the new industry, but Congress and the FCC have been preoccupied with sexual explicitness, profanity, and violence as well as the rising subscription rates; few in government seem concerned with oligopoly. The reluctance of government to become regulatorily involved in the winnowing-out process practically guarantees that big corporations will continue to devour smaller corporations on all levels of the business until, eventually, only a few megacorporations will remain.

This, however, is how capitalism works, particularly in the United States in a time of deregulation—or, as Chairman Mark Fowler of the FCC termed it, "unregulation." And given the enormous start-up costs required to launch a TV operation, be it cable or broadcast, it seems inevitable that only the wealthiest telecommunications operations will survive and control most of the business.

As far as it affects the average viewer, however, the more pertinent question concerns the effects that such developments will have on programming and culture. Even under the dominion of a few corporations, cable has several structural checks against its becoming a streamlined operation similar to the broadcast monopoly. Above all, because cable is subscriber-based, it must please its audience every month or run the risk of expensive disconnections. The promise and raison d'être of cable television is program diversity; failure to deliver what subscribers consider a sufficiency of choice could be fiscally self-destructive. In the era of broadcasting a disgruntled viewer could either write a letter of protest or turn off the set. The former usually had little obvious impact, and unless that viewer were also in a "Nielsen home" (one of the few thousand homes nationwide selected to provide the A. C. Nielsen Company with the information from which it computed program ratings) turning off the set had no impact on the broadcasters. In the new video order, the angry viewer is a potential defector from the system, and perhaps the harbinger of a costly exodus by others of similar mind.

Because cable TV is reliant on the economic stability of the national economy, it needs subscriber loyalty as a hedge against economic hard times. Cable must become relatively indispensable to its viewers. Again, to accomplish this it must deliver on its promise of something for everyone. If cable is treated by viewers as a luxury instead of a utility, economic downturns will have direct results in the loss of subscribers. Broadcasting has survived recessions and depressions—in fact, network radio proved invaluable to social morale in the 1930s, a decade marked by the worst depression in U.S. history. Cable TV might be hard pressed to survive such a collapse.

The potential of cable to streamline its programming is tempered by the fact that it operates as a supplement or complement to—but not an alternative or replacement for—free over-the-air video. Unless the broadcast networks were to collapse totally, or themselves move to cable exclusively, they will continue to balance the cable presence. The networks, moreover, will continue to earn the lion's share of the total advertising dollar because they still deliver the largest audiences. Network viewership is divisible by three; the full cable audience is divided among dozens of channels. Whereas a leading network rating in prime time may be 16.0 (as it was NBC for the 1988–89 season), a cable network rating of 2.0 is considered outstanding.

Although there has been fundamental change in the delivery of TV programming, what has not changed is the public preference for familiar types of entertainment and informational programming. To a disappointed Gitlin, writing in the early 1980s, this meant only that "sports, old movies, news, and syndicated shows are the staples of the new cable networks, and they are likely to remain so. What they offer is not so much different as more of the same."[22] In apparent frustration with the medium he had so well dissected, he was led to conclude:

> If there is ever to be an American television industry that aims to do something different, to challenge us rather than hook us and fawn on us and condescend to us, it would have to come because publics organize to resist it. . . . In the end, if public life were sufficiently rich and engaging people would already be communicating—literally, "making common"—rather than relying on the little electronic box to ease our days. . . . This is why the predicament of American television is the predicament of American culture and politics as a whole. Walt Whitman wrote: "To have great poets there must be great audiences, too."[23]

261

In such resignation is acknowledgment of the immutable nature of popular culture in a capitalistic United States, an explanation for the persistence of entertainment formats. As Gitlin suggests, to long for consistent quality or profundity or persisting originality in TV is to anticipate a restructuring of American television and culture along lines that most of the population would not necessarily applaud, or subscribe to, anyway. Commercial television, be it broadcast or cable, will never lead by example an aesthetic or moral transformation of the American people; as a business, it will seek only to service its constituency and make money doing it. This is not the precondition for television "to challenge us."

Along the way, however, there will be moments of uplifting programming—wonderful dance and theater, music from the masters, probative news and documentaries. But this will always be of a minority interest. The record of broadcasting in this matter has clearly been dismal; public television has performed considerably better. But only the narrowcasting capabilities of cable television have the potential to deliver such programming consistently.

To John Fiske, a leading theoretician of video culture, the functionality of television was based on its organization and purpose, and they were fairly obvious. "Television is, above all else, a popular cultural medium," he wrote in his book *Television Culture*. "Television is a conventional medium—its conventions suit both the audiences with their needs for a familiarity and routinization and the producers, for established conventions not only keep the costs of production down, they also minimize the risks in the marketplace. The economics of television gives it a conventional form, even when its content is more progressive."[24]

Given such determinants, the persistence of the familiar must be understood as inevitable in U.S. television. Since TV is filled with popular culture, and since popular culture appeals to the commonalities within the mass population, it will continue to dominate any medium of commercial entertainment and information. The strength of cable, of course is its ability—if not the necessity—to program "less-popular culture," entertainment and informational attractions of interest principally to intellectual, racial, occupational, or aesthetic minorities. Importantly, however, such programming is still within the boundaries of conventionality and familiarity required by the viewership and the medium.

The disconcerting part of the equation, however, is that the American people are having to pay directly for their video smorgasbord. Granted, so-called free television never really was without cost to the viewer. All those millions of dollars spent for advertising had to be recouped in the cost of advertised products. As indicated in late 1989 by Richard Gessner, president of Massillon Cable TV of Massillon, Ohio, and chairman of the Community Antenna Television Association, "the only thing that's free about 'free TV' is the free use of the public spectrum. . . . Whenever a person buys a new car, a box of soap powder, a frozen TV dinner, cosmetics, clothing, national chain store merchandise, or any product or service advertised on TV, a substantial portion of the price goes to pay for over-the-air free TV—even if the person does not own a TV set." Gessner calculated, moreover, that in 1988 the average American household paid $285.56, or $23.80 per month, to support free TV.[25]

With cable, however, subscribers must pay the televiser directly: about $15 monthly for basic cable and upward of $10 per month each for pay channels. Intrusive commercials continue to proliferate on most of the basic cable networks, presumably keeping prices from spiraling even higher; and those with narrow interests still are not satisfied with regularity. After forty years as the disseminator of the common culture, broadcast is now only part of the TV spectrum in the United States. Millions of people, especially the less wealthy, will never know television as it fully exists because TV is no longer free. The social implications of this development will require many years to materialize.

When they first surrendered the airwaves to private commercial companies, Americans set their culture on its present course. That most capitalist countries arranged their video service otherwise—France, Canada, and Great Britain, for example—proves neither that they served as many people as well as U.S. television nor that they produced as prolifically and attractively as the American industry. If anything, the recent drift in Europe toward privatization of telecommunications constitutes an admission of sorts that private business may run television more effectively and approvingly than government.

Entering the 1990s, the United States is left with a hierarchical television system in which broadcasting continues to serve those unwilling or unable to purchase TV, while alternative technologies satisfy those with money and access. Perhaps this was the only way a diverse population could produce the narrowcasting selection it needed to satisfy less than mass tastes. This may no longer be one nation under network television, but it remains the same nation still deeply under the beguilement of the medium.

the new

The early promise of TV had been "free television in the home." Not only was it the promise, but quickly it also became the reality that made the medium popular, national, and indispensable. Yet, given the way video has evolved since its emergence, the question now emerging is whether free television in the home will **video** survive into the next century. With modern technical capabilities, have Americans revised their expectations of TV, or are the pledges delivered since the RCA/NBC sales campaign at the New York World's Fair still sufficient to energize an industry and excite a mass population?

Perhaps Americans are tiring of the medium, network and cable TV alike. More precisely, the graying children of the baby boom may have become satiated after a lifetime with an industry unable or unwilling to keep abreast of their changing priorities. Young adults may be becoming bored with **order** the same forms and formats that entertained their parents and grandparents. Contemporary youth, so mobile and independent and affluent, may be finding TV irrelevant to their interests. Moreover, the foundation of modern broadcasting has been the faith of advertisers that the enormous sums they spend on commercials are necessary to reach large audiences to sell products and services. If this belief is ever shattered, and there are serious reevaluations of advertising effectiveness, the result would put in jeopardy all commercial television.

Whatever the ultimate resolution, as it enters the last decade of the twentieth century U.S. television is in flux. The hard control of the industry exercised by monopolistic networks is crumbling, and there is a desperate scramble for leverage and power. It is not a battle for the scraps of a collapsing industry; instead, it is about restructuring the business, rearranging electronic communications for the next century, when profits will be enormous. While viewers spend their time choosing programs for the evening, zipping and zapping through their choices, the fate of television is being decided by powerful men and institutions.

the battle for the twenty-first century

Vested interests are struggling fiercely for advantage, each hoping to refashion the medium to enhance its own bottom line. As for government officials, the protectors of citizen interests, they are entering the fray or retreating from it according to their ideological understanding of the role of the state in the regulation of private business affairs. Confused, destabilized, and uncertain, the industry is engaged in mortal conflict, the outcome of which will determine the future of television. In its essential form, it is a corporate war involving the traditional networks, major cable operators, Hollywood producers, and global communications interests.

The three broadcast networks have been the most aggressive in this struggle. Defensive and aware of their shrinking popularity, they have been fighting for their future viability. Network leaders have been loud in demanding regulatory assistance to meet the challenge of cable and Hollywood. They have demanded the right to produce much of their own entertainment fare, and they have been particularly hostile toward the old Financial Interest and Syndication Rules (FISR), which since 1972 have prohibited them from owning or syndicating entertainment programs. They assert that they are losing money as their rivals are making millions. At a time when series such as *The Cosby Show* are reaping hundreds of millions of dollars in syndication fees for Hollywood producers, and foreign sales of U.S. programming are rising to unprecedented levels, broadcasters claim that they should be able to own part of these shows and share in their profits, since network TV made them successful in the first place.

Moreover, they suggest that the need for the FISR has passed. The fin-syn rules were established in great part because of pressure from the major Hollywood studios, which were in financial difficulties in the late 1960s. But the movie business has never been more lucrative. Box office receipts for 1988 were $4.46 billion; for 1989 they were approximately $5 billion. Receipts for the *summer* alone were phenomenal: $1.7 billion in 1988 and $2.05 billion in 1989.[1] Conversely, network executives argue, without new revenue sources they will be unable to compete in the new video marketplace.

Unnerved, too, by the rapid spread of cable throughout the 1980s, the networks have moved against their rivals in the distribution of programs. Raising the prospect of the death of free TV, ABC, CBS, and NBC have called pay TV undemocratic and alien to American traditions. To protect the "universal free over-the-air broadcast system" they have asked for rules mandating that cable systems carry their stations and assign them the same channels they have on the VHF dial. Above all, the networks have demanded that the FCC or Congress begin regulating the burgeoning cable industry, an entity that Senator Howard Metzenbaum has labeled "an economic Goliath."[2] After decades in which three national programmers monopolized television, the president of the NAB, Eddie Fritts, told members of his pronetwork organization that the enemy was now monopolistic cable. "Together, we are agreed that cable TV's unregulated monopoly must be reined in," he noted. "The unfair competitive advantage Congress gave cable by virtually total deregulation of that industry must be rectified."[3]

The debate reached a momentous high point on June 21, 1989, when the Senate Communications Subcommittee, chaired by Daniel Inouye, conducted public hearings to obtain input from the contending interests.[4] Although network leaders were unfamiliar in employing antimonopoly rhetoric to defend their interests, Robert Wright of NBC complained about the rapidly diminishing economic vitality of network TV, which had seen its 74 percent share of dollars spent on video entertainment in 1970 tumble to 24 percent in 1988.

Wright's alarm was amplified by Laurence Tisch of CBS. "Make no mistake about it," he warned the senators, "the long-term availability of the Super Bowl, the World Series, and the Olympics to all Americans over free television is in serious jeopardy." He also threatened that if pay TV were not brought under control and networks allowed to compete in the video marketplace, over-the-air networks would have no one left to serve except the poor and socially neglected. "What if we then had a two-tier broadcasting system," Tisch wondered, "with a second-class, free programming service available to the less fortunate who are disproportionately minorities, children, and the aged located heavily in urban ghettos and rural areas?"

Describing network TV as "a service of irreplaceable value," Thomas S. Murphy of Capital Cities/ABC called attention to the deterioration of the national audience precipitated by expanded competition—in the past five years the average number of channels received by TV households rose from ten to twenty-seven—and continued application of FISR limitations. Murphy sounded another alarm. "Because what we broadcast is the staple of much of the television in the United States, the continued health of the network system is and should be a matter of public interest and concern. Today the health of that system is in jeopardy."

While pleading their collective case, however, the executives studiously avoided the embarrassing fact that their corporations remained amazingly wealthy (a pretax profit margin of 48 percent)—and their future contained a bright silver lining. Although they promised to make their own totals available to the subcommittee, the executives denied the accuracy of revenue and profit figures for 1988 as published in *Broadcasting* magazine.

Those totals belied the financial desperation claimed by the networks. While Robert Wright was bewailing the decline of NBC's share of the communications pie, the corporation grossed $3.018 billion in network TV revenues alone. When added to the money earned through its owned and operated TV stations, the network grossed more than $3.6 billion and realized profits of $537 million. Even more successful, Capital Cities/ABC, with substantial investments in radio and other video enterprises, grossed $2.382 billion in network TV revenues, and almost $3.8 billion for its total broadcast group; the final profit for CCB/ABC was $767 million. Bringing up the rear, narrowly invested CBS still grossed $2.777 billion and made profits of $232 million.[5]

As if such profitability were not enough, the networks stand to make even more money with the lapsing in November 1990 of the judicial consent agreement that imposed production caps on the number of program hours they could produce and own. Each network will regain the right to fill as much as 100 percent of its twenty-two prime-time hours per week with its own shows.

Already, they could produce and own five hours of prime-time shows weekly—if such programming were 100 percent network-financed—and the fall 1989 lineup was stocked with their own productions. From the fourteen pilots it produced, for example, NBC filled two of its four one-hour slots with series from NBC Productions. NBC also bought a third series from itself as a midseason backup in case of an early cancellation, and it received the right to produce segments for a Walt Disney hour-long show. CBS bought two in-house productions for the fall; and anticipating total liberation in 1990, ABC announced that it was forming a new in-house entity headed by Brandon Stoddard, a former ABC Entertainment president, to produce new programs for the upcoming season.

Clearly, the FISR remained the only substantial impediments to the domination of American mass communications by ABC, CBS, and NBC. Among the related areas in which the networks were already deeply involved were movie production, movie theater ownership, movie distribution, network program production, pay per view, pay television, cable networks, cable program production, direct-broadcast satellite, home video, foreign syndication of their own internally produced shows, book and magazine publishing, and the phonograph record industry.

Appearing before the Senate Communications Subcommittee to oppose the network CEO's were representatives of the Hollywood film industry: Stephen J. Cannell, a major independent producer, and Jack Valenti, president of the Motion Picture Association of America. As a spokesman for more than two hundred independent programmers, Cannell appealed for a continuation of the FISR. According to the man responsible for hit series such as *The Rockford Files, Hunter,* and *Wiseguy,* "I hope you understand how desperately the Hollywood production community views this situation. I'm not here alone, I'm really here for a lot of other people." He continued, "We're forced to live in an oligopoly with three dominant corporations, but at least we go from one to the other in our search for a home for our programming. It's not perfect, but it creates some balance, and it works." There was, however, a tone of industry and personal urgency in Cannell's concluding imploration: "I plead with you, don't repeal the Financial Interest and Syndication Rules. Without [them] I fear my company will perish."

Arguing passionately that the FISR should not be relaxed, Valenti explained that with all their wealth and power his constituents, the Hollywood movie studios, still needed regulatory protection against potential network coercion. He recalled the monopoly over production and distribution exercised by the three networks in the 1950s and 1960s, and he claimed that film studios now supplying so many TV programs could not survive a revival of unfair competition. Valenti forcefully asserted that "our government ought never allow any tiny group of corporate chieftains, or corporate entities, no matter how benignly managed, to ever reassert full dominion over prime-time television, which is the most pervasive moral, social, political, and cultural force in this country. The networks' monopoly troika just can't be allowed."

Above all, Valenti recognized that despite wondrous technological alternatives to TV and a dwindling network share of the prime-time audience, ABC, CBS, and NBC remained the most influential forces in American communications. "The three networks in prime time are the only national force in this country," he noted. "Cable only reaches 54 percent. The independent stations don't have that kind of reach. Only the three networks and their six-hundred-plus affiliates do. And they have total authority to say yes or no." As Valenti explained it to Senator Inouye, were network authority enhanced by a revocation of the FISR, "the most powerful media company, Mr. Chairman—Time, Warner, Paramount, Fox, if they all merged—would be helpless and hapless before a fuzzy-cheeked little network vice president who said, 'No, buster, get out of here!' They're gone, they don't have any power."

Despite the great divisions between networks and producers, there were circumstances that suggested the differences were not as heated as their proponents suggested. Of the three broadcasters, only CBS was wholeheartedly committed to over-the-air television. Here the influence of William S. Paley endured. Much as the corporation had performed in the mid-1940s—defiantly refusing to develop black-and-white VHF channels because it was certain that CBS color technology and UHF would be the ultimate victors—Tisch and CBS launched a concerted campaign in mid-1989 to rally network affiliates and public opinion to blunt the cable revolution. "This is our biggest, toughest battle and it will require a lot of effort and vigilance, but we must win," Tisch declared. As for collaboration with the cable enemy, the CBS leader was consistent and candid.

In late 1988 he declared disinterest in cable because he feared it would become "the newest toy in the house," distracting CBS management from the priority of lifting the network from the broadcasting basement.[6] Tisch reiterated this feeling six months later, noting, "I do not see cable TV as the right business for CBS to move into at this time. If we're going to get into any other kind of business, we'd be devoting our resources and attentions away from the core business that needs fixing. We would be distracted. This way we are singularly focused."[7]

Ironically, CBS had already invested in cable and lost heavily. In 1982 the broadcaster had created a fine-arts network, CBS Cable. Its short and disastrous life produced uplifting ballets, wonderful plays, and insightful interviews with cultural leaders, but it never captured enough viewers. The collapse of CBS Cable in less than a year cost the parent network millions of dollars. It was exactly the type of financial miscalculation that CBS by 1990 would no longer afford.

Tisch's broadcast allies were less zealous in their resistance to the encroachment of wire distribution. Aggressive investment policies at ABC and NBC suggested that these networks were becoming deeply involved in an emerging cable future. By the end of the decade cable ventures of Capital Cities/ABC included 80 percent ownership of ESPN and minority interests in the Arts & Entertainment (A&E) and Lifetime networks. NBC was even more drawn to the rival technology.

As well as owning 25 percent of A&E, through its parent company, General Electric, NBC in December 1988 concluded a $325 million arrangement with an MSO, Cablevision Systems Corporation. By this partnership NBC entered cable as a major force—especially in sports, and potentially in all-news programming—obtaining half of Cablevision's investment in Rainbow Program Enterprises (American Movie Classics, Bravo); Sports Channel America; seven regional Sportsvision channels; and News 12 Long Island, a regional all-news operation. The arrangement also gave NBC ready access to the 1.14 million households receiving cable service from Cablevision.

In return, Cablevision received 50 percent of the new NBC cable venture, the Consumer News and Business Channel (CNBC), that was launched in April 1989. Cablevision also opened its door to a lucrative future in sports pay-per-view programming. It contracted to join NBC in televising the 1992 Summer Olympics—the American TV rights for which NBC had already paid $401 million—by setting up an ad hoc, multichannel cable network to package up to six hundred hours of the Olympics on a PPV basis.

The third force in the corporate communications struggle, the cable TV industry, also appeared before the Senate Communications Subcommittee in June 1989. Operating in an atmosphere of deregulation established in 1983 by the FCC under Mark Fowler, and reinforced through the Cable Act of 1984 by which Congress formally established the operational parameters of the industry, cable enjoyed its greatest expansion. Annual revenues from advertising and fees mushroomed from $6.5 billion in 1983 to an estimated $15.4 billion in 1989.[8]

Yet after years of unfettered capitalistic maneuvering, there were many areas of contention. The exclusivity enjoyed by cable operators within their service areas raised questions of monopoly and the loss of consumer protection. The desire of local telephone companies (telcos) to string cable lines into subscriber homes—most likely fiber-optic cable, which, compared to the familiar coaxial wire, would provide improved picture quality and greater channel capacity—prompted cries of unfair practices from existing cable operators. Rising subscriber costs, which by mid-1989 averaged $24.26 per month, raised questions about coercion of an audience used to feeless video. Televising current R-rated theatrical films and the absence of censorship raised questions about sexual explicitness, profanity, and violence on premium channels. And the concentration of cable systems in the hands of fewer and fewer MSO's provoked inquiries about vertical integration and other monopolistic practices.

For John Malone, president and CEO of the largest MSO, Tele-Communications, Inc., such problems constituted no reason for Congress or the FCC to reverse course now. The imposition of regulations, he warned, would only slow the cabling of America. He explained increased subscriber fees as driven solely by the cost of programming. He felt, moreover, that the introduction of telcos into cable service would complicate matters and ultimately force government back into regulation. Malone contended, expectedly, that cable was already adequately regulated.[9]

Although Malone was supported by other cable interests— James Moody, president of the National Cable Television Association; Robert Johnson, president of Black Entertainment Television; and John Hendrick, CEO of The Discovery Channel —the senators seemed unconvinced. As Senator Inouye remarked, "After listening to this panel, if I were a cable operator, it is time for Rolaids."

There were those in government, moreover, already convinced that reform of cable industry practices was overdue. Senator Metzenbaum, who testified before the Senate Communications Subcommittee, declared that "Congress cannot sit idly by. We're going to have to see to it that there is continuation of competition."[10] And Senator Albert Gore, Jr., was openly critical of the coercive practices of some MSO's, practices that reminded him of network maneuverings in the years before the FISR.

In blunt questioning of the president of NBC, Senator Gore revealed practices now occurring within the unregulated cable industry. Gore wondered why NBC had decided to drop its original plans to convert CNBC into an all-news service competing against Cable News Network (CNN). He also questioned why NBC would pay $20 million for "a shell company" that was "an asset of limited value"—the grossly neglected Tempo Network, owned by the largest MSO, Tele-Communications, Inc. (TCI)— only to convert it into CNBC. Gore's question to Robert Wright was unequivocal: "Was that transaction demanded by TCI during those negotiations?"

Wright: *It'd been around for eight years, so it wasn't just an overnight issue. We elected to change the service entirely. Hence, the "shell company," I guess. But it was an existing service with seven million people. They owned it, we didn't. That was a way that we thought would give us an opportunity to, uh, instead of going from zero, we'd start with six or seven million.*

Gore: *Was this kind of a shakedown by TCI to ensure that you'd get access for CNBC?*

Wright: *No, I can't say that. We didn't have to buy it. We could have gone another route. We could have picked another service. Or, we could have started up from scratch. It's hard to say what things are worth. . . .*

Gore: *Did you agree not to compete directly with CNN in making CNBC a full-scale news operation in direct competition with CNN because TCI owns part of CNN's parent company? Was this part of the arrangement also that guaranteed you access for CNBC?*

Wright: *We have an agreement in our affiliation agreement that was requested—required, if you will—by most cable operators that we not enter into general competition with CNN.*

Gore: *Isn't that anticompetitive?*

Wright: *Well, it's not exactly what we would have preferred.*

Gore: *Isn't it anticompetitive?*

Wright: *Well, it's hard to say. It, it, it does on the surface, anticompetitive—*

Gore: *Why is it hard to say?*

Wright: *Because their whole theory is—*

Gore: *Because you don't want to offend TCI?*

Wright: *Well, we certainly have to deal with our own customer base. That's our customer base.*

Gore: *Well, you see, Mr. Chairman, this is an example of the kind of shakedown, and I use the word again, that cable engages in. And they just have the power and the arrogance to hold up one of the major networks and force them to agree not to compete and not to show news on cable television because the biggest MSO owns part of CNN and doesn't want the competition. And they just tell them, "We won't even let you enter the market unless you agree not to compete. And by the way, we have this mostly worthless company that we're trying to unload on somebody. How about giving us $20 million on the side for it?"*

narrowcasting and globalization

While mighty adversaries—government regulators, broadcast networks, cable, and program producers—battle for the future of American TV, the shape of that future remains uncertain. But the current trends suggest that by the next century U.S. video will crystallize somewhere between a minimalist system of network broadcasting/cable narrowcasting, and a maximalist arrangement in which globally organized megacorporations control mass entertainment and information at every stage of commercial exploitation.

Narrowcast TV would mean more channels, more choice, a medium more responsive to individual differences within the U.S. population. That was certainly the vista of Austin Ranney of the American Enterprise Institute, who in the early 1980s wrote about the narrowcast future possible through cable. He called particular attention to the prediction that new technology would soon make interactive cable a possibility. And when viewers could "talk back" to the sets and electronically vote on pressing issues, American TV would have achieved "the old dream of town-meeting-style direct democracy for millions of citizens, perhaps even for the national electorate." [11]

Less civic in its concern, the advertising agency Lintas: U.S.A. also foresaw the imminent death of mass media—from mass-circulation magazines to network television—in a fragmented, decentralized future that would render mass media irrelevant. Speaking before the American Advertising Federation in June 1989, the agency's executive vice-president for business development, Don Peppers, argued that in the contemporary "consumer information economy," where many different media compete to satisfy the predilections of individual consumers, the homogenized product offered in the past was rapidly losing its popularity. "Gathering the family around and watching *I Love Lucy* has declined," Peppers noted. "Network and program loyalty and attention spans have gone down." Alexander Kroll, head of the Young & Rubicam advertising agency, was even more direct when he claimed in late 1989 that "the individual is poking his head out of the mass tapestry and sticking his tongue out at us."

In the Lintas model, advertisers would require what Peppers called "precise information through a whole range of communications vehicles to reach people effectively." He predicted that marketing strategies would become increasingly narrow, to be based ultimately on information gathered from records of purchases that detail individual buying habits and personal tastes, a fine-tuning that Keith L. Reinhard, chairman of the DDB Needham Worldwide advertising agency, characterized as "personal media maps" that chart the reading and viewing habits of consumers.

Furthermore, in this future where fragmented media have replaced mass media, advertisers will be able to market to specific buyers rather than collections of buyers. General Motors, for example, is already researching interactive advertising techniques that would interrelate and exploit various electronic media now available in the homes of consumers, among them television, telephones, personal computers, and facsimile machines. As one GM executive explained it, the corporation's goal is to discover ways to employ all these media "to communicate with you on a one-to-one basis." [12]

As well as in predictions about a decentralized future, the inexorable slide toward television narrowcasting is indicated in the experiences of network radio four decades ago. When national video emerged in the early 1950s, it killed network AM radio, in great part because radio was limited in scope and size, and it was controlled by the same networks scrambling to board the TV bandwagon. AM radio became so unpopular and decentralized, in fact, that late-blooming FM radio soon carved out a formidable spot on the economic spectrum. To thrive, even to survive, stations on both radio bands were compelled to develop formats appealing to specific tastes within a diverse but local public. The result was narrowcast radio in which many formats appeared, and cumulative ratings above 6.0 were considered successes in markets where dozens of outlets competed for listeners and advertisers.

The major difference between audio and video, however, is that the former was and is considerably less expensive to program than television. Most radio stations remain relatively inexpensive community operations, and the rump services that now pass as national radio deliver only a few minutes of news and/or features to subscriber stations each hour. Although TV serves more people than radio, narrowcast video—even those outlets programming old movies and well-used reruns—has sizable expenses that must be borne by advertisers or subscribers.

Narrowcast television has within it, moreover, the potential of self-destruction. Because it is so lucrative, television invites economic concentration and monopoly. In American society, where profit-oriented businesses control the air, and federal regulation has been chronically weak, fewer and fewer large corporations inevitably maneuver to increase their leverage within the industry. In the name of stockholder dividends and efficiency, corporate concentration leads to standardization, mass marketing, and a lack of diversity—the exact opposite of narrowcasting. As discussed in Chapter 11, there are structural forces mitigating against such an eventuality. Yet sociologist Todd Gitlin recognized the potential of such a development when he concluded that "the brave new cornucopia is likely to create only minor, marginal chances for diversity of substance—and fewer and fewer as time goes on." He continued:

> *The workings of the market give Americans every incentive to remain conventionally entertainment-happy. Conglomeration proceeds apace. Homogeneity at the cultural center is complemented by consumer fragmentation on the margins. Technology opens doors, and oligopoly marches in just behind, slamming them. There can be no technological fix for what is, after all, a social problem.*[13]

Questions inevitably emerge after fifty years of network television: Will commercial broadcasting remain influential enough with viewers that it will remain feasible for business to use—or to begin using—TV strategies in marketing goods and services? If the medium is moving toward a mixed narrowcast and subscription future, what will be the fate of the networks as communicators of a homogeneous national experience? What will be the future of television as a medium of social and political importance? Who will control television?

These are questions that emerge from an industry in flux. Leveraged buyouts and threats of hostile takeovers may be creating massive communications corporations, but these are usually deep in debt and therefore creatively constrained. Network ratings continue to fall to the point that CBS, once the industry's leader, faces a dismal future with old series that are losing their appeal, new series that do not attract viewers, and billions of dollars invested in sports programming. Although the network continues to realize a profit, its loss of popularity is unprecedented. As the president of one CBS affiliate lamented in late 1989, "We have, in the November ratings book for Monday through Friday, a single-digit rating, which has never happened before in our history."[14]

Even the advertising industry is suffering because of the turmoil in television. As Michael Lev reported in the *New York Times* in November 1989: "Television has not experienced a year of robust advertising growth since 1984, when revenues grew 18.5 percent. Since then growth has been held to single-digit increases that have barely kept pace with economic growth." Whereas TV advertising revenues for cable and broadcast reached $26.9 billion in 1988, much of that 7.5 percent increase came from advertising during the Olympic Games. Growth in 1989 slowed to 6 percent in 1989, and it was anticipated to rise only 7 to 9 percent in 1990.[15]

The three broadcast networks continue, however, to convince advertisers that even with less than 68 percent of the prime-time audience and rising costs-per-thousand viewers delivered, they provide the largest possible exposure for commercial messages. But ABC, CBS, and NBC have had to adjust their economics to the new reality. Comparative statistics from the November sweeps in 1984 and 1987 illustrate that the networks have had to accept fifteen-second commercials as a normal part of commercial time. Swelling from 6 percent of prime-time advertising in 1984 to 36 percent in 1987 (and up from 11 percent to 43 percent in weekday advertising), the quarter-minute spot has triggered an increase in the monthly number of commercials on network TV —up in prime time from 3,952 to 4,667, and on weekdays from 8,474 to 9,877. Where there was only a slight rise in total commercial minutes in prime time (up from 1,916 to 1,954), and a decrease in weekday TV (down from 4,061 to 3,894), the bombardment of the audience has prompted outcries against commercial clutter.[16]

Although the networks by late 1988 attracted only 59 percent of the viewing audience from sign-on to sign-off (independents drew 25 percent; cable received 16 percent), they still received 81 percent of the advertising dollar. And presale of prime-time advertising for the 1989–90 season led media analysts to predict record profits for the three TV networks in 1990, possibly exceeding $600 million.[17]

Cable TV continues to expand the narrowcast reality. Although some predicted a slow growth rate for cable in the 1990s, peaking at about 60 percent penetration, the industry in mid-1989 reported wiring 10,000 homes each day, 300,000 households per month. And gross advertising revenues for cable in 1989 were expected to reach $1.5 billion, a rise of 40 percent over the previous year.[18] Even half of the audience for the leading broadcast network, NBC, now watched it on cable TV.

There were misgivings, however. Local operators, no longer under the control of city cable commissions, continued to wrestle with viewer complaints about everything from poor reception to

R-rated program content. Because local operators make money from home shopping services, the several networks selling trinkets and fashions—Home Shopping Network, J.C.Penney Television Shopping Channel, QVC Network—often occupied several channels, while local operators dropped more popular (but less profitable) networks. The arts, education, minorities, government, business, children, and other specific tastes continued to be served; but many such channels survive only through subsidies from large MSO's such as TCI, which then point to cable diversity as proof of their industry's value to a pluralistic society.

Attempting to understand the direction of television in this time of flux, *Electronic Media* in early 1988 asked several analysts to act as seers. For those seeking a return to the past glories of free programming, or for those wishing to discover calm in contemporary TV, these experts were not encouraging. Among their predictions were the following:[19]

- DURING THE 1990s ONE OF THE THREE MAJOR NETWORKS WILL EITHER CEASE OPERATIONS OR SELL OUT TO ITS AFFILIATES AND BECOME A COOPERATIVE ENTITY.

- U.S. TELEVISION WILL ACCEPT MORE FOREIGN PROGRAMS, THEREBY SPEEDING UP THE PROCESS OF GLOBALIZATION IN VIDEO.

- CONTINUED FISCAL WOES AND TECHNOLOGICAL ADVANCEMENTS WILL PRECIPITATE EVEN MORE CHANGES IN THE RESTRUCTURING OF TRADITIONAL TV AND PROGRAMMING.

- NETWORKS WILL COOPERATE MORE WITH CABLE IN PRODUCING JOINT PROGRAMMING VENTURES.

- THERE WILL BE FURTHER FRAGMENTATION OF THE NETWORK AUDIENCES AS CABLE PENETRATION INCREASES; RESULT WILL BE INABILITY OF THE NETWORKS TO COMMAND INCREASING PRICES FROM THEIR ADVERTISERS.

- TRADITIONAL NOTIONS OF MASS MARKETING MAY SOON BE ANACHRONISTIC AS TV MOVES INCREASINGLY TO TARGET MARKETING AND PROGRAMMING—AND THIS WILL ENHANCE CABLE STATIONS MORE THAN IT WILL NETWORK BROADCASTERS. IF THE NETWORKS DO NOT FOLLOW SUIT, THEY "COULD ONE DAY FIND THEMSELVES LIKE *LOOK* AND *LIFE*

MAGAZINES—WITH THE LARGEST AUDIENCE CIRCULATION
BUT SOME OF THE SMALLEST REVENUE SHARES."

■ "FROM NOW ON EVERYONE IS PLAYING BY DIFFERENT RULES.
EVERYTHING AND ANYTHING IS POSSIBLE."

Although such prognostications indicate that the TV business is in turmoil, they do little to promote clarity. It is possible, however, to discern that future by observing developments in other countries. Around the world vast conglomerates have been purchasing communications industries, synchronizing their video, radio, publishing, and phonograph subsidiaries into synergistic megacorporations. The goal has been to service vast geographic areas with operations able to take a creative idea and exploit, distribute, and market it from concept to rerun.

In this profitable process an idea could originate as a magazine article, then move through the continuum from book to big-screen motion picture—whose sound track is marketed on cassette and compact disc—to prerecorded videocassette, pay-per-view feature, pay-cable attraction, and first-run release to broadcast networks—then into syndication to cable or independent outlets. Along the way, too, it could be made into a radio or television show, a miniseries, or a full series—or a sequel, which itself could follow the same exploitative process.

The "warlords" maneuvering toward such vertical integration include the French publishing house and TV giant Hachette; corporations owned and/or controlled by the Australian-American Rupert Murdoch; the West German corporation Bertelsmann, AG; the Silvio Berlesconi conglomerate, headquartered in Italy; and the Robert Maxwell communications empire, headquartered in Great Britain. The cause of much of the tumult in American television has been the fact that until the creation of Time Warner in mid-1989, a U.S. warlord had not entered the field. And while its appearance was awaited by the industry, many foreign companies have been spending deflated U.S. dollars to acquire prime American communications properties for their own conglomerates. Among these have been:

■ SONY (JAPAN)
   CBS RECORDS
   COLUMBIA PICTURES ENTERTAINMENT (TV/MOVIES)

■ BERTELSMANN (WEST GERMANY)
   DOUBLEDAY (BOOKS)
   DELL (BOOKS)

BANTAM (BOOKS)
RCA RECORDS
THE LITERARY GUILD (BOOK CLUB)

■ *QINTEX PRODUCTIONS* (AUSTRALIA)
UNITED ARTISTS (MOVIES)
HAL ROACH STUDIOS (MOVIES)

■ *MAXWELL COMMUNICATIONS* (GREAT BRITAIN)
MACMILLAN (BOOKS)

■ *TELEVISION SOUTH* (GREAT BRITAIN)
MTM PRODUCTIONS (TV)

■ *THAMES TELEVISION* (GREAT BRITAIN)
REEVES COMMUNICATIONS (TV)

■ *PATHÉ ENTERTAINMENT/GIANCARLO PARRETTI* (FRANCE)
NEW WORLD ENTERTAINMENT (MOVIES)

■ *NEWS CORPORATION/RUPERT MURDOCH* (AUSTRALIA)
NUMEROUS MAGAZINES AND NEWSPAPERS
20TH CENTURY-FOX (MOVIES)
HARPER & ROW (BOOKS)
METROMEDIA (TV NETWORK)
FOX BROADCASTING (TV NETWORK)

Interestingly, the inability of the U.S. corporations to come together to compete with the emergent transnationals was upsetting the global balance. British communications magnate Robert Maxwell told ABC News in June 1989 that the United States needed a standard-bearer to represent American interests in the global telecommunications scramble. Speaking with Sander Vanocur on *Business World,* Maxwell approved the merger of Time, Inc., with any of its suitors—Paramount Communications, Cablevision, and the eventual winner, Warner Communications—as presaging the formation of a U.S. global conglomerate. These financial maneuvers, Maxwell said, were "very good for America. In particular, if the Time-Warner merger had gone through as was originally contemplated, that would have created a United States giant that would have matched any of what we could do in Europe, with or without the Japanese." Maxwell continued:

> *The information business is like energy or money: it is scarce, it is valuable, it is important, and it is moving globally. And this is*

why you see so many mergers on a national and international scale. It will continue until there are about ten megacorporations who will control communications in the world, without in any way harming national interests or regional newspapers or television and so on. The globe is becoming one village, and you need to have information and media companies to be global. . . . Time's a very very fine corporation. . . . the United States needs to have a major flag-carrying corporation.

Vanocur: *You've not mentioned, till this moment, synergy. Is that an overworked word?*

Maxwell: *It is not overworked. Synergy is a good thing in money terms. But the technology isn't yet completely in place where you can take an author's work, like your own, and convert it into a film, a radio play on CD-ROM disc. It's coming into place. It will be in place in about five years time. This is one of the reasons why globalism is so much to the fore.*[20]

Not all Americans shared Maxwell's transnational vision. Some, like media scholar Ben Bagdikian, have indicated that the appearance of any U.S. conglomerate would be inimical to the variety offered by competitive communications media. As Bagdikian explained it on ABC's *Business World* in June 1989: "I think we have to make a decision in this country on how much we want to sacrifice the diversity of media in this country—of news, of information, of television programs, of entertainment, of cable, of book publishing, of magazines—how much we're going to sacrifice our choice in those things in order to let a few American companies become as big as the supergiants around the world."

On the other hand, the situation is reminiscent of the dilemma perceived by the U.S. Navy following World War I when, with foreign radio companies threatening to get a jump on U.S. corporations, the navy helped to overcome antitrust conflicts and establish the Radio Corporation of America.

The most obvious U.S. player in global entertainment competition is the megacorporation Time Warner, Inc., which was formed in mid-1989 by the $14 billion purchase of Warner Communications by Time, Inc.—this following a costly legal battle with rival Paramount Communications. Time brought to the new union holdings in magazines *(Time, Life, Fortune, People, Sports Illustrated)*, basic and pay cable (BET, CNN, TNT, HBO, Cinemax, Viewers' Choice, The Fashion Channel), phonograph records (Time Records), book publishing (Time-Life Books; Little, Brown), and distribution (Book-of-the-Month Club, History Book Club).

Warner Communications provided film production and syndication (Lorimar Telepictures, Warner Brothers), home video (Warner), television stations (50 percent of United Television), cable systems (Warner Cable, 82 percent of American Television & Communications), cable programming services (Cable Value Network, The Fashion Channel, Movietime, Shop Television Network, 17 percent of Turner Broadcasting), phonograph records (Warner, Elektra, Atlantic), and music and book publishing (Warner Books, DC Comics).

As an interesting reflection of the times, the Time Warner deal quickly precipitated speculation about the next combinations: some suggested Time Warner would soon acquire Pathé Entertainment of France or Turner Broadcasting; or that Walt Disney Company would merge soon with either MCA or Columbia Pictures or Paramount Communications; or that Paramount would merge with MCA, Tele-Communications, Inc., the Tribune Company of Chicago, or perhaps even Time Warner.[21]

With potential profitability so enormous and such multibillion-dollar transactions happening or pending, the leap into transnational media has clearly been on the minds of the U.S. television networks. When Thomas S. Murphy of Capital Cities/ABC testified before the Senate Communications Subcommittee in 1989, he spoke about competition and the American public, but he concluded with a broader reference: "In order for us to compete effectively, I believe that the network companies must be freed from many of the restrictions that inhibit our ability to be full players in the burgeoning domestic and global programming industry." Capital Cities/ABC, however, had already demonstrated its desire to make foreign investments. In February 1989 the corporation purchased a sizable percentage of the West German media conglomerate Tele-München. ABC also pursued ventures in Spain and elsewhere.

At NBC Robert Wright was already on record predicting that by 1994 his corporation would be "a much bigger company engaged in multiple networks and the ownership and production of programs seen worldwide on cable and over-the-air television."[22] Appealing to the Senate Communications Subcommittee to make his corporate dreams come true, Wright again disclosed that NBC had global aspirations. In maintaining that the FISR "harm America's position in the exploding international video marketplace," he argued:

Only the networks, potentially this country's strongest competitors, cannot fully participate in the global arena. We watch as the Australian News Corporation and Qintex buy up Hollywood studios. But the American networks can't do what they do, at home or abroad. We can't produce programs in the United States with foreign money, and then export those programs. We can't buy the foreign distribution rights to a theatrical movie if it has ever been on television. About the only incentive, or the opportunity we have, in fact, is to produce abroad solely for foreign markets because that way we don't trigger the rules.

Indeed, television is moving toward rearrangement into global spheres of influence. At a time when TV around the world —broadcast, local, and cable—is controlled by fewer and fewer corporations, there are those in the United States who agree that the time is ripe for one or more American standard-bearers. Especially attractive to U.S. video interests is the integrated European Community to be finalized in 1992. This economic "United States of Europe," composed of twelve Western European nations, constitutes a rich and sophisticated market comparable to that of the United States. With its plan to foster a robust and cooperative European communications reality, "TV Without Frontiers," the EC has imposed quotas of 50 percent on foreign television product permitted on its screens. Still, possible financial rewards for entertaining the EC remain massive. And with the restructuring of Eastern European economies in the wake of the collapse of Communist authority, the European market for television appears all the more potentially profitable.

By the end of 1989 many U.S. communications corporations were rushing toward involvement in European television. By its purchase of 49 percent of Zenith Productions of Great Britain, Paramount Communications enhanced its European presence. When Warner Brothers, a division of Time Warner, acquired one-third of the Swedish pay-television market, one of its corporate presidents explained, "This is Warner Brothers' first investment outside the U.S. in a broadcasting pay television service. We will not stop in Sweden."[23]

Meanwhile, NBC solicited foreign partnerships, and Capital Cities/ABC announced plans to produce in Europe for Europe with European partners. As explained in September by J. B. Holston, the vice-president and general manager of NBC International, these were propitious times. "It's a good time for larger players in the entertainment industry around the world to sit down and find ways we can work together," he noted. "The marketplace is becoming increasingly global. We need real partnerships and alliances that would include swapping directors and equity. If not, we're going to wake up in three years and find the industry dominated by two or three individuals."[24]

To a degree, U.S. television has always been international. Industry success has been augmented by foreign syndication of American-made programs, network investment in foreign video infrastructure, and the reliability of profits from foreign dealings. But globalism transcends such limited exploitation of product. Instead of the old multinationalist view in which the world was approached as a collection of different countries and distinct markets, globalism is an integrationist mind-set that considers the world and its citizenry in singular terms: people everywhere eat the same, want the same, react the same. As Ted Levitt of the Harvard Business School explained it, "Increasingly, all over the world, more and more people's preferences regarding products and service and qualities and features are getting more and more alike." For Levitt, the global corporation is one that is "organized and operated to treat the world—or major segments of it—as being a single or similar category."[25]

Today, global advertising has been achieved through the universal attractiveness of sports and popular music and the ubiquity of television. Particularly attractive have been recent Olympic Games and World Cup soccer championships, which have drawn billions of viewers worldwide.[26] Tina Turner and Madonna have performed on soft-drink commercials that have been televised around the globe. The potential of music to maximize audience size was demonstrated, too, in the *Live Aid* concert in July 1985. This sixteen-hour rock 'n' roll concert linked musicians and a planetwide audience via satellite from Australia to Philadelphia to London to the Soviet Union in a selfless effort to raise money for Ethiopian famine relief. The affair generated more than $40 million in contributions, and it reached an audience estimated at 1.5 billion people.

In its extreme, globalism means the cultural homogenization of the world. Despite Robert Maxwell's pledge that it would not harm national interests or regional newspapers or television, its long-range implications are overwhelming. Much as national broadcasting was the fundamental industry that amalgamated the American people into a single cultural unit—in appreciation of and in subservience to an American popular culture—to envision the world as a single market is to play to the commonalities of the human experience while ignoring or denigrating the particulars that make people different. It is mass marketing to the maximum.

And much as this process leveled regionalism and deep cultural differences within the United States, so its success will be based on the glorification of an internationally common culture and the propagation of standardized values and attitudes throughout the planet.

One of the most important markets already experiencing the impact of globalism has been the Soviet Union. After decades of oppressive politics and similar TV programming, *glasnost* opened the Soviet window on the West and on the Far East—just as technologically advanced nations and the media conglomerates were recognizing Eastern Europe as a lucrative market for cultural software and hardware. Whether it is Sony selling TV sets in Moscow, Capital Cities/ABC feeding the 1989 Academy Awards to the entire U.S.S.R., Maxwell Communications peddling British television series to the drab Soviet TV system, or Turner Broadcasting sponsoring the U.S.-Soviet Friendship Games and allowing its CNN satellite signal to be used in preparation of Soviet newscasts, the impact on Communist culture promises to be enormous.

One Soviet broadcaster has told of the reaction to a British TV series televised recently in the U.S.S.R. The program from London included commercials for Kit-Kat candy bar and Singapore Airlines, both of which are unavailable in the Soviet Union. According to Uri Radzievsky, managing director of worldwide development at Maxwell/Berlitz, "the first showing of the Kit-Kat commercial was met with interest. It brought back some of the good memories about this forgotten bittersweet thing called chocolate that disappeared from stores years ago. The second time the reaction turned into curiosity. The third showing caused outright aggravation." And when the spots for Singapore Airlines showed "all the beautiful places it flies to"—none of which was in the Soviet Union—the audience was sent "into a state of deep depression."[27]

While some have criticized such distribution as destructive to cultural differentness, Jack Valenti, as spokesman for the major Hollywood studios, has suggested that an Americanization of the world via the export of U.S. television and film products would be a function of international democracy. Questioned by conservative political commentator John McLaughlin on the CNBC discussion show *McLaughlin*, Valenti expressed the attitude that is fueling globalism:

McLaughlin: *Europeans and Canadians complain that they're becoming too Americanized. Surely, you can appreciate the validity of that concern, Jack Valenti.*

Valenti: *Well, that's a decision that's taken by the citizens of that country. I mean, who's wise enough to say to the people of France or Germany or Great Britain, "You should watch this and not watch that"? These are free countries. And so if they're becoming "too Americanized" it's not anything that's being foisted on them by America. It's the people of that country making their own decisions about what they want to watch. I find that reasonable.*

McLaughlin: *You want to help them to be able to reject their own culture? Is that what you want to do?*

Valenti: *No, no, I want them to be able to be free to choose whatever they want. If anyone's culture is so flimsily anchored that a television show is going to cause them to rupture their connection to culture, it probably wasn't as deeply rooted as it should have been.*[28]

Clearly, the dominance of network broadcasting has been ebbing, irreversibly. And unless the American networks can become part of the larger transnational competition, they will become increasingly irrelevant in global telecommunications. A distinct era in the history of American mass communications has ended. One affiliate of each of three monopolistic networks, plus a few independent stations programming off-network reruns and local sports: in city after city this is the way commercial video was organized in the United States. The only new developments—UHF and public television—did nothing to undermine this basic design. UHF arrived too late to be important, and public TV never attracted audiences large enough to influence commercial television.

As American TV is being slowly rearranged, the dilemma foreseen by journalist E. B. White remains. Writing in 1939, he anticipated a critical, civilizing role for television, but he feared its effects might have cataclysmic results. As he expressed it,

I believe television is going to be the test of the modern world, and that in this new opportunity to see beyond the range of our vision, we shall discover a new and unbearable disturbance of the modern peace, or a saving radiance in the sky. We shall stand or fall by television—of that I am quite sure.[29]

Television in the United States has had an imperfect past. While it helped to educate the nation, it was neither as constructive nor as flawless as it might have been. Network TV evolved with chronic inefficiency and amid chronic controversy. Nevertheless, its effects have been widespread, for it became the nation's chief informant, offering the populace via entertainment and informational programming a value-laden perspective on reality.

TV has not been the "saving radiance in the sky" wished by E. B. White. Its primal ties to commercial and political interests and its emergence at the beginning of U.S. entry into the Cold War destined the medium to be a partisan force in the capitalist struggle against the international spread of rival political and economic doctrines.

On the other hand, TV did not become the "new and unbearable disturbance of the modern peace" feared by E. B. White. If anything, its slow but inexorable exposure of the brute ugliness of modern combat has done much to counter aggressive energies and recommend civilized processes. In recent years, when transmitting live pictures from the scene of popular uprisings, when bringing congressional sessions and political seminars, when interviewing international allies and enemies, when offering music and film and art of profound proportions, when encouraging public debate with articulate and balanced representation, when offering diversion that uplifts and entertainment that enhances and ennobles human experience, television is all that its most optimistic dreamers ever could have wanted. It just has never performed this well with consistency.

The legacy of television in the United States is mixed. With all its shortcomings, and there have been many, it has been a fascinating arena of popular interest. Through all its commercialism and banality, monopolistic practices and prepossessing concern over profitability, it has visually brought the world into the average home. TV has educated and diverted and stimulated, and often it has flattered its producers and programmers. Often, too, it has insulted and distracted, manipulated and exploited, even distorted, propagandized, and bored.

Whatever its fate in the last decade of this century and beyond, through fifty years broadcast TV has exercised a singular influence in molding and defining the nation. Because of what it did and did not show, Americans in many ways are what they are. Spiritually, morally, economically, intellectually, historically, ideologically: in these and other ways Americans have found in national video an influential medium of communication, the potent impact of which has touched popular thought and action.

As it moves toward a globalist twenty-first century, it seems certain that television may slowly but inexorably do to the rest of the world what it has done in the United States. The understanding of TV as a corporatized, profit-driven enterprise is catching on through the world. State-controlled systems are yielding to privatization. New channels, cable TV, home satellite dishes, and videocassette technology are sweeping the planet. The new European Community will be a major market for media. The Soviet Union and Eastern Europe, economically exhausted by forced collectivism, are now emerging as massive areas for broadcast investment and enterprise. The Far East, the Middle East, and Latin America are also geopolitical amalgams in which the world media revolution is occurring.

Already there are signs of international cultural homogeneity. Whether it is a Kentucky Fried chicken franchise on Tienanmen Square in Beijing, or *Dynasty* reruns in socialist Algeria, or Disneyland amusement parks in France and Japan, or National Football League games played in Sweden and Great Britain—and televised throughout the world—American popular culture and mass media are leaping borders, chronic enmities, and the traditions of centuries. Importantly, too, the U.S. corporations providing media and culture are only part of a patchwork of national entities, all laboring to sell leisure and information to one world under television. Whether there will be United States-based megacorporations in the forefront of the global movement, or whether American manufacturers will be devoured by foreign conglomerates, is ultimately immaterial. The process is in motion; globally arranged media and transnational culture seem destined in the next century to entertain and inform the world.

notes

preface

1. Erik Barnouw, *Tube of Plenty: The Evolution of American Television* (New York: Oxford University Press, 1975).
2. Paddy Chayefsky, *Network* (New York: Pocket Books, 1976), p. 98.

chapter 1: struggle for an industry

1. *Variety*, October 7, 1953, p. 1.
2. Joseph H. Udelson, *The Great Television Race: A History of the American Television Industry, 1925–1941* (University, Ala: University of Alabama Press, 1982), p. 100.
3. *The New York Times* (cited hereafter as *NYT*), January 25, 1925.
4. Samuel L. Rothafel and Raymond Francis Yates, *Broadcasting: Its New Day* (New York: Century, 1925), pp. 239–40.
5. *NYT*, September 13, 1925.
6. Erik Barnouw, *A Tower in Babel: A History of Broadcasting in the United States to 1933* (New York: Oxford University Press, 1966), p. 231.
7. *NYT*, February 23, 1930.
8. *Radio Retailing*, March 1940, p. 17.
9. Gladys Hall, "Are Comedians Through on the Air?" *Radio Stars*, February 1936, p. 73.
10. *NYT*, June 1, 1930.
11. Ibid., July 2, 1930.
12. Ibid., February 21, 1930.
13. Ibid., July 27, 1930.
14. *Variety*, February 10, 1937, p. 41.
15. Udelson, *The Great Television Race*, pp. 58–78; *Variety Radio Directory, 1937–1938* (New York: *Variety*, 1937), pp. 780–85.
16. For an effective summary of this historical development, see Ken Ward, *Mass Communications and the Modern World* (Chicago: Dorsey Press, 1989), pp. 168–93.
17. *NYT*, April 30, 1939.
18. George H. Gallup, *The Gallup Poll: Public Opinion 1935–1971*, vol. I (New York: Random House, 1972), p. 152.
19. Alfred R. Oxenfeldt, *Marketing Practices in the TV Set Industry* (New York: Columbia University Press, 1964), pp. 9–11; *Variety Radio Directory, 1939–1940* (New York: *Variety*, 1939), p. 885; Herman S. Hettinger,

"Organizing Radio's Discoveries for Use," *Annals of the American Academy of Political and Social Science*, January 1941, pp. 174–75.

20. Laurence Bergreen, *Look Now, Pay Later: The Rise of Network Broadcasting* (New York: New American Library, 1980), p. 139.

21. Eugene Lyons, *David Sarnoff: A Biography* (New York: Harper & Row, 1966), p. 216.

22. *NYT*, May 4, 1939; Jack Sher, "Before Your Very Eyes," *Radio and Television Mirror*, August 1939, pp. 22–23.

23. Kenneth Bilby, *The General: David Sarnoff and the Rise of the Communications Industry* (New York: Harper & Row, 1986), p. 8.

24. *Variety Radio Directory, 1940–1941* (New York: *Variety*, 1940), p. 357. NBC claimed by February 1940 that it had sold two thousand sets, but trade estimates ranged from fifteen hundred to eighteen hundred; see *Radio and Television Retailing*, February 1940, p. 52.

25. Bilby, *The General*, pp. 131–32.

26. Ibid., p. 5.

27. Ibid., p. 135.

28. William S. Paley, *As It Happened: A Memoir* (Garden City, N.Y.: Doubleday, 1979), pp. 200–201.

29. William S. Paley, "Broadcasting and American Society," *Annals of the American Academy of Political and Social Science*, January 1941, p. 63.

30. *Variety Radio Directory, 1940–1941*, p. 357.

31. *Variety*, August 30, 1939, pp. 1, 30. See also Red Barber, "The First Major-League Telecast," *TV Guide*, August 24, 1974, pp. 16–17.

32. Bud Gamble, "The Television Tour of 88 Department Stores," *Televiser*, Winter 1945, p. 48.

33. Bilby, *The General*, p. 45.

34. Ibid., p. 51.

35. Louis G. Caldwell, "Regulation of Broadcasting by the Federal Government," in *Variety Radio Directory, 1937–1938*, pp. 270–71.

36. James L. Baughman, *Television's Guardians: The FCC and the Politics of Programming 1958–1967* (Knoxville: University of Tennessee Press, 1985), pp. 5–15.

37. Barry G. Cole, *Reluctant Regulators: The FCC and the Broadcast Audience* (Reading, Mass.: Addison-Wesley, 1978).

38. James M. Graham and Victor H. Kramer, *Appointments to the Regulatory Agencies: The Federal Communications Commission and the Federal Trade Commission (1949–1974)*, as cited in Cole, *Reluctant Regulators*, p. 5.

39. Baughman, *Television's Guardians*, p. 9.

40. James Lawrence Fly, "Regulation of Radio Broadcasting in the Public Interest," *Annals of the American Academy of Political and Social Science*, January 1941, p. 102.

41. *The New Republic*, June 24, 1931, p. 140.

42. Erik Barnouw, *The Golden Web: A History of Broadcasting in the United States 1933–1953* (New York: Oxford University Press, 1968), pp. 24–25.

43. Armstrong Perry, "Weak Spots in the American System of Broadcasting," *Annals of the American Academy of Political and Social Science*, January 1935, pp. 23–24.

44. William S. Paley, "Radio and the Humanities," ibid., pp. 95–96.
45. Merlin H. Aylesworth, "Broadcasting in the Public Interest," ibid., p. 115.
46. Gilbert Seldes, "The Nature of Television Programs," ibid., January 1941, p. 138.
47. David Sarnoff, "Possible Social Effects of Television," ibid., p. 148.
48. Ibid., p. 152.

chapter 2: the arrival of tv

1. "WBKB, Chicago's War Baby, Dons Its Long Pants," *Televiser*, July–August 1946, p. 15.
2. Ibid., Summer 1945, p. 48; Fall 1944, p. 39.
3. Ibid., November–December 1947, p. 14; July–August 1947, p. 6.
4. Ibid., Summer 1945, pp. 20–21, 54.
5. Richard W. Hubbell, *4,000 Years of Television: The Story of Seeing at a Distance* (New York: G. P. Putnam's Sons, 1942), p. 219.
6. *Variety*, March 15, 1944, p. 1.
7. *Televiser*, Fall 1944, back cover.
8. Eugene Lyons, *David Sarnoff: A Biography* (New York: Harper & Row, 1966), pp. 277, 279.
9. Ibid., p. 275.
10. Christopher H. Sterling and John M. Kittross, *Stay Tuned: A Concise History of American Broadcasting* (Belmont, Calif.: Wadsworth, 1978), p. 233.
11. Ibid.
12. William Fay, "Program and Station Promotion," in Broadcast Music, Inc., *Television Talks 1957* (Great Neck, N.Y.: Channell Press: 1957), pp. 3–4.
13. Harriet Van Horne, "The Truth About Color TV," *Radio-Television Mirror*, March 1951, p. 33.
14. Kenneth Bilby, *The General: David Sarnoff and the Rise of the Communications Industry* (New York: Harper & Row, 1986), p. 195.
15. Lyons, *David Sarnoff*, p. 310.
16. *Televiser*, Summer 1945, p. 38.
17. George H. Gallup, *The Gallup Poll: Public Opinion 1935–1971* (New York: Random House, 1972), I, p. 551.
18. Marian Thomas, "What the 'Man-on-the-Street' Thinks of Television!" *Televiser*, Summer 1945, pp. 17, 37.
19. *Television*, April 1949, p. 40; July 1949, p. 25.
20. Ibid., June 1949, pp. 7, 27, 30, 33; Sterling and Kittross, *Stay Tuned*, p. 518.
21. *Television*, December 1949, p. 18.
22. Herbert S. Laufman, "Television's Impact," *Radio & Television News*, July 1949, p. 127.
23. *Television*, January 1949, p. 2.
24. *Television Forecast* (Chicago), January 10, 1949, p. 3.
25. *Chicago Tribune*, January 12, 1949.
26. *Television*, September 1949, p. 15.

27. William Hawes, *American Television: The Experimental Years* (University, Ala.: University of Alabama Press, 1986), p. 172.

28. *Television Forecast* (Chicago), December 17, 1949, p. 27; September 16, 1950, p. 16c.

29. *Television*, December 1949, p. 29.

30. *Variety*, April 12, 1989, p. 80.

31. Tim Brooks and Earle C. Marsh, *The Complete Directory to Prime Time Network TV Shows 1946–Present*, 3rd ed. (New York: Ballantine Books, 1985), pp. 1,050–54.

32. *Variety*, July 27, 1949, p. 41.

33. Charles A. Siepmann, *Radio, Television and Society* (New York: Oxford University Press, 1950), p. 52; *Variety*, April 20, 1949, pp. 1, 26.

34. *Variety*, July 28, 1948, p. 29.

35. *Television*, June 1949, p. 31.

36. *Variety*, August 17, 1949, pp. 32, 40.

37. Ibid., July 28, 1948, p. 41.

38. Ibid., April 20, 1949, pp. 1, 26.

39. Ibid., October 18, 1950, p. 23.

40. *Broadcasting*, May 26, 1952, p. 80.

41. *Television*, March 1952, p. 11.

42. *Variety*, May 6, 1953, p. 22.

43. Ibid., May 27, 1953, p. 25.

44. Ibid., December 21, 1955, p. 91; May 11, 1955, p. 29.

45. "Is Television an Asset or a Liability to Education?" *America's Town Meeting of the Air*, February 13, 1951.

46. *Variety*, July 16, 1952, p. 37.

47. Ibid., February 27, 1952, p. 20.

48. Frieda B. Hennock in O. Joe Olson, ed., *Education on the Air: Twentieth Yearbook of the Institute for Education by Radio* (Columbus: Ohio State University, 1950), p. 26.

49. William S. Paley, "Broadcasting and American Society," *Annals of the American Academy of Political and Social Science*, January 1941, pp. 67–68.

50. Mortimer W. Loewi in O. Joe Olson, ed., *Education on the Air: Nineteenth Yearbook of the Institute for Education by Radio* (Columbus: Ohio State University, 1949), pp. 22–24.

51. *Variety*, January 3, 1945, p. 73.

52. Ibid., July 28, 1950, pp. 1, 99.

53. *Broadcasting*, May 26, 1952, pp. 92–94; *Variety*, August 17, 1949, p. 40.

54. Stewart Louis Long, *The Development of the Television Network Oligopoly* (New York: Arno Press, 1979), pp. 82–88.

55. Sterling and Kittross, *Stay Tuned*, p. 535.

56. Richard F. Doherty, "Is the Television Industry Still in the Growth Stage?" *Analysts Journal*, November 10, 1954, pp. 35–36.

57. Lyons, *David Sarnoff*, p. 313.

58. Harry Hansen, ed., *The World Almanac and Book of Facts for 1956* (New York: *New York World-Telegram*, 1956), p. 791.

59. See Long, *Television Network Oligopoly*.

60. William S. Paley, *As It Happened: A Memoir* (Garden City, N.Y.: Doubleday, 1979), p. 242.

chapter 3: programming for a nation

1. Christopher H. Sterling and John M. Kittross, *Stay Tuned: A Concise History of American Broadcasting* (Belmont, Calif.: Wadsworth, 1978), p. 515. Sterling and Kittross cite incorrect figures for network TV affiliations in 1949–53; see Stewart Louis Long, *The Development of the Television Network Oligopoly* (New York: Arno Press, 1979), p. 87.

2. Cited in Kenneth Bilby, *The General: David Sarnoff and the Rise of the Communications Industry* (New York: Harper & Row, 1986), pp. 206–7.

3. Long, *Television Network Oligopoly*, p. 111.

4. Sterling Quinlan, *Inside ABC: American Broadcasting Company's Rise to Power* (New York: Hastings House, 1979); Laurence Bergreen, *Look Now, Pay Later: The Rise of Network Broadcasting* (New York: New American Library, 1980), p. 230.

5. Al Morgan, "Revelations of Former Network Presidents," *TV Guide*, April 29, 1972, p. 9; Bob Stahl, "The Men Who Run ABC," ibid., August 1, 1959, pp. 4–7.

6. Richard W. Hubbell, *4,000 Years of Television: The Story of Seeing at a Distance* (New York: G. P. Putnam's Sons, 1942), pp. 222–23.

7. *Television*, Annual Data Book, March 1954, p. 102.

8. *Broadcasting*, June 2, 1952, p. 73.

9. Milton Berle, "Guest Column," *Television Forecast* (Chicago), May 7, 1949, p. 8.

10. *Variety*, May 19, 1948, pp. 1, 63.

11. For CBS thinking on this strategy, see ibid., February 7, 1951, p. 27.

12. Ibid., December 14, 1955, p. 46.

13. For an interesting discussion of industry uncertainties in the early 1950s, see Quinlan, *Inside ABC*, pp. 3–28.

14. Michael Winship, *Television* (New York: Random House, 1988), p. 191.

15. David G. Walley, *The Ernie Kovacs Phile* (New York: Bolder Books, 1976), p. 109.

16. Chevy Chase, "The Unique Comedy of Ernie Kovacs," *TV Guide*, April 9, 1977, p. 39.

17. *TV Forecast* (Chicago), October 21, 1950, p. 17.

18. *Variety*, August 15, 1956, pp. 25, 44; January 31, 1951, pp. 1, 55.

19. Ibid., March 6, 1957, pp. 25, 36.

20. Ibid., August 17, 1960, pp. 23, 39.

21. Steve Allen, *The Funny Men* (New York: Simon & Schuster, 1956), p. 274.

22. O. Joe Olson, ed., *Education on the Air: Twenty-first Yearbook of the Institute for Education by Radio and Television* (Columbus: Ohio State University, 1951), p. 46.

23. *Variety*, July 27, 1949, p. 49.

24. See, for example, William I. Kaufman, ed., *The Best Television Plays of the Year* (Boston: Merlin Press, 1950); Paddy Chayefsky, *Television Plays* (New York: Simon & Schuster, 1955); Irving Settel, ed., *Top TV Shows of the Year 1954–1955* (New York: Hastings House, 1955); Gore Vidal, ed., *Best Television Plays* (New York: Ballantine Books, 1956); A. S. Burack, ed., *Television Plays for Writers* (New York: The Writer, 1957); Reginald Rose, *Six Television Plays*

(New York: Simon & Schuster, 1957); Writers Guild of America, ed., *Writers Guild of America Presents the Prize Plays of Television and Radio 1956* (New York: Random House, 1957); Rod Serling, *Patterns: Four Television Plays with the Author's Personal Commentaries* (New York: Simon & Schuster, 1957).

25. William I. Kaufman, ed., *The Best Television Plays*, Vol. III (Boston: Merlin Press, 1954), p. 354.

26. Museum of Broadcasting, *Produced by . . . Herb Brodkin: A Signature of Conviction and Integrity* (New York: Museum of Broadcasting, 1985), p. 10.

27. Nora Sayre and Robert B. Silvers, "An Interview with Paddy Chayefsky," *Horizon*, III:1 (September 1960), p. 51. Even earlier Chayefsky had written praisefully of Fred Coe in an elaborate tribute to the producer appearing in *Variety*, May 23, 1956, p. 31:

I don't suppose it will be too long before someone sits down to do a scholarly history of television. . . . In about 10 years or so, 50-year-old men will meet in bars and talk about "the early days" of television, and small legends and little fantasies will grow up about the pioneer personalities of our industry. I don't think there is too much doubt but that Fred Coe will be the Paul Bunyan of television. . . . There is nobody in the business who did more to give television its self-respect. If there is any renaissance of dramatic writing in our country, it will be directly traced to Fred's single-handed sponsorship of new playwrights in television. His arbitrary decisiveness, his acute story mind (the sharpest of any man I have known in show business), his passion for achievements make him the closest thing to an ideal producer.

28. *TV Guide*, August 6, 1955, p. 15.

29. Mrs. A. Scott Bullitt, "Toward Improved Programming," in O. Joe Olson, ed., *Education on the Air: Twenty-second Yearbook of the Institute for Education by Radio and Television* (Columbus: Ohio State University, 1952), pp. 14–15.

30. Paddy Chayefsky on David Susskind's *Open End* television program, November 18, 1958, as cited in *Advertising Age*, December 1, 1958, p. 76.

31. Rose, *Six Television Plays*, p. 107.

32. *TV Guide*, August 6, 1955, p. 15.

33. Robert Johnson, "Rod Serling Describes Headaches of TV Script Writing," ibid., May 11, 1957, p. 18.

chapter 4: shaping a national culture

1. *Television*, February 1949, p. 9.

2. Ibid., December 1950, p. 5.

3. Ibid. See also "California . . . and the Cable," ibid., April 1951, pp. 40, 46; November 1952, p. 23.

4. O. Joe Olson, *Education on the Air: Twenty-first Yearbook of the Institute for Education by Radio and Television* (Columbus: Ohio State University, 1951), p. 11.

5. Ibid.

6. Stan Opotowsky, *TV—The Big Picture* (New York: Collier Books, 1962), p. 33.

7. Stewart Louis Long, *The Development of the Television Network Oligopoly* (New York: Arno Press, 1979), p. 114.

8. *TV Guide*, September 4, 1953, p. 20.

9. *Television*, December 1950, p. 5.

10. Ibid., p. 21.

11. Frank Mayans, Jr., and Norman Young, "Ratings Study," *Television*, November 1952, p. 23. See also *Variety*, February 9, 1949, p. 30.

12. *Variety*, March 30, 1949, p. 2.

13. *TV Guide*, May 24, 1958, pp. 18–19.

14. *Variety*, May 22, 1955, pp. 30, 54; R. W. Sanders, "Freeing Area Television Reception," *Radio & Television News*, October 1949, pp. 44–46, 148–49.

15. *Ebony*, June 1950, p. 22.

16. *Variety*, July 18, 1951, p. 1.

17. Ibid., June 20, 1956, p. 17.

18. Ken Crossen, "There's Murder in the Air," in Howard Haycraft, ed., *The Art of the Mystery Story* (New York: Simon & Schuster, 1946), p. 304.

19. *Variety*, August 3, 1949, p. 25.

20. *Television*, November 1948, pp. 18, 32.

21. *Variety*, December 7, 1949, pp. 31, 36.

22. Ibid., May 2, 1951, p. 33.

23. *Broadcasting*, September 22, 1952, p. 28.

24. *Variety*, April 19, 1950, p. 1.

25. Ibid., August 29, 1951, pp. 1, 63.

26. *Broadcasting*, October 1, 1951, p. 90.

27. *Television*, February 1955, p. 30.

28. The Television Code was ratified October 19, 1951, and became effective March 1, 1952. See Charles S. Aaronson, ed., *International Television Almanac 1962* (New York: Quigley, 1961), pp. 760–68.

29. *Broadcasting*, September 29, 1952, p. 32.

30. Luigi Luraschi, "Censorship at Home and Abroad," *Annals of the American Academy of Political and Social Science*, November 1947, p. 148.

31. *Variety*, April 22, 1953, p. 25.

32. Ibid., May 9, 1951, p. 18.

33. Ibid., February 14, 1951, p. 34.

34. *TV Forecast* (Chicago), November 25, 1950, p. 6.

35. *Variety*, March 29, 1950, p. 42.

36. Ibid., August 22, 1951, p. 1.

37. *Broadcasting*, September 22, 1952, p. 28.

38. *Variety*, October 26, 1960, p. 28.

39. Ibid., May 9, 1951, pp. 1, 18.

40. *TV Forecast* (Chicago), December 29, 1951, p. 19.

41. Ibid., February 2, 1952, p. 7.

42. Aaronson, *International Television Almanac 1962*, pp. 760–68.

43. *Variety*, March 29, 1950, p. 42.

44. Ibid., June 20, 1956, p. 30.

chapter 5: streamlining culture/ streamlining industry

1. Nicholas Johnson, *How to Talk Back to Your Television Set* (Boston: Little, Brown, 1967), p. 102.

2. John Cogley, *Report on Blacklisting*, vol. II, *Radio-Television* (New York: Fund for the Republic, 1956), pp. 192–95.

3. *Variety*, May 1, 1957, pp. 1, 46.

4. Leo Burnett, foreword to Harry Wayne McMahan, *The Television Commercial: How to Create and Produce Effective TV Advertising* (New York: Hastings House, 1957), p. 8.

5. Christopher Schemering, *The Soap Opera Encyclopedia* (New York: Ballantine Books, 1985), pp. 302–7.

6. James L. Baughman, *Television's Guardians: The FCC and the Politics of Programming 1958–1967* (Knoxville: University of Tennessee Press, 1985), p. 173.

7. *Variety*, January 3, 1951, p. 101.

8. Ibid., December 19, 1951, p. 25.

9. Ibid., March 31, 1954, p. 27.

10. Ibid., August 4, 1954, p. 31; December 3, 1958, p. 27; *Billboard*, September 9, 1957, pp. 1, 10.

11. Tim Brooks and Earle C. Marsh, *The Complete Directory to Prime Time Network TV Shows, 1946–Present*, 3rd ed. (New York: Ballantine Books, 1985), p. 804.

12. Richard Bunce, *Television in the Corporate Interest* (New York: Praeger, 1976), p. 77.

13. *Broadcasting*, July 13, 1953, p. 87. On film in the early 1950s see Marjorie Thomas, "TV Film Has Joined the Hollywood Elite," *Broadcasting*, December 14, 1953, pp. 84–85, 88.

14. *Variety*, May 4, 1960, p. 23.

15. Thomas Schatz, *The Genius of the System: Hollywood Filmmaking in the Studio Era* (New York: Pantheon Books, 1989), p. 478.

16. Wilson P. Dizard, "American Television's Foreign Markets," *Television Quarterly*, Summer 1964, pp. 58–59.

17. Cited in Stan Opotowsky, *TV—The Big Picture* (New York: Collier Books, 1962), p. 52.

18. *Variety*, February 22, 1956, p. 1; December 31, 1958, p. 21.

19. Ibid., October 2, 1957, p. 26; October 30, 1957, p. 56.

20. *Broadcasting*, January 19, 1953, p. 77.

21. *NYT*, February 26, 1956.

22. Dan Jenkins, "TV Film Companies—A New Generation of Giants," *TV Guide*, January 17, 1959, pp. 9–10; *Variety*, May 6, 1959, p. 27.

23. *Variety*, January 11, 1956, pp. 43, 48.

24. Ibid., April 26, 1961, p. 185. That there was a demand for TV feature films was obvious since Hollywood studios produced only 250 new films per year, and in Los Angeles the 7 operating stations used 150 pictures weekly—

some, by early 1959, having been rerun as many as 18 times; ibid., March 11, 1959, pp. 33, 56.

25. Todd Gitlin, *Inside Prime Time* (New York: Pantheon Books, 1983), p. 66.

26. CBS News, *60 Minutes*, September 8, 1981.

27. A. Frank Reel, *The Networks: How They Stole the Show* (New York: Charles Scribner's Sons, 1979), p. 6.

28. *Variety*, December 19, 1956, p. 31; *Billboard*, July 22, 1957, p. 3.

29. *Variety*, January 6, 1965, p. 85.

30. Ibid., February 24, 1960, pp. 31, 34.

31. See Opotowsky, *TV—The Big Picture*, pp. 132–33.

32. Hubbell Robinson, "How to Get a Hit—*and Keep It*," *Television Quarterly*, Fall 1963, p. 30.

33. Gary H. Grossman, *Saturday Morning TV* (New York: Dell, 1981), p. 170.

34. David Levy to Robert W. Sarnoff, July 13, 1961, pp. 3–4. NBC Records, Wisconsin State Historical Society, Madison.

35. Cited in Barry Russell Litman, *The Vertical Structure of the Television Broadcasting Industry: The Coalescence of Power* (East Lansing: Michigan State University, 1979), p. 46.

36. Arthur M. Schlesinger, Jr., "Where Does the Liberal Go from Here?" *The New York Times Magazine*, August 4, 1957, pp. 36–37.

37. Richard Austin Smith, "TV: The Light That Failed," *Fortune*, December 1958, pp. 78–79.

38. Cited in Gary A. Steiner, *The People Look at Television: A Study of Audience Attitudes* (New York: Alfred A. Knopf, 1963), p. 235.

39. Christopher H. Sterling and John M. Kittross, *Stay Tuned: A Concise History of American Broadcasting* (Belmont, Calif.: Wadsworth, 1978), p. 536.

40. Frank Stanton, preface to "Free Television and the American People," published as a paid advertisement in *TV Guide* (Chicago edition), February 1, 1958, p. A-28.

41. MacDonald, *Television and the Red Menace: The Video Road to Vietnam* (New York: Praeger, 1985), p. 148.

42. Edward R. Murrow, "How TV Can Help Us Survive," *TV Guide*, December 13, 1958, p. 22. The article comprises excerpts from a speech Murrow delivered in Chicago on October 5, 1958, before the national convention of the Radio-Television News Directors' Association. See *Variety*, October 15, 1958, pp. 23, 46.

43. Eric Sevareid, "TV: Big Rock Candy Mountain," *TV Guide*, April 4, 1959, p. 5.

44. John P. Cunningham, "Creeping Mediocrity Brings Boredom to TV," *Advertising Age*, November 4, 1957, p. 68.

45. *Variety*, June 21, 1961, p. 23.

46. Baughman, *Television's Guardians*, p. 35.

47. Edward C. Shils, "Daydreams and Nightmares: Reflections on the Criticism of Mass Culture," *Sewanee Review*, Autumn 1957, as cited in Baughman, *Television Guardians*, p. 34.

chapter 6: of scandal and power

1. Kent Anderson, *Television Fraud: The History and Implications of the Quiz Show Scandals* (Westport, Conn.: Greenwood, 1978), p. 175.
2. *Variety*, March 31, 1954, p. 27.
3. Ibid., March 13, 1957, p. 23.
4. From congressional hearings as cited in Harry Hansen, ed., *The World Almanac and Book of Facts 1960* (New York: *New York World-Telegram*, 1960), p. 123.
5. Michael Winship, *Television* (New York: Random House, 1988), p. 158.
6. *Variety*, November 4, 1959, p. 51.
7. William S. Paley, *As It Happened: A Memoir* (Garden City, N.Y.: Doubleday, 1979), p. 247.
8. *Variety*, December 9, 1959, p. 37.
9. Ibid., November 4, 1959, p. 51.
10. Bruce M. Owen; Jack H. Beebe; and Williard G. Manning, Jr., *Television Economics* (Lexington, Mass.: D. C. Heath, 1974), p. 20.
11. *Television*, January 1954, pp. 22–26.
12. Jack Alicoate, ed., *1953 Radio Annual* (New York: Radio Daily, 1953), p. 840.
13. Stan Opotowsky, *TV—The Big Picture* (New York: Collier Books, 1962), p. 43.
14. *Business Week*, November 21, 1959, pp. 115–17.
15. Les Brown, *Televi$ion: The Business Behind the Box* (New York: Harcourt Brace Jovanovich, 1971), pp. 63–64.
16. A. Frank Reel, *The Networks: How They Stole the Show* (New York: Charles Scribner's Sons, 1979), p. 80.
17. Al Morgan, "Revelations of Former Network Presidents," *TV Guide*, April 29, 1972, p. 10.
18. Ibid.
19. A. D. Murphy in *Variety*, April 19, 1972, p. 38.
20. Reel, *The Networks*, p. 128.
21. David Halberstam, *The Powers That Be* (New York: Alfred A. Knopf, 1979), p. 416. See also Erik Barnouw, *The Sponsor: Notes on a Modern Potentate* (New York: Oxford University Press, 1978), pp. 555–58.
22. *Variety*, January 10, 1962, p. 83.

chapter 7: appearance and reality

1. "The Money Tree of Madison Avenue," *Forbes*, January 15, 1964, p. 20.
2. Leo Rosten, "A Disenchanted Look at the Audience" in *The Eighth Art* (New York: Holt, Rinehart & Winston, 1962), p. 33.
3. John F. Kennedy, "Television: A Force in Politics," *TV Guide*, November 14, 1959, pp. 6–7.
4. E. William Henry, "The 50-50 Rule," *Television Quarterly*, Fall 1965, p. 8.
5. William S. Paley, *As It Happened: A Memoir* (Garden City, N.Y.: Doubleday, 1979), p. 242.

6. Fred W. Friendly, *Due to Circumstances Beyond Our Control . . .* (New York: Random House, 1967), p. 113.

7. David Halberstam, *The Powers That Be* (New York: Alfred A. Knopf, 1979), pp. 416–17.

8. Daniel Karp, "TV Shows Are Not Supposed to Be Good," *The New York Times Magazine,* January 23, 1966, pp. 8, 40.

9. Hermann S. Hettinger, "Organizing Radio's Discoveries for Use," *Annals of the American Academy of Political and Social Science,* January 1941, pp. 179–80.

10. Gary A. Steiner, *The People Look at Television: A Study of Audience Attitudes* (New York: Alfred A. Knopf, 1963), pp. 228–29.

11. William Small, *To Kill a Messenger: Television News and the Real World* (New York: Hastings House, 1970), p. 42.

12. Richard Lemon, "Black Is the Color of TV's Newest Stars," *The Saturday Evening Post,* November 30, 1968, p. 42; see also J. Fred MacDonald, *Blacks and White TV: Afro-Americans in Television Since 1948* (Chicago: Nelson-Hall, 1983), pp. 108–9.

13. Lemon, "Black Is the Color of TV's Newest Stars," p. 84.

14. "Address by Sterling 'Red' Quinlan" in Robert H. Stanley, ed., *The Broadcast Industry: An Examination of Major Issues* (New York: Hastings House, 1975), p. 57.

15. Allen Kirschner and Linda Kirschner, eds., *Radio and Television: Readings in the Mass Media* (New York: The Odyssey Press, 1971), pp. 208–10, 214.

16. Rosten, "A Disenchanted Look at the Audience," p. 32.

17. Marya Mannes, "The Lost Tribe of Television," in *The Eighth Art* (New York: Holt, Rinehart & Winston, 1962), p. 29.

18. Ashley Montagu, "Television and the New Image of Man," ibid., p. 128.

19. Roy B. Huggins, "The Bloodshot Eye: A Comment on the Crisis in American Television," *Television Quarterly,* August 1962, p. 22.

20. James L. Baughman, *Television's Guardians: The FCC and the Politics of Programming 1958–1967* (Knoxville: University of Tennessee Press, 1985), p. 168.

21. Ibid., p. 125.

22. Address to NAB convention, March 23, 1965, as cited in Robert E. Summers and Harrison B. Summers, *Broadcasting and the Public* (Belmont, Calif.: Wadsworth, 1966), p. 368.

23. Baughman, *Television's Guardians,* pp. 142–43.

24. Summers and Summers, *Broadcasting and the Public,* p. 376.

25. *NYT,* November 14, 1969.

26. Robert T. Bower, *Television and the Public* (New York: Holt, Rinehart & Winston, 1973), pp. 100–01.

27. David Levy to Robert W. Sarnoff, July 13, 1961, p. 70, NBC Papers, Wisconsin State Historical Society, Madison.

28. Raymond L. Carroll, "Economic Influences on Commercial Network Television Documentary Scheduling," *Journal of Broadcasting,* Fall 1979, p. 415.

29. *Variety*, August 27, 1969, p. 39.

30. William O. Johnson, Jr., *Super Spectator and the Electric Lilliputians* (Boston: Little, Brown, 1971), pp. 32–46.

31. *Variety*, July 27, 1966, p. 33.

32. Ibid., June 28, 1967, p. 31.

33. *Advertising Age*, October 6, 1958, p. 3.

34. Grantland Rice, "For Better or Worse: TV," *The Story of Our Time: Encyclopedia Year Book 1954* (New York: The Grolier Society, 1954), pp. 385, 387.

35. Benjamin G. Rader, *In Its Own Image: How Television Has Transformed Sports* (New York: The Free Press, 1984), pp. 156, 196–97.

36. *Variety*, June 15, 1966, p. 29.

37. Among the highest-rated telecasts in the period 1960–88, five of the top ten and twelve of the top twenty-five were Super Bowl games. The seventeen games between Super Bowls VI (1972) and XXII (1988) were rated among the top fifty. "Nielsen Television Index Top 50 Programs Average Audience Estimates," *Nielsen Newscast*, Spring 1988, p. 17.

38. *Variety*, January 20, 1965, p. 47; September 29, 1965, p. 23; June 2, 1965, pp. 35, 48.

39. Cited in Merrill Panitt, "A Dark Perception—The Challenge," *Television Quarterly*, Fall 1968, p. 11.

40. This episode was tied for sixteenth position among the fifty highest-rated broadcasts of the period July 1960 to January 1988; "Nielsen Television Index Top 50 Programs Average Audience Estimates," *Nielsen Newscast*, Spring 1988, p. 17.

41. *Variety*, February 27, 1963, pp. 1, 40; June 5, 1963, pp. 22, 38. Richard Schickel, "The Problem of the Year," *TV Guide*, February 29, 1964, p. 17.

42. Joseph Turow, *Playing Doctor: Television, Storytelling, and Medical Power* (New York: Oxford University Press, 1989).

43. J. Edgar Hoover, *"The FBI," TV Guide*, May 20, 1972, p. 30.

44. Richard Gid Powers, *Secrecy and Power: The Life of J. Edgar Hoover* (New York: The Free Press, 1987), p. 436.

45. J. Fred MacDonald, *Television and the Red Menace: The Video Road to Vietnam* (New York: Praeger, 1985), pp. 111–21.

46. J. William Fulbright, *The Pentagon Propaganda Machine* (New York: Liveright, 1970), p. 114.

chapter 8: the networks at home and abroad

1. David Levy to Robert W. Sarnoff, July 13, 1961. NBC Papers, Wisconsin State Historical Society, Madison, pp. 36–38.

2. Erik Barnouw, *The Image Empire: A History of Broadcasting in the United States from 1953* (New York: Oxford University Press, 1970), p. 306. Barry Russell Litman, *The Vertical Structure of the Television Broadcasting Industry: The Coalescence of Power* (East Lansing: Michigan State University, 1979), p. 88.

3. *Variety*, September 16, 1970, p. 28.

4. Ibid., January 2, 1985, p. 25.

5. Christopher H. Sterling and John M. Kittross, *Stay Tuned: A Concise History of American Broadcasting* (Belmont, Calif.: Wadsworth, 1978), p. 518.

6. Erik Barnouw, *The Image Empire*, p. 113.

7. Charles S. Aaronson, ed., *1962 International Television Almanac* (New York: Quigley, 1962), pp. 752–58.

8. Wilson P. Dizard, "American Television's Foreign Markets," *Television Quarterly*, Summer 1964, p. 65.

9. *Variety*, September 11, 1968, p. 62.

10. Jon Frappier, "U.S. Media Empire/Latin America," *NACLA Newsletter*, January 1969, p. 2. See also Alan Wells, *Picture Tube Imperialism? The Impact of U.S. Television on Latin America* (Maryknoll, N.Y.: Orbis Books, 1972), p. 121.

11. Wells, *Picture Tube Imperialism?* p. 103.

12. Ibid., p. 102; Richard Bunce, *Television in the Corporate Interest* (New York: Praeger, 1975), pp. 82–83.

13. Barnouw, *The Image Empire*, pp. 108–9.

14. *TV Guide*, May 23, 1959, p. 3; November 2, 1957, pp. 14–15.

15. *Variety*, July 5, 1961, p. 27.

16. Henry Comor, "American TV: What Have You Done to Us?" *Television Quarterly*, Winter 1967, pp. 50–51.

17. Herbert I. Schiller, *Mass Communications and American Empire* (New York: Augustus M. Kelley, 1969).

18. Ross Drake, "Selling U.S. TV Abroad," *TV Guide*, April 29, 1972, pp. 33–38; Andrew R. Horowitz, "The Global Bonanza of American TV," in James Monaco, ed., *Media Culture* (New York: Dell, 1978), pp. 115–22; *NYT*, June 9, 1989.

19. *Variety*, May 13, 1970, p. 50.

20. Norman Horowitz, "Syndication," in Steve Morgenstern, ed., *Inside the TV Business* (New York: Sterling, 1979), pp. 72–73, 82–85.

21. A. Frank Reel, *The Networks: How They Stole the Show* (New York: Charles Scribner's Sons, 1979), pp. 188–89.

22. *Variety*, November 24, 1976, p. 85.

23. Ehrlichman to Nixon, September 11, 1972, in Bruce Oudes, ed., *From: The President: Richard Nixon's Secret Files* (New York: Harper & Row, 1989), p. 316.

24. Buchanan to Nixon, November 10, 1972, ibid., pp. 560–61.

25. *Variety*, December 16, 1970, p. 35.

26. Laurence Bergreen, *Look Now, Pay Later: The Rise of Network Broadcasting* (New York: New American Library, 1980), pp. 255–56, 262; Sterling and Kittross, *Stay Tuned*, p. 518.

27. *Broadcasting*, January 27, 1964, pp. 70–72; *Variety*, April 2, 1969, p. 38; April 4, 1973, p. 42.

28. *Variety*, October 21, 1970, p. 35.

chapter 9: the politics of television

1. *Variety*, July 6, 1960, pp. 29, 47.

2. Ibid., September 10, 1969, p. 89.

notes

notes

3. Edwin Diamond, *The Spot: The Rise of Political Advertising on Television* (Cambridge, Mass.: M.I.T. Press, 1984), p. 258.

4. *Variety*, April 29, 1953, p. 23.

5. Edwin Diamond, "TV and Watergate: What Was, What Might Have Been," *Columbia Journalism Review*, July–August 1973; *Variety*, June 27, 1973, p. 20.

6. Marilyn A. Lashner, *The Chilling Effect in TV News: Intimidation by the Nixon White House* (New York: Praeger, 1984), p. 151.

7. *Variety*, May 23, 1973, p. 42.

8. Ibid., July 12, 1972, p. 34; February 23, 1966, pp. 1, 46; June 7, 1967, p. 29.

9. Ibid., September 16, 1970, p. 35.

10. Donna McCrohan, *Archie & Edith, Mike & Gloria: The Tumultuous History of All in the Family* (New York: Workman, 1987), p. 33.

11. *TV Guide*, February 27, 1971, p. 18.

12. *Variety*, January 13, 1971, p. 48.

13. McCrohan, *Archie & Edith*, p. 149.

14. A. Frank Reel, *The Networks: How They Stole the Show* (New York: Charles Scribner's Sons, 1979), p. 53.

15. *Variety*, September 30, 1987, p. 36.

16. Barry Russell Litman, *The Vertical Structure of the Television Broadcast Industry: The Coalescence of Power* (East Lansing: Michigan State University, 1979), pp. 24–25.

17. Paul Klein, "Programming," in Steve Morgenstern, ed., *Inside the TV Business* (New York: Sterling, 1979), pp. 16–17. See also Paul Klein, "Why You Watch What You Watch," *TV Guide*, July 24, 1971, pp. 7–10.

18. Ibid., p. 18.

19. Laurence Bergreen, *Look Now, Pay Later: The Rise of Network Broadcasting* (New York: New American Library, 1980), p. 263.

20. Alvin H. Marill, *Movies Made for Television: The Telefeature and the Mini-Series 1964–1979* (Westport, Conn.: Arlington House, 1980), p. 9.

21. CBS, closed-circuit kinescope, fall 1974 (author's collection).

22. Gary Grossman, *Saturday Morning TV* (New York: Dell, 1981), p. 270.

23. Geoffrey Cowan, *See No Evil: The Backstage Battle over Sex and Violence in Television* (New York: Simon & Schuster, 1978), p. 158.

24. Ibid., p. 243.

25. Tim Brooks and Earle C. Marsh, *The Complete Directory to Prime Time Network TV Shows, 1946–Present*, 4th ed. (New York: Ballantine Books, 1988), pp. 895, 921.

26. Robert T. Bower, *The Changing Television Audience in America* (New York: Columbia University Press, 1985), pp. 18–22. See also Bower's earlier study *Television and the Public* (New York: Holt, Rinehart & Winston, 1973).

27. Myles Callum, "Exclusive Poll: What Viewers Think About TV," *TV Guide*, May 12, 1979, pp. 6–12.

28. *Variety*, November 18, 1970, p. 50.

29. Ibid., August 3, 1977, p. 43.

30. Ibid., October 18, 1978, p. 255.

31. Neil Hickey, "The Changing Shape of TV," *TV Guide*, April 22, 1978, pp. 9–10; see follow-up articles, ibid., April 29, 1972, and May 6, 1972.

32. U.S. House of Representatives, Hearings Before the Subcommittee on Telecommunications, Consumer Protection, and Finance, October 21, 1981, *Social/Behavioral Effects of Violence on Television* (Washington, D.C.: U.S. Government Printing Office, 1982), p. 5.

33. Eric Sevareid, "A Little Less Hypocrisy, Please," *TV Guide*, December 30, 1967, p. 9.

34. *Variety*, May 13, 1970, p. 32.

35. Ibid., August 16, 1972, p. 36.

36. Ibid., September 17, 1975, p. 56.

37. Kathryn C. Montgomery, *Target: Prime Time. Advocacy Groups and the Struggle over Entertainment Television* (New York: Oxford University Press, 1989).

38. *Broadcasting*, September 20, 1971, p. 36.; Erwin G. Krasnow and Lawrence D. Longley, *The Politics of Broadcast Regulation* (New York: St. Martin's Press, 1978), p. 44.

39. Sidney W. Head, *Broadcasting in America: A Survey of Television and Radio* (Boston: Houghton Mifflin, 1976), p. 452; Montgomery, *Target: Prime Time*, p. 25.

40. Richard Levinson and William Link, *Stay Tuned: An Inside Look at the Making of Prime-Time Television* (New York: St. Martin's Press, 1981), p. 191.

41. *Variety*, October 17, 1973, p. 23.

42. Ibid., May 22, 1974, p. 41.

43. Ibid., October 19, 1978, p. 255.

44. Ibid., January 9, 1980, p. 211.

45. U.S. Public Health Service, *Television and Growing Up: The Impact of Televised Violence* (Washington, D.C.: U.S. Government Printing Office, 1972), pp. 11–12.

46. U.S. House of Representatives, Report Together with Additional, Dissenting, and Separate Views by the Subcommittee on Communications, September 29, 1977, *Violence on Television* (Washington, D.C.: U.S. Government Printing Office, 1977), pp. 30–31.

47. *Variety*, January 3, 1979, p. 198.

chapter 10: the decline of network television

1. *Television*, January 1962, p. 48.

2. *Electronic Media*, March 28, 1988, p. 24.

3. *Nielsen Newscast*, Fall 1988, pp. 2–9; for 1989 statistics see *Variety*, August 16, 1989, p. 37.

4. *Variety*, August 18, 1982, p. 46.

5. *Broadcasting*, May 8, 1989, p. 34.

6. Jacques W. Oppenheim, *Code: télévision à la carte* (Paris: Edilig, 1988), p. 296.

7. A. C. Nielsen Company, *1988 Nielsen Report on Television* (Northbrook,

Ill.: A. C. Nielsen, 1988), pp. 2, 12; *Variety*, August 18, 1982, p. 46; March 16, 1988, p. 76; *Electronic Media*, April 11, 1988, p. 38.

8. *Variety*, September 30, 1987, p. 36; *Electronic Media*, April 24, 1989, pp. 58, 70.

9. *Broadcasting*, August 21, 1989, p. 35.

10. *Variety*, January 2, 1985, p. 25; January 8, 1986, p. 160; December 24, 1986, p. 75; December 30, 1987, p. 24.

11. *Electronic Media*, April 3, 1989, p. 3.

12. *Variety*, January 4, 1989, p. 26.

13. Bernard D. Nossiter, "The FCC's Big Giveaway Show," *The Nation*, October 26, 1985, p. 402.

14. Mark S. Fowler, "Broadcast Unregulation in the 1980s," *Television Quarterly*, Spring 1982, pp. 29–30. For an interesting rebuttal by a prominent consumer advocate, see Samuel A. Simon, "Mark Fowler's Challenge to the American Public Communications System," ibid., Summer 1982, pp. 47–55.

15. "The World World Is Watching," *PBL (Public Broadcasting Laboratory)*, December 22, 1968.

16. Robert Higgins, "Why ABC's News Innovation Fizzled," *TV Guide*, April 5, 1969, pp. 4–9.

17. David M. Stone, *Nixon and the Politics of Public Television* (New York: Garland, 1985), p. 266.

18. Jeffrey K. Hadden and Charles E. Swain, *Prime Time Preachers: The Rising Power of Televangelism* (Reading, Mass.: Addison-Wesley, 1981), pp. 135–39.

19. Mel Friedman, "Aftermath: Reflections on the Day After," *Television Quarterly*, XXI:1 (1984), pp. 7–17.

20. Harrison E. Salisbury, "*Amerika:* Could a Soviet Takeover Happen This Way?" *TV Guide*, February 14, 1987, p. 10. See also Erica Blair, "With *Amerika* Under Fire, the Stars Were Feeling the Heat," ibid., pp. 2–6.

21. *Variety*, March 4, 1987, p. 1.

22. Tom Engelhardt, "The Shortcake Strategy," in Todd Gitlin, ed., *Watching Television* (New York: Pantheon Books, 1986), pp. 88–89.

23. *Variety*, September 20, 1989, p. 124.

24. *NYT*, December 10, 1989.

25. *The American Mind* (Part 2), Public Broadcasting Service, November 29, 1989.

26. Sig Mickelson, *From Whistle Stop to Sound Bite: Four Decades of Politics and Television* (New York: Praeger, 1989), p. 167.

27. Don Kowet and Sally Bedell, "Anatomy of a Smear: How CBS 'Got' General Westmoreland," *TV Guide*, May 29, 1981, p. 15.

28. Lewis J. Paper, *Empire: William S. Paley and the Making of CBS* (New York: St. Martin's Press, 1987), pp. 338–40.

29. *NYT*, February 8, 1989.

30. Ibid., July 30, 1984.

31. William A. Henry III, "Is TV Getting Better—or Worse?" *TV Guide*, March 12, 1988, p. 6.

32. *Electronic Media*, May 2, 1988, p. 17.

33. *Variety*, January 20, 1988, p. 175.

chapter 11: broadcasting versus cable

1. George Mair, *Inside HBO: The Billion-Dollar War Between HBO, Hollywood, and the Home Video Revolution* (New York: Dodd, Mead, 1988), p. 25.

2. J. Fred MacDonald, *Who Shot the Sheriff? The Rise and Fall of the Television Western* (New York: Praeger, 1987), p. 123.

3. *Broadcasting,* June 19, 1989, p. 36.

4. *Variety,* January 20, 1988, p. 175.

5. Ibid., August 30, 1989, p. 73; *Broadcasting,* August 28, 1989, p. 55.

6. A. C. Nielsen Company, *Nielsen Newscast,* no. 3 (1986), p. 13.

7. A. C. Nielsen Company, *Television Viewing Among Blacks, January–February 1988* (Northbrook, Ill.: A. C. Nielsen, 1988), pp. 9, 20.

8. A. C. Nielsen Company, *Television Viewing Among Blacks, January–February 1986* (Northbrook, Ill.: A. C. Nielsen, 1986), pp. 26–27.

9. Nielsen, *Television Viewing Among Blacks, January–February 1988,* pp. 24–25.

10. Tim Brooks and Earle C. Marsh, *The Complete Directory to Prime Time Network TV Shows, 1946–Present,* 4th ed. (New York: Ballantine Books, 1988), pp. 964–75.

11. *Broadcasting,* July 24, 1989, p. 33.

12. *Variety,* January 6, 1988, p. 80; Cabletelevision Advertising Bureau, *Cable TV Facts 1989* (New York: Cabletelevision Advertising Bureau, 1989), p. 40; *NYT,* July 24, 1989.

13. Survey by Talmet Research & Strategy televised on "Media Watch," CNBC, July 2, 1989.

14. *Variety,* May 3, 1989, p. 49.

15. Ibid., March 22, 1989, p. 48.

16. Ibid., May 17, 1989, p. 1.

17. "The Business of Sports," April 1, 1989, ESPN. *NYT,* November 10, 1989; December 3, 1989; *Broadcasting,* November 6, 1989, p. 41.

18. *Electronic Media,* January 18, 1988, pp. 8, 57.

19. *NYT,* April 18, 1983.

20. *Variety,* January 6, 1988, p. 80; A. C. Nielsen Company, *The Television Audience 1988* (Northbrook, Ill.: A. C. Nielsen, 1988), p. 10.

21. *Electronic Media,* April 27, 1987, pp. 3, 49.

22. Todd Gitlin, *Inside Prime Time* (New York: Pantheon Books, 1983), p. 328.

23. Ibid., pp. 328, 334–35.

24. John Fiske, *Television Culture* (London: Methuen, 1987), pp. 37–38.

25. *Broadcasting,* December 4, 1989, p. 30.

chapter 12: the new video order

1. *Variety,* August 30, 1989, p. 1.

2. Ibid., April 19, 1989, p. 43.

3. Ibid., May 3, 1989, p. 37.

4. All quotations from the subcommittee hearings are taken from a videotape recording of the proceedings as televised on C-SPAN.

5. *Broadcasting*, May 1, 1989, p. 35.

6. *Variety*, December 28, 1988, p. 23.

7. *Electronic Media*, June 12, 1989, p. 1.

8. *NYT*, July 9, 1989.

9. For more on Malone's views see also Peter Ainslie, "Malone Alone," *Channels*, June 1989, pp. 30–36.

10. *Electronic Media*, June 19, 1989, p. 4.

11. Austin Ranney, *Channels of Power: The Impact of Television on American Politics* (New York: Basic Books, 1983), p. 160.

12. *NYT*, July 11, 1989; October 3, 1989.

13. Todd Gitlin, *Inside Prime Time* (New York: Pantheon Books, 1983), p. 332.

14. *Electronic Media*, December 11, 1989, p. 72.

15. *NYT*, November 15, 1989.

16. A. C. Nielsen Company, *The Television Audience 1988* (Northbrook, Ill.: A. C. Nielsen, 1988), p. 47.

17. *Variety*, January 4, 1989, p. 25; *Broadcasting*, July 3, 1989, p. 19.

18. *NYT*, July 9, 1989.

19. *Electronic Media*, January 4, 1988, pp. 48, 119; February 22, 1988, pp. 24, 220, 222.

20. ABC News, *Business World*, June 21, 1989.

21. Ibid., July 31, 1989, p. 30; *Variety*, June 14, 1989, p. 1; July 26, 1989, p. 1.

22. *Electronic Media*, January 30, 1989, p. 1.

23. Ibid., October 16, 1989, pp. 1, 44.

24. *Variety*, September 13, 1989, pp. 1–2; October 4, 1989, p. 1.

25. *MacNeil/Lehrer Newshour*, PBS, September 29, 1987, as cited in Cynthia Schneider and Brian Wallis, eds., *Global Television* (New York: Wedge Press, 1988), p. 182.

26. For more on the Olympics as global ritual, see Michael R. Real, *Super Media: A Cultural Studies Approach* (Newbury Park, Calif.: Sage Publications, 1989), pp. 230–49.

27. *Electronic Media*, July 10, 1989, p. 28.

28. *McLaughlin*, CNBC, June 25, 1989.

29. As cited in Daniel Schorr, "Go Get Some Milk and Cookies and Watch the Murders on Television," *The Washingtonian*, October 1981, p. 190.

bibliography

archival sources

NBC Papers, Wisconsin State Historical Society, Madison, Wis.

newspapers and magazines

ADVERTISING AGE

BILLBOARD

BROADCASTING

BUSINESS WEEK

CHICAGO TRIBUNE

EBONY

ELECTRONIC MEDIA

FORBES

THE NEW REPUBLIC

THE NEW YORK TIMES

NIELSEN NEWSCAST

RADIO MIRROR

(RADIO-TELEVISION MIRROR)

RADIO RETAILING

RADIO AND TELEVISION RETAILING

TELEVISER

TELEVISION

TELEVISION FORECAST

(TV FORECAST)

TV GUIDE

VARIETY

almanacs, videographies, and reports

Aaronson, Charles S., ed. *International Television Almanac 1962*. New York: Quigley, 1961.

Alicoate, Jack, ed. *1953 Radio Annual*. New York: Radio Daily, 1953.

Brooks, Tim, and Earle C. Marsh, eds. *The Complete Directory to Prime Time Network TV Shows, 1946–Present*, 3rd and 4th eds. New York: Ballantine Books, 1985, 1988.

Cabletelevision Advertising Bureau. *Cable TV Facts 1989*. New York: Cabletelevision Advertising Bureau, 1989.

George H. Gallup, ed. *The Gallup Poll: Public Opinion 1935–1971*, 3 vols. New York: Random House, 1972.

Gianakos, Larry James, ed. *Television Drama Series Programming: A Comprehensive Chronicle, 1947–1982*, 5 vols. Metuchen, N.J.: Scarecrow Press, 1978–88.

Hansen, Harry, ed. *The World Almanac and Book of Facts for 1956*. New York: *New York World-Telegram*, 1956.

———. *The World Almanac and Book of Facts for 1960*. New York: *New York World-Telegram*, 1960.

Kirschner, Allen, and Linda Kirschner, eds. *Radio and Television: Readings in the Mass Media.* New York: Odyssey Press, 1971.

Merrill, Alvin H. *Movies Made for Television: The Telefeature and the Mini-Series 1964–1979.* Westport, Conn: Arlington House, 1980.

Nielsen, A. C., Company. *1988 Nielsen Report on Television.* Northbrook, Ill.: A. C. Nielsen, 1988.

———. *The Television Audience 1988.* Northbrook, Ill.: A. C. Nielsen, 1988.

———. *Television Viewing Among Blacks, January–February 1986.* Northbrook, Ill.: A. C. Nielsen, 1986.

———. *Television Viewing Among Blacks, January–February 1988.* Northbrook, Ill.: A. C. Nielsen, 1988.

Olson, O. Joe, ed. *Education on the Air: Twenty-first Yearbook of the Institute for Education by Radio and Television.* Columbus: Ohio State University, 1951.

U.S. House of Representatives. Hearings Before the Subcommittee on Telecommunications, Consumer Protection, and Finance, October 21, 1981. *Social/Behavioral Effects of Violence on Television.* Washington, D.C.: U.S. Government Printing Office, 1982.

———. Report Together with Additional, Dissenting, and Separate Views by the Subcommittee on Communications, September 29, 1977. *Violence on Television.* Washington, D.C.: U.S. Government Printing Office, 1977.

U.S. Public Health Service, *Television and Growing Up: The Impact of Televised Violence.* Washington, D.C.: U.S. Government Printing Office, 1972.

Variety Radio Directory. 4 vols. New York: Variety, 1937–40.

primary sources—books

Burack, A. S., ed. *Television Plays for Writers.* New York: The Writer, 1957.

Chayefsky, Paddy. *Television Plays.* New York: Simon & Schuster, 1955.

Fulbright, J. William. *The Pentagon Propaganda Machine.* New York: Liveright, 1970.

Hawes, William. *American Television: The Experimental Years.* University, Ala.: University of Alabama Press, 1986.

Johnson, Nicholas. *How to Talk Back to Your Television Set.* Boston: Little, Brown, 1967.

Kaufman, William I., ed. *The Best Television Plays,* vol. III. Boston: Merlin Press, 1954.

———, ed. *The Best Television Plays of the Year.* Boston: Merlin Press, 1950.

Mickelson, Sig. *From Whistle Stop to Sound Bite: Four Decades of Politics and Television.* New York: Praeger, 1979.

Museum of Broadcasting, ed. *Produced by . . . Herb Brodkin: A Signature of Conviction and Integrity.* New York: Museum of Broadcasting, 1985.

Oudes, Bruce, ed. *From: The President: Richard Nixon's Secret Files.* New York: Harper & Row, 1989.

Paley, William S. *As It Happened: A Memoir.* Garden City, N.Y.: Doubleday, 1979.

Quinlan, Sterling. *Inside ABC: American Broadcasting Company's Rise to Power.* New York: Hastings House, 1979.

Rose, Reginald. *Six Television Plays*. New York: Simon & Schuster, 1957.

Rothafel, Samuel L., and Raymond Francis Yates. *Broadcasting: Its New Day*. New York: Century, 1925.

Serling, Rod. *Patterns: Four Television Plays with the Author's Personal Commentaries*. New York: Simon & Schuster, 1957.

Settel, Irving, ed. *Top TV Shows of the Year 1954–1955*. New York: Hastings House, 1955.

Vidal, Gore, ed. *Best Television Plays*. New York: Ballantine Books, 1956.

Writers' Guild of America, ed. *Writers Guild of America Presents the Prize Plays of Television and Radio 1956*. New York: Random House, 1957.

primary sources — articles

Aylesworth, Merlin H. "Broadcasting in the Public Interest." *Annals of the American Academy of Political and Social Science*, January 1935, pp. 114–18.

Barber, Red. "The First Major-League Telecast." *TV Guide*, August 24, 1974, pp. 16–17.

Berle, Milton. "Guest Column." *Television Forecast* (Chicago), May 7, 1949, p. 8.

Bullitt, Mrs. A. Scott. "Toward Improved Programming" in O. Joe Olson, ed. *Education on the Air: Twenty-second Yearbook of the Institute for Education by Radio and Television*. Columbus: Ohio State University, 1952, pp. 13–18.

Burnett, Leo. Foreword to Harry Wayne McMahan, *The Television Commercial: How to Create and Produce Effective TV Advertising*. New York: Hastings House, 1957, pp. 7–8.

Cunningham, John P. "Creeping Mediocrity Brings Boredom to TV." *Advertising Age*, December 2, 1957, pp. 65–68.

Fay, William. "Program and Station Promotion." *Television Talks 1957*. Great Neck, N.Y.: Channell Press, 1957, pp. 1–9.

Fly, James Lawrence. "Regulation of Radio Broadcasting and the Public Interest." *Annals of the American Academy of Political and Social Science*, January 1941, pp. 102–8.

Fowler, Mark. "Broadcast Unregulation in the 1980s." *Television Quarterly*, Spring 1982, pp. 7–30.

Hennock, Frieda. "Do We Need a New National Policy for Radio and Television?" in O. Joe Olson, ed., *Education on the Air: Twentieth Yearbook of the Institute for Education by Radio*. Columbus: Ohio State University, 1950, pp. 7–12, 22–33.

Henry, E. William. "The 50-50 Rule." *Television Quarterly*, Fall 1965, pp. 7–12.

Hoover, J. Edgar. "The FBI." *TV Guide*, May 20, 1972, pp. 28–30.

Horowitz, Norman. "Syndication" in Steve Morgenstern, ed., *Inside the TV Business*. New York: Sterling, 1979, pp. 71–94.

Huggins, Roy B. "The Bloodshot Eye: A Comment on the Crisis in American Television." *Television Quarterly*, August 1962, pp. 6–22.

Kennedy, John F. "Television: A Force in Politics." *TV Guide*, November 14, 1959, pp. 5–7.

Klein, Paul. "Programming" in Steve Morgenstern, ed., *Inside the TV Business*. New York: Sterling, 1979, pp. 13–36.

———. "Why You Watch What You Watch." *TV Guide*, July 24, 1971, pp. 7–10.

Murrow, Edward R. "How TV Can Help Us Survive." *TV Guide*, December 23, 1958, pp. 22–27.

Paley, William S. "Broadcasting and American Society." *Annals of the American Academy of Political and Social Science*, January 1941, pp. 62–68.

———. "Radio and the Humanities." *Annals of the American Academy of Political and Social Science*, January 1935, pp. 94–104.

Quinlan, Sterling. "Address by Sterling 'Red' Quinlan" in Robert H. Stanley, ed., *The Broadcast Industry: An Examination of Major Issues*. New York: Hastings House, 1975, pp. 53–64.

Sarnoff, David. "Possible Social Effects of Television." *Annals of the American Academy of Political and Social Science*, January 1941, pp. 145–52.

Sayre, Nora, and Robert B. Silvers. "An Interview with Paddy Chayefsky." *Horizon*, III:1 (September 1960), pp. 49–56.

Seldes, Gilbert. "The Nature of Television Programs." *Annals of the American Academy of Political and Social Science*, January 1941, pp. 138–44.

Sevareid, Eric. "A Little Less Hypocrisy, Please." *TV Guide*, December 30, 1967, pp. 6–9.

———. "TV: Big Rock Candy Mountain." *TV Guide*, April 4, 1959, pp. 5–8.

Stanton, Frank. Preface to "Free Television and the American People." *TV Guide* (Chicago edition), February 1, 1958, pp. A-28–A-29.

secondary sources—books

Allen, Steve. *The Funny Men*. New York: Simon & Schuster, 1956.

Anderson, Kent. *Television Fraud: The History and Implications of the Quiz Show Scandals*. Westport, Conn.: Greenwood, 1978.

Barnouw, Erik. *The Golden Web: A History of Broadcasting in the United States 1933–1953*. New York: Oxford University Press, 1968.

———. *The Image Empire: A History of Broadcasting in the United States from 1953*. New York: Oxford University Press, 1970.

———. *The Sponsor: Notes on a Modern Potentate*. New York: Oxford University Press, 1978.

———. *A Tower in Babel: A History of Broadcasting in the United States to 1933*. New York: Oxford University Press, 1966.

———. *Tube of Plenty: The Evolution of American Television*. New York: Oxford University Press, 1975.

Baughman, James L. *Television's Guardians: The FCC and the Politics of Programming 1958–1967*. Knoxville: University of Tennessee Press, 1985.

Bergreen, Laurence. *Look Now, Pay Later: The Rise of Network Broadcasting*. New York: New American Library, 1980.

Bilby, Kenneth. *The General: David Sarnoff and the Rise of the Communications Industry*. New York: Harper & Row, 1986.

Bower, Robert T. *The Changing Television Audience in America*. New York: Columbia University Press, 1985.

————. *Television and the Public*. New York: Holt, Rinehart & Winston, 1973.

Brown, Les. *Television: The Business Behind the Box*. New York: Harcourt Brace Jovanovich, 1971.

Bunce, Richard. *Television in the Corporate Interest*. New York: Praeger, 1975.

Cole, Barry G. *Reluctant Regulators: The FCC and the Broadcast Audience*. Reading, Mass.: Addison-Wesley, 1978.

Cowan, Geoffrey. *See No Evil: The Backstage Battle over Sex and Violence in Television*. New York: Simon & Schuster, 1978.

Diamond, Edwin. *The Spot: The Rise of Political Advertising on Television*. Cambridge, Mass.: M.I.T. Press, 1984.

Fiske, John. *Television Culture*. London: Methuen, 1987.

Friendly, Fred W. *Due to Circumstances Beyond Our Control . . .* New York: Random House, 1979.

Gitlin, Todd. *Inside Prime Time*. New York: Pantheon Books, 1983.

Grossman, Gary H. *Saturday Morning TV*. New York: Dell, 1981.

Hadden, Jeffrey, and Charles E. Swain. *Prime Time Preachers: The Rising Power of Televangelism*. Reading, Mass.: Addison-Wesley, 1981.

Halberstam, David. *The Powers That Be*. New York: Alfred A. Knopf, 1979.

Head, Sidney W. *Broadcasting in America: A Survey of Television and Radio*. Boston: Houghton Mifflin, 1976.

Hubbell, Richard W. *4,000 Years of Television: The Story of Seeing at a Distance*. New York: G. P. Putnam's Sons, 1942.

Johnson, William O., Jr. *Super Spectator and the Electric Lilliputians*. Boston: Little, Brown, 1971.

Krasnow, Erwin G., and Lawrence D. Longley. *The Politics of Broadcast Regulation*. New York: St. Martin's Press, 1978.

Lashner, Marilyn A. *The Chilling Effect in TV News: Intimidation by the Nixon White House*. New York: Praeger, 1984.

Levinson, Richard, and William Link. *Stay Tuned: An Inside Look at the Making of Prime-Time Television*. New York: St. Martin's Press, 1981.

Litman, Barry Russell. *The Vertical Structure of the Television Broadcast Industry: The Coalescence of Power*. East Lansing: Michigan State University, 1979.

Long, Stewart Louis. *The Development of the Television Network Oligopoly*. New York: Arno Press, 1979.

Lyons, Eugene. *David Sarnoff: A Biography*. New York: Harper & Row, 1966.

McCrohan, Donna. *Archie & Edith, Mike & Gloria: The Tumultuous History of All in the Family*. New York: Workman, 1987.

MacDonald, J. Fred. *Blacks and White·TV. Afro-Americans in Television Since 1948*. Chicago: Nelson-Hall, 1983.

————. *Television and the Red Menace: The Video Road to Vietnam*. New York: Praeger, 1985.

————. *Who Shot the Sheriff? The Rise and Fall of the Television Western*. New York: Praeger, 1987.

Mair, George. *Inside HBO: The Billion-Dollar War Between HBO, Hollywood, and the Home Video Revolution*. New York: Dodd, Mead & Company, 1988.

Montgomery, Kathryn C. *Target: Prime Time. Advocacy Groups and the Struggle over Entertainment Television*. New York: Oxford University Press, 1989.

Opotowsky, Stan. *TV—The Big Picture*. New York: Collier, 1962.

Oppenheim, Jacques W. *Code: télévision à la carte*. Paris: Edilig, 1988.

Owen, Bruce M.; Jack H. Beebee; and Williard G. Manning, Jr. *Television Economics*. Lexington, Mass.: D. C. Heath, 1974.

Oxenfeldt, Alfred R. *Marketing Practices in the TV Set Industry*. New York: Columbia University Press, 1964.

Paper, Lewis J. *Empire: William S. Paley and the Making of CBS*. New York: St. Martin's Press, 1987.

Powers, Richard Gid. *Secrecy and Power: The Life of J. Edgar Hoover*. New York: The Free Press, 1987.

Rader, Benjamin G. *In Its Own Image: How Television Has Transformed Sports*. New York: The Free Press, 1984.

Reel, A. Frank. *The Networks: How They Stole the Show*. New York: Charles Scribner's Sons, 1979.

Schatz, Thomas. *The Genius of the System: Hollywood Filmmaking in the Studio Era*. New York: Pantheon Books, 1989.

Schiller, Herbert I. *Mass Communications and American Empire*. New York: Augustus M. Kelley, 1969.

Siepmann, Charles A. *Radio, Television and Society*. New York: Oxford University Press, 1950.

Small, William. *To Kill a Messenger: Television News and the Real World*. New York: Hastings House, 1970.

Steiner, Gary A. *The People Look at Television: A Study of Audience Attitudes*. New York: Alfred A. Knopf, 1963.

Sterling, Christopher, and John M. Kittross. *Stay Tuned: A Concise History of American Broadcasting*. Belmont, Calif.: Wadsworth, 1978.

Stone, David M. *Nixon and the Politics of Public Television*. New York: Garland, 1985.

Summers, Robert E., and Harrison B. Summers. *Broadcasting and the Public*. Belmont, Calif.: Wadsworth, 1966.

Turow, Joseph. *Playing Doctor: Television, Storytelling, and Medical Power*. New York: Oxford University Press, 1989.

Udelson, Joseph H. *The Great Television Race: A History of the American Television Industry 1925–1941*. University, Ala.: University of Alabama Press, 1982.

Walley, David G. *The Ernie Kovacs Phile*. New York: Bolder Books, 1976.

Ward, Ken. *Mass Communication and the Modern World*. Chicago: Dorsey Press, 1989.

Wells, Alan. *Picture Tube Imperialism? The Impact of U.S. Television on Latin America*. Maryknoll, N.Y.: Orbis Books, 1972.

Winship, Michael. *Television*. New York: Random House, 1988.

secondary sources—articles

Ainslie, Peter. "Malone Alone." *Channels*, June 1989, pp. 30–36.

Blair, Erica. "With *Amerika* Under Fire, the Stars Were Feeling the Heat." *TV Guide*, February 14, 1987, pp. 2–6.

Caldwell, Louis G. "Regulation of Broadcasting by the Federal Government" in *Variety Radio Directory 1937–1938*. New York: *Variety*, 1937, pp. 269–303.

Callum, Myles. "Exclusive Poll: What Viewers Think About TV." *TV Guide*, May 12, 1979, pp. 6–12.

Carroll, Raymond L. "Economic Influences on Commercial Network Television Documentary Scheduling." *Journal of Broadcasting*, Fall 1979, pp. 411–25.

Chase, Chevy. "The Unique Comedy of Ernie Kovacs." *TV Guide*, April 9, 1977, pp. 39–40.

Crossen, Ken. "There's Murder in the Air" in Howard Haycraft, ed. *The Art of the Mystery Story*. New York: Simon & Schuster, 1946, pp. 304–7.

Diamond, Edwin. "TV and Watergate: What Was, What Might Have Been." *Columbia Journalism Review*, July–August 1973, pp. 20.

Dizard, Wilson P. "American Television's Foreign Markets." *Television Quarterly*, Summer 1964, pp. 57–73.

Doherty, Richard F. "Is the Television Industry Still in the Growth Stage?" *Analysts Journal*, November 10, 1954, pp. 35–36.

Engelhardt, Tom. "The Shortcake Strategy," in Todd Gitlin, ed., *Watching Television*. New York: Pantheon Books, 1989, pp. 68–110.

Frappier, Jon. "U.S. Media Empire/Latin America." *NACLA Newsletter*, January 1969.

Friedman, Mel. "Aftermath: Reflections on the Day After." *Television Quarterly*, XXI:1 (1984), pp. 7–17.

Gamble, Bud. "The Television Tour of 88 Department Stores." *Televiser*, Winter 1945, p. 48.

Hall, Gladys. "Are Comedians Through on the Air?" *Radio Stars*, February 1936, pp. 44–45, 70–73.

Henry, William A. III. "Is TV Getting Better—or Worse?" *TV Guide*, March 12, 1988, pp. 2–6.

Hettinger, Herman S. "Organizing Radio's Discoveries for Use." *Annals of the American Academy of Political and Social Science*, January 1941, pp. 170–89.

Hickey, Neil. "The Changing Shape of Television." *TV Guide*, April 22, 1978, pp. 4–10; April 29, 1978, pp. 33–40; May 6, 1978, pp. 31–40.

Higgins, Robert. "Why ABC's New Innovation Fizzled." *TV Guide*, April 5, 1969, pp. 4–9.

Jenkins, Dan. "TV Film Companies—A New Generation of Giants." *TV Guide*, January 17, 1959, pp. 8–11.

Johnson, Robert. "Rod Serling Describes Headaches of TV Script Writing." *TV Guide*, May 11, 1957, pp. 17–19.

Karp, Daniel. "TV Shows Are Not Supposed to Be Good." *The New York Times Magazine*, January 23, 1966, pp. 6–7, 36–38.

Kowet, Don, and Sally Bedell. "Anatomy of a Smear: How CBS 'Got' General Westmoreland." *TV Guide*, May 29, 1981, pp. 2–15.

Laufman, Herbert S. "Television's Impact." *Radio & Television News*, July 1949, pp. 30–31, 125–27.

Lemon, Richard. "Black Is the Color of TV's Newest Stars." *The Saturday Evening Post*, November 30, 1968, pp. 42–44, 82–84.

Luraschi, Luigi. "Censorship at Home and Abroad." *Annals of the American Academy of Political and Social Science*, November 1947, pp. 147–52.

Mannes, Marya. "The Lost Tribe of Television" in *The Eighth Art*. New York: Holt, Rinehart & Winston, 1962, pp. 23–29.

Mayans, Frank, Jr., and Norman Young. "Ratings Study." *Television*, November 1952, p. 23.

Montagu, Ashley. "Television and the New Image of Man" in *The Eighth Art*. New York: Holt, Rinehart & Winston, 1962, pp. 125–34.

Morgan, Al. "Revelations of Former Network Presidents." *TV Guide*, April 29, 1972, pp. 40–44.

Nossiter, Bernard D. "The FCC's Big Giveaway Show." *The Nation*, October 26, 1985, pp. 402–5.

Panitt, Merrill. "A Dark Perception—The Challenge." *Television Quarterly*, Fall 1968, pp. 7–13.

Perry, Armstrong. "Weak Spots in the American System of Broadcasting." *Annals of the American Academy of Political and Social Science*, January 1935, pp. 22–38.

Rice, Grantland. "For Better or Worse: TV" in *The Story of Our Time: Encyclopedia Year Book 1954*. New York: The Grolier Society, 1954, pp. 385–87.

Rosten, Leo. "A Disenchanted Look at the Audience" in *The Eighth Art*. New York: Holt, Rinehart & Winston, 1962, pp. 31–38.

Salisbury, Harrison E. "*Amerika:* Could a Soviet Takeover Happen This Way?" *TV Guide*, February 14, 1987, pp. 10–12.

Sanders, R. W. "Freeing Area Television Reception." *Radio & Television News*, October 1949, pp. 44–46, 148–49.

Schickel, Richard. "The Problem of the Year." *TV Guide*, February 29, 1964, pp. 15–19.

Schlesinger, Arthur M., Jr. "Where Does the Liberal Go from Here?" *The New York Times Magazine*, August 4, 1957, pp. 7, 36–38.

Schorr, Daniel. "Go Get Some Milk and Cookies and Watch the Murders on Television." *The Washingtonian*, October 1981, pp. 190–93ff.

Sher, Jack. "Before Your Very Eyes." *Radio and Television Mirror*, August 1939, pp. 22–23, 58–59.

Simon, Samuel A. "Mark Fowler's Challenge to the American Public Communications System." *Television Quarterly*, Summer 1982, pp. 47–55.

Smith, Richard Austin. "TV: The Light That Failed." *Fortune*, December 1958, pp. 78–81, 161–62.

Stahl, Bob. "The Men Who Run ABC." *TV Guide*, August 1, 1959, pp. 4–7.

Thomas, Marian. "What the 'Man-on-the-Street' Thinks of Television!" *Televiser*, Summer 1945, pp. 17, 37.

Thomas, Marjorie. "TV Film Has Joined the Hollywood Elite." *Broadcasting*, December 14, 1953, pp. 84–85, 88.

Van Horne, Harriet. "The Truth About Color TV." *Radio-Television Mirror*, March 1951, pp. 32–33, 98–99.

subject index

index of television and radio programs

about the author

J. Fred MacDonald is internationally recognized as an expert on U.S. popular culture, particularly in the area of radio and television history, on which he has written five previous books. He is a professor of history at Northeastern Illinois University, and curator of the Museum of Broadcast Communications in Chicago. Dr. MacDonald was educated at the University of California, Berkeley, and at UCLA, where he received a Ph.D.